The Christian
Understanding of Atonement

DATE DUE

The
Christian Understanding
of
Atonement

F. W. Dillistone

SCM PRESS LTD

334 01936 2

First published 1968
Reissued 1984 by
SCM Press Ltd
26–30 Tottenham Road, London N1 4BZ

Typeset in the United States of America
and printed in Great Britain at
The Camelot Press Ltd
Southampton

PREFACE

Since the first edition of this book was published in 1968 I have become increasingly conscious of a major deficiency in the first chapter. Whereas the later part of the book is structured in pairs, the first chapter attempts to focus attention on a single word or category in order to portray the human situation to which the gospel of atonement can be addressed.

I am now convinced that this was an over-simplification. From the view-point both of past traditions and of present experience *two* fundamental needs or predicaments may be discerned. That there have been and still are between societies and between individuals bitter *alienations* I have no doubt. This has ever been an outstanding problem when (as in the history of the Jewish people described in the Old Testament) tribes and nations are on the move, seeking for riches or lands or conquests. But alienation does not equally apply to a situation where a people is settled relatively securely on its own land, dependent on an agrarian economy.

In this latter case, the major threats are infertility, failure of crops, disease, decay, death. In a strikingly impressive book Robert Parker has summarized these concerns (deeply felt by the Greeks) by the one term which forms the title of his book: *Miasma.* Perhaps the most expressive word in English is *pollution,* and therefore I would now want to make the first chapter dual rather than singular and to develop the two themes of pollution and alienation as the negative preludes to the positive affirmation of the Christian doctrine of reconciliation.

Since 1968 a number of important studies have appeared in the general field of the understanding of atonement. Martin Hengel's two books, *Crucifixion* (1977) and *The Atonement: The Origins of the Doctrine in the New Testament* (1981), have helped us to gain a clearer view of the social context within which the crucifixion on Golgotha was enacted and subsequently the ways in which it was related to human needs. Jürgen Moltmann's book *The Crucified God* (1974) constitutes an outstanding theological event. The author sees the Cross not only as having a powerful bearing on contemporary social issues but also as challenging us to reinterpret radically our whole conception of God.

Over the past decade the demand for conciliation, for mediation, and for go-betweens in human relations has become increasingly clamant. Is the Christian 'word of reconciliation' (II Cor. 5.19) a viable response? Social anthropologists have, I think, increasingly taken note of the importance of *sacrificial* ceremonies and theories in non-Western cultures. Do their researches help us to interpret the Cross by means of sacrificial imagery and language? Novelists have explored human relationships by drawing upon the theme of vicarious suffering. Can we regard what was manifested at Calvary as the supreme example? Everywhere people are being awakened to the possibility of total annihilation. Can we still embrace the vision of cosmic reconciliation through the blood of Christ's cross (Col. 1.20)?

But perhaps the most remarkable development in the past fifteen years has been the way in which Jewish theologians have sought to come to terms with the horrendous event of the Holocaust by interpreting it as meaning for Israel something parallel to what the Cross has meant for Christians. To a degree a common consciousness concerning the divine way of atonement has emerged. How far this common understanding may progress further cannot be foretold. But that undeserved suffering and cruel death cry out for interpretation and deeper understanding if we are to continue to believe in the providence and mercy of God seems obvious.

The search for analogies and parables (which can be viewed as extended metaphors) continues. No single pattern of language is adequate to encompass the total meaning of the Cross: a model which may have aroused gratitude and trust in an earlier age may not stir our imaginations today. I hope that what was written in the 1960s is not already outdated. Certainly I am grateful to SCM Press for its willingness to reissue a book which has for some years been out of print.

Christmas 1983   F. W. DILLISTONE

CONTENTS

CHAPTER I

ALIENATION AND ATONEMENT

The words 'Atone' and 'Atonement' are seldom used in the modern world. Indeed it is not easy to think of an occasion when either would be heard in ordinary conversation. It would be a rare thing for a public speaker to speak of 'atonement' outside a church or theological lecture hall. And if any reader of newspapers and general literature keeps watch for the occurrence of 'atone' or its cognates he will be fortunate if he encounters a single example during any specified period of time. Several years ago I tried the experiment. In a span of several months I found the London *Times* announcing that the English bowlers had 'atoned' for a failure of their batsmen in Australia. I chanced upon a reference in the New York *Herald Tribune* to the future of Alger Hiss: only if he makes a 'voluntary atonement for his crime' should he be received back 'into respected circles of American life'. But nothing else came to my notice.[1]

The case is very little different in more serious literature. It is significant, for example, that when a character in Mr. T. S. Eliot's play, *The Cocktail Party*, ventures to use the word 'atone' it is with hesitancy and with no assurance that it will be understood in her own particular circle.

> It's not the feeling of anything I've ever *done*
> Which I might get away from, or of anything in me
> I could get rid of—but of emptiness, of failure
> Towards someone, or something, outside of myself
> And I feel I must—atone—is that the word?

Yet the absence of the actual words 'atone' and 'atonement' does not for a moment imply that the Christian doctrine of the Atonement has no relevance to the world in which we live. Indeed I am confident that there is no doctrine of the Christian Faith which has more

---

1. A strange and perhaps significant example of the use of the word 'atone' recently came to my notice. An Associated Press story from Santa Monica, California, on 9th August 1962 reported that:
'Nearly 100 traffic violators watched a police traffic accident film today to atone for their violations. Two had to be treated for nausea and shock . . .
' Viewers were offered a $5.00 reduction in fines if they agreed to see the movie, Signal 30, made by the Ohio State Police.
'It showed twisted wreckage and mangled bodies and recorded the screams of accident victims.' Marshall McLuhan: *Understanding Media*, p. 30.

points of contact with life in the modern age. If Paul Tillich is in any way right in his assertions that 'the Christian message provides the answers to the questions implied in human existence'; that the Christian answers are, so far as their form is concerned, directly dependent upon the questions which they answer; if, in other words, it is true that the leading questions of any particular era supply the language-forms necessary for expressing the essential Christian affirmations within that era, then everything points to the fact that it is precisely the doctrine of the Atonement (even though the actual word 'atonement' may not be used) which is needed to answer the most pressing enquiries of our own time. For in whatever direction we look—in the realms of race, of colour, of class, of culture, of community, of personal relationship, of psychological adjustment—one question overshadows all others. It is the question of Alienation,[2] or Estrangement.

A

It was in the writings of Hegel that the concept of 'Alienation' first gained forceful expression. To him, history itself could be regarded as the history of man's alienation, though he regarded a loss of unity, both in individual and social life, as peculiarly the mark of the modern era. Man is in conflict with nature, he is estranged from his fellow, he is alienated from his own essence and end. All these alienations are to be viewed as manifestations of a still more fundamental conflict between subject and object in which man in his subjectivity stands over against the objective world of physical necessity. Indeed reality itself is a 'structure of contradictions' but it is man's task to hold together these contradictions in his mind and thereby to resolve them within a living unity.

This theory was taken up by Marx but interpreted in a different way. For him the source of man's total alienation is found in the conditions of his labour. The institution of private property and the system of capitalist production are such that man cannot fail to be alienated both from nature and from the product of his work and this means that he is alienated in his total existence. In Marx's own words: 'The object which labour produces, its product, is encountered as an *alien entity*, a force that has become *independent* of its producer. The realization of labour is its objectification. Under

---

2. 'It has become steadily clearer to me that alienation is one of the determining realities of the contemporary age: not merely a key concept in philosophy, literature and the social sciences—but a cultural and psychological condition implicating ever larger sections of the population.' R. A. Nisbet: *Community and Power* (Galaxy Edition. p. VIII).

the prevailing economic conditions, this realization of labour appears as its opposite, the negation of the labourer. Objectification appears as loss of and enslavement by the object and appropriation as alienation and expropriation.'[3] Further, the very fact of his being a commodity alienated from his work makes possible the division of labour which in its turn brings about the estrangement of man from man. In fact, whenever conditions of labour are such that things and the relations between things are of first importance, while men and the relations between men occupy a subordinate and dependent position, then an overall estrangement in the human situation is inevitable.

Here then we see two of the greatest minds of the nineteenth century interpreting human life in terms of total alienation and asking the question of unification or reconciliation. For Hegel, the estrangement was to be found within the very structure of life universal. For Marx, it was to be found within the structure of man's conditions of labour which compelled him to be alienated from his work, from himself, and from his fellow men. The answer to man in his predicament Hegel sought through a philosophical system, corresponding to the dialectical process of the Universal Mind. Marx, on the other hand, sought it through a revolutionary change in man's economic conditions which would make possible a complete harmony between man and his work. But whatever may be thought about their proposed solutions, the centrality of the category of 'alienation' in their respective diagnoses of the human situation can scarcely be questioned.

The theme of man's self-alienation has been explored and elaborated in a somewhat different way by the leaders of the modern psycho-analytical movement. For all such, man's basic problem lies in his inner tensions and conflicts. In Freud's view the child, from the time of its birth, is subject to a variety of strains and tensions within the inner self, which can be analysed in a scientific way by means of observation and experimentation. This diagnosis of inner conflicts and warring desires is not, of course, new. Plato was fully aware that man's involvement in a transitory and shadowy world meant that he was separated from the eternal and real world to which he essentially belonged and that this separation or estrangement inevitably resulted in inner pain and disharmony. Paul and Augustine, in their classical accounts of their souls' experiences, showed clearly that the higher and the lower, the ideal and the actual, are constantly opposed to one another within the human psyche and that at times the strain of this inner dividedness becomes almost unbearable. But Freud and his successors have sought to classify

3. Quoted H. Marcuse: *Reason and Revolution*, p. 276.

and arrange the evidences of the inner conflict in such a way that its general nature can become clear and the way of its resolution plain.

The chief new category which has been introduced by modern psycho-analytical theory is that of the unconscious. And it is within this area of the personality, it is claimed, that the roots of the most intense inner conflicts are to be found. For instincts which have been denied their full emotional satisfaction tend to be repressed and driven back into the unconscious where they remain unresolved and a potential source of almost intolerable strain in days to come. When the alienation within the self passes beyond a certain stage, when feelings of anxiety or guilt or fear have become so intense that the self is virtually divided against itself, then the terms neurosis and neurotic are usually employed to describe the situation. 'Neurosis,' Jung has written, 'is an inner cleavage—the state of being at war with oneself. What drives people to war with themselves is the intuition or the knowledge that they consist of two persons in opposition to one another. The conflict may be between the sensual and the spiritual man, or between the ego and the shadow. It is what Faust means when he says: "Two souls, alas, dwell in my breast apart". A neurosis is a dissociation of personality.'[4]

Dissociation of personality—this is the disease of which the modern world is becoming increasingly conscious. The number of those actually admitted to mental hospitals constitutes a significant index of the growing alienation between man and his inner self. But even when the help of the skilled mental doctor is not sought, the questions are still being asked: What is the secret of the integration of the personality? How can man be adjusted to his environmental situation? Where can he find peace of mind and of soul? How can he be reconciled to his essential being? The traditional vocabulary of atonement may not be used (though 'peace' and 'reconciliation' are important terms in the witness to the nature of the work of Christ as given in the Authorized Version of the New Testament) but the questions to which the doctrine of the Atonement is related are certainly there. If the theological answer can express itself in terms of the existential questions the doctrine can hardly fail to be relevant to some of the most important aspects of the modern situation.

Taking one more example from the contemporary scene what are the themes of modern art, especially of the novel? In her book on the Twentieth-Century American City Novel, Blanche H. Gelfant affirms that the modern artist has 'certain obsessive concerns—to name some, a concern over man's aloneness and alienation, over

4. *Modern Man in Search of a Soul*, p. 273.

the collapse of his community and the breakdown of tradition, the ineffectuality of love and religion, the impact of mechanization, the materialism of modern life and the conflict between artist and society'.[5]

Man, in other words, is alienated from himself, from his fellows, from the past, from nature, from cultural standards. And this means that a constantly recurring theme in city fiction is 'personal dissociation': 'the prototype for the hero is the self-divided man'.[6] 'The irony, pathos and tragedy of City fiction,' Miss Gelfant goes on, 'lie in the fact of dissociation. Ironically, the city novel shews that the chaotic conditions of urban society create man's intense need for conscious self-integration while they also constitute the obstacles to personal fulfilment.'[7]

So painful is this personal dissociation and social estrangement that man will do almost anything to overcome it. The 'alienated' intellectual will sacrifice his standards of intellectual integrity in order that he may really *belong* to the masses: the 'estranged' activist will engage in violence and destruction in order that he may overcome his personal frustration and win the *approval* of a gangster society: the 'dissociated' artist will surrender himself to the allurements of the bar and the brothel in order that he may find the comfort of oblivion and the warmth of an embrace. In the last resort there is the way of suicide, a way which is more commonly taken in modern urban society than in any other; 'This,' as Miss Gelfant strikingly indicates, 'is a method of resolving conflicts by running away from them forever.'[8] But in all of these typical cases the driving force is one and the same. It is the intense longing of the alienated and dissociated individual to find integration either by immersing himself in some greater whole or by discovering some form of selfhood which can gain the approval of his fellows. The question of reintegration, of reconciliation is as urgent as any of our day: and no artist who attempts to interpret the contemporary scene can afford to ignore it.

B

Is then the sense of Alienation a feature peculiar to the modern culture of the west? To such a question no simple and immediate answer can be given. There are undoubtedly certain strains and tensions in Western society which have become ever more acute

5. p. 21.   7. p. 22 f.
6. p. 26.   8. p. 39.

during the period of technological expansion which has extended over the past 500 years. Man's relationship with nature has changed: his increasing mobility has led to change in his relationship with his fellow man: his growing awareness of his own individual existence has brought about changes in his attempts to deal with the problems of his own inner psyche. But such changes may not be peculiar to our modern Western civilization. May it not rather be the case that whenever in human history dynamic movements occur within the life of a society, vibrations are set up which inevitably cause stresses and strains to develop and make the question of alienation far more acute than in relatively stable and settled times?

On general grounds this would seem to be a reasonable expectation. For what are the chief components of the human structural situation at all times and in all places? First of all man is related to the all-encompassing environment within which he dwells—what we may call Nature, or Life Universal. Secondly he is related in a more specialized way to the particular society to which he belongs. Thirdly there are relationships with the intimate family group within the wider society, a group which cannot strictly be defined so far as its limits are concerned but which is such as to make possible an ever deepening mutual understanding and sympathy. Finally man is related to the mysterious inner world of his own personality, a world which may include conscious as well as unconscious elements. These four relationships—with Life Universal, with the great Society, with the intimate Family group, and with the inner Self—are of paramount importance[9] and although it is possible to analyse any one of them in a more detailed way, they provide a sufficiently comprehensive framework for all ordinary purposes.

To be sure a form of human existence can be conceived in which any vivid consciousness of these relationships has scarcely begun to emerge. In the case of the newly-born child there is virtually no differentiation: the all-encompassing environment is provided by the mother. And even when there begin to be contacts with the world of objects and with the wider society of other persons the initial movement of desire is towards bringing all these new experiences within the enveloping embrace of the mother herself. Similarly

9. I prefer at this stage to speak of Life Universal rather than of God in the way that Arnold Toynbee does:
'Our field of human affairs articulates itself into four provinces occupied respectively by the soul's diverse relations with God, with his own self, with a relatively small circle of human beings, with whom he is in direct personal communion, and with a relatively large circle of people with whom he is in indirect impersonal contact, through the mechanism of institutions.' *A Study of History*, Vol. IX, p. 169.

in the case of many primitive societies, especially those living within a bounded area and having no contact with other groups, any sense of the individual standing over against the tribe or entering into relationship with natural forces is virtually non-existent. There are bound to be spasmodic movements towards some minimal form of differentiation but these are quickly countered by movements to return to that integrated unity which is the symbol of security and peace.

Erich Neumann discusses this primeval condition of things in an interesting passage which stresses the importance of three out of the four elements to which I have already referred. 'The essential fate of man,' he writes, 'at least of the mature modern man, is enacted on three fronts which, although interconnected, are none-theless clearly marked off from one another. The world as the outside world of extrahuman events, the community as the sphere of inter-human relationships, the psyche as the world of interior human experience—these are the three basic factors which govern human life, and man's creative encounter with each of them is decisive for the development of the individual. In the initial stage, however, these territories have not yet become separated from one another, neither man from the world, nor individual from the group, nor ego consciousness from the unconscious. Nor is the human world which is composed of individuals and the group in any way distinguished from what we call the external world of objects. Although we know the original condition of things only as a borderline experience, we can still describe its symptomatology because, with those parts of our psyche which are not our ego consciousness, we continue to participate in this archetypal stage.'[10]

Almost certainly Neumann is right in postulating an original condition of virtually undifferentiated unity. Yet just as the child is, from the moment of its conception, a separable entity even though for a long period, and perhaps for the whole of its life-span, it remains closely dependent upon the mother, so the individual in any society *has* a separate identity, however much that identity may seem to be swallowed up in the corporate wholeness. And this means that there have always been tiny ripples on the surface of what Neumann calls the 'anonymous collectivity', even though the constant tendency is towards the restoration of the smooth pattern of unity which may have been temporarily disturbed. But it is always possible that the individual may break out in some unexpected way and then the reintegration of the society may constitute a far more serious problem.

10. E. Neumann: *The Origin and History of Consciousness*, p. 267.

While the settled pattern of the original unity remains intact, any small variation brought about as a result of the individual's growth in self-consciousness tends to be corrected by the employment of certain prescribed forms. These may consist mainly of words or of actions. By repeating certain formulas, formulas which have to do with the individual's identity with the comprehensive whole, the movement of return to the primitive unity gains strength. Or again, by performing certain actions, actions which symbolize a participation in the life-force or the life-pattern of the original unity, that unity is gradually re-established.

Such a restoration, however, can hardly be called 'atonement'. There has been no real *break* in the original unity. A slight tremor, a minor aberration, a momentary upheaval, a faint movement towards independence, but nothing more. All that is needed is to re-assert the essential unity of the individual with the whole, to reaffirm that all apparent brokenness is illusion, to re-experience in accentuated and even exaggerated form the union with the ultimate one-ness which is the be-all and end-all of existence. Oriental religions, the mysteries of Hellenism and indeed mystical cults of all ages have been designed to gather together within the embrace of the One all phenomena within or without the self which show any signs of movement towards independent existence of their own. We may call this Re-Absorption, Fusion or even Re-Union: it is hardly atonement or reconciliation.

But from time to time there have been more serious disturbances within the original unity of a human situation. Climatic conditions may have altered: a change of habitat may have become necessary: and men have become aware of a painful cleavage between themselves and the natural order on which they depend. Or again, an increase in population may have brought about changes of internal organization: the unusual skill or pertinacity of one family may have aroused the envy and jealousy of another: and again men have become aware of a serious tension between themselves and their fellows. Still further men may begin to sense the dividedness within their own selves. Above all a growing knowledge of the totality within which they live may reveal the gap that seems to exist between higher and lower, between permanent and transitory, between spiritual and material and it may seem that the wholeness of things has been pulled apart so that man, who by his body is held within the lower material order, is separated grievously from the higher spiritual order to which he essentially belongs.

When divisions of this magnitude are recognized no minor adjustment any longer suffices. Nor can there be a simple return

Don't see D's definition of alienation as pertaining to women

to the condition which existed before the breach appeared. Yet man is so made that he cannot be content to remain in a state of perm- anent separation either from his world or from the Divine Order to which he belongs. He seeks some creative process whereby the sundered elements may be rejoined, the divided wholeness re- integrated. Such a process may more fitly be called Atonement or Salvation. It is the establishment of a new wholeness which is not independent of the original unity but at the same time is not identical with it. It is the extension or expansion of the original wholeness in such a way as to retain the essential pattern while weaving into that pattern the unforeseen elements which the slow movement of time has brought in its train.

Yet there is another and that a very different aspect of human experience. I have spoken of man as set within a four-fold framework which may demand periodic readjustments and reintegrations but which retains its essential pattern. What now happens to him if a structure of social life appears which is radically different from that of his original society? How such a structure *could* appear is, of course, a large question. Movements of sections of the human race have seemed at time to be comparable to the swarming of bees or the migration of birds. An individual with his family, maybe a small group of families, has felt an irresistible compulsion to go forth into the unknown. Or a whole collection of clans has left an area where conditions of life were hard and unpromising in order to seek a home in more congenial surroundings. But that in the course of human development radically different structures of society have come to be established and that at times of special crisis these divergent social entities have become aware of one another's existence, are unquestionable facts of history.[11]

When once it becomes plain that a structure of natural or social life different from one's own actually exists, the effect is far-reaching and may even be catastrophic. For the fact is that every individual and every social group experiences a sense of being threatened when confronted by an order of life which is unfamiliar and utterly un- predictable. If there are a reasonable number of points of conformity with its own accepted pattern the threat is obviously not so great. But where language, behaviour, appearance, customs are all different the reaction to the situation may be irrational and even violent.

what original unity was there for women? what it means to be a woman/girl in this society means alienation from self inherent in language

11. It is possible to argue that the human race has not evolved from a single stock but that in different parts of the world families of *homo sapiens* developed an independent existence. Even if this were so it would not affect our immediate concern about what happens when at length such families meet.

In general, the witness of history is that when through group migrations or tribal wanderings critical encounters between differently-structured peoples take place, the outcome takes one of two forms. Either the disparity seems so great that one side sees no possibility of maintaining its own existence while the other is at large: or creative relationships begin to be set in motion whose ultimate aim is some form of co-existence. In the latter case the determination to seek these inter-relationships is likely to be signalized by some striking form of initial encounter. Let us look at these two main results of the coming together of divergent social orders a little more closely.

Of the first kind of reaction history holds many tragic examples. Fear is one of the most unmanageable emotions of the human heart and fear of the unknown is one of the strongest of its kind. Fear may induce flight but when flight seems to be impossible it may lead to a despairing attempt to obliterate that which threatens to destroy. The great East-West conflict of the twentieth century illustrates in a hitherto unparalleled way what happens when one society feels itself to be threatened in an ultimate way by another of a different pattern. 'A war to end all wars', 'unconditional surrender', 'a knock-out blow'—such are the phrases which come readily to the lips when the differences between societies seem absolute and irreconcilable.

But any kind of war of extermination constitutes a final confession of despair of the future of the human race. Even a complete subjugation of the kind which makes one individual or social group accept in its entirety the life-pattern of the other is substantially the same. It establishes a certain kind of unity but it is a monolithic unity from which all elements of creative criticism have been excluded. Moreover it brings about a kind of unity at the heart of which there is now a putrefying mass of death rather than a possibility of new life. It crushes the opposing force, it does not in any sense change it. It may claim that the other structure of life is so irredeemably evil that it deserves to be blotted out from the face of existence. But such a judgment implies either that the human race has been hopelessly divided from the very beginning and that the safety of one species of humanity can only be purchased at the expense of annihilating the other: or that it is possible for one section of humanity to become corrupted beyond reclaim and that again it must be exterminated for the good of the other section. Such a view of the nature and destiny of man involves a final dualism and means that the unification of society at any particular time can be achieved only by mass destruction. Atonement and Reconciliation are ruled out: the key-words are compulsory unification and 'forcible over-throw of all existing institutions'.[12]

2. In the second type of social encounter fear is not absent but fear is constantly checked by its polar opposite—fascination. Not only is there the sense of being threatened by the life-pattern which is unfamiliar though obviously powerful: there is also the sense of being attracted by certain novel and probably desirable features of this new way of life. Moreover there is in all likelihood a half-conscious recognition that marks of a common origin of the two societies still exist and that at least some common ground is available on which representatives of the two sides can take their stand and make approaches towards creative inter-relationships. If no common interests, no common structures, no common forms of communication can be found, relationship must be ruled out as impossible and a war of attrition must begin. No individual or society can achieve its own purposes if they are totally irreconcilable with the aims and interests of another.

But where there is the recognition of some common interest, coupled with a sense that the other person or social group has succeeded in acquiring some fuller knowledge or some more effective technique for the pursuance of that aim, that in fact the other party in the encounter has elements within its pattern of life which are greatly to be desired for the fulfilment of one's own purposes and ambitions, then a move is bound to be made sooner or later towards the bridging of the gulf that divides and the cementing of the common aims that unite. And as I have already suggested, this movement is likely to be launched in a decisive way by an act of coming together which in the form of dramatic symbolization goes far beyond what is immediately possible in actual life. On each side there is a genuine recognition of a need to be filled and of a possession to be shared: the fear of the unknown other and of the unexplored future causes anxiety, hesitation, even dread. Yet the leap is taken, the commit-ment is made, the grace is received, the community of intention is sealed. An act of reconciliation has been effected.

C

Alienation has been experienced in many forms but it is hard to think that there is ever a time, either in the development of the individual or of the society, when the notion of separation or estrangement becomes entirely meaningless. And if the question of estrangement is being asked, the answer of reconciliation must at

12. *Communist Manifesto*.

least be possible. Moreover, the more painful the sense of alienation, the more hope there should be of an open ear to the message of atonement.

It is not enough, however, simply to have on hand certain terms which awaken an element of response in the minds of those who hear them. The reconciliation about which I speak may not be an answer to the precise problem of estrangement with which my neighbour is concerned. It is an initial advantage that my language should be related to his vocabulary but that advantage may be entirely lost if it emerges that the problem to which my answer refers is not his real problem at all. Single words are not in themselves normally sufficient and it is desirable therefore to look more carefully at the general framework within which the language of estrangement and reconciliation gains meaning.

The framework *may* be filled in in such detail that it becomes indistinguishable from a total philosophy of life. But it is not my purpose to attempt any such elaboration at this stage. I am rather concerned to ask what is the minimum of statements which needs to be made in order that I may know that I am talking within the same framework of reconciliation language as that of my neighbour. It seems to me that at least four propositions of a general character must be accepted before the concept of 'alienation' can gain any kind of meaning. They are:

(1) That a distinctive creature exists that can be designated 'man'. What precisely constitutes his distinctiveness—his capacity for self-transcendence or his ability to project himself through symbols—need not be debated in this context. All that matters is the agreement that there is one genus 'man', and not a number of completely separable racial strains.

(2) That this creature is activated and motivated by numerous 'drives' which cry out for satisfaction.

(3) That these instinctual 'drives' can be thwarted and even dammed up, either by resistance from without or by negation from within.

(4) That as a result of any such frustration which separates him from the goal of his desire, man becomes alienated and estranged and conscious of a malaise which he is seldom able to explain fully in rational terms.

All the leading doctrines of man's nature and destiny at the present time make use of this simple analysis. Marxism, for example, talks quite generally about 'universal man' even though in the final dénouement one section of humanity has to be entirely liquidated. This creature man is motivated in all his activities, even in what might be called the manifestations of mind or spirit, by his material needs. To satisfy these needs, in whatever environment he lives, he must engage in some form of labour. By this labour he not only obtains food to eat and a habitation in which to live: he also develops his own nature. Thus material needs driving man to engage in particular modes of labour form the determining factors of his existence. But then in Marx's theory, many kinds of frustrating and even negating influences have to be taken into account. There are natural conditions such as climate and soil: there are the techniques of production which are developed to supply human needs within any given situation: there are the social institutions which emerge as a result of these technical developments. These all lead, by a highly complicated process of a dialectical kind, to a condition of total alienation. Thus the pattern of an original unity, activated by certain dynamic forces but checked and thwarted by factors not only from without but also evolved from within, and leading to a state of overall estrangement belongs to the essential analysis of the human situation provided by the Marxian theory.

Again in the Freudian theory and in many of its more recent modifications, man is treated as a homogeneous subject, open to scientific enquiry, regardless of whatever distinctions have to be made between normal and abnormal, between neurotic and psychotic behaviour. In Freud's view man is a creature who is activated by numerous instincts all of which are regulated by what he calls the 'pleasure-principle'. Further, for the experiencing of pleasure, nothing is to be compared in importance with the gratification of sexual desire. Even the instincts which seem to be directed towards self-preservation are not unrelated to impulses of a sexual or libidinous kind. In fact if the term 'sexual' is given a sufficient latitude of interpretation it becomes true to say that Freud regarded the sexual instincts as the driving force determining the whole of man's individual and social development.

Obviously, however, these instincts are never allowed free and unrestrained expression. There are factors of many kinds acting as obstacles: physical conditions, social conventions, and above all religious taboos which have evolved in the course of human history. There are also certain internal factors which emerge as the direct negation of the sexual life-instincts: they can only be regarded as 'death-instincts', directed against the ego and serving to increase the complexity of man's conscious and unconscious existence. The final outcome of the inter-action of all these forces is a state of alienation in which the conscious is opposed to the unconscious, the super-ego to the ego, the death-instincts to the life-instincts, the wish-illusions to reality. The analysis is different from that of Marx but it conforms to the four-fold pattern which I have postulated as necessary to a meaningful analysis of the alienation-situation

How then does the Christian view of the human situation fit into this framework? There have been many variations in the precise formulation of this view but common to all is the conviction that man is neither a self-originating creature nor a chance production: it is God who created him in His own image and predestined him to find the fulfilment of his nature in a personal relationship with his Creator. It is true that the phrase 'the image of God' has provided an almost limitless field for speculation and detailed interpretation but this need not deter us from fastening upon the central truth which it enshrines—that God is the originator of man's distinctive quality and that that quality consists essentially in the capacity to respond to God's invitation to conscious relationship. This may reach man in an infinite variety of ways but that man is open to receive it and to respond to it is a necessary presupposition of any Christian interpretation of atonement.

It would be possible to describe at length how this essential conviction is set forth in the writings of the New Testament. But it will, perhaps, suffice at this stage to refer to three short summaries of this conviction which are to be found in familiar formulations of later Christian history. No saying of St. Augustine is better known than that which occurs in the first book of his Confessions: Thou hast created us for thyself (*ad te*—with a direction towards thyself) and the heart is restless until it finds its resting-place in thee (*in te*—in relationship with thyself). Without such an initial conviction any elaboration of Christian doctrine is impossible.

Again, in the first chapter of the second book of the *Cur Deus Homo*, Anselm of Canterbury states as an unquestionable axiom that 'rational nature has been created righteous, that it may be blessed in the enjoyment of the highest good, that is, God. It follows then, that man, who is of a rational nature, was made righteous that he might be blessed by the enjoyment of God.' But even behind this statement there lie two more fundamental assumptions—that God created man and that He created him with a 'rational nature'. Without such assumptions it is doubtful whether it is possible to *reason* about God and man at all: possibly sounds could be uttered which would have an emotional reference but any kind of ordered sequence of language would be out of the question. With these assumptions, however, Anselm can go on to argue that man's rational nature would have been created in vain unless it gave him the capacity to discern between good and evil. But then, further, this capacity of discernment would have been given in vain unless it enabled man actually to choose the good and reject the evil and this in turn means that man is capable of loving and choosing the highest good as his proper end. The final conclusion follows that if it is possible for him to love and choose the highest good—which can be none other than God Himself—he must be destined to attain that good or he would have been created with these capacities in vain. In other words Anselm's initial assumption that God created man with a rational nature leads him to the inescapable conclusion that his rational nature can find its fulfilment only in the blessed enjoyment of God Himself. Whatever may be thought about Anselm's argument itself, there can be no doubt that he considered it impossible to speak about a condition of alienation unless the initial presuppositions were allowed—that God had created a rational creature and that his rational nature could attain its true end only in God Himself.

At a still later stage and within the context of Reformed theology stand the famous answers which act, as it were, as door-keepers guarding the way into the mysteries of the Larger and Shorter Catechisms agreed upon by the Assembly of Divines meeting at Westminster. In almost exactly the same terms they affirm that 'Man's chief end is to glorify God and to enjoy Him for ever'. Here at the very threshold of all instruction concerning man's defection and restoration are to be found the assumptions that there is a distinctive creature, man, that he has been created with the capacity of reflecting the glory of God and that he gains the fulfilment of his destiny in enjoying God for ever. Thus we find three of the most influential traditions of Christian thought agreeing upon certain basic presuppositions: that there is a universal creature man whose essential being is determined by what we may call the 'pull' towards God and that his being can only find its satisfaction and fulfilment when all his instincts find a harmonious co-ordination in relation with God Himself and with His purpose for man's good.

Immediately, however, the further assumption appears: that this 'pull' has been thwarted and resisted and even in a measure negated by all that is involved in what is comprehensively designated the sin of mankind. Not that the word sin in itself is a particularly helpful one. It has the advantage of expressing a very general failure and deficiency but can easily become too vague and abstract. It really only gathers proper meaning when interpreted in the context of God's comprehensive design for human life and of his increasing activity directed towards its fulfilment. Every perversion of this design, every hindrance to its fulfilment must be regarded as sinful. Some of the opposing forces may appear to come from outside the precise sphere of human life and its complex of inner relationships. Vast, impersonal, 'demonic' influences seem to be working against God and His purposes. Of these it will be necessary to speak more fully at a later stage in the book. But more obviously the opposition comes from within humanity itself where man, sensing the 'pull' towards that which is above and beyond his own limited existence, seeks to transcend his limitations not by a positive but by a negative response to that which lays its hand upon him. In fact the all-determinative magnetic attraction exercised upon man by God Himself is thwarted and, as it were, driven into reverse, by the strange medley of other forces which operate within the human scene.

The final proposition of our general framework naturally and inevitably follows. Within the Christian view man is 'restless', 'fallen', 'frustrated', 'disobedient', 'hostile', 'estranged'. The Divinely-created design has been marred and spoiled: the Divinely-activated drive has been resisted and repressed. Man is alienated, therefore, in every part of his being and only because this is so is it possible to speak meaningfully about restoration and reconciliation within the human situation. Certain postulates or presuppositions there have to be. It is altogether possible that my presuppositions will not be the same as those of my neighbour. But it is at least significant that three of the leading interpretations of the human condition at the present time—the Marxian, the Freudian and the Christian—all make use of roughly the same framework of description. Where of course they differ radically is at the central place where the nature of the instinctual 'drives' is expounded. Even here there may be points of contact but in the final instance there can be no compromise between a faith which regards a living and personal God as the original creator and final goal of human existence and one which finds the origin in the interaction of impersonal forces or the goal in the complete satisfaction of sensuous desires. In the former case the essential problem of atonement is the restoration of a torn fabric of personal relationships. In the latter case the problem is rather that of adjusting, in a world ultimately determined by material structures and physical needs, the temporary aberrations which have resulted from man's failure to relate himself rightly to the ongoing processes of natural evolution or historical determination. In each case the words estrangement and reconciliation may be used but the meanings attached to them are profoundly different.

D

Can the Christian interpretation of atonement, then, be derived simply from certain fundamental assumptions concerning the nature and destiny of man? Can we, following Anselm's method, prove by necessary reasoning from these fundamental presuppositions ('Christ being left out of the question as though nothing were known of Him'[13]) that there is no other way of reconciliation for mankind than that made possible through the work of the God-Man? Even if it were possible to proceed in these ways it would have little chance of commending itself to the temper of an age that has increasingly demanded factual foundation and historical verification. Such a temper may have gone to extremes through a too-hasty assumption that it must be obvious to all men what exactly the term 'historical fact' means and implies. But the appeal to history has become so general that it would be foolish of the Christian interpreter to think that he could avoid any such appeal in his attempt to put forward his own distinctive doctrine.

As it happens few things in the history of Christain thought have been so impressive as the response made by Christian scholars and teachers to the challenge of the 'historical' as it has developed during the past two centuries. In conformity with the general pattern of the culture stemming from the Graeco-Roman milieu, early Christian thought emphasized the patterns belonging to the order of nature and the Divine truths accessible to human reason. To a very large extent its theology was constructed with these emphases in view. Nevertheless it never abandoned the testimony to unique events which actually happened during a particular period of the world's history; this was enshrined in its credal and liturgical forms, in its painting and carving and above all in its canonical Scriptures. Anselm's proposal to leave Christ out of the question as though nothing were known of Him could only be brought into effect by a very deliberate disregard of something which was at the very heart of the living Christian tradition. The stuff of history was there even though the historical method was not yet being employed in any conscious or systematic way.

With the coming of the great change in the climate of Western thought however—a change which showed itself pre-eminently in the new concern for scientific and historical *fact*—the focus of interest began to shift away from the abiding principles of the Divine order to the precise character of the Divine ingressions into history.

13. *Cur Deus Homo:* Preface.

What, above all, could be said about the historical figure through whom, according to the firm tradition of the Catholic faith, God had manifested Himself within the bounds of space and time? What could be said with confidence about His birth, His words, His deeds, His death, His resurrection? What, further, appeared to be well-authenticated in the development of the early Church? Such questions prompted the most searching and extensive historical enquiries and the altogether distinctive quality of Christian thought since the beginning of the nineteenth century has been its continuing effort to establish firm *historical* bases at a time when many of its traditional *philosophical* supports seemed to be threatened. It would be quite impossible to give even a summary of the long struggle for defensible historical positions which Christian scholars have waged but it is essential to ask how the situation stands today in regard to that event which has always been at the centre of Christian interpretations of the Atonement, namely, the death of Jesus Christ upon the cross of Calvary.

In every historical investigation it is necessary to begin somewhere and here the obvious place from which to start is the living Christian community as we know it today. The variations and even contradictions within this community seem to be legion and yet there are a few elements which constitute a common and essential pattern. Let us seek to enumerate them, noting incidentally that they may be regarded as the minimum requirements for the stability of any substantial social entity.

① There is a definition of the *pattern* which distinguishes the particular Christian community from the totality of mankind. This definition is made explicit in a rite which both separates and incorporates.

② There is a definition of the *quality* which the Christian community seeks to make manifest through its corporate existence. This definition is made explicit in a rite which both denies and affirms.

③ There is a definition of the *significance of history* for the particular Christian community. This is made explicit in a story which both judges the past and anticipates the future.

④ There is a definition of the *relationship* of the Christian society to other groups in history. This is made explicit in a record of separation which unveils the causes of past antagonisms and reveals the secret of final reconciliation.

Let us now consider each of these in turn:

① Throughout Christendom today a rite is in common use which serves to distinguish the Christian community from the great

Baptism:
death & rebirth

society to which in other ways it belongs. Those who have been baptized have in some way been initiated into a death: they have also in some sense been incorporated into a new life. This double experience is dramatized in a water-rite accompanied by ritual formulae and the significant thing is that both the actions and the words form themselves into a coherent pattern around the central theme of death or burial and rebirth or renewal of life. Furthermore, this is no merely general death and rebirth: all is related to the death and resurrection of the Christ Himself. Thus the structure of the Christian community today is defined by reference to the death and resurrection of a representative person in history.

(2) Again in almost every section of Christendom the regular practice of a central community rite is to be found. Those who take part in the Eucharist actually participate in the death of Christ: they are also in some sense made partakers of His Divine life. This double experience is dramatized in a rite in which bread is broken and wine outpoured but in which also bread is eaten and wine consumed. In this way the whole quality of the life of the Christian community is made manifest: it is a self-denial leading to self-affirmation, it is a self-immolation leading to self-fulfilment, it is a corporate expression of humiliation leading to a corporate experience of enrichment. But all of this only finds its origin and secret of continuity in the actual self-oblation of the Christ to death and in His glorification in the resurrection. The quality of the Christian community today is defined therefore by a constant return to the death and resurrection of its Saviour and Lord.

(3) But a community is not only defined by its structural pattern and its continuing life but also by its place in history. What is its significance within the total movement of history? What is its pattern of its relationships with other groups? In answer to the first of these questions it has been the persistent claim of Christian witnesses that the story they tell about Jesus Christ (the Gospel) is the key to the understanding of all history. It gives meaning to an individual's life-span, to the corporate experience of God's people, and to the universal history of mankind. And at the heart of this story there is the witness to a great reversal when the death which symbolized the triumph of evil was negated by the resurrection which symbolized the victory of all that was good. For those who accept and live by this story the past stands constantly under judgment, the future is irradiated by hope. In the death and resurrection of Christ the Christian community finds *the definition of its own historical existence* and the key to the interpretation of the life and destiny of mankind.

(4) Finally the Christian community justifies its own separate development in history by recalling the record of the treatment of the Son of God by the rulers of this world. 'Him ye have taken and by wicked hands have crucified and slain.' 'Whom they slew and hanged on a tree.' 'Who . . . suffered under Pontius Pilate.' What happened to the Lord and Leader of the Christian community has happened again and again to His followers. They have been cast out, cut off, rejected, persecuted. But this very treatment marks them out as belonging to the community of Christ and as destined to share in His final triumph.

> They suffer with their Lord below
> They reign with Him above.

In the death and resurrection of the Christ the Christian community finds the definition of its own *relationship* to the other dynamic-groups of history and the pledge of the final triumph of the cause to which it is committed.

Thus amidst all the strange divergences and variations that are to be found within the total life of Christendom we find certain elements that can be described as perennial and universal. Baptism, the Eucharist, the Gospel, the Passion-Story: these are to be found in greater or lesser degree of emphasis wherever the Christian community is a reality. But the significant thing is that every element of this common pattern has as its central motivating power *the death and resurrection of Jesus Christ*. And wherever we test the records of the Christian community in history we find that the same is true. Most important of all, when we press back to the earliest credal and liturgical forms, to the earliest record of the life and worship of the Church, to the New Testament documents themselves, the witness is the same.

Baptism in the New Testament stamps upon the Christian community the mark of the death and resurrection of Christ: the Eucharist shows forth the Lord's death in the assurance of His victorious resurrection and thereby manifests the quality of the Church's continuing life: the Gospel proclaims that the meaning of the historical mission of the infant Christian community was to be found in the recapitulation of the judgment and salvation which had been brought to a crisis in history in the death and resurrection of Jesus: the Passion and Persecution records declare that the tension between the Church and the World in history was to be explained in terms of the casting out of the Christ in death and His vindication by God in the glory of resurrection. If every cross-section of the history of Christendom reveals a community with the cross and the resurrection established at the very centre of every major aspect of its corporate life: if this is true of the earliest pattern of the Christian community of which we possess records: if creeds, hymns, liturgical fragments, doxologies, sermons, sacramental practices, all find their central point of reference in His death and resurrection: then surely we may claim that if any event in history may be regarded as firmly attested and strongly supported it is this.

In saying this I am not suggesting that the detailed records of events leading up to His death are necessarily to be taken at their face-value. Nor am I suggesting that the records of the resurrection can be accepted uncritically or unquestioningly. What I am affirming is that the whole distinctive quality and significance of the Christian community is derived from the firm conviction that Jesus the Christ died on the cross and was restored to life again. Apart from the conviction that this double-sided event had actually happened within the boundaries of space and time it is impossible to think that the total Christian community in its earliest form or in any subsequent form could ever have come into existence. This does not *prove* that the event took place exactly as it is recorded in the New Testament. It makes it virtually certain, on the other hand, that some event of unusual magnitude occurred and in the absence of any other identification we are surely justified in accepting the testimony provided by so many of the symbolic forms and structures of the Christian community which are available for our examination. That Jesus in some sense died and in some sense rose again is the minimal conclusion that can be drawn from the historical evidence.

E

'Christianity is not the religion preached or taught by Jesus. It has for its content the drama of redemption accomplished by his death and resurrection . . . It is not concerned with the life of a holy man or a hero who serves as an example for those who follow him, but with a series of historical facts, which are interpreted as revealing redemptive acts of God.'[14] This contrast between the life and teaching of Jesus on the one hand and the drama of redemption on the other is probably expressed in too extreme a fashion. But the passage serves to point up a distinction which has far-reaching implications. On the one side Goguel sets a series of historical facts—in particular, the death and resurrection of Jesus: on the other side he sets an interpretation—in particular, interpretation in

14. Maurice Goguel: *The Birth of Christianity*, p. 5.

terms of redemption. In other words Christianity, in his judgment, has as its central concern the historical facts of the death and resurrection of Jesus: but these facts were interpreted in certain ways which are determinative for a true understanding of historical Christianity.

This distinction between 'fact' and 'interpretation' is of the greatest importance in any discussion of the doctrine of the Atonement for it corresponds to the distinction between 'fact' and 'theory' which has played so large a part in the history of the doctrine. Is it possible, for example, to speak of the *fact* of the Atonement as independent of any *theory* of the Atonement? Or is it possible to speak of the *event* of atonement as independent of any *interpretation* of the event? Such language is often used but in my judgment to employ the words *fact* or *event* in relation to such a concept as atonement is to confuse discussion seriously. Fact and event are surely better confined to that which has taken place within the familiar framework of time and space and has brought about some observable change in existing conditions. It is true that the words are notoriously difficult to define precisely. It can easily be asserted, for example, that it is possible to refer to a certain process of thinking at a particular time as a 'fact': it is a fact that I thought of my mother at a particular moment. It can be claimed that a certain 'event' took place which has changed existing conditions enormously but which was observed by nobody. But the first of these could hardly be called a historical fact as it cannot be tested by any of the usual methods of historical investigation and the second can only be called an event in history insofar as its effects can be observed or measured at a later time.

Can we then speak of the death and resurrection of Jesus as historical fact? I have tried in the previous section to approach this question from the standpoint of the social historian seeking the origin or origins of an existing social group. All lines of evidence seem to converge upon the death and resurrection of Jesus the Messiah and it appears therefore that one is entirely justified in speaking of this death and resurrection as historical fact or as an event in history. Yet

(*a*) this is not to affirm that the precise *manner* of the death and resurrection can be historically determined;

(*b*) this is not the same as saying that the *Atonement* is a historical fact or that the reconciliation effected by God in Christ is an established historical event;

(*c*) this is not sufficient in itself to explain the emergence in history of the Christian society or its continuance until today. It is only

because from the very beginning the fact was interpreted, the event
was set within the framework of a *theory*, that it began to have
profound social consequences and to affect observably the life of
mankind;

(*d*) this is not sufficient in itself to engage our interest or concern
today. The bare historical fact, the isolated event, even though all
the evidence points to its actually having happened, cannot become
important until it is set within what the noted historian Marc Bloch
calls 'a certain range of comparison'.[15] This is what the witnesses
to the event were doing from the very beginning: they were seeing
it within *a certain range of comparison*, they were viewing it within
a certain framework of interpretation, and it is these comparisons
or interpretations which are of supreme interest and importance for
all later generations.

It is altogether too simple, then, to affirm that we are only concerned with the *fact* of the Atonement and that *theories* are an
optional extra. It is nearer to the truth to say that we can be confident
about the historical *fact* of the death and resurrection of Jesus but
that *theories* are secondary and vary from age to age. Yet even
this is not a fully satisfactory analysis of the relationship between
fact and theory. Perhaps it can best be put this way. All the available
evidence leads us to conclude that a certain event of far-reaching
importance happened at a particular time in history. Those nearest
to the event were unanimous in affirming that Jesus of Galilee had
died and risen again and their words and deeds immediately showed
that this death and resurrection was, in their view, directly related
to every aspect of individual and social life. But we nowhere see
this death and resurrection as bare, isolated, disinterestedly-reported
event. Every witness to it moves within a certain 'theory':[16] it
may be the theory of Jesus' Messiahship, it may be the theory of a
new redemption, it may be the theory of a new covenant. The fact
is set within the framework of the theory but simultaneously the
theory is affected by the introduction of the new fact. So the mysterious dialectical relationship between fact and theory, between event
and interpretation, may be said to have been operating at the
beginning and to have continued in operation ever since. For long
periods, indeed, it seemed that theory was triumphing over fact:
more recently it has often seemed that bare facts were on the point
of banishing theory. But time and again the fruitful inter-relationship

15. 'There is no true understanding without a certain range of comparison.'
Marc Bloch: *The Historian's Craft*, p. 42.
16. It needs perhaps, to be emphasized that the Greek word *theoria* is essentially concerned with *seeing*, viewing in perspective.

has been restored and I shall seek as far as possible to work within it in all that follows.[17]

Two other things need to be said in this connection. In the first place it must be allowed that theories themselves can become matter for historical investigation. Here, indeed, is the place where the sharpest disagreement has revealed itself in recent times. The enquiry about the events leading up to the death of Jesus still goes on. The precise sequence of events on the night of His betrayal and the exact form of His trial are still matters for careful investigation as are the resurrection appearances as they are reported in the different Gospels. There is still the possibility that some new light may be thrown upon the *meaning* of the great event by some fuller knowledge of the facts—though I would emphasize again that these can never be entirely independent. But the storm-centre of historical investigation is in another area at the present time. It concerns theory rather than what is usually called fact and the dispute shows incidentally how hard it is to separate the one from the other.

The chief difference of opinion arises from the question as to whether Jesus Himself held a particular theory of His own death and resurrection, and if so what it was. Did He view his own future within the framework of Traditional Messianism or within the dual framework of Messiah and Suffering Servant? Did he see his work as that of a new Moses—Redeemer, Shepherd, Covenant-mediator? And if so did he communicate such theories in any significant way to his Disciples? Even in their own case, is it certain that they were ready at once to view the death and resurrection within the theoretic framework of suffering service and the mediation of the forgiveness of sins? Or were these, in fact, later interpretations introduced by those who had had time to meditate upon the event in the light of Old Testament images? None of these questions is easy to answer and yet they are all of great importance as we seek to understand the New Testament basis of Atonement doctrine.

Again in the case of Paul there is the difficult question concerning his own use of the imagery of sacrifice. Did this form his own leading interpretive category? Was he unaware of or indifferent to the Suffering Servant imagery? And how far was he influenced by Rabbinic conceptions, how far by Hellenistic ideas, as he sought to interpret the death and resurrection of Christ to his own contempor-

---

17. 'Christianity is built upon a life that was actually lived; and the first preaching was the proclamation of the fact that Christ is risen. But the Christian Gospel is not only facts: it is the meaning of those facts. And when we come to convey meaning, we have to resort to picture language—we cannot help it . . . though our picture language ought to grow up along with us and not stay arrested at an infantile level.' (M. V. C. Jeffreys, in a Broadcast.)

aries? Yet again there are questions raised by the Fourth Gospel. Is the use of sacrificial imagery incidental or central and determinative? What is the framework within which the references to the eating of the flesh and drinking of the blood of the Son of Man moves? What is the background of the symbol of the Lamb of God bearing away the sin of the world? Here are some of the most difficult historical problems of the New Testament, and no final answers are in sight.

Thus the process of examining documents and comparing texts and interpreting symbols and inspecting contemporary literature must go on continuously. To understand better how Jesus viewed the future and how the apostles viewed the past is of the greatest importance to the interpreter of the Atonement. Yet there is far less likelihood of settled conclusions here than in the case of the investigation of the open, observable events of death and resurrection. More complicated factors of a psychological and literary kind are involved, and subjective judgments play a much larger part in the historian's conclusions. This means that while the interpreter of the Atonement will seek ever to be attentive to the results which emerge from the work of the New Testament historian he will be more concerned with the developed *imaginative comparisons* which the book undoubtedly contains than with the difficult and detailed questions of who was responsible for originating them and how they came to establish themselves in the author's mind. In saying this I do not seek in the least to disparage the work of the Biblical historian to whom the systematic theologian owes so great a debt. I am only suggesting that it is unnecessary for the theologian himself to attempt to engage in a discussion of these intricate historical problems. He regards certain leading theories and imaginative comparisons as firmly established within the general testimony of the early Church and seeks mainly to understand what was their power at that time and what their abiding importance for the imagination of the man of today.

In the second place the question rather naturally arises as to what is the criterion for determining whether one theory of the atonement is to be preferred to another. I have already implied that more than one theoretical framework is to be found in the New Testament itself. It would be sufficient to give a brief description of the backgrounds of the words Redemption, Justification and Propitiation to show that such is the case. But if there are varying theoretical formulations of atonement in the New Testament how much more is this the case in later periods of the history of the Church. One attempt after another has been made to show that the death and resurrection of Jesus gains meaning and power when set within a particular framework of human experience which is already reasonably familiar. How then can we decide upon the relative value of these different theories?

Some would urge that whatever is most prominent in the New Testament should be given the place of supremacy in every age. If, for example, it could be proved that a theory worked out in terms of penalty and a substitutionary bearing of punishment occupied the position of primacy in New Testament thought, then, it might be said, this theory must stand first in every period. Or if it could be demonstrated that the theory in which Christ is seen as victor over all the forces that oppress and enslave men is the most prominent, then that should for ever hold pride of place. But the immediate difficulty in the way of such a solution is the fact that there is no kind of general agreement about which theoretical framework is the most frequently used and the most widely favoured in the New Testament. And the second difficulty is that even if one could be seen to hold an obvious priority in the New Testament, it does not necessarily follow that it must hold the same advantage in every age. My own conviction is that the New Testament contains a richly comprehensive interpretation of the death and resurrection of Christ and that we cannot afford to neglect any facets of this interpretation in any age. Yet it is altogether likely that the sociological and psychological needs of a particular era will manifest themselves in such a way that a particular theory or explanation will commend itself as most relevant and meaningful at that particular time. If the question of redemption from oppressive forces is being asked poignantly and urgently, the theory of atonement which is expressed in terms of a redemption situation is likely to make the most powerful appeal—and so on. To say this is not to adopt a light-hearted relativism. It does not mean that any well-established theory can be entirely ignored unless it can be shown to be a perversion of essential Christian doctrine. But it does mean that no absolute sanction can be accorded to any human formulation and that every Christian theologian must be constantly seeking to relate himself imaginatively to the particular needs of his own age. In this way, it may be claimed, the theory most to be preferred in any given situation will gradually become evident. This may be an empirical solution but it is the only alternative to accepting a formulation imposed by authoritative decree.

F

Let me finally draw together some of the main conclusions to which this chapter has pointed. We have seen that the very *idea* of atonement only becomes possible within a situation where an original design has been damaged or an expressed purpose disrupted. Within a specifically religious context, atonement means to deal with man's alienation in such a way that a general restoration of harmony becomes possible. But in the Christian tradition this restoration has always been associated with the death and resurrection of Christ. We saw how various strands of evidence serve to establish the firm historicity of this death and resurrection but the bare historical fact would of itself stimulate little interest and carry little meaning. It therefore becomes necessary for some vital connection to be established between the historical event and the transcendent effect. Such a connection, I have claimed, can only be made by means of a *theory* an imaginative *pattern of comparison* which somehow links the record of the death and resurrection of Christ with the wider experiences of mankind.

Generally speaking there are two main types of theory. The first type focuses attention on *patterns* of *corporate* experience which have recurred again and again in human history. It seeks to show that within these patterns suffering and death have played an essential part: that they have, in fact, formed the necessary pathway to the enhancement and enrichment of life. Once this point is established it becomes relatively easy to urge that in a similar, though obviously higher way, the suffering and death of Jesus, acting in his corporate capacity, proved the essential means of the regeneration and enlargement of the life of the whole world.

The second type looks rather at outstanding *examples of individual achievement* recorded in human history. It seeks to show that when a man has encountered death, actually or symbolically, and has faced it with dignity and courage, then, in some mysterious and surprising way, light has flashed forth from the darkness, life has leapt forth from the very jaws of death. Is it not then possible to imagine that something at least comparable to such a dramatic event happened in the case of Jesus himself? May it not be that He encountered and wrestled with forces which are the ultimate intensification of all that man has ever had to encounter? And may it not be that out of his agonising struggle redemption and release have become possible for all who follow in His train?

In the following pages we shall be looking at examples of each of these leading types of theory. I shall try to keep as close as possible to the witness of the New Testament to the death and resurrection of Jesus, within the context of the eve:ts which preceded and followed it. The nearer we can come to the actual event and to its setting in space and time the more likely we shall be to give a true interpretation of its meaning for the life of mankind. On the other hand the more we know of the general patterns of human experience, its rhythmical regularities and its startling surprises, the more comprehensively and the more imaginatively shall we be able to suggest what is the significance of the central historical fact for the recurring crises of human existence. In other words to see the *fact* within a certain *range of comparison* is to fashion *a theory*. No fact can ever be completely known: no range of comparison can be absolute in its outreach. So the fashioning and refashioning of theories will never cease, although I think there is good reason to believe that the frameworks now available cover the major structures of corporate and individual life. Whether this is so or not will perhaps become more evident after we have examined some of the leading theories in greater detail.[18]

minor exception women

18 I have called the first type—the patterns of corporate experience—*analogues*. They serve to lift the imagination upward from the partial realization within humanity to the perfect fulfilment in the reconciliation wrought by the God-Man Himself. I have called the second type—the examples of individual achievement—*parables*. They stir the imagination to make a leap from that which within human relationships is achieved in face of seemingly overwhelming odds to that which not only *seemed* overwhelming but which actually brought Him to the death of the Cross.

CHAPTER II

THE ETERNAL SACRIFICE

First Analogue - Pattern
Corporate experience

The whole universe as originally created was perfect in conception and form. Yet through some primordial catastrophe—either the pre-mundane fall of an angelic spirit or the post-creation fall of primeval man—the original perfection was disrupted. Disorder, decay and death threatened to ruin the archetypal design irretrievably. A complete reversal, a comprehensive recapitulation was essential if final disaster was to be averted.

What has been called 'The Myth of the Eternal Return' describes in varying ways the process by which such a reversal could be effected. Normally the process is regarded as costly, involving the self-oblation of a representative victim who sums up in his own being the life of nature and of humanity. He enacts symbolically the drama of regeneration and thereby restores the universe to a condition of wholeness.

Within the Christian context the victim is none other than One Who in His humanity revealed the perfect image of the invisible God: Who entered re-creatively into the fallen situation and by His career of self-offering reversed and negated the bias towards evil. Supremely He offered His very life-blood in a sacrifice which renews the whole life of the universe and restores the disordered cosmos to the perfection of its design within the mind and purpose of God. ?

A

Myths of creation and their corresponding rites have enabled man to come to terms with his universe and to share in the renewal of its life. He embellishes processes already familiar through ordinary experience and uses them to describe the way in which the world itself came into existence. For example he imagines the whole universe as a cosmic egg brought to gestation by a super-human agent. Or he employs a water-ritual to portray the emergence of life from the cosmic deep and to promote fertility in his immediate surroundings. Or again he spills blood on the earth in order, it

29

appears, to fertilize the cosmic womb by applying to it so obvious a carrier of life-potency.[1]

Other common themes in early creation-myths are those associated with the union of two partners in human generation and those linked with the fabrication of pots and vessels by the moulding of some kind of clay. These stories were told and corresponding ritual actions were performed not primarily for the entertainment of those involved but for a practical end. Man needed to be sure that the sun would rise again on the morrow, that spring would return in its proper season, that water would come from above to nourish the crops, that life would continue in the home and the fold. The totality of his environment needed in fact to be constantly reinvigorated and the only way to do this was to return to the beginnings, to repeat the sequence of words and actions which were operative in the original creation. Through the recitation of the proper myth and the performance of the appropriate ritual, Life Universal could be sustained.

So far I have referred to motifs which constantly recur in early creation-myths. The general pattern becomes even clearer if we look at the cult-practices of some of the great centres of civilization in the ancient world. Let us begin with Egypt. From the very beginnings of the settlement in the Nile valley two natural phenomena have commanded the attention, the wonderment and the concern of the settlers, viz. the Sun and the River. The waters are clearly the source of life. Yet life only becomes actual when small heaps of slime raise their tops above the swirling waters and receive the fertilization of the gracious rays of the sun. In the Egyptian-creation myths, then, the all-important event is the emergence of the creator from the waters of chaos to take his stand upon a mound or pyramid of dry land. This primeval hillock is regarded as the centre of the universe, the Sun-god rising erect upon this sacred spot is regarded as the creator and giver of life, the essence of the creative act is regarded as the bringing of order and design where previously there was the teeming confusion of the watery abyss.

The extension of this prototypal pattern of creation may be seen in the later, often competing cosmogonies which were constructed at the various cult-centres in Egypt. Always the particular mound on which a temple was built was regarded as the centre of the universe and the place of creation: always the King was regarded as the vicegerent and representative of the Sun-god and as the one upon whom the continuing vitality of the realm in all its parts completely

1. Cf. E. Neumann: *The Origin and History of Consciousness*, p. 6 f.

depended. Nothing therefore was more important than the daily rebirth of the king not only to life but to full vitality. This rebirth was in a very real sense the renewal of the creative act and the ritual and myth through which it was accomplished were essentially parts of a re-creative cult. The very existence of night with its dangers and disorders, the occasional experience of eclipse or storm or pest invasion, served to remind the Egyptian that his seemingly ordered and stable existence could not be simply taken for granted. Only by the regular re-enactment of the daily liturgy of rebirth could Life-Universal be sustained and the great act of cosmic reconciliation be constantly renewed.

But there were also two more serious threats to life which could never be forgotten. One was the coming of physical death to the individual: the other was the waning of the Nile waters, and the consequent death of vegetation in the autumn of the year. It was these threats which were mainly responsible for promoting the worship of the second most notable divinity of Egypt—Osiris, the Nile-god. Osiris was familiar with the kingdoms of the dead. In the annual vegetation cycle the Nile-god seemed to die and rise again and for the common people an identification with this river-deity on whom their food supplies so obviously depended seemed the altogether desirable state to achieve. So the cult of Osiris flourished alongside that of the Sun-god though in point of fact the actual ritual-pattern differed but little from that of the state religion. The Sun's cycle was a daily one, the Nile's cycle was annual. Yet the general framework of myth and ritual for both was cast in the pattern of a daily liturgy in which the god's representative or image was purified, clothed, censed and regaled with suitable foods. Through water purification and eucharistic offerings, all related to a single representative of both god and people, order was re-established, life was renewed and the cosmos was re-created in its primeval state of perfection.

Let us look next at the ancient civilization of India at a time after the Aryan invasions when a relative degree of settlement had been achieved and when elaborate regulations for the ordered life of the community were being framed. Here a different motif occupies the central place in the creation-myth. Not the sun nor the river but an original universal man is held to have been the source of all creation. This primeval man, Purusha by name (Rig Veda X 90), consisting of 'Whatever hath been and whatsoever shall be', was divided up and dismembered in a prototypal sacrifice. This sacrifice, moreover, is designated an 'all offered sacrifice', one, that is to say, in which the whole body is surrendered upon the altar and regarded as gathering all time into its embrace. In other words creation and sacrifice are virtually interchangeable ideas.

In the elaborate ritual directions which are to be found in the later Brahmanas every sacrifice is held to be a renewal of this act of creation. It is not exactly a *repetition* for the passage of time plays little part in the world outlook of classical Hinduism. Rather the sacrifice performed at any place, at any time, is identical with the original sacrifice at the centre of the universe, at the centre of time, through which the All came into phenomenal existence. Every new act of building—a house, a temple, a bridge—is celebrated by sacrifice and is thereby gathered up into the cosmic creative act for 'the periodical sacrifice is nothing else than a microcosmic representation of the ever-proceeding destruction and renewal of all cosmic life and matter'.[2]

It is true that in spite of the emphasis upon the timelessness of the sacrifice and upon the continuity of the creative act there is a certain recognition of the break in the original wholeness which came about through the process of dismemberment, as well as a sense that death is a threat to the perfection of the Life Universal. So it comes about that Prajāpati (the name given to the god offered in the sacrifice) is regarded as needing to be built up again in every sacrificial act and to be restored from any inroads which death may have made upon him. No strict distinction can be made between the successive stages of the sacrifice but the raising of the altar (usually in the shape of an eagle or falcon) is seen as the reproduction of the original cosmogonic act, the actual offering of the victim in the fire as the restoration of the primordial unity of the divine whole.

In every renewal of creation through sacrifice, the sacrificer is himself renewed and restored. For 'whosoever knowing this, performs this holy work, or he who but knows this (without practising any ritual) makes up this Prajāpati whole and complete'.[3] In short, according to the ancient myth-and-ritual pattern of the Brahmanas, the original universe came into being through a divine act of self-sacrifice[4] and in every re-enactment of sacrifice the sacrificer himself, the god of sacrifice, and the whole life of the universe are renewed and restored to their true primordial unity.[5]

2. S.B.E. 43 XV.
3. S.B.E. X 4.3.24.
4. Though it was created in order to be *eaten*. The process is *circular*: the god creates from himself in order to offer to himself. Cf. E. Neumann. Op. cit. p. 29 f.
5. Cf. M. Eliade: *The Myth of the Eternal Return*, p. 78 f.

For one further example of a re-creation myth-and-ritual complex we may turn to the ancient civilization of China under its earliest emperors. Probably none of the world's great cultures has ever stressed the importance of harmony in the universe so strongly as the Chinese. The amazingly comprehensive word Li is capable of being applied to every department of life—the regularity of natural phenomena, properly ordered government, good social relations, correct religious ceremonial: nothing has been more important than to promote and maintain Li and in early days no actions were more important towards this end than the offering by the Emperor of the requisite regular sacrifices.

At the centre of the nation's life stood the Ming T'ang or Hall of Light in which the Emperor performed the necessary ceremonies. His was the responsibility of directing the movements of sun, moon and stars, and of providing the correct calendar for his subjects' guidance. He was the Son of Heaven, the one Man central to the cosmic scheme, the medium between Heaven and Earth. Only through his control of the seasons by means of the proper ceremonies could the harmony of heaven, earth and man be sustained and the fullness of life in farm and home be constantly renewed. And of all the ceremonies none were so important as the sacrifices in which bullocks, rams and boars were offered to the appropriate divinities.

If it be asked why the sacrificial cultus held so important a place in early Chinese civilization it may be suggested that no ceremony could more adequately symbolize the rising of earth to heaven in response to heaven's descent to earth. For in Chinese outlook all creative life consists in the polar relationship between heaven and earth. In a famous passage of the Li Chi where the author is dilating on the perfect harmony which exists when heaven and earth is each performing its right function he states:

'The aura of earth ascends, the aura of heaven descends. Negative and positive meet in friction. Heaven and earth are in commotion, drummed by thunder-claps, fanned by wind and rain stirred by the four seasons, warmed by sun and moon. Thus all transforming processes arise.'[6]

And in the great sacrifices on the Altar of Heaven, accompanied as they were by drumming and music, the aura of earth could indeed rise to heaven and the creative processes necessary for the reinvigoration of the universe could again be set in motion.[7] Though

6. Quoted by W. E. Soothill: The Hall of Light, p. 223.
7. It is of interest that the word Li itself has a root bearing the meaning 'an offering on a platter'.

it cannot be proved that the myth of creation was so intimately associated with the sacrificial ritual as in the case of India, yet the general context is that of the renewal of the creative life of the universe and the inference may be confidently drawn that in China, as well as in India, the primordial state of harmony was restored whenever the appropriate myth-and-ritual pattern was performed.

In these three examples no complete uniformity of pattern can be discerned. No doubt in each case the settled ritual of which we have records came into existence as the result of a long process of development in which varying historical circumstances played their part. Yet it is striking to see that at the centre of the picture in each case is a divine-human figure (the primeval man, the representative man, the son of heaven) whose rebirth or whose offering of sacrifice is regarded as necessary for the constant reintegration and renewal of the life of the universe.

B

How far does this particular pattern appear in the Hebrew and Greek cultures which provided the language-forms for the proclamation of the earliest Christian Gospel? Taking the Hebrew first it is clear that so far as the Old Testament is concerned there is little interest in what might be called cosmological speculation and little explicit reference to renewal-of-life ceremonies. There are indeed passages which speak of the coming of a new creation, a blessed state in which earth's disparate elements will be reconciled as the wolf and the lamb dwell together and the lion eats straw like the ox: a state too in which Jerusalem will take its place as the centre of the earth and springs of living water will flow out to renew the land wherever they go. All this is related to the coming of the Messianic Age which, it was increasingly believed in later Judaism, would undo the effects of the Fall and restore the earth to its original splendour.

For in spite of a general discouragement of speculation concerning the story of creation and a steadily continuing conviction that all the powers of life and re-creation were in the hands of Yahweh alone, the bitter experiences of the sixth and following centuries B.C. almost compelled men to ask whether there were evil forces at work in the earth which were ultimately the cause of the dislocation of Yahweh's handiwork. This led, as is well known, to a new focussing of attention upon the Fall stories of Genesis and to an increasing emphasis upon the dire effects which followed upon

Adam's sin. The whole creation, it was believed, had been involved in corruption and decay. Sterility and death spoiled the fair face of the earth and only the merciful forbearance and loving-kindness of Yahweh preserved the earth from final disaster. Was there then no hope of better things? Yes, it was increasingly affirmed in late Judaism, the coming of Messiah would undo the evil consequences of the Fall and restore all things to the state of harmony which they originally enjoyed.[8] As we shall see later, other aspects of the Messianic deliverance tended to occupy the most prominent place in men's imaginations and expectations but that there was a certain movement of interest in pre-Christian Judaism towards the possibility of cosmic reconciliation and universal re-creation through the advent of a Divine figure who would undo the consequences of the first Man's disobedience can scarcely be doubted.

In the matter of the sacrificial ritual of late Judaism it is not easy to speak with confidence. In very large measure, it seems, it was concerned either with the celebration of festal occasions when great acts of Yahweh's historical deliverances were commemorated or with the outward expression of obedience to the Divinely-given regulations for sacrifice—piacular and expiatory—contained in the Law. Yet the cult-acts associated with the nature-festivals and with the beginning of the New Year almost certainly carried some suggestions of life-renewal and life-enhancement such as were to be found in other sacrificial rituals of the Near East. I shall refer to this question again in Chapter IV but meanwhile it seems possible to affirm that within the sacrificial cultus as practised in the Temple at Jerusalem in the period of late Judaism there was a pattern which suggested that through the identification of the offerer with the offering and through the slaying and subsequent oblation of the victim, life-universal—of the land, of the flocks, of the human species, of society at large—could be purified from corruption and reinvigorated with its original life-force. Explicit teaching along these lines could not, in all probability, be found but the very existence of the regular ritual practices meant that from Israel as well as from other ancient cultures a ritual-pattern of recapitulation could be derived.

But it is within the richly-varied culture of the Mediterranean basin that we find the most notable precursors of the pattern of re-creation and renewal of life. Here the difficulty is to take account of the many strands of religion and philosophy and mysticism contained within the Graeco-Roman civilization and to sift out the motifs which are of importance for later Christian formulation. It

8. See W. D. Davies: *Paul and Rabbinic Judaism*, p. 33 ff.

will only be possible to touch on those that seem of greatest significance for our immediate purpose.

Perhaps the point which needs most to be emphasized is that in all this welter of thought and speculation one general conviction held firm. It was that the universe was without beginning and without end, that the life which animated it might rise and fall like the tides of the ocean but could not be conceived as finally extinguishable. It is true that there were wide varieties in the formulation of these convictions, the philosophers tending towards a naturalism where the creative activity of neither god nor man had any significant part to play, the common people toward a ritualism in which man sought to unite himself with the gods in the unending process of preserving and restoring life. But behind all these variations lay the general assumption that all life was ultimately one and that the cycle of existence was of eternal duration.

Yet however tenaciously men might cling to this ultimate belief in the indestructibility of their universe, there were certain obvious experiences of daily life which had, in some way, to be reconciled with it. There were the motions of the heavenly bodies, rising and setting, waxing and waning; there was the annual cycle of nature with spring and autumn, seed time and harvest: there was the rhythm of human life with the promise and potency of new birth, the decline and foreboding of death: there were the delights associated with the clear light of day, the dangers associated with darkness and night: there was order and proportion within a situation controlled by reason, chaos and shapelessness when ignorance and wilful obtuseness held sway. The combined effect of all these common experiences was to create (save perhaps in the minds of the most exalted philosophers) a constant concern for life in all its manifestations, a burning desire to gain assurance of sharing in the reinvigoration of life whensoever and howsoever it might be achieved.

In the great days of Athens the deity most widely venerated for her association with the processes of life was the corn-goddess Demeter. Here was a saviour who died and rose again and in her rising brought fertility to the land and immortality to men. A typical passage from the fourth century B.C. indicates something of the veneration in which she was held:

'Demeter arrived in our land,' says Isokrates, the spokesman of Athens, 'and showed the goodwill that she bore to our ancestors by means of those blessings which it is not possible for any but the initiated to hear. Two gifts she gave, the greatest of all gifts: on the one hand the fruits of the field, which have been the instrument whereby mankind is raised above the life of beasts, and on the other hand initiation, participation in which gives sweeter hopes concerning the end of life and all eternity'.[9] Here there is no exclusive emphasis on sacrifice though sacrifices were probably included within the initiation ceremonies and certainly sacrifice was the major event in the great spring *dromenon* which marked the renovation of earth and the refertilization of human life. But a general pattern of a descent to the cold earth and death followed by resuscitation and ascent to new life was familiar not only in the Eleusinian mysteries from which the Athenians derived the Demeter-cult but also in the later importations from Anatolia and Egypt. The worship of Isis in particular was replete with this symbolism and no myth-and-ritual complex impressed itself more deeply upon the popular imagination in the pre-Christian Mediterranean world than did that of the dying and rising god (or goddess) by identification with whom the initiate might be gathered up into the universal renewal of life.

Other motifs, however, may also be discovered. There is the constantly recurring emphasis on the need for purity, an emphasis which is particularly to the fore in formulated Orphic doctrine. But this purity is not to be conceived simply as an outward mark of cleansing from ceremonial impurities: it is essentially connected with death and from the pollution which comes from having contact with death in any of its forms. To touch a dead body, to have any dealings with the world of the dead, to be contaminated by corruption of any kind—these were eventualities which demanded a solemn *Katharsis* for only through such a purgation could the threat of death be countered and the fullness of life be renewed. In earlier days Apollo was essentially the god of purification but at all times the concern for a *Katharsis* which would counteract the infection of death and infuse new potencies of life was a motivating force within the common life of Greece.

Further, and still related to the thirst for life, we find in the cult of Dionysus a vivid testimony to the lengths to which men[10] will go in their endeavour to enjoy the experience of a vitality fuller than that which they possess in themselves. In all probability Dionysus-worship came into Greece from Thrace and was in time assimilated with the rites of the bull-god which formed so popular a part of the religion of Crete. But whatever may be the true story of its origins and development, by the fifth century it was not

9. Quoted by W. K. C. Guthrie: *The Greeks and their Gods*, p. 286.
10. And in this case women even more. In the rites of Bacchus they found an extraordinary release and fulfilment.

only firmly established in Greece but was also spreading into the surrounding countries which were influenced by Greek culture. In almost every respect this cult seems foreign to the love of moderation and proportion which characterized the typical Greek. Yet so great has been the desire for enhancement of life and for union with the young god who is the source of vitality in plants, animals and men that not only in Greece but also in the lands to which Christian civilization came, the rites of Bacchus have exercised a strange fascination and have caused men and women to abandon all self-control in their eager longing to be caught up into the surging life of this god.

Finally in the writings of the philosophers attempts were made to interpret the nature of the universe and the manifold variety of life in an ordered and rational way. If men could only come to a proper understanding of the truth of their world and of their existence within it, they could then order their lives in conformity with the movement of the wholeness of creation as it presses forward to the destiny designed for it by the Divine Mind. For Plato, the perfect, timeless and changeless world is the world of Ideas which can only ultimately be known by thought or reason. But man dwells in the world of objects apprehended by the senses and must at first be largely directed by his sense-impressions. Nevertheless he becomes dimly aware of patterns of regularity and permanence even in his phenomenal world and is thereby reminded of the eternal world from which he came—the world of unchanging forms to which he should be always aspiring. His task, then, is to rise above the body and the things of sense. By feeding the soul with true knowledge and by directing the reason to the Eternal Ideas which are its concern, man can gradually loose himself from the cramping ties of mundane existence and return to his true home in the heavenly world.

Aristotle shared with Plato the conviction that there is an eternal perfection towards which all that belongs to the phenomenal world is being drawn. But he differed radically from his master in holding that there was no body of changeless ideas or forms laid up in heaven, but that the forms were immanent in every existing object and that each object must, by realizing its own specific form, be ever moving towards the perfection of pure form which is God Himself. For him it was impossible to separate form from matter: rather within every existent material object there is a certain potentiality waiting to come to the actuality which is its own proper destiny. I say 'waiting' yet nothing in the world is static or at rest but everything is in process of movement from the potential to the actual. How then is this movement sustained? In the last resort only through the operation of the final cause, the unmoved Mover, God Himself. This God, though external to the universe and not subject to the motion from potentiality to actuality, exerts by his very perfection an attractive force upon all material phenomena and causes them to move forward each towards its own fulfilment within the ordered whole.

I have referred briefly to the systems of Plato and Aristotle because each was destined to exert a most powerful influence upon the development of later Christian doctrine.[11] Plato's general framework of thought lends itself the more easily to a doctrine of universal reconciliation for according to him all life consists of a movement out from itself, *through* a medium which is in some measure formless and resistant, and *back* to its home in the world of perfect ideas or forms. Such a scheme allows room for the notions of compassion, of travail with the hard stuff of the world's complexities, of the union of man with the divine in the ongoing process of reconciliation. Indeed it may be said that the reconciliation-pattern which is expressed in terms of an original perfection becoming involved in the stresses of necessity and returning to its perfection through suffering and sacrifice, is ultimately derivable from the Platonic myth, however much it may have been transformed by the moulding influence of the Christian mind.

In the case of Aristotle the framework is not so easily adapted to a Christian theory of atonement. It is, as we have seen, of the very essence of his teaching that God is external to the world, that He does not go out to the world, that in fact he is not involved in its pain or travail in any way. He is constantly drawing it to himself and this allows room for the conception, which has often been prominent in Christian theology, of man, acting as the priest of creation and making his constant oblation in this capacity, being the instrument through whom the Divine Lover is bringing all things toward their true end as conceived within his perfect plan. Supremely the God-man may be conceived in this way but only at the cost of separating the character of his earthly activity sharply —and it would seem absolutely—from that of the eternal activity of the Unmoved Mover. For unless suffering and travail be in some

11. The problem of the One and the Many was always central in Greek philosophy. It was a virtually unquestioned assumption that the manifold variety of things must have been derived from an original unity and that in consequence the possibility always existed of a return to this unity. Thus the problem of reconciliation was set for Greek religious thinkers in this form: 'Why has the universe become so diversified and how can a true unity be restored?'

way included within the reconciling act, the God-man becomes far removed from the Christ of the Gospel story.

Summing up this short survey of the cosmological motifs which attained greatest prominence in the life and thought of the Mediterranean world in the centuries immediately preceding the coming of Christ, we may say that in general the view of the universe was stable and relatively confident. Men had little conception either of a sudden beginning or of a sudden ending. The world had its regular rhythms and periods and these were likely to continue unendingly. At the same time there were certain causes for anxiety—the recurring question of fertility in man and beast and field, the decline of vegetation year by year, unusual natural portents such as storm and flood, pestilence and drought, the incidence of death in its many forms. So whether through ritual celebrations such as the sacrifice and the dance or through mythological recitations or through initiation into some secret knowledge or through the gaining of wisdom by philosophic discipline, men's energies were constantly bent towards the undoing of the depredations of corruption and sterility and decay and towards the promotion of universal life. When all things were working together in harmony and proportion, when lands were flourishing and spirits were soaring, the Greek felt that the face of the earth was being renewed and that the universe was being restored to that perfect condition in which its true form and essence lay.

C

It is within this general 'range of comparison' that a theory of atonement can be expressed. Yet the New Testament witnesses did not readily speak in these terms just because their own training had been mainly in Jewish circles where speculation on cosmological questions had never been encouraged. It was only when Paul and the writer of the Epistle to the Hebrews and the Fourth Evangelist found it necessary to interpret Christian truth to those who had some familiarity with the vocabulary and questionings of the Hellenistic world that possible intimations of this theory began to appear.

There is, for example, the fascinating and beautiful passage in Romans 8 which is full of suggestiveness though not easy to interpret with confidence. Probably its background is still mainly Jewish though it contains certain parallels to the mythological thinking of the contemporary pagan world. The whole created order, Paul says, has been subjected to 'futility' and is groaning in the pains of travail as it strains after some mighty deliverance. In the light of what we know of Rabbinic speculation on the results of Adam's Fall, it is altogether likely that Paul regards the 'futility' of the created order as the direct result of Adam's sinful disobedience. It will never be restored to its proper harmony and coherence until man himself has been delivered out of *his* bondage of corruption into the glory of the liberty of the children of God.

But although there appears at first sight to be a sense of real sympathy with 'nature' and a suggestion of the total 'reconciliation', (including both man and the natural order) comparable to that which we have encountered in other cultural traditions, it is doubtful whether the apostle, in this particular passage, looks beyond man's immediate 'natural' environment. Man's physical body, the earth which according to the Genesis narrative lay under a curse, vegetation and the animal creation—these will be delivered when man is delivered. But the cosmos as a whole is probably still regarded in this passage as the abode of vast malignant forces which need to be overcome and finally subjected to the will of the God against whom they have rebelled. In Romans 8: 38 at least four of the words used are technical astrological terms and the implication seems to be that the cosmological powers are doomed, even though they may continue to exercise their hostile influence against those who have been saved by Christ.[12] In fact the general tenor of Romans 8 seems to be more in harmony with the Jewish view of a final Divine victory over cosmic antagonists than with the Hellenistic conception of a fallen universe being raised again to its original perfection.

With a remarkable passage in the Epistle to the Colossians (1: 15–20), however, the case seems to be different. Here Paul[13] is not only writing to a Gentile Church: he is specifically dealing with teachings emanating from a Gentile environment. The main question at issue seems to be that of the scope and range of the work of Christ. Allowing that Christ was a Redeemer who had delivered his devotees from certain of the evils with which they had been surrounded, was it certain that he possessed authority over *all* the powers of the universe? Paul has no hesitation in claiming that God has, through Christ, reconciled *all things* unto Himself. Did not the Christ exist *before* all things? Did they not all come into existence by Him and for Him? Are they not all sustained by Him? In other words there is no single force in the whole universe which is finally independent of the Divine Son.

12. See W. L. Knox: *St. Paul and the Church of the Gentiles*, p. 106. G. V. Jones: *Christology and Myth in the New Testament*, p. 156 f.
13. If he is the author.

Yet all too clearly discord and alienation characterize the vast cosmic whole at the present time. Man himself is caught up within this universal disharmony and only if there is a *complete* reconciliation can man himself be assured of his own final salvation. But this end cannot be achieved through any available myth-and-ritual pattern of life-through-death with which man can identify himself. It is rather 'through the blood of his cross'—a phrase which calls up memories of blood-ceremonies and sacrificial-rites and renewal of life through death but which also anchors us firmly in historical event—that God in Christ reconciles all things to Himself, whether they be things in earth or things in heaven. Through Him all things were created: through Him all things are being re-created. Through Him all things have been preserved from an otherwise inevitable disintegration: through Him all things are being brought forward to a goal of universal integration.[14]

One other very significant passage may be found in the Pauline writings in the first chapter of Ephesians. In a verse (v. 10) whose grandeur of conception is unmistakable but whose detailed interpretation is far from certain, the writer speaks of God's purpose in Christ which is 'in the dispensation of the fullness of times' (alternatively 'a plan for the fullness of time' i.e. the purpose has not yet been fully realized) to 'gather together in one all things in Christ, both which are in heaven and which are on earth'. The Greek word translated 'gather together in one'[15] is the key to the whole passage and came to occupy a place of immense importance in later theological discussion. It clearly contains within it the ideas of consummation, the summing up of a speech or a series, the gathering together of a multiplicity of members within the perfect integration of the head. The Latin word used to translate it—*recapitulatio*—contains the same suggestion of 'headship' but it is questionable whether the 're' gives the precise equivalence of 'ana'. There has always been the danger in Latin theology of over-emphasizing the idea of sheer repetition—a process which *could* happen an indefinite number of times—rather than that of a reversal or restoration which can only happen once and for all.

Commentators translate the word into English as 'unite all things in Him', 'sum up all things in Him' and interpret the idea as 'the restoration of a lost unity', 'the restoration of universal harmony', 'the reconstitution of the essential oneness of mankind'. Perhaps the most thorough-going attempt in recent times to draw out the

14. An illuminating account of recent thought on this passage is to be found in C. K. Barrett: *From First Adam to Last*, p. 83 ff.
15. anakephalaiosis.

meaning of the passage has been made by L. S. Thornton.[16] He defines God's purpose as the summing up of all creation in the Christ 'through the power of his resurrection, through his exaltation over the universe, and through his headship of the Church'. This summing up will mean that man and the whole created order will participate in the glory which belongs by right to the exalted Christ. Creation in the Son will find its consummation in the new creation which is under the headship of the risen and exalted Christ. True harmony will be restored as all things find their fruition and fulfilment in Him.

Father Thornton believes that by taking account of the context of the whole Epistle it becomes possible to expound this key-idea in an even more detailed way. The headship of Christ is being fulfilled, he says, within His universal high-priestly ministry. This He performs 'towards and on behalf of the world of creatures' by His ministry of sacrificial oblation. Having identified Himself with the things of the created order through all that is involved in Incarnation, He consecrates the natural world to God through all that is involved in His high-priestly Sacrifice. Thus *all things* are being brought forward to their true fulfilment as they are gathered up into the sacrificial oblation of the Christ and restored to their true harmony in the eternal life of God.

Whether Father Thornton is justified in deriving so comprehensive an interpretation from this one key-verse may be debatable but at least there are suggestions of the idea of cosmic reconciliation in the Colossians-Ephesians corpus of writings. In Ephesians, as in Colossians, there is the reference to 'redemption through his blood' with the clear implication that the summing up of all things has only become possible through the sacrificial-oblation of the Redeemer-Son. The cosmos which has become disordered and corrupted through man's self-inturning and self-aggrandisement can only be brought to its true goal through an all-embracing representative act of self-outpouring and self-sacrifice. Though the actual New Testament material is meagre it was sufficient to provide a starting-point and a fount of inspiration for those who were later to interpret the Doctrine of Atonement in these terms.

So far as the Epistle to the Hebrews is concerned, while the opening chapter gives promise of expounding the universal quality of the reconciliation wrought by Christ, subsequent chapters focus attention almost exclusively upon the way in which it has affected the children of flesh and blood whose nature He assumed. In the

16. See *The Common Life in the Body of Christ*, pp. 178 ff, 296, and *Revelation and the Modern World*, pp. 137 f, 268.

splendidly comprehensive exordium of the Epistle the writer refers to Jesus as the Divine Son, as the Heir of the universe, as the Agent of creation, as the Sustainer of all things, as the Expression of the essential glory of God: He is, in fact, the Wisdom or Logos of God, titles familiar in current cosmological speculation. As such He is greater than the angels who were in some quarters regarded as intermediaries between God and the world. As such, too, He is destined to remain, even when the created order dissolves and vanishes away. That through the Divine Son the whole of creation was fashioned and created and sustained and controlled could hardly be more clearly affirmed.

Yet the writer makes no explicit reference to the way in which the sin of man has affected the created order or indeed to the presence of evil within the non-human world. He touches upon man's failure to occupy the position of dominance over nature which God had appointed for him: he proclaims the universal dominion which Jesus now exerts by reason of His passage through suffering and death: he dwells at length upon the eternal priesthood which Jesus exercises, a priesthood which consists essentially in the offering of His own body and the application of His own blood. These themes might easily have been developed into a full-scale doctrine of recapitulation in which the Agent of creation might have been set forth as the agent also of re-creation, the Priest-King of Melchizedek's line might have been viewed as restoring all things through His own all-inclusive sacrifice, the Body-imagery might have been related to the world-organism which came into being through the Divine self-expression and which is returning again to its origin through its association with the eternal self-oblation of the Logos. But none of these possible themes is pursued in any systematic way though later writers develop in more detail ideas and suggestions which this Epistle contains. The altogether dominating concern of the author is to remind his hearers of the way in which the priestly sacrifice of Christ has affected and still affects their life-in-community. Through Him all may now draw near to God in confident worship: through Him all may now live the life of faith and move towards the goal of their promised rest in God Himself.

The chief connecting-link between the Johannine writers and the pagan religious-systems described earlier in this chapter is to be found in their deep interest in and concern for *life* and *light*. The world lies in darkness: the world is dying. Through his witness to life-giving words and to light-bringing events the Evangelist seeks to convince his readers that *the* Life has been manifested, that *the* Light has come into the world. This eternal Life and this authentic

Light have come in the person of the only-begotten Son of the Father who descended from heaven into the sphere of darkness and death. But as He has come from heaven, He is able to ascend to heaven again and in so doing He opens the way for those who have been living in darkness and under the shadow of death to arise and ascend into the same realm of light and life which is His eternal abode.

This is the general framework of these writings and although the eschatological thrust is not absent yet the constantly reiterated theme is the movement from above to below and the return from earth to heaven. Again and again our eyes are directed to the vision of one who was with God, who was as a son in the bosom of the Father, who was in heaven, who shared the glory of the eternal God, who was 'above' in the realm of spirit and of light, and yet who became flesh, descending to earth, entering into the realm of darkness, actually coming to grips with death, laying aside His glory, falling like a corn of wheat into the ground. From the heights of heavenly bliss to the depths of earthly woe—this is one of the dominant motifs of these unique books.

But this is not the only motif. There is equally the stress on the Son of Man rising, ascending where He was before, sharing again the glory which He had with the Father before the world was. Yet in this case the movement is not so direct or unchecked as was the downward plunge. The ascent involves a 'lifting up', not to immediate glory but to pain and death. This 'lifting up' is no sham movement, no mere illusion. Like the serpent in the wilderness, the Son of Man is lifted up: like the Lamb of God, the Son is offered in sacrifice. Only by being lifted up upon the tree can He begin the upward ascent to the heavenly home. Only by being displayed as the saving victim can He break through the darkness which distorts men's vision and raise their eyes towards the eternal Light. By beginning His upward ascent in this shocking and startling way He stabs men broad awake, makes them aware of their condition and draws them to Himself. Thus they begin the upward movement to the eternal spheres as the Lord of Life and Light leads captivity captive and brings men to their true destiny as sons of the living God.

Yet can this be called a cosmic reconciliation? Is there any indication that the world itself is being redeemed, that universal nature is being restored to its primal condition, that through the ascent of the Son of Man *all things* are returning to their true home in God? It would be hard to find any *direct* reference to such a process. It is true that the writer does not hesitate to proclaim that the darkness is passing away but he also declares that the world is passing away. He glories in the fact that God so loved the world but he also speaks of the Christian overcoming the world. In an unforgettable phrase he affirms that the Word became flesh but in a further passage he warns against the lustful desires of the flesh which are doomed to destruction. His main concern is clearly with the world of *persons*: the world of *things* was created through Christ but little if anything is said about its redemption or its ultimate destiny.

The fact is that an undertone of dualism runs through the Johannine writings and we are constantly reminded that there is a powerful force of evil in the world (the sin of the world, the prince of the world, the lust of the world) from which humanity needs to be delivered. Moreover this evil force works havoc by operating through the flesh or through the eyes and thereby brings man under captivity to that which is contrary to the will and purpose of God. In a sense it is only possible for man to enjoy his redemption to the full when he is altogether released from the flesh and from the mundane order of existence. Earthly things *can* be made sacramental channels for spiritual realities: they can also become ends in themselves and thereby instruments of anti-God and antichrist. Man will only finally be safe when he enters into his heavenly inheritance and the world is left behind.

It would be highly precarious, then, to attempt to fit the Johannine writings into any scheme of universal cosmic redemption. Their leading concern is with the redemption of *men* from sin and darkness and death. 'The world' is not the universe as such but the whole of human society especially in its godlessness and sensuality and materialism. God loves this world but His all-consuming purpose is to redeem men out of this world. The Son of Man entered into the conditions of *this* world, He draws men to Himself that they may be exalted to the blessedness of *that* world. Possibly the author envisaged a redemption which would include *all things* in heaven and earth. It is more likely that he looked for a new spiritual order in which the evils of man's earthly existence would be finally removed and in which even the need for sacramental media would no longer be felt. The 'captivity' which the ascending Son of Man takes with him into the heavenly spheres certainly includes *men*: it is not clear that we dare say more so far as this writer's thought is concerned.[17]

17. I recognize that the writer of the Epistles and the Fourth Evangelist may not have been one and the same person. As I have been concerned with the general standpoint of the Johannine writings I have not attempted to distinguish between the two.

D

From the New Testament then there come hints, suggestions, even daring affirmations of a comprehensive cosmic reconciliation but this particular pattern of imagery cannot be said to figure largely in the apostolic witness. This is not surprising seeing that metaphysical speculation and ontological systematization were alike foreign to Hebrew ways of thought. It was not until early Christian witnesses found themselves confronted by pagan systems in which a full theory of cosmic redemption played a prominent part that the effect of the work of the Christ upon the cosmos at large began to receive serious consideration. Almost certainly the Epistle to the Colossians must be set against a background of Gnostic speculation and the Johannine writings must have been circulated in a milieu where Hellenistic, Hermetic and Gnostic ideas were claiming men's attention and influencing their religious outlook.

It was in the second century, however, that Gnosticism made its full impact upon the early Christian Church and ultimately one of two courses had to be taken. Either the Christian apologist had to affirm that his was the true Gnosis and that the Christ to whom he bore witness was the true integrating agent of the Gnostic world-picture: or he was driven to regard the whole Gnostic system as false and the Christian interpretation of reality as both radically different and exclusively true.

As an example of the first approach (not perhaps entirely typical but of special interest in this connection) let us glance at the teaching of Origen. He shares with the Gnostics and indeed with Oriental thought generally the height-depth framework in which the pure and the good and the perfect belong to the celestial regions above and all others are regarded as existing on descending levels of reality. These various levels of inferiority are the result of a general Fall which injured some more than others. At the lowest level the Prince of Evil, lord of gross matter, commands a host of beings whose constant aim it is to drag down to their own level of existence those who belong to higher spheres of life. In the whole system, degrees of disobedience correspond closely to degrees of involvement in visible matter: the negation of the spiritual leads to an equal and opposite affirmation of the material and to a corresponding degree of imprisonment within it.

When the Fall is viewed as a descent from pure spiritual existence, Redemption can hardly fail to be regarded in terms of ascent to the original beatitude. And in common with the Gnostics, Origen holds that this ascent can only be made by those who possess true *knowledge*. As against the Gnostics, on the other hand, Origen affirms that this knowledge comes to men through the Christ who was the supreme teacher and who Himself showed man the way from the lower to the upper world. By learning His way of obedience man becomes refined in his whole being and rises into realms to which he could not previously have attained. Within this redemptive process set in motion by Christ, matter becomes ever more refined and men become ever more conformed to the Divine pattern. Finally a purifying fire will remove all remaining grossness and the whole creation will be restored to its original perfection.

But can we define this way of obedience which the incarnate Christ pioneered more precisely? Origen seems to give a double answer to this question. In the first place he constantly refers to the defiling and destructive influence of sin in human nature. This results in a thorn-infested condition and the thorns need to be burned out of man by a consuming fire. Or to use another metaphor it results in a condition of intoxication and man needs to be shocked into sobriety. Sin must be rooted out, purged out, burned out and this can only be done by the enactment within human nature of a burning, cleansing process. Such a process was the suffering and dying of the Lamb of God. Through baptism into His death, through imaginative participation in His sufferings, through 'the eye of the mind' gazing 'fixedly at the very death of Christ', man can master sin and death and move upwards into the enjoyment of his true life in God.

In the second place Origen appeals to the imagery of the sacrificial-rite. In this rite it is normal for the offering to be submitted to the fire and as the heat begins to consume the material substance the vapour rises up into the higher and more ethereal regions. Something of this imagery seemed appropriate to apply to the Christ who offered Himself a pure offering and allowed His body to be consumed in the fire of suffering and death. The result of this process however was not destruction but etherealization. He rose up into the pure regions of eternal life and leading captivity captive lifted into the realm of blessedness all who believe in Him. The pattern and image of this mystery were already disclosed to Abraham. 'For he had believed, when he was ordered to sacrifice his only son, that God was able to raise him even from the dead; he had also believed that the transaction then set afoot did not only apply to Isaac but that it was sacramental, and that its full meaning was reserved for that descendant of his who is Christ. It was then with joy that he offered his only son, because he saw therein not the death of his issue, but the restoration of the world, the renewal of the whole creation, re-established through the resurrection of the Lord.'[18] Through the sacrifice of Christ, i.e. through death issuing in resurrection, the whole creation is renewed and man is restored to his true destiny in God.[19] The suffering and death and resurrection of Christ, in other words, provides the pattern of activity by which all nature is renewed and man, insofar as he is identified with this pattern sacramentally or actually, discovers the ultimate meaning of his own existence.

Another famous treatment of this general theme is that of St. Athanasius in the *De Incarnatione Verbi Dei*. In this treatise man's fundamental predicament is described as two fold. On the one hand he has become subject to corruption and is declining towards eternal death. On the other hand he has lost the true knowledge of his Creator and is obsessed with the pursuit of visible and material things. For these two reasons it was imperative that there should be some new development if God's original purpose for man was not to be entirely frustrated.

St. Athanasius argues that the former of these situations has been effectively met by the advent of the incorruptible Word into a body capable of death. This body, by partaking of the Word who is above all, 'was worthy to die in the stead of all' and, 'because of the Word which was come to dwell within it', remained incorruptible. Corruption was stayed from all by the grace of the resurrection. Such a conception raises immediate and obvious difficulties but Athanasius does not attempt to deal with particular points of objection. He is concerned rather to present the broad picture of a monarch taking up his abode in a threatened city and the consequent immunity of the city from further attack: or of indestructible life being clothed with mortality in order that mortals might become clothed with incorruption by the promise of the resurrection. The incorruptibility and indestructibility of the Word are beyond question. Hence even the offering of His assumed body to death was entirely possible seeing that His own restoration to life was assured and all others could gain the hope of resurrection through Him.

The other serious aspect of man's condition is his ignorance. If he does not know and comprehend his Maker, he utterly fails to attain that for which he has been created. Yet in point of fact man through his carelessness and neglect had given himself up to the

18. *Commentary on Romans* 4: 23–5.
19. Cf. A. D. Galloway: *The Cosmic Christ*, p. 84 ff. B. Drewery: *Origen and the Doctrine of Grace*, p. 121 ff.

contemplation of material things and was failing to look upwards to the source of all his good. Not even the coming of holy men nor the provision of a law made any serious difference. 'What then was God to do? Or what was to be done save the renewing of that which was in God's image, so that by it men might once more be able to know Him? But how could this have come to pass save by the presence of the very Image of God, our Lord Jesus Christ? Whence the Word of God came in His own person, that, as He was the Image of the Father, He might be able to create afresh the man after the Image. But again, it could not else have taken place had not death and corruption been done away. Whence He took, in natural fitness, a mortal body, that while death might in it be once for all done away, men made after His Image might once more be renewed.'

This basic proposition is expanded and expounded by Athanasius in subsequent sections as he dwells on the teaching office of the Incarnate Word. He shows that the life and signs and works of Jesus were necessary to teach men of the Father and to show that He was indeed God the Word. But something more was necessary. It was essential for Him to die a particular death—openly, publicly, on a tree, with hands spread out, between earth and heaven—all in order that man might know that his mortality, his curse, his bondage, his impotence had been removed and the way opened to resurrection and incorruptibility. Athanasius never wavers in his conviction that the Word by entering into the human situation has restored life to man and the universe. Yet he is equally convinced that man, if he is to attain his true stature, needs to know that all this has happened. He needs to *know* that God is His Father, that the Word was made flesh, that he himself has passed from death to life, that all things have been restored by Christ. In the tradition of true Gnosis, man only enjoys eternal life insofar as he *knows* the only God and Jesus Christ Whom He has sent.

As an example of the second approach the obvious choice is Irenaeus. The famous Bishop of Lyon worked in the midst of a missionary situation where he was in touch not only with pagan religious systems but also with rivals who might possess a veneer of Christian terminology and yet be actually anti-Christian in their doctrines. As a means of opposing the more popular mythologies he employed his own mythological description of the work of Christ with which we shall be concerned in Chapter III. But in opposing the more sophisticated heretical systems he developed a remarkable doctrine of recapitulation which deserves recognition not only as a viable alternative to the theories of his own time but also as generally applicable to later situations when philosophical systems were becoming serious rivals to the Christian faith.

Central to all Gnostic speculations was a doctrine of a fall. It was because man had fallen from some blissful state of pure spirit or pure contemplation that some kind of restoration became necessary. But if there had to be an *undoing* of a process which had brought about dereliction and disaster, it was natural to assume that the undoing would bear some resemblance to the doing. Every view of the universe which is monistic rather than dualistic in its basic assumptions must tend to think in terms of cycles and circular motion rather than in terms of sudden reversal and radical change. Hence the mind delights in seeing similitudes between the process of doing and the process of undoing, parallels between the stages of the fall and the stages of the restoration. The more striking the relationships between types and anti-types, the more impressive the total pattern of development becomes.

For Irenaeus the all-important narratives for comparison and contrast were the story of Adam and the story of Jesus Christ. The comparison may be seen for example in a succinct statement at the beginning of the eighteenth chapter of the third book of the *Adversus Haereses* where Irenaeus writes: 'The Son of God, when He was incarnate and was made man, recapitulated in Himself the long line of men, giving us salvation compendiously, so that what we had lost in Adam, viz. that we should be after the image and similitude of God, this we should receive in Jesus Christ'.[20] In this brief quotation the framework of his thought appears. God created Adam as an inclusive human organism containing the potentiality of expanding into a total humanity bearing the image and similitude of God. Adam was created from virgin earth and was called to pursue the pathway of complete obedience through all stages of his growth and development. But it only needed a minor test for Adam to fall into disobedience, thereby defiling both himself and his descendants and making impossible the attainment of the incorruptibility and immortality which had been God's intention for the human race. Mankind in its totality was affected— all ages, all races, all generations. The pattern and destiny originally implanted in the human organism were not entirely obliterated but the mark of disobedience had been inscribed upon humanity

20. 'He has therefore in his work of recapitulation summed up all things, both waging war against our enemy and crushing him who at the beginning had led us away captive in Adam in order that, as our species went down to death in a vanquished man, so we may ascend to life again through a victorious one.' (5.21.1.) Professor H. E. W. Turner translates the phrase in 3.19.1: 'He recapitulated in Himself the long evolution of human history'.

at large. Only the entrance of a quite new potency into the human situation could lead to the recovery of that which had been lost.

But such an entrance is in fact described in the story of Jesus Christ. He was generated in the womb of a Virgin: He 'recapitulated in Himself all the dispersed peoples dating back to Adam, all tongues and the whole race of mankind': 'He came to save all through Himself, infants and little children, and boys and young men and older men'—this by passing through every age and thereby sanctifying it. The altogether decisive factor in the recapitulation was the unswerving *obedience* of the Son of Man. This was revealed in critical fashion through the temptation-conflict in the wilderness. Here already His victory spelt victory for the human race—the victory over disintegration through a true obedience. This obedience formed the unbroken pattern of the life of the second Adam, enabling him to reverse just those acts of disobedience which had been so characteristic of the life of the first Adam. And the career of total obedience was gathered into a final concentration when He performed the act of supreme self-abnegation: 'in obliterating the disobedience of man originally enacted on the tree, He became obedient unto death, even the death on the cross, healing the disobedience enacted on the tree by obedience on a tree'. The fitness of such a recapitulation as that enacted by the Son of Man is still further emphasized through the fact that 'what the virgin Eve bound by means of incredulity, this the virgin Mary loosed by faith'. Thus the contrast between the two Adams, originally set forth in principle by St. Paul, is expounded in the most detailed way by Irenaeus, the main point of course being that the inclusive defection of Adam could only be remedied by an even more inclusive reversal in the career of Jesus the Christ. 'Jesus Christ because of His unmeasurable love was made what we are, that He might make us completely what He is.' 'The son of God became the Son of Man that man . . . might become the Son of God' (V.6.1).

So far, in spite of our modern unfamiliarity with an outlook in which inclusive and organic categories are taken for granted, we do not find it too difficult to respond to Irenaeus's general ideas. The disobedience of Adam (however precisely we interpret 'Adam') has been reversed in the obedience of Christ. Man's weakness in succumbing to temptation and the wiles of the flesh has been turned into strength through the coming of the Son of God into the human situation. But it is when we pass on to a further aspect of Irenaeus's teaching that we begin to encounter major difficulties. This teacher of the second century finds it altogether natural to regard the created order as essentially one. Man is derived from the earth, the earth is dependent upon man. Irenaeus assumes without question that man was created out of the virgin earth and in a sense therefore carries the earth or the natural world in his very being. His own fall cannot fail to affect the earth: his own restoration in like manner is bound to have cosmic repercussions. The recapitulation is concerned not only with man but with the whole creation, animals, plants and trees.

It is true that Irenaeus does not speculate in detail upon what might be called the cosmic fall. He is sure that it was through the Word that creation took place and that the mark of the Word upon the created order has never been obliterated. But man who could have been the instrument by which creation could have developed towards its intended fulfilment had betrayed his trust and thereby introduced corruption and mortality into its very midst. Thus creation was hindered from moving towards its true destiny. Man and nature were alike involved in carnality and death. God did not cease to draw them towards His own perfection through the Word. But without some new intervention, the weakness of man was such that any hope of a final attainment of that perfection seemed out of the question.

In a very impressive and often beautiful way Irenaeus unfolds his theme. He affirms that the entrance of the Word into human flesh and into the world meant the recapitulation of man and the world within a new divine organism. Through the Incarnation God was recapitulating in himself the original creation, primarily of man but also of nature itself. Never at any time had He ceased to operate within the world of nature—the processes represented by sunshine, growth, harvest, fruitfulness are all signs of His beneficence. But with the coming of the Word in person into the world, these processes were all, as it were, gathered up into a concentrated activity and directed to their true end. He took the loaves and sanctified them to a divine use. Similarly the water at the wedding feast. In fact He summed up all things in Himself, and taking to Himself the pre-eminence drew 'all things to Himself at the proper time'.

What Christ did in His incarnate life is continued in the life of the Church which is His Body and the whole process will come to its completion when the bodies of the dead are resurrected and a new heaven and a new earth come into being 'in which the new man shall remain, always holding fresh converse with God'. While the present order continues, the most vivid example of the things of earth being sanctified and lifted up to heaven is to be found in the Eucharist.

Here the Church offers to God the first-fruits of His own creatures and thereby proclaims harmoniously 'the unity of flesh and spirit'. 'For as the bread of the earth, receiving the invocation of God, is no longer common bread but Eucharist, consisting of two things, an earthly and a heavenly; so also our bodies, partaking of the Eucharist, are no longer corruptible, having the hope of eternal resurrection.' In such a statement the general picture becomes clear. Material things are sanctified and receive spiritual character through the operation of the Word. Irenaeus does not say that matter is evil in itself but he is convinced that all material things have been corrupted by man's disobedience and are in danger of being directed in upon themselves instead of towards God to whom they belong. It is therefore all-important that the process of spiritualization, characteristic of the work of the Word in the natural order in His pre-incarnate existence, concentrated and openly shown forth by the Son in the days of the flesh, should be continued by redeemed man as an essential part of his new life in the Body of Christ. His calling is to be the priest of creation, spiritualizing the material order and bringing all things to their true fulfilment in the life of God.

Whatever difficulties there may be in capturing the background and formulation of Irenaeus's thought, certain general themes stand out clearly. Creation is to be regarded not as something ready made but rather as a potentiality to be fulfilled. This potentiality was made to depend upon Adam, representative man, who in God's purpose was to be head of the created order, the one called to lift it up to God, to lead it forward to its predestined end. 'But the tragedy of creation lies in the fact that man by seeking to usurp divine prerogatives ceased to fulfil rightly his priestly service on behalf of the created world.'[21] Only by the restoration of man could creation be restored. Hence the 'recapitulation' by which Adam was saved in Christ and creation was saved in the redeemed Adam. The macrocosm (the world) was included in the microcosm (the body of Adam) and all was recapitulated in the second Adam, the great High Priest, who by identifying Himself with humanity within the created order restored the totality to its harmony within the design and purpose of God.

The majestic conception of cosmic regeneration and renewal has never been lost from the liturgy and theology of the Orthodox Church of the East. The constantly re-enacted celebration of the Holy Mysteries serves not only to restore and refresh the worshipping Church: it is believed to be effective also in renewing the face of the earth and maintaining the fullness of the cosmic cycle. The

21. L. S. Thornton: *Revelation and the Modern World*, p. 138.

joyful exultation in the triumph of Christ's Resurrection is related not only to humanity but to the whole order of creation which is assured of rebirth through Him.

But thought and imagination in the West have travelled on different lines. In the ordinary life of the Church there has been the tendency to embrace, if sometimes furtively, the basic dualism of the Manichees and to long for release from the body and the material order rather than for their redemption. In more intellectual circles the attempt has often been made to set up a double standard with God's activities in grace occupying the higher level, His operations in nature occupying the lower. 'And even though that inferiority is described in terms of privation rather than in terms of positive evil', as A. D. Galloway writes in an illuminating comment 'its practical outcome in relation to the doctrine of cosmic redemption was the same as that of the Gnostic dualism. It meant that the hardships and evils in and associated with man's physical environment could be accounted for as inevitably arising from an essential defectiveness in nature without in any way blaming or holding the true God responsible for that defectiveness. Therefore His ways were already justified in nature and the question of cosmic redemption did not arise.'[22]

Such an outlook prevailed throughout the Middle Ages and no serious challenge to it arose in the West until the rise of the modern scientific era. It is true that the Reformation and the Renaissance each in its own way affected man's attitude to nature. The Reformers were inclined to place nature lower in the hierarchy of Being: the devotees of the Renaissance inclined in the opposite direction. But there was no radical change. God had created the natural order: He retained it under His absolute control: man could learn lessons from it about the Divine operations: but it was no part of man's responsibility to concern himself unduly about the ultimate destiny of nature: his duty rather was to make sure of his own destiny within the heavenly realm. He could indeed use the resources of nature for the glory of God and God in His grace employed nature in sacramental ways for man's benefit. Just as man's Fall had seriously corrupted nature so, it must have been assumed, man's restoration would serve to remove corruption from nature. But except in such exercises as the popular practice of alchemy there seems to have been little interest in a possible radical change in nature, a redemption of the cosmic order itself.

Gradually, however, the change came. Man's growing confidence as he began to explore the detailed structures of the natural order

22. A. D. Galloway: *The Cosmic Christ*, p. 129.

led to a marked shift in attitude. His interest began to centre in things in themselves and the ways in which they could be adapted to his own purposes rather than in things as constituting part of a providentially ordered system. Even Calvin had spoken of the Creator driving 'the machinery of the world and all its parts in a universal motion'.[23] Might it not be that man could learn the laws of this universal motion, adapt himself to them and even in course of time become a kind of under-driver, using the laws of nature for his own advantage? And might he not, by employing the methods of the new sciences to other aspects of his existence—his morals, his politics, his culture—arrive at a more reliable picture of the universe than he had hitherto conceived?

The general view of an empirically learned, patiently investigated universal order was at first strongly resisted both by theologians and philosophers. The former held firmly to the idea of a special and all-sufficient revelation which the activities of science might illuminate at certain points but could never repudiate. The latter clung strenuously to the notion of what can best be described as the principle of *a priori*—that man in his moral and intellectual and emotional make-up possessed capacities and structures independent of the world outside and that the universe must be understood in terms of these rather than they in terms of it. Such a conviction led naturally to the construction of a massive system of ethics (as by Kant), a comprehensive system of metaphysics (as by Hegel) and a wide-ranging system of aesthetics (as by Schleiermacher). Each began with certain simple assumptions about the nature of man, particularly about his mental structure, and, with these as starting-points, proceeded to weave an amazingly complex theory to which all facts of human experience must be regarded as ultimately comfortable.

The fascinating thing is that neither of the great thinkers just mentioned regarded himself as opposed to the essential doctrines of Christianity. Kant believed that he had provided a true exposition of the ethics of the Kingdom of God: Hegel that he had given a true interpretation of the doctrine of the Trinity: Schleiermacher that he had shown the true meaning of Christian salvation. Yet as subsequent events have revealed, none of these systems has been able to deal adequately or realistically with the two greatest challenges of the nineteenth and twentieth centuries—the advance of the scientific method and the proliferation of historical information. By constructing an all-inclusive framework of a mental or theoretical kind and assuming that all man's experience of the natural and

23. *Institutes*, 1.16.1.

historical orders could be included within it, they gained an initial
success but suffered an ultimate rejection. Though their influence
on modern thought has been immense, yet none was able to reinterpret the Christian doctrine of recapitulation, the 'restoration
of all things' for the new scientific age.

The thinker who was deeply concerned with the problem and
came nearest to throwing new light on it was Hegel. For him one
comprehensive principle governs the whole of reality. It is the
principle variously described as dialectic, as *coincidentia oppositorum*,
as the reconciliation of contraries, as the movement of thesis—
antithesis—synthesis. That this is a supremely suggestive principle
for the interpretation of reality as man experiences it can scarcely
be doubted. Any concept contains the possibility of its own negative.
The human psyche gains an extraordinary satisfaction in passing
through the stages of affirmation—negation—reintegration. It
becomes possible then to imagine that this is indeed the ultimate
pattern of reality and that the manifestation in Christ is first and
last a revelation in temporal, finite form of this eternal and infinite
principle. In particular His death is seen as the death of God—
the unique revelation in terms of earthly existence of what is forever
true in the sphere of heavenly reality. His resurrection is again
the unique manifestation to human sense-experience of that which
is an indispensable part of the eternal order. Thus life—death—
resurrection is the notion which governs the whole of reality. It
has been revealed once, in one unique Subject, perfectly. We now
have assurance that reality itself, the final structure of all existence,
is the reconciliation of opposites in a higher unity.

Hegel's religious philosophy was reflected in modified form in the
idealisms of the nineteenth and early twentieth centuries but so far
as the interpretation of natural processes is concerned its greatest
influence by far has been exercised through the negation of its
central principle in the system of Karl Marx. For Hegel the principle
operated in the realm of eternal spirit though its symbolic manifestations could be seen in the material order and in historical
events. For Marx the principle operated in the realm of natural
history though its symbolic manifestations could be seen in the
realm of cultural and artistic creation. As Bertolt Brecht was to
write:

> Dreams and the golden 'if'
> Conjure the promised sea
>   of ripe corn growing.
> Sower, say of the harvest
> You will reap to-morrow
> But it is your own to-day.

In the dialectical process the ultimate harvest is assured. Meanwhile, as the artist engages in a dialectical struggle with his material, the momentary realization of the 'end' is already achieved.

The nineteenth and early twentieth centuries proved to be a time of unparalleled expansion for the countries of Western Christendom. Expansion geographically and economically was important but of still greater significance was the expansion in knowledge of the past (which was recorded in countless historical publications) and of the structural dynamisms of the universe (which was recorded in innumerable scientific papers). So great was the enthusiasm for the discovery of new 'facts' that questions of meaning and purpose were allowed to remain in the background. Certain broad assumptions about progress and the good of the greatest number were popular but amongst historians and scientists themselves there was little probing to discover the inner significance and the ultimate end of the universal process. At length, however, such questions began to be asked with ever greater insistence and the nature of the tasks, both of the historian and of the scientist, to be more searchingly scrutinized. In view of the vast store of information about the past of the human race which was now available could anything be said about the meaning or goal of the historical process? By the help of the immense resources of scientific knowledge upon which the philospher could now draw, could some tentative sketch of a world picture be constructed to show whether nature was in any way related to ultimate human interests or whether it was a great neutral phenomenon to be used or despoiled by man at his will?

These questions have only begun to be dealt with seriously and vigorously and the enquiry is likely to continue indefinitely. But for the purpose of this book the question of greatest importance is whether there is any sign that Christian interpretations of history and nature inherited from the past, and particularly from the Apostolic period, can have any relevance to a world which has undergone a major revolution in its outlook over the last 200 years. Can the Christian interpretation of atonement be reconciled with what is known about the great movements of human history— the emergence of civilizations, the rise and fall of imperial powers, the upsurging of revolutionary political changes, the clash of economic interests? Can it help to make sense of the vast accumulation of the results of scientific observation and experiment—the expansion of the universe, the origins of life, the processes of growth, the evidences of form? I believe that a beginning has been made in this direction and I propose to draw attention to one or two interesting examples. But the subject is vast and in this particular area of Christian doctrine the output so far is quite meagre. We must speak in terms of promise rather than of achievement.

E

Perhaps the most widely hailed and at the same time most severely criticized attempt of our time to relate the total world-process as interpreted by the scientist to the essential Gospel of the life, death and resurrection of the Christ as proclaimed by the man of faith, has been that of Père Teilhard de Chardin. This celebrated palaeontologist who had spent most of his life in active field work sought at length to sum up his view of universal process in a volume *The Phenomenon of Man*. This has since been followed by other volumes of a more personal or specifically religious nature and it is now possible to see how in Teilhard's imagination the Cross of Christ is related to the whole sweep of the development of the natural order. The concluding sentence of the Appendix to *The Phenomenon of Man* is:

'In one manner or the other it still remains true that, even in the view of the mere biologist, the human epic resembles nothing so much as a way of the Cross.'

The general pattern of this, his most famous book, is as follows. Evolution is described in four stages: pre-life, life, thought and hyper-life. In the first, matter passes into a structure of organized forms: in the second, living forms are built up into more and more highly organized species: in the third 'earth finds its soul in man': finally humanity continues to develop, particularly in the direction of richer differentiation, within a more closely knit unity. The whole dynamic movement has been marked by a deepening of the inner human consciousness in conjunction with an expanding of external complexity. Man's pre-eminence arises from the fact that he is the most conscious and at the same time the most highly organized of living creatures. And in the process of on the one hand the intensification of inner consciousness and on the other hand of the complexification of outer organization energies are generated which are carrying man and his world forward to more exalted heights of psycho-social activity and ultimately to a pole of final reconciliation or convergence which he names Omega but which for the Christian believer seems to be the near equivalent of 'the summing up of all things in Christ.'

An original aspect of Teilhard's system is his treatment of the concept 'energy'. Whatever theory of the evolution or development of the universe is entertained, the phenomenon of 'energy' is obviously central to it. In the limitless applications of scientific theory to practical problems today, 'energy' always has a part to play. But Teilhard was concerned and deeply concerned to discover an interpretation of energy which would hold together the physical and the moral, the spiritual and the material in nature and in man. In other words he was searching for a theory which would make sense both of the obvious fact of unlimited resources of energy in the physical world and of the equally obvious fact of an unlimited potential of psychic or spiritual energy in man himself. He did not pretend to have found a finally satisfactory solution to the problem. He believed, however, that he had outlined a possible interpretation of what he called 'an integral science of nature'.

A picture of total development in which the whole movement seemed to be from the lower to the higher, from the simple to the complex, from the diffuse to the concentrated, immediately invited criticism. What place did it give for evil, for regression, for surds, for catastrophe and primordial deviation? Teilhard was by no means unaware of this difficulty and referred to it in an appendix from which I have already quoted the final sentence. He offers only a hint and a suggestion of the way in which he would be prepared to deal with it more fully. The picture which he has sketched does not, he holds, preclude the appearance within it of varying types of evil (disorder, decomposition, anxiety, travail). 'A universe which is involuted and interiorized, but at the same time and by the same token a universe which labours, which sins and which suffers. Arrangement and centration: a doubly conjugated operation which, like the scaling of a mountain or the conquest of the air, can only be effected objectively if it is vigorously paid for—for reasons and at charges which, if only we knew them, would enable us to penetrate the secret of the world around us.'[24]

The hints given in this appendix can be amplified by referring to some of the author's more devotional and theological utterances. The fullest exposition available in English is to be found in the section entitled 'The Meaning of the Cross' in his book *Le Milieu Divin*. His favourite image to describe the specifically Christian interpretation of the universe is that of the 'upward road', 'the impulse towards the heavens', 'the unfolding and bursting open upward in the direction of God'. The Cross must involve tension and antagonism and sifting. Yet it is not to be regarded as a symbol of sadness, limitation and repression. 'In its highest and most general sense, the doctrine of the Cross is that to which all men adhere who

24. *The Phenomenon of Man*, p. 313.

believe that the vast movement and agitation of human life opens on to a road which leads somewhere and that that road climbs upward. Life has a term: therefore it imposes a particular direction, orientated, in fact, towards the highest possible spiritualisation by means of the greatest possible effort. To admit that group of fundamental principles is already to range oneself among the disciples—distant perhaps and implicit, but nevertheless real—of Christ Crucified.'[25]

Teilhard proceeds to deepen and clarify this general conception. He points us to the historical Christ, 'the Master of the world, leading, like an element of the world, not only an elemental life, but (in addition to this and because of it) leading the total life of the universe, which He has shouldered and assimilated by experiencing it Himself. In His death we see that there is no finality in the temporal zones of this visible world. Rather He beckons us beyond towards the peaks—by a path which is the way of universal progress. To sum up, Jesus on the Cross is both the symbol and the reality of the immense labour of the centuries which has, little by little, raised up the created spirit and brought it back to the depths of the divine milieu. He represents (and in a true sense, He is) creation as, upheld by God, it reascends the slopes of being, sometimes clinging to things for support, sometimes tearing itself from them in order to pass beyond them, and always compensating, by physical suffering, for the setbacks caused by its moral downfalls. We can now understand that from the very first the Cross was placed on the crest of the road which leads to the highest peaks of creation. But, in the growing light of Revelation, its arms, which at first were bare, show themselves to have put on Christ: Crux invincta— the Christian is not asked to swoon in the shadow, but to climb in the light of the Cross.'[26]

If climbing was his favourite image, transformation through offering was a conception equally congenial to him. Man himself, responding to and energized by the Cross, would himself be transformed in the process of the upward climb. Concurrently he could, by gathering up the material order and offering it to God, be instrumental in the transforming and spiritualizing of matter so that it also can attain its true destiny. As we climb towards the light we pass through 'a given series of created things which are not exactly obstacles but rather foot-holds, intermediaries to be made use of, nourishment to be taken, sap to be purified and elements to be associated with us and borne along with us'.[27] There is,

25. *Le Milieu Divin*, p. 85 ff.
26. Op. cit., p. 87.
27. Op. cit., p. 92.

it is true, a kind of downward drift in matter and man may be included within it. But the Christ has by His enfleshment stayed the downward drift and by His ascension actualized the process of spiritualization. Now in and through the Body of Christ the 'drift' is being reversed and all is moving towards God *in Christo Jesu*.

Naturally and inevitably Teilhard's thoughts turn towards the priestly work of Eucharistic offering in which this universal process of reconciliation is sacramentally realized. In a notable section[28] of *Le Milieu Divin* he expounds this thought theologically and devotionally. In addition he wrote a poem, 'Mass upon the altar of the world', in which he conceives his whole work, his scientific labours and his liturgical offerings, as one—as part of the total offering of the Christ who is reconciling all things to God.

'Since once more, my Lord, not now in the forests of the Aisne but in the steppes of Asia, I have neither bread, nor wine, nor altar, I shall rise beyond symbols to the pure majesty of the real, and I shall offer you, I your priest, on the altar of the whole earth, the toil and sorrow of the world.'[29] In his sacramental doctrine Teilhard draws very close to the more detailed theological expositions of recent Roman Catholic writers who have sought to reinterpret the meaning of the Eucharistic Sacrifice. His great achievement has been to set this theology firmly within the context of a theology of universal reconciliation and to support it by language and symbolic forms derived from his own intimate knowledge of the structures of the world and of the human body. However deficient Teilhard's system may be in its dealing with radical evil in nature and the proud rebellion of man to which I shall be referring later, it is an immensely impressive attempt to interpret the groaning and travailing of the natural order in the light of the experience of a life-time spent in first-hand scientific investigation.[30]

28. Pp. 110–18.
29. *Letters from a Traveller*, p. 141.
30. The contribution of Teilhard de Chardin to Christian Theology has received a warm welcome from many scholars both in Europe and in North America. None perhaps was more enthusiastic than Canon Charles E. Raven whose life was also spent in the task of reinterpreting the Christian doctrine of the summing-up of all things in Christ in terms of experience gained from the investigation of the created order. A paragraph from the second volume of Dr. Raven's Gifford Lectures reveals the heart of his own concern and shows the affinity of his system with that of Teilhard.

'The fact is that if we are to see the creative process as a whole and culminating for us in Christ we shall regard it as at every level reflecting in its own measure something of the quality of deity: from atom and molecule to mammal and man each by its appropriate order and function expresses the design inherent in it and contributes so far as it can by failure or success, to the fulfilment of the common purpose. We can refer to it in three main terrestrial phases, as a preparation for the organism, as a process of organic individuation, as a

A second exceedingly impressive attempt to reinterpret the doctrine of recapitulation in modern terms was made by L. S. Thornton in his books *The Incarnate Lord, The Common Life in the Body of Christ* and his final trilogy *The Form of the Servant*. Even a cursory inspection of these volumes reveals the author's deep interest in organismic theories and analogies. One of his earliest studies was devoted to the theology of Richard Hooker whose exposition of the doctrine of the mystical body of Christ aroused his admiration. A few years later he was linking the concepts of the body and process and organism with the thought of A. N. Whitehead whose combination of detailed scientific analysis with imaginative philosophic construction he found wholly congenial. To interpret to the modern world the meaning of the series Creation, Israel, Christ, The Church, Recapitulation became henceforward his major task.

It was one of Thornton's basic principles that we can only speak about God, we can only worship God, if God has in fact revealed Himself to us. Assuming that such a revelation has been made, what is its *form*? Without hesitation the Christian answers that God has made Himself known in Jesus Christ who is 'the way, the truth and the life'. But Jesus Christ does not come to us as an isolated phenomenon having no connections or associations with other aspects of our experience. As incarnate in flesh and blood He is related to the totality of the created order: as born under the Law He is related to the totality of Israel's history: as performing in His career on earth acts of healing and saving and redeeming and

culmination in a community of persons, and can interpret these phases as due to the continuous *nisus* of the indwelling Spirit. If so, then it is surely congruous that at a definite stage in the process, as the partial reflexions of the divine reach their human fullness, that they should be consummated in the perfect image of God; and that thus the goal of the whole adventure should be interpretable in terms of the attainment by mankind of its true nature and significance, the stature of Christ and the significance of the family of God. The cost of the process, in terms of error and frustration, suffering and pain, sin and rebellion, can only be appreciated by those who have themselves experienced heartbreak and dereliction. Even for them the effort to hold together a full acknowledgment of evil and a conviction of the continuity and victory of good demands a range of sensitiveness and a sense of proportion only attainable by the saints. Those who have shared the Pauline experience and learned that the true symbol of reality is neither power nor wisdom but a Man on a Cross, have a clue to the resolution of the paradox. If Christ crucified be the one perfect manifestation of the Godhead to us, then we shall expect to find foreshadowings of it at every preliminary stage of the creative process. These will necessarily be conditioned by the limitations of the level at which they are disclosed—Wheeler Robinson is right in recognizing that this "self-emptying" of the divine Spirit is a *kenosis* similar to that of the Word when he became flesh and dwelt among us.' (Natural Religion and Christian Theology, II, p. 157 f.). See also Charles E. Raven: *Teilhard de Chardin, Scientist and Seer*.

renewing He is related to the totality of the world's future. In fact, the ministry of Christ stretches in all directions: downwards and upwards, backwards and forwards. His work has gathered up all in nature and history that can be redeemed and lifted up to God: at the same time He is renewing and carrying forward to their true goal all the processes of the created order which are consonant with the final design of God Himself.

Thornton appeals particularly to the doctrines of St. Irenaeus whom he regards as the most reliable guide to the 'structure of orthodoxy' as it appears just after the last personal links with the apostolic age had been severed. Irenaeus was in a sense near enough to the apostles to be cognizant with their teaching, far enough away to see it in perspective. Hence his conception of the wholeness of revelation can be of the highest value to all subsequent interpreters of the Christian faith.

Following Irenaeus, Thornton lays immense emphasis upon the early chapters of Genesis. Here we see a pattern of creation and disintegration, of man's derivation from nature and yet his despoliation of nature, of one created to be the head of creation falling to become the slave of creation. Clamant voices in Irenaeus's day were calling for the separation of the new creation in Christ from all that had gone before. The very thought that the pure world of spirit could become enshrined in or contaminated by the world of gross matter was abhorrent to them. The very suggestion that the experiences and disciplines of the people of Israel were signs and pointers to the pattern of God's way of redemption was to them unthinkable. Yet in face of all opposition Irenaeus held fast to his faith in the one Creator God who was also Redeemer, to the creation of the world and man as having been the outcome of the design and purpose of a beneficent creator who would not allow His design to be finally thwarted but instead initiated a long process of redemption to undo all the evil effects of man's apostasy. Thornton stresses the necessity of an adequate span of time in order that the necessary processes of spiritual growth and development could take place. Within any organismic philosophy the key-words are growth, process, fulfilment rather than change, crisis, revolution. 'As harvesting is neither more nor less important than sowing, so the biological significance of an organism does not lie specially in the earlier stages of its development nor in the later, but rather in the development as a whole.'[31]

In an important summary paragraph Thornton defines his own conception of 'recapitulation'. It is closely linked, he says, with the

31. *Revelation and the Modern World*, p. 133.

undoubtedly primitive motif of 'repetition' (an experience in life which gives us confidence and enables us to gain our bearings) for it implies 'that the events of the first creation are repeated in the new creation. The repetition of a previous pattern of events is, so to speak, a hall-mark of genuineness. By it the divine activity can be recognized to be truly present and efficacious. Moreover the familiarity of the pattern ensures the possibility of a definite human response to something which can be known and appreciated for what it is. In the present instance "repetition" is the means through which the effects of Adam's Fall are undone, and thus the order of creation is restored in Christ to its true harmony once more. "Recapitulation" is a word which seems capable of several shades of meaning according to the precise context of thought in which it is used. Fundamentally it means that the divine plan of creation is to be summed up "representatively" in Christ its true head, so that its whole wealth of significance is brought to fulfilment in Him. In this function of headship our Lord fulfils the part assigned to Adam in the story of Genesis. That is to say, as the redeemer Christ fulfils that universal high-priestly ministry, towards and on behalf of the world of creatures, which is the proper function of our human nature.'[32]

The mention of priestly ministry naturally suggests the thought of sacrifice and in point of fact the sacrificial act is of supreme importance in Thornton's system. He looks back to primitive man's concern about two matters of urgency—the preservation of fertility in man and beast and the proper functioning of the annual cycle (the seasons and the celestial bodies). In both cases ritual actions had an essential part to play. And seeing that the focus of interest was the mysterious processes of life and death it was not surprising that a life-and-death cult-form constituted the most significant ritual action of the society. Through sacrifice (which was in fact this cult-form) the renewal of the natural and social environment was ensured and man himself was identified again with the universal process. As Mircea Eliade vividly remarks: Sacrifice served always to promote 'the circulation of sacred energy in the cosmos'.

Thornton traces the development of sacrificial ritual from the early practices of primitive peoples, on through the myth-and-ritual pattern of the empires of the Near East, a pattern in which Israel itself was to some extent involved, on still through the covenant-sacrifices by which the Hebrews celebrated God's redemptive acts in their history, on finally to the Son of God taking upon himself

32. Ibid., pp. 137–8.

the role of the divine-human priest-king. 'In so doing he repeated the original pattern of nature-religion in historical acts of redemption. In this fusion of nature with history the original pattern is finally brought to completion. For the death and the resurrection are physical events wrought out in the flesh of the God-man. Moreover this repetition is wholly unique in kind, since it has a once-for-all character which can never occur again in human history. All previous repetitions of the original pattern are here recapitulated. For in the death and resurrection of Jesus the truth of them all is included. For that very reason the divine-human victim in whom the gospel events were wrought out may be regarded as the Whole in whom all the age-long events of sacrifice are summed up.'[33]

The sacrifice at the centre of history was once-for-all and complete. Yet as within the total organismic development of the universe a process of ritual enactment led up to it, so a further process goes forth from it. 'The passage of the Christ from death to resurrection inaugurated, not a New Year of physical events in the cycle of nature, but a New Age of mystical events in the domain of history. Yet here too nature and history are fused together into one whole. For the mystical events have two foci of reference in the sacramental dispensation of the Church. On the one hand elements of nature, such as bread and wine, are taken into redemptive history to become the media in which the historical redemption is continually renewed; and on the other hand the participants in this new order of ritual action are the persons who together make up the redeemed community. In that sacramental order the old cycle of identification comes to fulfilment in a more august manner. Repetition now means a total, yet voluntary surrender of human life and all its powers to be conformed in character to that eternal sacrifice of God's Son which is the heart of the Church, as it is the core and centre of history.'[34]

The strength of Father Thornton's doctrine of recapitulation consists partly in its firm hold on the necessity for a Christian interpretation of the Divine activity in creation, partly in its interpretation of atonement in terms of a comprehensive reconciliation of all things in Christ. So often the Atonement has been regarded as related exclusively to the salvation of individual souls with no proper recognition of the fact which Dr. Thornton so powerfully emphasizes—that no soul can be isolated from its bodily and historical and even its universal environment, and that Christ Himself insofar as He became truly incarnate, became necessarily

33. Ibid., pp. 279–80.
34. Ibid., pp. 280–1.

related to all structures of the created order, and of cultural life. If the Christian God is Lord over all then He is Lord of soul and body, of creation and redemption, of patterns of calling and of patterns of response, of imaginative myth and of ritual identification. If the Christ has become man He is intimately and inextricably related to all these structures and His death and resurrection must be interpreted in terms of them all. If the Holy Spirit is continuously active in the world He must be operating in nature and in history as well as in the realm of personal relations to bring all into one harmonious working order under the suzerainty of Christ.

The weakness of his doctrine, as it seems to me, is that it is inclined to be too abstract and generalized without sufficient reference to the concrete realities of the scientific and historical orders. It is true that he gives detailed attention to the patterns of events (and their representation in symbolic forms) of the Biblical record. Certain correspondences with the wider ancient world of the Near East are noted. But his theoretic scheme of organic development becomes all-inclusive and little place is found for the Fall interpreted as a shattering rebellion against God, for the irrationalties and the catastrophes, the cruelties and the conflicts which the universe reveals, for the Cross seen as the critical realization and symbolization of conflict and antagonism and tearing asunder. The organic wholeness to which Thornton looks forward is a noble and inspiring ideal. It seems to correspond to a large portion of the evidence gained by observation both of the order of nature and of the structures of humanity. But it is not sufficient to encompass the totality of the human experience of the Divine revelation.

<h3 style="text-align:center">F</h3>

If Teilhard de Chardin's writings may be regarded as the most ambitious recent attempt to give a religious interpretation of *nature*, Arnold Toynbee's work and especially his *A Study of History* must be given pride of place in modern attempts to see a religious significance in the movements of *history*. In sharp reaction to Spengler who had viewed civilizations and cultures as strictly comparable to the trees of the field which grow to maturity and then decline and perish, Toynbee saw them rising and falling, growing and disintegrating in accordance with laws and regularities whose patterns man himself could at least in part discern and by which he could modify his own future if he would.

Toynbee's general terminology has become world famous. He selects twenty-one civilizations for investigation and proceeds to examine the geneses, the growths, the breakdowns and the disintegrations which meet the observer's eye. Can these be explained in terms of cause and effect? Are they determined by the gods, by man himself, by particular natural forces and environments or by a combination of all? One clue is found in the concept of Challenge and Response for there is good evidence that it is through the stimulus of hard circumstances that societies (like individuals) have advanced towards maturity. On the other hand if the pressure of adversity is too great there can equally be a decline and even a collapse. Again a clue is found in the concept of Withdrawal and Return for there are striking examples of individuals and even groups gathering in and reorganizing their resources in order to engage in a new and creative advance. On the other hand if the disengagement is too prolonged the possibility of return to the world of reality becomes increasingly remote.

When it comes to analysing the reasons for the breakdowns and disintegrations of civilizations, Toynbee lays greatest stress on the dangers inherent in any kind of fixation or idolization of static forms—techniques, institutions, policies. Especially he points up the danger of being attached to 'formal institutions and formulated ideas' belonging to a remote period of the past though there is also great peril in taking a 'flying leap' into the future and attaching all one's energetic longings to a goal which can never in fact be reached. Nevertheless it becomes clear that as between the claims of archaism and futurism Toynbee does not hesitate to show where his own sympathies lie. The fatal mistake is to turn back nostalgically to the past. The leap into the future can be creative and constructive if it is consciously directed towards a transcendent purpose: if men 'have ceased to set their heart upon the old mundane purpose of Futurism and have put their treasure, instead, in a purpose which is not Man's but God's and which therefore can only be pursued in a spiritual field of supra-mundane dimensions'.[35]

At this stage of his exposition Toynbee seems to reach a turning-point. So far he has been searching for general patterns *within* the world of space and time, the narrow stage that has hitherto set the limits of our field of vision and action. But the look into the future can only be justified and substantiated if the future is not in fact a void, a random mixture of possibilities, but is rather governed by purpose, a purpose which 'is not Man's but God's', a purpose which has begun to be revealed in This World but which belongs in its fullness to an Other World. And if it be asked in what terms the

35. A. J. Toynbee: *A Study of History*, VI, p. 128.

revelation has been made Toynbee's answer is unambiguous. It is through the disappointments of mundane expectations that man's eyes have been turned to a supra-mundane hope and in this very turning of his eyes there has come an epoch-making spiritual reorientation: It is through the *sufferings* of this present age that man's affections have been set upon the glories of the Kingdom of God and in this very redirection of his desires there has come to pass what can rightly be called a 'transfiguration'.

But does man make this profoundly important readjustment through his own wisdom and strength? In part he may, for history has already shown that πάθει μάθει (Suffering teaches) is one of the most well-attested principles of human living. Yet both in periods of growth (by way of example) and in periods of disintegration (by way of saving action) *the creative individual* has an indispensable part to play. This conviction leads Dr. Toynbee to undertake his famous survey of would-be saviours in the history of mankind—the Saviour with the Sword, the Saviour with the Time-Machine, the Saviour with both wisdom and authority and finally the Saviour who is believed to be a god-incarnate. The very appearance of these saviours underlines man's need to live within the framework of a pattern of meaningful existence. Only if his universe shows *some* signs of being the outworking of a transcendent purpose can he go forward with confidence and hope.

After surveying the saviour-heroes of the past, all of whom in one way or another have sought to bring purpose and meaning into mundane existence, Toynbee comes at length to a remarkable conclusion. Though the passage has often been quoted it bears repetition, especially as it represents the most ambitious effort of our time to relate the Passion and Death and Resurrection of the Christ to the total universal drama. Toynbee's system has been searchingly and even bitterly criticized as having no claim to be regarded as authentic history: it is mythology perhaps, morphology perhaps, but not history. Be that as it may, my own conviction is that this distinguished author has drawn together sufficient evidence to show that there *are* regularities in man's relationships both with nature and with his fellow-men. Man has sought to express and exploit these —through art, through science, through philosophy, through politics, through techniques. But sooner or later he must ask himself whether there is any evidence of a pattern of coherence, a factor of integration, a symbol of unified purpose. Is there any suggestion of that which would give meaning to the Whole? This is Toynbee's answer:

'This is the final result of our survey of saviours. When we first set out on this quest we found ourselves in the midst of a mighty marching host; but, as we have pressed forward on our way, the marchers, company by company, have been falling out of the race. The first to fail were the swordsmen, the next the archaists, the next the futurists, the next the philosphers, until at length there were no more human competitors left in the running. In the last stage of all, our motley host of would-be saviours, human and divine, has dwindled to a single company of none but gods; and now the strain has been testing the staying power of these last remaining runners, notwithstanding their superhuman strength. At the final ordeal of death, few, even of these would-be saviour-gods, have dared to put their title to the test by plunging into the icy river. And now, as we stand and gaze with our eyes fixed upon the farther shore, a single figure rises from the flood and straightway fills the whole horizon. There is the Saviour; "and the pleasure of the Lord shall prosper in his hand; he shall see of the travail of his soul and shall be satisfied".'[36]

Another remarkable attempt to interpret universal history in terms of Reconciliation through suffering and travail may be found in the writings of Nicholas Berdyaev. Here was a man whose early framework of thought and imagination had been formed by the tradition of Orthodox spirituality, though he was also deeply involved in the social and intellectual stirrings of the Russia in which he grew to maturity. Then came the move to Paris and contacts with Western ways of life and thought, contacts which undoubtedly influenced him but did not prevent him from being still regarded as an authentic representative of Eastern mysticism.

Like Dostoievsky, whose writings he so brilliantly interpreted, Berdyaev was gripped, shaken, tormented by the existence of suffering in the world. If πάθει μάθει has been Toynbee's guiding principle, Leon Bloy's aphorism 'Souffrir passe, avoir souffert ne passe jamais'[37] was Berdyaev's. Suffering was to him only tolerable

36. Op. cit., VI, p. 278.
Commenting on Mr. Toynbee's total achievement, a by no means uncritical reviewer in the *Times Literary Supplement* (22nd October 1954) made this interesting judgment:
'Christ, Socrates and Lycurgus died that others might live, the bodhisattvas, like Plato's philospher, have chosen to return to the cave. And so civilizations must die that new civilizations may be born. There is a profound intimation here of a broad moral and psychological truth to which empirical facts are almost irrelevant. Does not every creative act involve both violence and suffering? Must we not *payer de nos personnes*, if not harm others, in everything we do? Do we not see everywhere in animal life and in plant life, as much as in human life, perhaps even also in the inanimate world of physics, a constant dissolution and transcendence? It is this interpretation of the meaning of the Cross which may well be Dr. Toynbee's most lasting contribution to our moral understanding.'
37. 'Suffering disappears, but the fact of having suffered remains always with us.'

if it could somehow be integrated into the pattern of ultimate reality. He found no difficulty therefore in conceiving spirit in terms of a dynamic movement which included pain and suffering. And it followed naturally that the pattern of the career of the Christ revealed in the Gospel-story was to him the central and crucial exteriorization of that which belongs to the timeless order of spiritual reality. The startling symbol of John the Seer, 'The Lamb slain from the foundation of the world', has always exercised a particular appeal in Eastern circles and to Berdyaev it became the essential expression of his ultimate faith.

In the first chapter of his book *Freedom and the Spirit* there is an important section which summarizes his interpretation of universal history. Redemption and Calvary are not in the first place realities which can be learned from recorded history. They constitute 'an inner mystery of the spirit which is accomplished in the secret depths of being. Calvary is an interior moment of life and of spiritual development, the submission of all life to sacrifice. The Christ is born in the depths of the spirit, He passes through life, dies upon the Cross for the sin of the world and rises again. This is the inner mystery of the spirit. It is revealed in spiritual experience and everyone who is born of the spirit knows it.'[38] Such an experience is primary and indispensable. Without it nothing can be gained by focussing the attention upon the empirical, exterior world. Yet once the clue has been revealed, once the flash of illumination has been received, once man in freedom has entered consciously into the experience of new life through death, of transfiguration through suffering, of communion through separation, then the whole exterior universe begins to be seen as displaying the same essential pattern.

'The Christian mystery of the spirit is objectified and exteriorized in the natural world and is symbolized in history. Christ is born, He dies and rises again, not only in the depths of the spirit but in the natural, historical world. The birth of Christ, His life, His death upon the Cross and His Resurrection are authentic facts of the natural world. That which we read in the Gospel really happened in history, and in space and time. But the reality of the truth which happened in history, in space and time, is the same in this case as in that of all reality in the natural world, that is to say, it is a symbolic reality reflecting the happenings of the spiritual world.'[39]

This statement applies to *all* events which have taken place in the natural, objective world. Yet a grading or hierarchy can be observed.

38. N. Berdyaev: *Freedom and the Spirit*, p. 33 f.
39. Ibid., p. 34.

'The life of Christ revealed in the Gospel symbolizes and reflects events of the spiritual world of an importance, a unity and a determining value, infinitely greater than anything else in world history.' And beyond the Christ of the Gospel is the Christ of the Church: 'The Church is not a reality existing side by side with others; it is not an element in the historic and universal whole. The Church is all—It possesses a cosmic nature—It is in the Church that the grass grows and the flowers blossom, for the Church is nothing less than the cosmos Christianized.[40] Christ entered the cosmos, He was crucified and rose again within it, and thereby all things were made new. The whole cosmos follows His footsteps to crucifixion and to resurrection.'[41] Particularly in the offering of the 'bloodless sacrifice of love' in the Eucharist 'we have inner mystical communion with Christ and participate in the work which He has accomplished'.[42]

Berdyaev would not be accepted as an official or authorized interpreter of Eastern spirituality. Yet it seems to me that his general interpretation of atonement conforms to the age-long tradition of this section of Christendom. I find myself imagining a series of concentric spheres. At the heart of the system is a burning centre. (The nature of spirit, Berdyaev remarks at one point, is Heraclitic and not Parmenidean. Spirit is fire and energy.) This burning centre may be described in terms of sacrifice and particularly of the sacrifical *Lamb*: or in terms of suffering and particularly of the suffering *Servant* of humanity: or in terms of the sequence birth—passion—death—resurrection. This fire burns perpetually and is not consumed. This fire is the energy which activates the whole of the cosmos. In a kind of pulsating movement all things are transfigured as they are drawn towards the burning centre from which they originally withdrew.

He that is near me, is near the fire. Through suffering, fulfilment. Through sacrifice, renewal. Through death, newness of life. Whatever may appear to be happening in the world of nature and of universal history these are the images of ultimate reality which have sustained the faith of the Eastern Church and confirmed the age-long tradition that only through suffering can nature, societies, individuals, yes even the God-man Himself, enter into glory.

40. Cf. another striking passage in which Berdyaev writes: 'Not only human nature but the whole universe and the whole of cosmic life was transformed after the coming of Christ. When the Blood of Christ shed upon Calvary touched the earth, earth became a new thing, and it is only the limitation of our receptive faculties which prevent us from seeing it with our very eyes.' p. 179.
41. Ibid., pp. 331–2.
42. P. 180.

G

I have tried to look at the way in which Christian interpreters have, through the centuries, used my first general range of comparison to bring home the meaning of the Cross to their contemporary world. Until the beginning of the modern scientific era and the new concentration upon the ascertainable 'facts' of history this comparison proved immensely serviceable and rewarding. But over the past two centuries it has become increasingly difficult to sustain. To what 'patterns' of nature or history can we confidently appeal? How can the human mind even begin to envisage the reconciliation of *all things*, the summing-up of *all things* in Christ? There is no formula, no comprehensive image which can claim to be in any way world-embracing.

Yet what is at present impossible within the realms of strict scientific analysis and historical enquiry may at least be suggested in the realm of art. Certain notable images have established themselves in the course of history and they can still move us as we contemplate the theme of universal reconciliation. For example, Franks claims that in the ancient view the work of Christ was regarded as operating in a mode inaccessible to human reason. Rather men loved to speak in mystical terms of this work acting as a *ferment* in humanity 'destroying sin and death and imparting righteousness and immortality'. Or there is the image of the sacrificial *Lamb* again not open to precise logical explanation but exercising it would appear an extraordinary appeal to the Eastern imagination. The Lamb on Mount Zion, the Lamb slain from the foundation of the world, the Lamb holding the banner of victory— the Lamb sacrificed to save and restore the whole world has been a central symbol of devotion throughout Christian history.

Yet the image which in our present range of comparison seems to have been the most effective and appropriate of all has been *the cosmic tree*, which is the tree of life. In a section of his Exposition of the Orthodox Faith which extols the Cross on account of the countless blessings which it has brought to mankind, John of Damascus concludes by drawing out parallels between it and the tree of life planted in the Garden of Eden. 'The tree of life,' he writes, 'which was planted by God in Paradise prefigured this precious Cross. For since death was by a tree, it was fitting that life and resurrection should be bestowed by a tree.' (4.a). Or as a medieval account of the Harrowing of Hell expresses the same ideas—'Out of that very tree that made us suffer through Eve's primal sin began our salvation after it had carried him who was both God and man.'

The origins of this image can be traced far back in human mythology and it is not entirely without meaning in our modern world.[43] Mircea Eliade makes frequent reference to the sacred Tree in his writings[44] and shows how intimately it is associated with another symbolic archetype—the Centre of the World. It seems that the primitive imagination regarded the *centre* of any region or space as peculiarly sacred. Above all the centre of the cosmos (which might have its manifestation at varying centres) was the supremely holy place—the locus of creation, the support of the axis on which the whole of the created order revolved, the place of meeting of the three zones, Heaven, Earth and Hell.

'The most widely distributed variant of the symbolism of the Centre is the Cosmic Tree, situated in the middle of the Universe, and upholding the three worlds as upon one axis.'[45] In the rites designed to renew creation, a tree standing near the centre is felled and out of its wood a sacrificial stake is fashioned and set up. This stake now becomes a pillar or ladder connecting earth and heaven and the sacrificer, mounting the stake, believes that he is ascending into the heavenly regions and thereby gaining the boon of immortality.

Here then is a notable symbolic pattern. The centre or navel of the earth where creation originally took place: the tree growing at the centre: the sacrifice at the centre in order that creation may be renewed: the setting up of a sacrificial stake derived from the living Cosmic Tree and the ascent upon this stake by the man offering the sacrifice. Small wonder that 'Christianity has utilized, interpreted and amplified this symbol. The Cross, made of the wood of the tree of good and evil, appears in the place of the Cosmic Tree; the Christ Himself is described as a Tree (by Origen). A homily of the pseudo-Chrysostom speaks of the Cross as a tree which "rises from the earth to the heavens. A plant immortal, it stands at the centre of heaven and of earth; strong pillar of the universe, bond of all things, support of all the inhabited earth; cosmic interlacement, comprising in itself the whole medley of human nature." And the Byzantine liturgy sings even now, on the day of the exaltation of the Holy Cross, of "the tree of life planted on Calvary, the tree on which the King of ages wrought our salvation" the tree which

43. One of Teilhard de Chardin's most significant diagrams represents the total process of evolution in the form of 'The Tree of Life'.
44. M. Eliade: *Images and Symbols*, pp. 44 ff. and 161 ff.; also *Myths, Dreams and Mysteries* passim.
45. *Images and Symbols*, p. 44.

"springing from the depths of the earth has risen to the centre of the earth" and "sanctifies the Universe unto its limits".[46]

There can be little doubt that the essential pattern of *universal regeneration through a central cosmic sacrifice*, of the *attainment of eternal life through the efficacy of a sacrificial stake* were motifs which had established themselves firmly in the human imagination long before the Christian era. The transfiguration of Calvary was therefore assured. This was the new tree of life: this was the noble tree of sacrifice: this was the central ladder linking earth to heaven. In the sixth century A.D. Venantius Fortunatus could hail the Cross as

> Tree of beauty, Tree of light!
> Tree with royal purple dight!
> On whose dear arms, so widely flung,
> The weight of this world's ransom hung.
> The price of humankind to pay,
> And spoil the spoiler of his prey.

In the seventh century the famous *Dream of the Rood* tells how the Saviour-warrior ascended the tree to save mankind, how the tree itself was then felled and hid in the earth until its hour of vindication came:

> Lo, me, the prince of Glory, heaven's Lord
> Hath glorified above all forest trees.

And in the art of early Christianity the Cross as the centre of universal reconciliation finds its most frequent expression through the picture of the tree of life. The Cross is the tree of life which brings healing to the whole world. The Cross is the sacrificial pillar which now supports and sustains the whole cosmos.[47]

> We think that Paradise and Calvarie
> Christ's Crosse and Adam's tree, stood in one place.
> Looke, Lord, and finde both Adams met in me;
> As the first Adam's sweat surrounds my face,
> May the last Adam's blood my soul embrace. (John Donne)

---

46. Op. cit., pp. 161–2.
47. See E. Stauffer: *New Testament Theology*, p. 133 for examples.

CHAPTER III

THE UNIQUE REDEMPTION

First Parable

The universe, as we know it through observation and experience, bears the marks of enmity and conflict. Good against evil, truth against falsehood, light against darkness, order against chaos, life against death. And the destructive powers—darkness, disease, death—seem often to be winning the day. How can their reign be brought to an end? How can mankind be released from their tyranny? Only, it would appear, through some critical and comprehensive victory by which the powers of evil can be subdued and their stronghold broken.

But in point of fact the One Who is the Divine Hero, the Champion of light and goodness, has entered the fray and challenged the demonic powers who lord it over the created order. The final battle has been joined. The Hero has taken upon himself the full fury of the forces antagonistic to the Divine sovereignty. Stricken down, He has not been vanquished by these hostile powers, even though they accomplished His death on a cross. God vindicated Him and raised Him from the dead and designated Him prince and leader of a new victorious humanity. Moreover the creation itself is now assured of deliverance from its frustration and of ultimate participation in the glorious liberty of the sons of God.

A

Let us try to explore the 'range of comparison' presented in this summary expression. Immediately we recognize that in certain respects this theory seems antithetical to that which has been outlined in Chapter II. There the over-riding conception was of a single cosmos which had become disordered and deranged and therefore needed to be restored to its proper wholeness. Here the dominant idea is that of radical division between two groups of antagonistic forces, each of which is seeking to destroy the other. There man's world-view, though reflecting certain distortions and disharmonies, maintained its essentially unified character. Here his

76

world-view, reflecting antagonisms and conflicts, approaches an ultimate dualism. Taken to their limits, these two conceptions would become either an absolute monism or an unqualified dualism and in neither case would the thought of reconciliation or atonement carry any further meaning. It seems desirable therefore to retain both world-views, recognizing that each is a valid attempt to express a theory corresponding to a major area of human experience.

For what in fact is the common experience of mankind in relation to its natural environment? Basically it is a *mixed* experience. There are evidences of regularity, of rhythm, of ordered movement, of predictable occurrences. There are also unmistakable indications of revolutionary changes, of critical events, of dangerous possibilities. At certain times, in certain places, the ordered will seem to be in control: at other times, in other areas, the struggle of conflicting forces will seem to fill the picture. For example in his book *Kingship and the Gods* Professor Henri Frankfort was at pains to emphasize how the world-views characteristic of Egyptian civilization on the one hand and Mesopotamian on the other were in marked contrast to one another just because of the differing climatic and geographical conditions belonging to the respective environments.

It is true that this contrast was not absolute. In each area a remarkable river-valley civilization emerged and each society was aware of certain rhythms and regularities which provided the framework of an ordered cosmos. Society adapted itself to the succession of the seasons and moved in harmony with nature by means of its festival observances. Yet there is a remarkable contrast between the atmosphere of these religious occasions in the two countries. Mesopotamia was never free from a feeling of anxiety. At all times there was a sense of strife between the good principle of cosmic order and the malignant principle of chaotic disruption. Religion had its full share of wailing and lamentation as worshippers sought to identify themselves actively with their divine representatives who seemed to be overshadowed or overwhelmed within the cosmic strife. Only after an experience of uncertainty and painful apprehensiveness could the community move forward into a new experience of confidence and victory.

Yet in Egypt 'the festivals provided occasion to reaffirm that all was well. For Egypt viewed the universe as essentially static. It held that a cosmic order was once and for all established at the time of creation. This order might occasionally be disturbed, for the forces of chaos were merely subdued and not annihilated. Nevertheless revolts against the established order were bound to remain mere ripples upon the surface. The feeling of insecurity, of human frailty, which pervades every manifestation of Mesopotamian culture is absent in Egypt.'[1] The Nile was predictable, its valley was easily protectable. The Tigris on the other hand was turbulent and dangerous, its valley readily open to invaders.

It is not hard to construct a list of hostile elements with which man has had to contend in his journey towards an ordered and civilized life. Every night has brought darkness in its train and darkness has always been associated with danger. Sterility and infertility are obvious threats to existence and these are associated with the wilderness and the salt sea. The unsown land and the untamed water may at any time encroach upon that which has been tended and cultivated and reduce it to waste. Storm and drought, earthquake and flood, are phenomena which affect the existence of most peoples to a greater or lesser degree while fire and plague, in spite of all that man has done to bring them under control, still threaten the life of every society. Moreover, at least until comparatively modern times man has viewed these phenomena not as mere sports of his universe, not even as inescapable elements in a complicated physical environment, but rather as the direct manifestations of supranatural forces intent on causing him harm.

A notable proportion of the early myths of mankind deal imaginatively with this general situation. The enemy is normally represented as a monster, an exaggerated form of a frightening natural phenomenon. Occasionally a bird appears in this role, and sometimes a fierce animal such as a bull or lion. But the enemy-form *par excellence* is the serpent or dragon. In ancient mythology an almost universal motif is the struggle with the dragon. The dragon seems to focus in the human imagination the ultimate terror, the threat of final destruction.

In Greek mythology the story of Herakles's conflict with the seven-headed Hydra (dragon) is perhaps the most famous of all saviour-myths. In Egypt an animal drama celebrated the Festival of Victory by a harpoon ritual in which a male hippopotamus (akin to the dragon) was destroyed. And the Ras Shamra tablets have revealed the Canaanite god Baal in many combats of which that with the serpent Lotan may be the most primitive. But it is in Babylonian mythology that the struggle between the saviour-god and the fearsome dragon is most vividly depicted and there is little doubt, as I shall note later, that this myth played no small part in the imaginative vocabulary of Biblical writers.

The myth Enuma elish may have originated in the third millen-

1. H. Frankfort: *Kingship and the Gods*, p. 4.

nium B.C. but seems to have passed through various recensions before attaining the form in which it appears with Marduk as hero and central figure. The forces hostile to man are represented by Apsu, the god of the sweet water and his wife Ti'amat, goddess of the salt waters of the sea. First Apsu is tamed through the casting of a sacred spell but the real conflict is with Ti'amat. She is the leader of the forces of chaos thus described in the myth:

> Angry, scheming, restless day and night,
> they are bent on fighting, rage and prowl like lions.
> Gathered in council, they plan the attack.
> Mother Hubur—creator of all forms—
> adds irresistible weapons, has borne monster serpents,
> sharp toothed, with fang unsparing;
> has filled their bodies with poison for blood.
> Fierce dragons she has draped with terror,
> crowned with flame and made like gods.
> So that whoever looks upon them shall perish with fear,
> and they, with bodies raised, will not turn back their breast.

When the battle is finally joined Ti'amat's supporters quickly lose heart but she herself confronts the young god Marduk alone. Then 'spreading his mighty net, Marduk envelops Ti'amat in its meshes. As she opens her jaws to swallow him he sends in the winds to hold open. The winds swell her body and through her open mouth Marduk shoots an arrow which pierces her heart and kills her. When her followers see Marduk treading on their dead champion, they turn and try to flee; but they are caught in the meshes of his net and he breaks their weapons and takes them captive.'[2] Finally the champion cuts Ti'amat's body in two and lifts up one half to form the sky, making sure in the process that the waters above the sky are securely under control.

I have recounted the Marduk-Ti'amat myth in some detail because of the widespread significance of the struggle with the dragon in the early mythology of mankind. Even in very early Sumerian culture where the idea of conflict has no place in the myth of Creation, the dragon still appears in another context. It seems that in the depth of the human consciousness the serpent or dragon stands for all that is the object of fear in the devouring mother, the waters of the flood, the surging ocean, the return of chaos. Man is fascinated and in some measure attracted by a snake on land though he is aware of the danger which lurks in its deadly poison. Still more is he attracted yet terrified by monsters of the deep—the crocodile, the sea-serpent, the whale. So it appears that a variety of motifs—chaos identified with the waters out of which

2. H. Frankfort: *Before Philosophy*, p. 194.

a created order first emerged, infantilism identified with the womb out of which man himself first emerged, the *status quo* identified with the fixed social order out of which the pioneering hero himself first emerged—find their mythological concretion in the dragon or serpent which has to be overcome and dismembered if universal life is to be sustained.

In this comprehensive mythology the key figure is the saviour-hero who delivers his fellow-men from the tyrannical clutches of the dragon. In point of fact salvation may have come about in a wide variety of forms corresponding to the various ills which threaten the disruption of universal life. But the common factor in all these salvation events is the setting free of creative life, ordered life, purposive life. The dragon is emptiness, meaninglessness, the bondage of death. The pioneering hero attacks the forces which divide and confuse and destroy and rescues man from the vacuity and futility into which his universe can so easily disintegrate. It is significant that in one culture after another we find the same essential struggle with the dragon depicted in a variety of forms. All the threats to creative life in an ordered universe are gathered up into the one sinister mythological figure, the dragon. All the acts of deliverance into purposeful and creative existence are seen as the exploits of the hero who through renunciation, conflict and even death brings salvation to mankind.

B

This salvation-mythology of the ancient Near East is taken up and used extensively in the Old Testament. It is examined in detail in an essay by Professor F. F. Bruce contributed to the symposium *The Saviour God* edited by Professor S. G. F. Brandon. I quote his main conclusion because of its importance in relation to the general subject of our enquiry:

> 'The picture of a deity or hero procuring deliverance by fighting and conquering a serpent or dragon is widespread in the ancient Near East and farther afield as well. The dragon may be the dragon of chaos or of drought or (and this is specially marked in Old Testament literature) he may symbolize some historical figure. In the Old Testament it is uniformly Yahweh who destroys the dragon, no matter what malign power may be denoted by the dragon from one place to another.'[3]

In his survey of Old Testament references to this divine salvation Bruce adopts the following classification. Most vivid of all are the

3. *The Saviour God*, p. 53.

descriptions in the book of Job of the victory over the monster of chaos (Rahab) and the fleeing serpent:

> By his power he stilled the sea;
> by his understanding he smote Rahab.
> By his wind the heavens were made fair,
> his hand pierced the fleeing serpent.
>
> (Job 26: 12–13)

The natural phenomenon chiefly represented by this imagery seems certainly to be the sea. At all times feared by the Hebrews, the sea had, they believed, been curbed and bound when the waters burst out from the womb of creation (Job 38: 8); it had been vanquished and divided in the mighty victory at the Red Sea.

> Thou didst divide the sea by thy might;
> thou didst break the heads of the dragons on the waters.
>
> (Psalm 74: 13)

> Thou dost rule the raging of the sea;
> when its waves rise, thou stillest them.
> Thou didst crush Rahab like a carcass,
> thou didst scatter thy enemies with thy mighty arm.
>
> (Psalm 89: 9–10)

The sea, the Red Sea, Egypt the tyrant, whose dominion was associated with the sea—all these were identified with Rahab, the dragon, the fleeing serpent, Leviathan, and in joyful acclaim Yahweh was hailed as the victor over all these mythological enemies of his people.

Many psalms celebrate some kind of personal salvation enjoyed by God's servant and a concluding paean in the prophecy of Habakkuk seems to refer to a signal deliverance from the agonies of drought. But by far the greatest emphasis in the Old Testament rests upon the great redemption from the bondage of Egypt, a redemption which is sometimes described in terms drawn from an earlier mythological vocabulary but which has always constituted for Israel the firmest foundation of its historical existence. Whatever conclusion may be reached about the patriarchal stories—how far they contain reliable accounts of what actually happened in the period before the Exodus—there can be little doubt that a group of Hebrews who had been enslaved in Egypt were brought out into a new kind of freedom under the leadership of Moses and that the general pattern of this redemption has never been erased from the national memory. Though Moses was the human agent, the true Saviour and Redeemer had been Yahweh Himself. By this outstanding event He had manifested His power as a saviour and mighty deliverer. He had chosen this people, He had called them to respond in faith, He had broken the bonds of their affliction, He had led them out in safety to begin a new life. The triumph song of Exodus 15 stands for all time as a redemption-hymn whose pattern can be applied to every kind of slavery and dereliction which may befall the children of God.

Moreover, those who came after were not slow to draw the inference that what Yahweh had done once in the history of His people He could and would do again. For the Old Testament never attempts to disguise the fact that the triumph at the Red Sea was followed almost immediately by faithlessness and disobedience on the part of those who had enjoyed so great a salvation. Harassed and distressed in the wilderness journey, often defeated and plundered in the promised land, led at last into exile to experience a new slavery under the power of the great empire of the East—how could this people have survived had it not been that again and again Yahweh made bare His arm on their behalf and brought salvation to His chosen people. Ragnar Leivestad may overstate the matter when he says that ' "The Book of the Wars of the Lord" might have been a suitable title of the whole of the Old Testament' but at least it can be said that no pattern of imagery is of more frequent occurrence than that which displays a people down-trodden, defeated and distressed being brought out into a new experience of life and liberty through the intervention of a power not their own, through the saving acts, in fact, of Him whom they acknowledged, at least through their prophets and spiritual leaders, as God and Saviour of Israel.

The famous chapters 40–55 of the book of Isaiah contain some of the noblest redemption songs of the whole Old Testament. Here past and future mingle together. There is the imagery and the historical reference drawn from the past: there is the triumphant assurance that a similar redemption will yet be the lot of God's people in an age to come.

> Awake, awake, put on strength,
> O arm of the Lord;
> awake, as in days of old,
> the generations of long ago.
> Was it not thou that didst cut Rahab in pieces,
> that didst pierce the dragon?
> Was it not thou that didst dry up the sea,
> the waters of the great deep;
> that didst make the depths of the sea a way
> for the redeemed to pass over?
> And the ransomed of the Lord shall return
> and come with singing to Zion.
>
> (Isaiah 51: 9–11)

> Break forth into singing you waste places of Jerusalem,
> for the Lord has comforted his people, he has redeemed
>   Jerusalem.
> The Lord has bared his holy arm before the eyes of
>   all the nations;
> and all the ends of the earth shall see the salvation
>   of our God (Isaiah 52: 9–10)

No words could more eloquently express the prophet's faith that in spite of all the oppression and cruelty that seem to be rampant in the world, God would yet come to defeat the arch-enemy and restore the fortunes of His people. And not only would this mean the resettlement of Israel in its rightful land: it would mean also the renewal of creation and the rescue of the animal and the vegetable kingdom from the ills by which they had been harassed and in part destroyed.

The hope of the re-establishment of the Divine community in the holy city under the rule of God's vicegerent has never faded entirely from the Hebrew imagination. Yet there is another tradition in Hebrew theology, appearing in some of the later oracles of the Old Testament and gaining still fuller expression in the literature of the two centuries preceding the Christian era. In this tradition any partial restoration, any renewal through the return of the exiles to Zion is virtually despaired of. Instead attention is focussed upon 'that day', the great day of the Lord yet to come, the day of what Professor S. H. Hooke has called 'one great final revolution of the wheel of the divine purpose, setting all things right, in the New Testament writer's phrase, the *apokatastasis*, the restitution of all things'.[4]

The apocalyptic tradition to which I have just referred is not by any means uniform in its treatment of the restoration which the day of the Lord will bring. Perhaps the most striking common feature is the emphasis upon the Messianic agent through whom Yahweh effects the final salvation. Most frequently he is named Son of David and his special task is to deliver Jerusalem from the yoke of the nations that oppress her and to reign righteously in their stead. Sometimes he is called Son of Man and in this role his task is to mete out judgment to the nations and to establish righteousness in the world. Still another strand of tradition names him Son of Levi and describes his work in more mythological terms. The evils that oppress mankind are concentrated into a single figure Beliar with his attendant spirits (also referred to as Satan, the devil, the enemy). This arch-enemy of God and His people

4. S. H. Hooke in *The Labyrinth*, p. 221.

will certainly be destroyed though it is not always clear whether the champion who defeats him is God Himself or His Messiah. But the result of the conflict is assured. Beliar and his hosts are defeated, those whom he has taken captive are rescued and the souls of the righteous enter into peace. There is a proliferation of motifs in Jewish apocalyptic literature and no consistent pattern of imagery can be found. But the picture of Beliar or Satan or the Dragon being overcome by Messiah and his captives being thereby released was destined to play a notable part in Christian apocalyptic and in the imagery of Christian interpreters of the Atonement in a later age.

Did this mean, however, that the Messianic victor emerged unscathed? In the theology of pre-Christian Judaism there is constant emphasis upon the sufferings of God's people and, for reflective minds, the Messiah or leader of the people could hardly fail to be involved in some way in this suffering. This is essentially the background of the Emmaus story as recorded by St. Luke. Jesus seems to take for granted that a reflective Jew would be aware that it was the lot of God's faithful people in olden times to endure persecution and suffering. And although the Old Testament contains no explicit reference to the suffering of the Messiah as such, yet as He is the very embodiment, the authentic representation of the people of God, He surely cannot escape some identification with their suffering and distress. 'What Luke is here claiming,' writes Professor G. B. Caird, 'is that, underlying all the Old Testament writings, Jesus detected a common pattern of God's dealings with his people, which was meant to foreshadow his own ministry.'[5] Only through suffering could they fulfil God's purpose for them. Only through suffering therefore, could the true Messiah go forward to His glory. And the pattern which had been foreshadowed so often in the partial experience of the holy people under the Old Covenant had now been brought into clear focus, at a central point in history, in and through the sufferings of the Son of Man. Through the humiliation and apparent defeat of their champion God had in fact visited and redeemed His people. And even though their own sufferings in the world might continue, they could rest assured that these too were necessary preliminaries to the final overthrow of the Adversary and the climactic vindication of the saving power of God.

In this whole area there is much that is uncertain and open to differing interpretations. What is however abundantly clear is that one pattern of imagery holds a place of supremacy in the minds of the writers of the Old Testament: it is the Exodus-pattern.[6]

5. G. B. Caird: *The Gospel of St. Luke*, p. 258.
6. See David Daube: *The Exodus Pattern in the Bible*.

And as Dr. Caird remarks in his admirable comment on Luke 24: 25–27, whatever variations there may be in the Old Testament interpretation of the sufferings of God's people 'in each case the common pattern is the Exodus pattern; for at the outset of her history Israel had been constituted a nation when God brought her from the humiliation of Egyptian bondage into the glory of a new day, so that the Exodus, annually celebrated at the Passover, had become the prototype of the messianic deliverance. Thus Moses and all the prophets could be said to bear witness to the one divine method of dealing with the problem of evil. But if Israel was called to suffer in order to break the power of pagan despotism . . . then this must be *par excellence* the vocation of the Messiah, Israel's symbolic head and leader. Thus the Cross, so far from being a cause for dejection, was a necessary element in the divine purpose of redemption.'[7]

C

The New Testament contains a wealth of analogies and metaphors whose function it is to make dramatically present to human minds and imaginations the power and meaning of the death of Jesus. There can be little doubt that to all the Cross was mystery and yet it was also saving revelation. It was terrible in its condemnation of certain accepted human values yet it was also wonderful in its affirmation of the eternal righteousness of God. Most appealing of all it would seem: The Cross was the supreme victory of the powers of darkness yet it was also their place of final defeat. It will be the aim of this section to examine the New Testament appeal to this range of comparison.

No one can read the Gospels without being conscious of the writers' concern not only with sinister tyrants such as Herod and Caiaphas, not only with the evil machinations of groups such as the Pharisees and Sadducecs, but still more with the devil as prince of the kingdoms of this world, with the unseen forces operating under his domain and with human beings whose behaviour was such as to mark them out as being possessed by demonic influences. In the Synoptic Gospels Jesus indeed speaks of His own activity as contributing in some way to the overthrow of the Satanic powers. But still in the Acts of the Apostles we find records of encounters between the apostles and evil spirits and it is clear that whatever may have been accomplished through the life and death and resurrection of Jesus, the Church believed that it must still engage

7. Op. cit., pp. 258–9.

in a warfare with more than human adversaries. The whole emphasis is upon Jesus and the Spirit of God as being demonstrably stronger than the devil and the spirits of evil.

It is in the Epistles however, and especially in the writings of Paul that we find the repeated affirmation that through the death and resurrection of Jesus an altogether critical act of deliverance had been accomplished. A hateful tyranny had been broken. Men and women had been brought out of bondage. Apparent defeat had been turned into dramatic victory. Not that the full results of the victory had as yet been made manifest. The redeemed people could expect to be subjected to the attacks of the demonic host. But equally they could be assured that neither principalities nor powers could separate them from their divine leader and that because of His triumph their own victory was secure.

How this was all worked out in more detailed exposition can be seen to full advantage in Ragnar Leivestad's fine monograph, *Christ the Conqueror*. Here we are given a careful survey of the rich complex of ideas of conflict and victory as they are found in the New Testament, a comprehensive view of the imagery brought from the athletic stadium, the amphitheatre and the battlefield into the service of the Gospel. And naturally the writings of Paul occupy the largest area of the author's attention.

No one in Christian history, it could be claimed, has felt more keenly than Paul the pressure of intangible forces intent on compassing his personal destruction and inimical to the whole purpose of God for His people. These forces include the Devil and Antichrist (the latter a manifestation of the former), the principalities and powers in heavenly places, sin and death, the law and its curse, the flesh and its lusts. Rather strangely St. Paul lays no stress upon any direct conflict between Christ and Satan. Christians are summoned to beware of him and to resist him but the most strenuous part of their conflict is described in another way. This is with the host of cosmic powers designated by such titles as princes, authorities, lords, thrones—a somewhat vague totality originally subservient to God but now the enemies of His purpose for His people. Their enmity is such that they must be held finally responsible for the crucifixion of the Lord of glory (1 Corinthians 2: 8). But this very crucifixion spells their own defeat, as is clearly implied in Colossians 2: 14–15, even though the detailed exposition of the passage presents very great difficulties and is never likely to receive a uniform interpretation.

Whatever uncertainties there may be in the details of the imagery, the central affirmation of the passage stands out the more clearly. It is that the stranglehold of the law, rigidly retained while obligations remained unfulfilled, has been dramatically broken: at the same time the demonic powers have been disarmed and their usurped lordship over the human creation for ever shattered. Moule paraphrases the section in this way:

'Deleting the adverse bond signed by us as committing us to the decrees of law—the bond which was opposed to us—he has removed it, nailing it to the cross. Divesting himself of the rulers and authorities, he boldly displayed them, leading them in triumphal procession on the cross.'[8] And as the result of an exhaustive examination of the whole passage Leivestad comments:

'What really happened the moment the hostile powers triumphed, nailing Christ to the cross, was that God nailed the charge against us to the cross and disarmed the powers, triumphing over them in the crucified. Christ became the end of the law the moment he submitted to the verdict of the law. . . . It is not of great significance whether we imagine a humiliating degradation of the powers, whereby their mantles and other insignia are taken from them, or a military conquest at which they are deprived of arms and weapons by the conqueror. The important thing is that the crucifixion of Jesus is, in one way or other, depicted as a divine triumph over the cosmic powers.'[9]

The bondage of the law has been annulled at the Cross. The grip of 'the powers' on our lives has been broken. What then of Sin and Death? That the dominion of sin has been ended is the clear testimony of Romans 6–8. Though man has since the Fall been sold under sin and unable to act according to the express wishes of his own mind: though the penalty of such a subjection to sinful desires must inevitably be death: though the Law which might have eased the situation has proved impotent to deliver man because of the weakness of human flesh: yet God, in His great mercy, has put an end to the dominion of sin by sending His Son into the very midst of the situation, exposing Him to the penalties which necessarily descended upon one who was hung in the flesh under the reign of law, and annulling them finally in Him.[10]

8. C. F. D. Moule: *The Epistles to Colossians and to Philemon*, p. 102.

9. R. Leivestad: *Christ the Conqueror*, pp. 102–4.

10. 'The stronger had to enter the house of the strong one to deprive him of his prey and arms. The flesh is the territory that is to be liberated from the occupation of sin. The incarnation of Christ means an invasion of territory occupied by the enemy. Sin must be defeated ἐν τῇ σαρκί. It reads ἐν τῇ σαρκί, not ἐν τῇ σαρκί αὐτοῦ because the flesh of Jesus is representative of all flesh. If sin is conquered in the flesh of Jesus it implies that the dominion of sin over flesh is broken. From that moment it is no longer sin that is master, but Christ.' Leivestad: op. cit., p. 118.

In proclaiming the victory over death Paul rises to the very heights of inspired exultation. The key passage is 1 Corinthians 15. The universal reign of death is regarded as an unquestioned reality, unquestioned because death follows upon sin and all have in fact sinned. The only serious question is whether it is conceivable that this tyranny could be breached and man thereby delivered. On the level of ordinary humanity it is unthinkable. But here is One Who has actually risen from the dead. Here is One Who is not just an isolated individual but head of a new humanity, the first-fruits of a new harvest. By passing through death He, the sinless One, has destroyed death and opened the gate of everlasting life to all who believe. 'Thanks be to God Who giveth us the victory through our Lord Jesus Christ' (1 Corinthians 15: 57).

Nowhere else in the New Testament is the theme of deliverance through the saving work of Christ celebrated so lyrically and so comprehensively as in the Pauline writings. Deliverance from the past, the present and the future, deliverance from the sinister control of evil cosmic influences, deliverance from the burden of a law from whose injunctions there seemed no way of escape, deliverance from the unbreakable chain of evil habit, deliverance from the awful power of the final enemy, Death—all this, Paul believed, had been achieved by the death and resurrection of the Redeemer. All who had been united with him in Baptism became partakers of the emancipating power of His double-sided saving act. United with Him in death they stripped off all subservience to cosmic powers, all indebtedness to legal systems, all enslavement to self-destroying habits. United with Him in resurrection they became more than conquerors through Him Who loved them.

But although this wide ranging exposition of the victory-theme is without parallel in the rest of the New Testament, the note of exulting triumph is certainly not absent from other writings. The Epistle to the Hebrews for example finds this theme entirely congenial. Indeed in commenting on 2: 14, the verse which describes Jesus as victor over him who possessed the power of death, i.e. the devil, Leivestad goes so far as to say that 'along with Colossians 2: 14 f. this passage represents the most dramatic interpretation of the death of Jesus in the New Testament'.[11] In this drama man's supreme enemy is death. And the principle is assumed that the only way of breaking its power is for someone stronger than death to assume a mortal body and as it were gain the victory within death's own territory. Moreover if death can be conquered, the devil also, who uses death to keep men in bondage (chiefly by playing on the

11. Op. cit., p. 182 f.

emotion of fear—2: 15) will suffer an ignominious reverse and his dominion will be destroyed.

The characteristic title assigned to Jesus in this Epistle is 'captain of salvation' (2: 10, Cf. 12: 2). The idea behind this title is precisely that of a pioneer or champion who enters into a threatening situation daringly and representatively. As man he shares the weaknesses of flesh and blood, becomes subject to every kind of trial and testing and passes through the valley of suffering on the way to his final engagement with death. But in fact death cannot hold him. The God of peace brings him again from the dead (13: 20) and in this victory which He, 'the perfecter of faith', wins essentially through His faith in the God Who raises the dead, the devil is defeated and men are released from an age-long bondage. In every respect Jesus is the perfect leader or champion. He goes on ahead, He clears the way, He displays an unswerving faithfulness, He is deterred by no obstacle, He challenges man's ultimate foes. In the most astonishing paradox of all time He, through death, destroys death. Through His resurrection He brings to all men the pledge of their own and thereby delivers them from the debilitating fear which otherwise haunts their lives.

In different language and within a different symbolic framework the same victory-theme is unfolded in the Fourth Gospel. Though there is no record of temptations in the wilderness nor of exorcisms in Galilee nor of conflict with unsympathetic disciples nor of struggle with cosmic powers yet, in the striking words of Leivestad, 'the Johannine literature is to a higher degree than any of the documents hitherto discussed permeated by an antagonistic dualism and depicts Jesus as the triumphant victor more emphatically than all of them'.[12] The adversaries are named differently—the world, darkness, falsehood, death—but the conviction of universal, once-for-all victory is as strong as anywhere in the New Testament. In a dramatic passage 12: 20–33 the prince of the world is cast out and the crucified reigns from the tree.

No exposition of the theology of the Johannine writings can fail to emphasize their dramatic representation of the victory of the Redeemer from heaven over all the foes that oppress mankind. The world and the prince of this world are bitterly hostile to the champion who has invaded their territory and threatened their authority. They resist him, they accuse him, they condemn him. He on his part bears witness to the light, defends his chosen disciples, allows the truth to sift men. The process of judgment moves to its climax. The king to whom all authority has been committed, the

12. Op. cit., p. 192 f.

judge whose verdicts are always righteous, is condemned and cast out. Yet 'the world has sentenced the innocent to death and Christ allows the execution of the verdict. That means the decisive testimony for truth and against the world. The triumph of injustice seals its ultimate defeat. The world lifts Jesus up on the cross, God lifts him up to heaven. The world judges him; God justifies him. In appearance it is Christ who is judged and executed; in fact it is the world which is condemned and the accuser cast out.'[13] God did not send His Son into the world to condemn the world but that the world through Him might be saved. Yet it is the testimony of this gospel that although men have indeed been delivered from the tyranny of the prince of darkness through the saving illumination of Calvary yet many have still loved darkness rather than light and that the victory of the Son of Man will only be complete at the final judgment on the last day.

It is the concentration of attention upon the End which marks the characteristic contribution of the Apocalypse to the imagery of the Divine victory. As Leivestad points out the pattern of conflict and victory appears in this book in two main forms. First there is the often moving and poignant description of the suffering of the saints who follow the Lamb in His sacrificial witness to the truth and righteousness of God. They suffer with Him: they will reign with Him. They have washed their robes in His blood: they will stand vindicated and triumphant around His throne. But there is a second application of this basic pattern. It is the mythical-eschatological, the unfolding of the drama of the Lamb Who has been slain from the foundation of the world, Who in His historic manifestation has loosed men from bondage by the shedding of His own blood and Who at the end will stand triumphant on Mount Zion. He it is who has conquered death once and for all and will finally cast death and hades out from His Kingdom (XX:14). Furthermore the Devil's final doom is assured, however damaging his writhings and lashings may be in the period before the End. When he has been cast into the lake of fire the victory of God and the Lamb will be complete.

It only remains in this brief reference to the Apocalypse (a book rich in symbols of conflict and victory) to mention one chapter in which there seem to be clear connections with ancient cult-myths. This is Chapter 12, a chapter full of complexity for the interpreter, but one in which the defeat of the dragon is explicitly elaborated even though his influence on earth is not brought finally to an end. Martin Kiddle in his imaginative commentary on the chapter draws

13. Leivestad: op. cit., p. 206.

special attention to the colour of the dragon, to his heads and horns and particularly to the suggestive links with Egypt and the Exodus which appear in the context. The redness of the dragon links him with the Egyptian monster Typhon who persecuted the sun-goddess Osiris, his tail with the snaky Nile so prominent in Hebrew memory. There is much to support Kiddle's contention that here at the heart of the Apocalypse we find the pattern of the dragon, Rahab, Egypt, the Red Sea, in a new eschatological context. The final victory will partake of the same character as that of the initial victory through Moses the servant of God. The Lamb is the leader moving towards the final contest. He has already won the battle on the Cross when by the outpouring of His own blood He revealed Himself as worthy to be the shepherd of the ransomed people of God. And this battle on earth had its counterpart in heaven: 'The great dragon was thrown down, that ancient serpent who is called the Devil and Satan, the deceiver of the whole world—he was thrown down to the earth and his angels were thrown down with him. And I heard a loud voice in heaven, saying,

"Now the salvation and the power and the kingdom of our God and the authority of his Christ have come, for the accuser of our brethren has been thrown down, who accuses them day and night before our God.

"And they have conquered him by the blood of the Lamb and by the word of their testimony, for they loved not their lives even unto death." '

Kiddle is surely right when he claims that the ejection of the dragon from heaven is nothing other than a pictorial expression of the Atonement.[14] It links the remote mythological past with the far-off eschatological future. It unites the redemption from Egypt with the exodus accomplished at Jerusalem and the final salvation of the people of God. It reveals the Christ as victorious over all that is opposed to the Divine purpose and therefore as the One Who restores to its true harmony a universe torn asunder by the pride and presumption of those who had originally been created to serve God and to enjoy Him for ever.

D

In the second and third centuries A.D., Christian missionaries and pastors had to proclaim the message of reconciliation to those who were surrounded by pagan cults and customs. In a few great centres of learning—Ephesus, Rome, Alexandria—the gospel had

14. M. Kiddle: *The Revelation of St. John*, p. 232.

to be related to a culture of a somewhat sophisticated kind and full attention is naturally given in histories of Christian doctrine to the attempts of the early Apologists and the Alexandrine theologians to follow the example of the writer of the Fourth Gospel in adapting the essential good news to the thought-forms current in educated circles. But an equally important task is that of examining the way in which the gospel was proclaimed amongst ordinary people uneducated in Greek philosophical concepts. How did early preachers and teachers seek to interpret the meaning of the death and resurrection of Christ in this more normal context?

Whereas a sophisticated mind tends to move naturally within a unified framework—a framework within which distortions and disharmonies can be reconciled—a more popular outlook tends to be preoccupied with the dangers which threaten normal human existence and to find a dualistic framework a more realistic structure for the representation of ordinary experience. When misfortune comes, surely it must be due to some evil and unseen influence: when disease and plague attack the body, surely they are themselves malevolent forces: when death strikes, surely it is the most implacable enemy of all. If the good news of redemption in Christ was to have any relevance to the needs of the ordinary people of the Mediterranean world it must be shown to be a way of salvation from the tyranny of these malign powers and as a means of leading men into a new assurance of victorious life.

It is not surprising then that although, as we have seen in Chapter II, a more philosophical interpretation of the great reconciliation in Christ was not without its distinguished representatives in the early centuries, by far the most popular 'range of comparison' was the appeal to men's awareness of the world as a place where hostile forces were constantly in opposition to one another: light and darkness, health and disease, life and death. Other religious systems —in particular varying forms of Gnosticism and the Mysteries— were attracting initiates by promising a way of escape from the ills of mortal life and it was natural that Christianity should make its appeal along the same lines and in so doing expose the inadequacy of other myths of salvation. Emil Brunner comments in one place on the strangeness of the fact that the idea of 'ransom' is almost the only one drawn from 'the whole range of ideas in the New Testament which the Early Church laid hold of and used in order to describe the significance of the Work of Jesus'.[15] But it is surely not very strange when one recalls the fear and apprehension which affected so much of human existence and the popularity of any myth

15. E. Brunner: *The Christian Doctrine of Creation and Redemption*, p. 309.

which could stir the imagination and provide a hope of redemption.

But the ransom-idea was only one particular expression of the conflict and victory pattern which had become woven into the very texture of the New Testament. In sermon and liturgy, in hymn and rite, in apologetic and catechetical teaching the same theme is celebrated again and again: Christ the Redeemer has, through His death and resurrection, overcome the devil and all his hosts and rescued the sons of men from every form of bondage. Let us glance at the way this central affirmation of faith assumes varying forms in differing contexts.

(i) *In the anti-heretical writings of S. Irenaeus*

Irenaeus was well aware of the attractiveness of other systems which were the rivals of the Christian faith. In fact it was the very pressure of these systems which led Irenaeus not only to denounce them as alien to the authentic apostolic tradition but also to construct a positive theology which would provide a true picture of the redemption of mankind. For if anything is clear about the Gnostic systems of the second century it is that they held out to men the promise of *redemption*. They assumed, in the vivid words of Rudolf Bultmann, that 'man is the lonely victim of a dreadful fear—fear of infinite space and time, fear of the turmoil and hostility of the world, or rather, fear of the demonic powers at work in it, seeking to lead him astray and alienate him from his true self. He is also afraid of himself, for he feels he is in the clutches of the demonic powers. He is no longer his own master, but the playground of demons. He is estranged from his own spiritual life, the impulses of his desire and will. Physical and sensual life . . . is the enemy of his Self and even his soul can be his enemy.'[16]

The only hope is redemption from above, from the world of pure light. In all kinds of ways the Gnostic teachers bore witness to the descent of a heavenly being bringing the secret formula for the release of the true Self. And in the time of Irenaeus many of these sects had adopted elements from the Christian tradition, claiming in some cases that Christ had come to release men from their bondage to the god of the Jews, the god who had created the world, the god of stern justice, the god who was responsible for holding them fast in their condition of misery. Contaminated by the matter which he had created, their situation was hopeless unless a redeemer could be found who would deliver them from the dominion of this evil god and bring them into the realm of a god of light and love. Just because these ideas and notions were being

16. R. Bultmann: *Primitive Christianity*, p. 197.

propagated so vigorously it was essential that a revised interpretation of salvation, true to the essential Christian gospel, should be proclaimed. It was the great achievement of Irenaeus to make such a proclamation through his work *Adversus Haereses*, a proclamation which, with all its curiosities by modern standards, provided a norm of atonement-doctrine for Eastern Christendom over the next millennium.

How then did Irenaeus perform his task? In the first place he rejected entirely any form of ultimate dualism. However clever and powerful the Devil might be, he was certainly not a second god, a demiurge. Neither in nature nor in history was it necessary to postulate an ultimate dualism such as could be resolved only by the annihilation of one dominion or the other. In the second place he gave a position of dignity and significance to man as made in the image of God. Man had indeed fallen from his high estate and needed to be rescued. But no comprehensive salvation could be effected except from within humanity itself. A heavenly being salvaging sparks of light from a world in almost total darkness could not be a true redeemer. Irenaeus delights to speak of the Redeemer as the second Adam who not only annuls the disastrous consequences of the primal Fall but brings humanity to the attainment of its true destiny—incorruption and immortality in union with God Himself. 'In the second Adam we were reconciled' (A.H.5.16.3).

In the third place Irenaeus anchors his thought firmly within the Biblical narrative and Biblical categories even though his detailed interpretations may at times seem fanciful and over-elaborate. He makes the most of the fact that the Fall was reversed and that defeat was turned into victory and discovers all manner of correspondences and antitheses in the two events. But what he is determined to preserve at all costs is the faith that it was the same God Who created the world and rules over it in righteousness Who also redeemed the world and made it possible for man to recover what he had so grievously lost. There can be no place for injustice in God's Kingdom. Yet His original design in creation cannot for ever be thwarted. Hence the beauty and fittingness of the Christian way of salvation for through the work of the Redeemer who was both true Man and Word of God the devil's apostasy was annulled and man was set free. An oft-quoted passage provides what is perhaps the best summary of Irenaeus's teaching and includes the seminal idea which was to be expanded and elaborated in remarkable ways in the following centuries:

'He Who is the Almighty Word and true Man, reasonably

redeeming us by His blood, gave Himself as a ransom for those who were led into captivity. And since he (the Devil) unjustly ruled over us by an apostasy and whereas we by nature belonged to Almighty God, alienated us contrary to nature, making us His own disciples, He, the Word of God, powerful in all things, and not failing in His own justice, behaved justly even as against the very apostasy; redeeming what was His own from that apostasy, not violently (or arbitrarily) inasmuch as that apostasy dominated over us from the beginning—not insatiably seizing on what was His own, but by way of persuasion, as it beseemed God to get what He wanted by persuasion, and not by employing violence; so that neither should the law of justice be violated nor the ancient creation of God perish' (A.H.5.1.1).

(ii) *In the more detailed expositions of the Eastern Fathers*

Irenaeus had made certain leading affirmations—that man created in the image of God had been tempted by and overcome by the Devil in the form of a serpent, that the result of this downfall was the loss of immortality and the consequent triumph of Death, that the Devil could not be justly arraigned for a disaster in human affairs to which man himself had given his assent and yet that if the situation continued indefinitely the whole purpose of creation would be brought to nought: that the second Adam had come in the flesh, had been tempted by the Devil but had not succumbed, had been brought under the dominion of Death but had emerged victorious, had in fact taken upon himself the whole human situation and reversed its disastrous failure by his own perfect obedience and integrity. And in all this God had not in any way acted violently or arbitrarily against the Devil but had, as it were, accepted his limited suzerainty before proceeding to deliver his prey out of his grasp. Irenaeus refused to countenance the Gnostic dualistic theories of redemption but committed himself rather to a doctrine which could claim considerable Biblical support and which was undoubtedly a gospel of victory in a period of darkness and despair.

But what Irenaeus had expressed in paradoxical yet restrained terminology, later writers, either by way of more detailed explanation or as a spur to their audience's imagination, proceeded to elaborate and embellish. How exactly had the redemption been affected? If the transaction could be described as a 'ransom' to whom had the ransom been paid? And what was the precise nature of the ransom price? It was Origen who was first responsible for pressing the matter further.

'If then we were "bought with a price" as also Paul asserts, we were doubtless bought from one whose servants we were, who also named what price he would for releasing those whom he held from his power. Now it was the devil that held us, to whose side we had been drawn away by our sins. He asked, therefore, as our price the blood of Christ' (in Rom. 2: 13).

'To whom gave He His life "a ransom for many"? It cannot have been to God. Was it not then to the evil one? For he held us until the ransom for us, even the soul of Jesus, was paid to him, being deceived into thinking that he could be its lord, and not seeing that he could not bear the torment of holding it.' (In Matt. 16: 8.)[17]

Gregory expands the image still more fully in the important twenty-third chapter of his Great Catechism. From the beginning the devil has caused havoc by his ingrained propensity to envy the happiness of others. Originally he envied man and brought about his downfall. Now when the God-man appears in human form the devil is more envious than ever. He is ready even to surrender 'those who are shut up in the prison of death' if only he can gain possession of the pearl of great price (whose human beauty he has recognized without in any way being aware of His unique Divine origin). It is the devil who proposes the bargain and it is a hard bargain for he is in fact already in possession of humanity at large but judges that this single soul is worth more to him than all the rest. Yet God in His infinite goodness and wisdom accepts the proposed arrangement and thereby achieves a glorious and comprehensive redemption.

'His choosing to save man is a testimony of his goodness; His making the redemption of the captive a matter of exchange exhibits his justice; while the invention whereby He enabled the enemy to apprehend that of which he was before incapable is a manifestation of supreme wisdom.'

Thus the Divinely inspired stratagem achieves three purposes. It sets imprisoned humanity free: it preserves the requirements of perfect justice: it even benefits the adversary by teaching him a supreme lesson which previously he had been quite incapable of learning. It is interesting to note the concern of all the Eastern Fathers that what may be called natural justice should in no way be impugned. At the same time there is respect for the devil's rights in as much as he is a creature of God and not an independent rival deity. Of course, the Fathers say, God could have used His omnipotent power to crush the devil or to snatch man violently

17. Quoted L. W. Grensted: *A Short History of the Doctrine of the Atonement*, pp. 37–8.

out of his grasp. Yet God does not act that way. God in His pity and love for man (in the words of John of Damascus) wished to reveal man himself as conqueror and became man to restore like with like. It is the love of perfect correspondence and the preservation of the rhythmic order of the universe which marks the attempts of the Eastern Fathers to commend Christian Doctrine to their disciples.

So much for the image of the market-place. But there is one other prominent image which proved its effectiveness, partly because of its associations with motifs which, as we have seen, appeared in some of the earliest myths of the human race, partly because of its links with the symbol which, with that of the shepherd and his sheep, captivated the imagination of the earliest Christians. The imagery to which I refer is that connected with the art of fishing. From time immemorial man, having recognized the advantages of living in the neighbourhood of river or lake for his water supply, has exercised his ingenuity by adding to his food supply whatever he could capture from their depths. Fishing is exciting and, often rewarding. Its imagery is familiar to all. Its metaphorical possibilities are obvious.

So it comes about that in a succession of writers from Gregory of Nyssa to John of Damascus we find an elaboration of bait-and-hook images, coming perhaps to fullest expression in Gregory the Great's *Moralia on the Book of Job*. Gregory was convinced that Job, who had wrestled with the problem of evil more tenaciously than any other Biblical writer, had mystically prefigured the atoning work of Christ. The sea-monster, the great Behemoth, symbol of man's arch-adversary, was ever eager for prey. But his doom was being cleverly planned. From Abraham on to Mary the virgin a kind of line was spun to the end of which the Incarnate Lord was destined to be suspended in the dark waters of the human race, His divine virtue acting as the hook, His human flesh the bait. Attracted by our Lord's humanity, the devourer was wounded by His divinity; excited by His open infirmity, the spoiler was pierced through the jaw by His hidden virtue.

'The bait tempts that the point may wound. Our Lord, therefore, when coming for the redemption of mankind, made as it were a kind of hook of Himself for the death of the devil.'

Other images are employed dramatically by Eastern writers—the Cross as a net for catching birds, as a trap for catching mice—but the hook and bait motif is the most popular of all. Viewed literally these images become bizarre and repulsive but it is quite unfair to these writers to interpret their concepts in this way. The images are poetic, parabolic, dramatic. They are taken from the commonest experiences of the contemporary world. They are designed to celebrate the goodness and justice and wonder of God, the self-humbling and faithful obedience of the Divine Son, the triumph-in-defeat, the victory-in-death of man's Redeemer, the deliverance of man from sin and death through the blood of Christ, the final restoration of a harmonious universe through a just reckoning with all the power of darkness. We do not read Shakespeare literally when he makes Angelo exclaim:

> O cunning enemy, that, to catch a saint,
> With saints dost bait thy hook!

We do not need to read the Gregories literally when they elaborate the fish-hook concept in the context of their witness to man's redemption through Christ.

(iii) *In the myth of the Harrowing of Hell*

Throughout the Middle Ages the myth of the harrowing of hell maintained an extraordinary hold on the popular imagination. Whereas in Eastern Christendom the 'dominant theme in liturgy and popular devotion was the *resurrection* of Christ—His triumph over the grave, His defeat of the Devil who held the keys of death—in Western Christendom the ground of exultation for the common man tended rather to be the despoiling of hell, the rescue of souls from its dreary shades. Whereas in the East the idea of ransom gave an excellent framework for vivid imagery drawn from the worlds of trading and angling, in the West the idea of the descent into hell provided equal possibilities for the imagination to expand in terms of ancient mythology or of border raiding.

For just as the myths of the dismemberment of the sea-monster and the defeat of the dragon lie behind the victory imagery of the East so the myths of the descent into the underworld and the rescue of lives enchained lie behind the victory imagery of the West. There were types in the Old Testament which could easily be fitted into the general pattern—Noah saving his family from the Flood, Moses delivering his people from Egypt, Samson despoiling Gaza, Jonah emerging safely from the jaws of hell—and there was one famous passage in the First Epistle of Peter which gave abundant scope for the exercise of the imagination.[18] Other passages in the New Testament (e.g. Matthew 12:39 f., Romans 10:7, Colossians 1:18, Acts 2:27–31) at least suggested that the Christ went down

---

18. 1 Peter 3:18–22. Especially 'being put to death in the flesh but made alive in the spirit; in which he went and preached to the spirits in prison . . . who has gone into heaven and is at the right hand of God with angels, authorities and powers subject to him'.

to the place of the departed between His death and His resurrection and this thought came to frequent expression in the writings of the early Fathers. In the middle of the fourth century a credal statement included a reference to the descent to the underworld and to the shuddering of the gate-keepers of hell when the Redeemer came to set things in order. And in the sixth century the bare clause 'He descended into hell' appeared in certain Spanish creeds. All this time the popular imagination was interpreting the descent in terms of a victorious combat in the underworld and the release of countless souls from the devil's grip.[19] It is highly probable that this development came about just because of the existence of an age-long mythological complex which provided the mould into which the good news of Christus Victor could be poured.

Mircea Eliade has a valuable section in his book *Images and Symbols* in which he discusses the way in which Christianity has taken over ancient patterns and transformed them by relating its own central affirmation to them. He recalls the common theme in shamanistic cults of the descent of the shaman into Hell to seek and bring back the patient's soul which has been snatched away by demons. 'Orpheus, similarly,' he continues, 'descends into hell to bring back his wife Eurydice who has just died. There are analogous myths elsewhere; in Polynesia, in North America, and in Central Asia . . .; a hero is said to descend into hell to recover the soul of his dead wife. In the Polynesian and Central Asian myths he succeeds in this: in the North America myths he fails, in the same way as Orpheus.'[20] It may be of significance that the hero has often established himself already as a healer, a tamer, an agent of culture and civilization. But his altogether distinctive mark is his willingness to brave danger and to endure physical distress *in order to save a single soul from doom*. This is a new element in stories of initiations and exploits. 'The symbolic death is no longer undertaken solely for one's own spiritual perfection but for the salvation of *others*.'[21]

All that was now required was an imaginative writer who could embody the saving action of Christ within a compelling myth of this kind. For as E. M. W. Tillyard remarks 'once a way of feeling or a mode of action has been embodied in the mythology of a large

19. Cp. for example an extract from a sermon by St. Caesarius of Arles quoted by J. N. D. Kelly: *Early Christian Creeds*, p. 382:—
'Because this Lion, that is, Christ, of the tribe of Judah, descended victoriously to hell, snatching us from the mouth of the hostile lion. Thus He hunts us to save us, He captures us to release us, He leads us captive to restore us liberated to our native land.'
20. Op. cit., p. 165.
21. Ibid.

group of people it acquires an incalculable power'.[22] Such a genius was to arise in the person of the unknown author of the apocryphal Gospel of Nicodemus. The substance of the story probably derives from the second century A.D. though it was not until two centuries later that it attained a fully developed form. It has been acclaimed as one of the finest works in primitive Christian literature[23] and its theme was being taken up by Christian artists as early as the time of Constantine. In the twelfth and thirteenth centuries it gained enormous popularity in the literature, art and drama of Northern Europe. Tillyard, for example, draws attention to the fact that the window in the Chapel of King's College, Cambridge, which depicts the harrowing of hell seems even more dramatic and more important than that which proclaims the Resurrection.

The general pattern of the story in the Gospel of Nicodemus is as follows. Two men having risen from the dead on the day of Christ's crucifixion when graves were opened, were ultimately induced to write down an account of what they had witnessed in the underworld. Their narrative begins with the advent of a golden light like the sun which caused Adam and the righteous patriarchs to tremble with joy. But Hell and the prince of Tartarus were disquieted. Then come two mighty challenges: 'Lift up your gates, O ye princes, and the King of Glory shall enter in'. In spite of resistance by the infernal legions 'the King of Glory, in his majesty treading Death under foot, and laying hold on Satan deprived hell of its power and led Adam to the light of the sun. And the Lord said, "Come to me, all my saints, who have borne my image and likeness". And all the saints, reunited in the land of God, sang his praises.'

This story, so full of dramatic appeal, was eagerly seized by the artists of the thirteenth century. Emile Male, speaking out of his great authority on the art of the Middle Ages, gives as his judgment that 'of all the legends which gathered round the Passion of Christ that of the descent into Limbo was the most impressive and was destined to take an unequalled place in the history of art. . . . As conceived by the thirteenth century (it) is an almost literal translation of the Gospel of Nicodemus. The Saviour comes as a conqueror carrying the cross of victory—to which the fourteenth century attached a white oriflamme like the pennon on a knight's lance— and He treads on the gates torn from their hinges, which falling had overwhelmed Death and Satan. Before him hell opens in the form of the jaws of a monster, the gaping jaws of the biblical

22. E. M. W. Tillyard: *Mythical Elements in English Literature*, p. 28.
23. E. Male: *The Gothic Image*, p. 224.

leviathan which seem ready to devour him. But in them He plants the foot of the cross and holds out His hand to Adam.'[24]

The painter was followed by the dramatist. In a mystery play of the early fourteenth century belonging to the Northern Passion cycle the Harrowing of Hell is thus described: 'And furthermore, when Christ was dead, his spirit went in haste to Hell. And soon he broke the strong gates that were wrongfully barred against him. The devils were so greatly afraid that they would have fled had they been able. But they may never flee beyond Hell, for it is their lot to stay there. He bound Satan fast with eternal bonds; and so shall Satan ever remain bound till the day of doom. He took with him Adam and Eve and others that were dear to him; John the Baptist, Moses too, Abraham and others, whom he had redeemed through His heavy pains—all these he led out of Hell and set in Paradise, where there is ever joy and endless bliss. Thus out of the very tree that made us suffer through Eve's primal sin began our salvation after it had carried him who was both God and man.'[25]

There can be little doubt that it was this story which exercised 'an incalculable power' over the imaginations of men and women in northern Europe in the later Middle Ages. The fear of demonic influences and above all of Hell and the power of darkness was oppressively real. If the doctrine of the Atonement was to mean anything to such people it must be couched in terms which would enable them to overcome their fear and regain the assurance that they were in God's hands in a universe which had no areas (not even hell) outside his ultimate control. The essential theme Christus Victor needed to be expressed vividly, realistically, relevantly. The use of the legend of the Harrowing of Hell enabled this to be done. The matter is summed up so well by Dr. Tillyard that I propose to quote his statement in full:

'The idea of Christ rescuing Adam from Hell between his death and his resurrection came from a sublime imaginative effort to fulfil Scripture in its account of the central episode of the Christian creed and to establish connections within that episode. In the New Testament it is clearly asserted that through the fall of Adam he and all his progeny were incriminated: that a debt had been incurred that no ordinary man could fulfil, and that the Son of God chose out of his goodness to fulfil it through dying in human form; but nothing is said specifically about what happened to Adam when the debt was fulfilled. So, relying on vague texts to the effect that the spirit of Christ went and preached to the spirits in prison, interpreters of the Bible supplemented the text by defining what happened to Adam once the debt, what Milton called "the rigid satisfaction, death for death", was paid.

24. Op. cit., pp. 224, 226.
25. See Tillyard: op. cit., p. 34.

The resultant myth was strictly logical. The moment Christ died, Adam could be freed, there was no need to wait for the Resurrection: and the central doctrine of the Redemption could be rounded off by Christ's rescuing Adam from Hell at the earliest possible moment. Was it not indeed self-evident that Christ would at once perform the act, the performance of which was the very reason of his Incarnation and Passion? As to establishing connections, the concrete rescue of Adam by Christ corresponded precisely with the perdition of Adam by Satan through the concrete act of eating the forbidden fruit.

'There is a special reason why the rescue of Adam, in itself so congenial to the imagination, should have been made prominent, indeed advertised, by medieval artists and writers. These men intended or were employed to *teach*; and what they produced was aimed largely at the eyes or the ears of illiterates, on whom they wished to make the deepest possible impression. To such recipients Adam was Everyman, the embodiment of humanity, or, if you like, one of themselves. If the doctrine of the Redemption could be put in terms of Adam it would penetrate the simple man's mind more quickly and surely than through any other means. Looking at a mosaic or a fresco of Christ taking Adam by the hand, he could reflect: There am I, or there I could be, if I followed the commands of the Church.'[26]

E

One of the most striking developments in the theology of the Atonement during the past half century began with the publication of Gustaf Aulén's book *Christus Victor* in its English translation in 1931. Up to that time the emphasis of the early Church on Christ's death as a grim struggle issuing in victory and thereby ransoming captive souls, though recognized, tended to be regarded by theologians as a somewhat naïve and even crude interpretation of the central mystery of the faith. But Aulén vigorously challenged such a view. The idea of the victorious Christ who through his death and resurrection overcame all the powers of evil and brought mankind the assurance of liberty and life—this, he said, is the altogether classic idea of Atonement. This was the altogether dominating conception in early Christianity. It tended to be overshadowed and superseded by a penal view more congenial to the scholasticism of the Middle Ages. It was recovered in startling fashion by Luther, only to be relegated again to the background through the advance of idealism in the eighteenth and nineteenth centuries. In Aulén's view, however, the classic idea had no right to be put at the mercy of historical changes of fashion. It is of perennial significance and deserves to be the determining perspective through which at all times the atoning work of Christ should be rightly viewed.

Aulén's book immediately attracted interest and opened up an

26. Op. cit., pp. 26–8.

important debate. This centred around two issues. Could such a historical interpretation be vindicated? And could the so-called dramatic theory be regarded as meaningful in the twentieth century? So far as the first question is concerned the general consensus of opinion seems to have been that whereas Aulén performed a most valuable service in focussing attention upon an aspect of New Testament and Patristic thought which had been neglected in the prevailing atmosphere of the nineteenth century, it was doubtful whether the 'classic' view had ever dominated men's minds to the extent suggested in *Christus Victor*. Perhaps the major test case was that of Luther. Aulén claimed that Luther had been gravely misrepresented so far as his atonement teaching was concerned. Though he sometimes uses terms which seem to be those of the Latin or penal view of atonement, in actual fact Luther's imagination was gripped by the vision of Christus Victor, Christ as the conqueror of sin, death and the everlasting curse, Christ as the manifestation in time of the omnipotent God Who is alone able to overcome the devil and his hosts.

That Luther loved to speak paradoxically, almost shockingly, of the conflict between the divine and the demonic there can be no doubt. He used the imagery of the fisherman's angle-hook with Christ's humanity as the worm: he drew a parallel between David killing Goliath with the giant's own sword and Christ vanquishing the devil by employing one of his own weapons: he celebrated the great victory in vivid song and hymn. In the following passage his thought gains specially clear expression:

'For God's proper work is "life, peace, joy" and the other fruits of the Spirit. Yet in this God made marvellous his holy one, and is made wonderful in His saints, that he destroyed the Devil, not with the work of God, but even with the work of the Devil himself. For this is the most superb of all victories, to confound the adversary with his own weapon, and slay him with his own sword, as we sing "Prostrate he lies with his own dart". For thus God sets forward his own work and fulfils it by means of his "strange work" and with wonderful wisdom forces the Devil, by means of death to work nothing other than life, and thus when it seems to work most against the work of God, it works with his "own work" for God. For thus it was with the work of Christ, his death, which Christ through the immortality of his divinity swallowed up altogether and gloriously rose from the dead.'[27]

Furthermore Luther went beyond the Fathers who had celebrated the victory over sin, death and the devil by adding to the victims the

27. W.A. 57.128.7. Quoted in Gordon Rupp: *The Righteousness of God*, p. 206.

Law, the Curse and the Wrath. For him these were no merely abstract categories. They had become vividly personal. He sees the Law advancing menacingly upon the Saviour who had shouldered the burden of the sins of all men. The Law attacks him and slays him. But in so doing it actually brings about the destruction of sin and enables righteousness to conquer and live. So too he sees the curse (which inevitably follows upon a broken law) fighting with the blessing—God's eternal mercy and grace in Christ. He sees the wrath (which must descend upon sin wherever it exists) struggling with the love of God. It is in this contrast of Law-Grace, Curse-Blessing, Wrath-Love that Luther's paradoxical utterances reach their limit. To postulate a desperate conflict in the very being of God Himself obviously constitutes dangerous doctrine. Yet only in this way, it seemed, could Luther assure himself and his fellow-sufferers (for he and many another had suffered torments as they stood under the law, the curse and the wrath and contemplated the power of the devil, death and hell) that they were more than conquerors through Him Who loved them and that nothing could separate them from the love of God in Christ Jesus.

Yet when all this is recognized the question still remains whether the *Christus Victor* theme is indeed the very core of Luther's theology. The Righteousness of God, Justification by Faith, The Freedom of the Christian Man, Faith and Works—a claim could be made on behalf of each of these contenders for the primacy. Aulén may have overstated his case. But that no one in history has proclaimed the victory of the Son of God more daringly, more paradoxically, more comprehensively, can surely be affirmed.

I turn to the second question. Has it been possible for theologians of the twentieth century to reinstate the 'classic' theory by making it obviously relevant to the circumstances of modern life? Let us first look at Aulén's own teaching. In an article some twenty years after the publication of *Christus Victor*, he explains his position more clearly. It was never his intention, he declares, to say that the 'classic' view 'ought to be considered as a complete doctrine, standing beside and parallel to other doctrines. It was rather my intention to emphasize that the outlook of the Atonement as a drama, where the love of God in Christ fights and conquers the hostile powers, is a central and decisive perspective which never can be omitted and which indeed must stamp every really Christian doctrine of the Atonement.' This perspective he believes is characteristic of the whole Bible. 'The message of the Bible is focussed on the drama—the *mirabile duellum*, the war that God fights against the resistance, against the hostile powers, against all the evil that holds mankind in bondage. . . . We must see the work of the Atonement from this comprehensive, cosmos-encompassing dramatical perspective. It must be fitted into this drama. The Atonement is the turning point of the war that God fights with the powers of evil. God did not begin his war when he sent Christ into the world. From this point of view the New Testament does not set forth a beginning of something quite new in relation to the Old Testament. The New Testament means rather that the war is continued but that, at the same time, it enters into a new and decisive phase—the phase of victory—and that this victory is realized through Christ and all his work.'[28]

In this statement the two most striking categories seem to me to be 'war' and 'drama'. To these Aulén constantly returns and they are categories which have been very much with us in the past half century. The devastating effects of two world wars are known only too well. What is not perhaps so readily recognized is the way in which through the advent of the mass media of communication the drama has become an increasingly familiar art-form in the lives of millions of people. But a drama is constructed by the imagination—it is not necessarily dependent upon events which have happened in space and time though it may take such events into its structure. Aulén then is affirming that in all periods of the Church's existence God's activity may rightly be seen as a dramatic encounter with the forces of evil in which the victory of Christ is the supreme vindication of His sovereignty. But his very language seems to me to be deliberately adapted to our twentieth-century situation when for example he speaks of 'a turning point in the war', 'a new and decisive phase'; such expressions would not, I think, have been used in earlier times in this context, partly because the imagery is normally that of a single battle, partly because the relation of Christ's atoning act to the long outworking of the historical process had scarcely begun to be taken into account. Man's time-consciousness was of a different kind.

An extensive exposition of the ideas suggested by Aulén's image of the turning-point in the *mirabile duellum* is to be found in Oscar Cullmann's widely read book *Christ and Time*.[29] In this the author is concerned to throw light upon the specifically Hebrew-Christian view of God's redeeming work in history. To do this he uses as a determinative analogy the pattern of events which became familiar to countless people in the Second World War: a long period of

---

28. *Interpretation:* January 1951, pp. 156–8; Cp. *The Faith of the Christian Church*, p. 226.
29. See especially Chapter 5.

attrition during which the final outcome of the struggle was uncertain: a decisive battle or at least the emergence of a new factor
which was seen later to have been decisive in its influence: and finally
a long period of 'mopping-up operations' in which the effects of
the critical engagement were being exploited and the final triumph
secured. 'The decisive battle in a war may already have occurred
in an early stage,' Cullmann writes, 'and yet the war continues.
Although the decisive effect of that battle is not perhaps recognized
by all, it nevertheless already means victory'. So the event on
the cross, together with the resurrection, was the decisive battle in
the age-long struggle between God and all that is opposed to His
purpose. Since the decisive battle was won the Church has gone
forward in the assurance of final victory. The central feature of
'Victory Day' will be the deliverance of man and the earth into
a new freedom as the Holy Spirit lays hold of the entire world
of the flesh and re-creates it. Then will the victory be complete.

Cullmann's book appeared just at the end of the Second World
War when the terminology of D-day and V-day was constantly
on men's lips and in their minds. A little later Anders Nygren was
using similar imagery but in a slightly different way. He asked his
readers to think in terms of an occupied country—a concept which
has become more poignant and sinister in the twentieth century
than ever before in history. In such an emergency some citizens go
underground, some languish in prisons. All are deprived of any
ultimate freedom of movement. Then one day a message comes,
at first perhaps as rumour, then fully authenticated: Your country
is free! The forces of the occupying power have been decisively
defeated and in due course he must abandon the field everywhere.
Such a message not only gives the assurance that an objective
change in the theatre of world history has actually taken place:
it brings comfort to every individual who believes the good news
and enters into freedom. This, said Nygren, constitutes the illustration capable of bringing home to people of our time the good news
of Christ's victory over all the powers that enslave mankind.[30]

It may not be without significance that the finest exposition (in
my judgment) available[31] of the ideas of conflict and victory in
the New Testament was written by a distinguished scholar of an
'occupied country'. And Bishop Aulén, commenting on the fact
that in the early years of this century there was a tendency to
regard the Gospel narratives of Jesus' encounter with demons as
accommodations to current popular ideas and not therefore very

30. *Scottish Journal of Theology*, IV: pp. 364–5.
31. Leivestad: op. cit.

important, continues: 'Since then we have learned quite a lot. In fact, it would be rather striking if the thought of demoniacal powers, devastating in our world, would be unfamiliar to men in the present age. Indeed, we have experienced beyond measure how such powers have swept over us like a pestilential infection; we know very well their might to poison and lay waste.'

It is the massive evil revealed in war and preparation for war which has reawakened interest in the imagery of the 'dramatic' or 'classical' theory. This imagery has not unnaturally been most in vogue when groups or societies have been living under the threat of some impending doom. Man's whole world seems to be torn asunder by opposing forces and the question arises whether there *can* be any kind of reconciliation or at-one-ment. Where can he gain any confidence that the powers of evil will not be finally victorious? Aulén and Nygren and Leivestad and Cullmann and Karl Heim and many another would answer that only in the Cross and Resurrection of Christ can such confidence be won. A side glance may be cast at the record of the wilderness temptation or of the casting out of demons from those possessed. But the real focus of attention is the Cross, set within the context of the cosmic drama. Here the champion of the people of God wins the decisive victory. A total restitution of all things is assured.

Though such a view of the universe involves what Heim in this context has called 'impenetrable mystery' and 'insoluble contradiction' it is tenable if it be not regarded as the sole and final 'range of comparison' by which atonement in Christ can be interpreted. Alone it implies an ultimate dualism. Aulén it is true is at pains to affirm that his 'dramatic' view is not dualistic in a metaphysical sense 'nor in the sense of the absolute Dualism between Good and Evil typical of the Zoroastrian and Manichaean teaching in which Evil is treated as an eternal principle opposed to Good. It is used in the sense in which the idea constantly occurs in Scripture, of the opposition between God and that which in His own created world resists His will; between the Divine Love and the rebellion of created wills against Him. This Dualism is an altogether radical opposition but it is not an absolute Dualism.'[32] But the only way to prevent a lapse into absolute dualism is to recognize the full validity of other 'ranges of comparison', and in particular that which engaged our attention in Chapter II. If the focus of attention is always the activity of the living God there need be no fear that either an absolute monism or an absolute dualism will prove finally acceptable to the questing imagination.

32. *Christus Victor*, pp. 20–1.

F

In this chapter I began with a general mythical model (whose varieties in detail are almost unlimited). I then passed on to historical events of which the Exodus as attested by the Old Testament and the Death-Resurrection of Jesus as attested by the New are all important in the Christian tradition. Beyond this I tried to consider certain ways in which the *Christus Victor* theme has been proclaimed in the history of the Church. Now in a concluding section I shall enquire whether this way of speaking about the Atonement, this 'range of comparison', has any relevance or meaning for the world of today.

I have already indicated that the most notable recent expositions of the theme of Christ's victory over the power of darkness have come from the pens of Lutheran theologians. Partly this may have been due to the frequent vivid affirmations in Luther's own writings that God in Christ has conquered every power that exalts itself against His just rule and purpose. Partly it can have been due to the fact that these theologians have during the greater part of their careers been living close to the centre of active conflict or to threats of tyrannous oppression. In circumstances of this kind an immediate affinity is discovered with Christian witnesses of the First or Third or Sixteenth Centuries—all periods of wars and rumours of wars, of persecution and threat of death.

Let us look at a book which has enjoyed wide popularity in Germany and has obviously appealed to the imaginations of those who lived in other parts of war-torn Europe. Ethelbert Stauffer completed his *New Testament Theology* in 1938 and successive editions were called for in the next ten years. To Anglo-Saxons the general arrangement and many of the chapter titles are unusual. 'Creation and Fall' includes 'The Adversary' and 'Human and Cosmic History'. 'Law and Promise' includes 'The Passion of Christ's Forerunners'. 'The Coming of Christ' includes 'The Kingdom of God and the Demonic Powers' and 'Deliverance from the Enemy'. In fact it soon becomes evident that Stauffer's writing of *New Testament Theology*, though undergirded by an immense knowledge of pre-Christian material and by a thorough familiarity with the New Testament writings themselves, has a particular 'slant'. He is convinced of certain priorities. He believes that certain aspects of the New Testament witness to Christ stand out with unique prominence. Consequently, in a forceful and well-substantiated fashion, he draws out from his sources a theology of conflict and victory in which the struggle of Christ with the demonic powers occupies a central position.

In his introductory sections Stauffer depicts the Adversary as the survival of the primordial power of chaos and its hostility to creation—as 'the spirit of constant negation'. He gives evidence of man's age-long struggle with the Adversary and of his longing for redemption. In ancient art, for example, a favourite theme is the conflict of gods, heroes, rulers or knights with demonic monstrosities: in one after another of the ancient religions 'the cry comes for a deliverer, the dream for a saviour'. In the religion of the Old Covenant, above all, the way is prepared through law and prophecy for the advent of the Saviour who can inflict a crushing defeat upon the Adversary and deliver those who through fear are all their lifetime subject to bondage.

The Cross then is to be interpreted chiefly (though Stauffer does not say exclusively) in terms of *victory* and *salvation*. The paragraph which summarizes the victory-theme I have found particularly impressive:

'The antagonistic form of the *theologia crucis* thinks of the cross as the decisive turning-point in the history of the *civitas dei* and its fight with powers hostile to God. This mode of thought had its preparation in the basic apocalyptic ideas of universal history as warfare and of the special place of martyrs in that war. It has its basis in a saying of Jesus: Only when the night of death is past can the fire blaze forth that Christ must kindle on the earth—and will (Luke 12: 49 f.). So the death of Christ brings about a new disposition of the battle and a new situation in the world. This basic idea is presented in all sorts of ways in the christology of the primitive Church. But it was in particular Paul who took up the idea and developed it. The humiliation of the Son signified his subjection to the powers controlling this age. His rising signified his elevation above those demonic opponents who seemed to be victors when he hung on the cross. The early Church put these thoughts into an eloquent formula when it intensified one of the favourite conceptions of the old biblical theology of martyrdom: Christ is the "Victor" who has beaten down the ancient enemy in the battle of His passion. That is the picture of Christ that later found its monumental expression in the Ravenna of Theodoric and which was generally characteristic and normative for the young Germanic peoples.'[33]

It is not difficult to see how relevant and enheartening the conflict-and-victory symbolism must have seemed to hard-pressed Europeans who so often in the past half century have found themselves in danger not only of their lives but even of their inner integrity. But how far could this be true of a very different part of the world—

33. Pp. 130–1. An unusual but invaluable aspect of Stauffer's exposition is his frequent reference to the witness of art both pre-Christian and Christian.

the North American continent which until the last ten years had never known the threat of serious attack from an outside power? Perhaps unexpectedly it is yet in fact true that the imagery of a vast struggle with evil powers, which has never been entirely absent from the American tradition, has sometimes over the past forty years received fresh and powerful expression. It is, I think, possible to claim that whereas for European theologians the demonic powers have been more easily conceived in terms of *historic* phenomena, the emergence of tyrannical empires, dictatorial rulers, armies of destruction—for American thinkers, at least until recently, demonism has been more easily associated with hostile forces in *nature* (including human beings whose *nature* seems somehow threatening). Thus Richard Chase in discussing the imagery of the American Novel writes:

'As apprehended by the literary imagination New England Puritanism —with its grand metaphors of election and damnation, its opposition of the kingdom of light and the kingdom of darkness, its eternal and autonomous contraries of good and evil—seems to have recaptured the Manichaean sensibility. The American imagination, like the New England Puritan mind itself, seems less interested in redemption than in the melodrama of the eternal struggle of good and evil, less interested in incarnation and reconciliation than in alienation and disorder. If we suppose ourselves correct in tracing to this origin the prevalence in American literature of the symbols of light and dark, we may doubtless suppose also that this sensibility has been enhanced by the racial composition of our people and by the Civil War that was fought, if more in legend that in fact, over the Negro?'[34]

The titanic forces of Nature (the sea, the storm, the flood, the forest), the cunning and cruelty of wild beasts, the mysterious and sinister behaviour of men of red or black skin—these were the enemies over whose evil designs the servant of the Good needed to be assured of victory. But with the expansion of industry and the growing recognition of the weakness of the individual in the midst of a vast mechanical organization, governed, it appeared by rigidly impersonal economic laws—the conflict came to be interpreted in a new way. For example, the theology of Reinhold Neibuhr took shape as a result of the author's experiences of life in a great industrial city with its assembly-line techniques and its struggles between management and labour. If the cosmos is nothing more than an impersonal and irresponsible machine man's lot is a sorry one indeed. Niebuhr fought against such an interpretation and in his first major book set up the general theological framework within which his brilliant application of the Christian Gospel

34. *The American Novel and its Tradition*. p. 11.

was to be made in the ensuing years. It was a modified dualism, a dualistic polarity, a full recognition of 'the conflict which disturbs the harmonies and unities of the universe'. It was, he believed, a rediscovery of the general outlook of the primitive Church and especially the early theology of the Cross.

> 'Its (i.e. early Christianity's) symbols lacked philosophical precision but they did give vivid and dramatic force to the idea of a conflict between evil and the redemptive and creative force in life. Thus it could fulfil the two great functions of religion in prompting men to repent of their sins and in encouraging them to hope for a redemption from them. No mechanical or magical explanations of the Crucifixion have ever permanently obscured the helpful spiritual symbolism of the Cross in which the conflict between good and evil is portrayed and the possibility as well as the difficulty of the triumph of the good over evil is dramatized. An absolute dualism either between God and Universe or between man and nature, or spirit and matter, or good and evil, is neither possible nor necessary'.[35]

To expose radical evil in its new forms, to focus attention upon the Cross as the place where good and evil, God and the Devil, have been engaged in deadly combat, to proclaim the victory of the Cross, to summon men to play their part in the continuing conflict— these have been the aims of Reinhold Niebuhr throughout his notable ministry. And the imagery of *Christus Victor* has become relevant and meaningful in an era when, as at Calvary, inhuman impersonal forces seemed to defy God and to do everything in their power to prevent His saving purpose from being fulfilled. 'The Cross, which stands at the centre of the Christian world-view, reveals both the seriousness of human sin and the purpose and power of God to overcome it. It reveals man violating the will of God in his highest moral and spiritual achievements (in Roman Law and Jewish religion) and God absorbing this evil into Himself in the very moment of its vivid expression.'[36] Such an interpretation has meaning in the scientific and industrial world of the twentieth century as well as in the custom-dominated and agrarian world of the first and second centuries A.D.

Turning to a quite different area, though one which at first sight has more affinities with the Middle East in which the Christian Gospel was first preached, how does the situation stand in Africa? It is certainly dangerous to make generalizations about a continent still in the throes of rapid social change but it is at least possible to notice how certain patterns of interpretation make a special appeal to the African mind. No one possessing even the slightest

35. Reinhold Niebuhr: *Beyond Tragedy*, Preface, p. x.
36. From 'Does Civilization Need Religion?'. Quoted H. Hofmann: *The Theology of Reinhold Niebuhr*, p. 32.

acquaintance with normal social behaviour and conversation in that great continent can fail to be impressed by the way in which the reality of a spirit-world surrounding and impinging upon the world of human affairs is implicitly assumed. Whatever means may be employed for gaining the spirits' friendship or restricting their power to hurt, the fact of their influence upon human life is scarcely questioned.

This being the case it is not surprising that within the Christian context the good news that Christ has gained a decisive victory over the powers of evil and that He protects His followers in their continuing struggles with the sinister influences which are still abroad in the world is of paramount significance. It is noticeable that however African pastors' sermons may vary in their detailed development the essential framework remains unchanged. God's good creation, man's fall and consequent subjection to the devil and his agents, his sad predicament, the descent of the Redeemer into the hopeless situation, His struggle with the powers of evil and His wonderful victory, the possibility now open to man of sharing in this triumph—the pattern recurs again and again.

No one has made a more careful investigation of this aspect of African life than has Bishop Bengt Sundkler. In his book *The Christian Ministry in Africa* he recounts a particularly vivid Easter sermon by a celebrated Zulu preacher. It followed the customary pattern—Creation, the Fall, death, the disaster of the Flood, the succession of Old Testament heroes who yet shared the sin of Adam. At length the dark background was complete with Adam as the central figure bearing an intolerable load of suffering and sorrow all on account of the primal sin. Then, in a moment of supreme drama, the Victor was depicted in a blaze of light. 'Zulus, men and women, consider that incredible joy, that indescribable jubilation which filled Adam's heart on the First Easter Morning, as the Hero of Heaven came in through the Gate of Heaven, with His Crown of Thorns, now a brilliant Crown of Victory, walking the central aisle in the heavenly Temple, straight up to the throne of the Almighty. There He gave His report that from this day Satan and Sin and Death had been overcome. For now He, the Second Adam, had won the victory.

'And the First Adam had peace.'[37] This, Sundkler comments, is living African theology. It is linked with the archetypal myths of their own culture, it is grounded in the pattern of Old Testament theology, it is related to the most moving of the common experiences of tribal life. The parallels between the Church in Africa

37. Pp. 283-4.

today and the Church in Syria and Asia Minor in the first three centuries are not hard to discern.

Finally what can be said of the world of *the imagination* which is perhaps less tied to particular countries or areas (though my illustrations are taken from British writers)? Does the image of a Divine-human protagonist, engaged in deathly combat and winning a decisive victory which ensures the final reconciliation of the whole universe—does this image appeal any longer to the human imagination or must it be now rejected as an outmoded interpretation of atonement?

Perhaps the most ambitious recent attempts to reinterpret the work of Christ in terms of a supreme victory over the powers of evil are to be found in the imaginative novels of Charles Williams and C. S. Lewis. Each of these writers had a profound sense of the reality of evil. The universe for them was not simply defective in certain respects, imperfect because unfulfilled; rather it was groaning and travailing, the scene of a grim conflict, the field of a real battle in which more than human forces were engaged. Williams wrote of the *War in Heaven*. Lewis through his *Screwtape Letters* gave a brilliant exposition of the conflict in the human heart. Through such fantasies as *Perelandra* and *That Hideous Strength* he raised the conflict to its ultimate dimensions in the invisible world. To Lewis, good and evil were so real and powerful in their antagonism that it became altogether natural for him to embody their conflict in a myth of the eternal world.

In a moving tribute to Lewis, Valerie Pitt has told how the reading of *Perelandra* was for her a critical stage in her journey into faith. '*Perelandra*', she writes, 'is not concerned only with unfallen worlds; it reverts to the ancient Christian vision, the myth of the struggle between the powers of God and those of darkness. But for Lewis it was not remote, not a question of Michael and his archangels battering the dragon down, but of our personal involvement in a cosmic battle. For "we", St. Paul says, "wrestle not against flesh and blood but against principalities and powers". The Prince of Darkness (however we conceive of darkness) is defeated not beyond time but in the affairs of men. The myths . . . are not fictions, nor even simply the way our ancestors expressed their understanding of things, they are patterns of reality. Ransom's great battle in *Perelandra* is Beowulf's battle against Creudel's mother and St. George's against the dragon, but it is also Horatius at the Bridge and Thermopylae and the Battle of Maldon, to say nothing of more recent battles in which—I was about to say the spirit of man but let us rather say *men*—pitched themselves for what they conceived to be good against what they dimly understood as evil. It is also the battle which—as the poet of *The Dream of the Rood* expresses it—Christ the young hero fought against Death and won. The certainty Lewis had[38] was precisely the certainty we most need, which we already have. . . . It is that the issue of our struggle is already decided. The Kingdom of God is neither created nor won by our efforts. What we have to do is to enter into a world already ours.'[39]

The Victor in the battle of the passion, the Saviour from machine-controlled existence, the Hero of Heaven, the Knight who absorbs the darts of evil in his own breast, the Champion of the Truth, the young Conqueror of death—these are, all in their own ways, modern attempts to express the glowing conviction that Christ through His atoning work has delivered the death blow to all systems that seek to obstruct the gracious purpose of God and has pioneered a way of victorious living for all who follow in His train. The great *Reversal* has been achieved. The ultimate *Triumph* is assured.

> O Captain of the wars, whence won Ye so great scars?
> In what fight did Ye smite, and what manner was the foe?
> Was it on a day of rout they compassed Thee about,
>   Or gat Ye these adornings when Ye wrought their overthrow?
>
>   "Twas on a day of rout they girded Me about,
>   They wounded all My brow, and they smote Me through the
>   side:
> My hand held no sword when I met their armed horde,
>   And the conqueror fell down, and the Conquered bruised his
>   pride.'
>
> What is Thy Name? Oh, show!—'My Name ye may not know;
>   'Tis a going forth with banners, and a baring of much swords:
> But My titles that are high, are they not upon My thigh?
>   "King of Kings!" are the words, "Lord of Lords!";
>   It is written "King of Kings, Lord of Lords". '

38. I would prefer to say 'faith' rather than certainty.
39. *Prism*, January 1964, pp. 38–9.

CHAPTER IV

THE SUPREME TRAGEDY

Second Analogue

The whole pattern of man's life in society was intended in God's original design to reveal harmony and balance and proportion. By discovering and conforming to the structures of his natural environment man could live with his fellows in peaceful and fruitful relationships. But in actual fact human societies constantly reveal conditions of distortion and disharmony. By excess in one direction, by neglect in another, the authentic pattern·of communal relations has been disturbed and things have become 'out of joint'. How can true order be restored? How can the social wound be healed?

In the development of the human imagination a particular figure has assumed an immense significance within this situation. This is the *tragic* figure, the *victim* of the disjointed structure who, though relatively innocent himself, is caught in the toils of tangled and ambiguous forces and suffers accordingly. Yet through his patient suffering, social evils are purged, the entail of the past is arrested and the healing of the community is made possible.

Within the Christian context it has been claimed that amidst all such tragic figures One stands out pre-eminently. He it was who made himself vulnerable to the total interplay of conflicting loyalties and vested interests which characterized the human situation. He is the Lamb of God bearing innocently and patiently the sin of the world. He is the bleeding victim within whose suffering the distortions and diseases of human society are exposed and ultimately dispersed. He is the suffering servant by whose stripes mankind is healed.

A

Until about the beginning of the nineteenth century the Christian view of law and morality had been determined by two major traditions inherited from the past. On the one side, and that the most influential, there was the legacy of the Old Testament with its extension and revision in the New. The Old Testament contained a clearly defined body of laws—social, ritual, political. The New

115

Testament contained a new body of ethical injunctions, new inter-pretations or adaptations of Old Testament commands and a small body of regulations of a ritual or political kind. In course of time it had come to be assumed that the basic *social* laws of the Old Testament constituted a permanent and required pattern of human behaviour. The ritual and political laws, however, were regarded differently. Either they were considered to have been brought to their fulfilment in Christ and as therefore no longer binding on Christians or they were interpreted as foreshadowing in a typological way important elements in Christian worship and political organization.

On the other side there was the notable legacy from Greece and Rome. The ethical ideals of the Greeks, the civil laws of Rome—these must surely fall within the area of Christian concern if only because of their continuing influence within the civilizations of Eastern and Western Europe. One of the major tasks therefore of Christian theologians and moral philosophers was to work out the relationship between obligations for conduct derived from the Biblical revelation and those framed by Greek philosphers and Roman lawyers. That there were *natural* laws governing human behaviour was widely assumed. The major question was how they were to be reconciled and even synthesized with the direct commands of God revealed in Old and New Testaments. Thus the Christian was expected to conform to the requirements both of revealed moral law and of basic natural law. At times the attempt was made to establish a society on the basis of the Biblical revelation alone but this was really only practicable for an isolated and relatively static group. A dynamic community in vigorous relationship with its wider social environment was compelled to look for a body of ordered regulations beyond what was incorporated in the legislation of Old and New Testaments. At other times there was a tendency to minimize the distinctiveness of Biblical ethics and to focus attention upon a few basic principles which could be regarded as within the scope of realization by all reasonable men. But whether the emphasis was in one direction or the other there was a wide and continuing recognition that a transcendent moral law was essential for the proper ordering of stable and civilized life.

All this was to receive a gradually intensifying challenge as doors opened upon wider vistas both of man's historical past and of the social life of contemporary peoples. The work of the philo-logist, for example, threw a flood of fresh light upon the ancient civilizations of India and China. The explorations of missionaries and traders collected wholly unexpected information about the complicated social structures of so-called primitive peoples. Inscriptions were deciphered, time-honoured customs were recorded, tribal organizations were compared and contrasted. Two things became increasingly clear. The first was that the ten commandments and other ethical injunctions contained in the Old Testament were by no means unique amongst the legislative codes of ancient peoples. Other civilizations had their laws, their judiciaries, their wisdom-sayings, their schools of instruction. The reference of 'given law' could no longer necessarily be confined to the Hebrews though it was still possible to claim that their code was the best and the only one possessing timeless and universal validity. The second obvious fact was that any definition of 'natural law' must now take into account not only the social ideals and regulations of ancient Greece and Rome but also those of cohesive communities wherever found. The very concept of 'law' became a matter of debate. Was there evidence to show that *any* social obligations were recognized by all men everywhere? Could taboos practised in any particular society be shown to possess significance or relevance in a quite different context? The law of God, which had seemed so majestic and unchanging in the seventeenth and eighteenth centuries when revolutions were taking place amongst the nations, might after all be only one amongst a world-wide collection of legal systems now gradually coming into view.

A century which has combined careful historical investigation and analysis of documents with first-hand anthropological field-studies and comparisons has brought us to a point where we can make at least a few basic generalizations about the nature of laws and their place in human life. The old distinction between natural and revealed law can perhaps be better framed today in terms of *custom* and *formal law*. There are generally speaking two operative forces which maintain cohesion and continuity in society. On the one hand there are unwritten and not easily definable obligations recognized by the members of a particular social group, often with centuries of tradition behind them yet often with no clear-cut rationale to explain the constraint which they undoubtedly exercise. On the other hand there are definite precepts and prescriptions expressed in their earliest stages in terse, epigrammatic fashion in terms of a positive 'shalt' or a negative 'shalt not'. These can be easily committed to memory and handed on orally from generation to generation. Simple symbolic devices may represent them openly and publicly but only after the invention of writing can they be completely formalized. In general a 'religious' official is needed to deal with questions relating to 'custom', a 'secular' official with questions relating to formal social law. But it is highly dangerous to press such distinctions too far for until comparatively recently the life of a community has been regarded as an organic whole and its two aspects of 'custom' and 'formal law' have been closely intertwined.

Let us now turn to consider in more detail what I have broadly called 'custom'. In his valuable account of the place of 'law' among the Kapauku Papuans, Leopold Pospisil tells how often he heard the phrase 'One does not act like this, this is *prohibited*' (*daa* in the Kapauku language). But, he points out, daa does not by any means confine itself to matters of dispute about rules and regulations which have already been formulated—rules relating, for example, to property or injury or contract. Rather, he says, 'a non-punishable breach of etiquette, a prohibition sanctioned by the supernatural as well as by the society, a purely religious taboo which defines a relation between an individual and the supernatural and the violation of which does not concern anybody else except the actor, and, finally, a moral but not enforced creed, all these various phenomena are assigned the same name'.[1] In other words deep in the tribal consciousness lies the conviction that certain attitudes and actions are prohibited, banned, taboo—they simply are *not done*, 'one does not act like this'. And this holds for man in relation to his *total* environment—physical, human, supernatural.

Within such a system, so long as man avoids any transgression of that which is prohibited his social life will be preserved in health and harmony. Yet it is all too clear that disturbances of the equilibrium do occur. Something, as we so often say, goes wrong. A man falls and injures himself: a woman breaks a household pot: a conflict of interests arises between parent and child: the tamed animal is refractory, the wild animal predatory: lightning strikes, a tree falls: in countless ways the harmony of the total environment is disturbed and the question immediately arises whether the disturbance is serious and whether some offence has been committed against the mysterious Power which holds all things in check. There may have been some excess or over-confidence on the part of the living. Alternatively there may have been some fault or mistake on the part of the dead, a fault which has never been righted and whose evil influence continues therefore to be felt.

To speak of good and evil in this context is liable to be misleading just because today these words have come to be interpreted in an almost exclusively moralistic way. But in earlier and less sophisticated societies the all-important distinction is between a situation in

1. *Kapauku Papuans and their Law*, p. 144.

which the current of life flows along undisturbed, in which the body politic is in an altogether healthy (in the sense of all its parts functioning harmoniously) condition and one in which there is strife, abnormality, disease and death. That there are rhythms or oscillations of this kind in the history of every social group can scarcely be doubted. The great questions are: Can these disturbances be prevented? If society is in a state of 'evil' can the situation be put right? If there are excesses in one direction can the balance be redressed? If there is an entail of evil remaining from the past can it be expiated and its evil effects nullified? If the due requirements of the 'holy' have not been met can some kind of readjustment be effected?

It is immediately evident that such questions can lead to all kinds of quack remedies. Man has always been hungry for a panacea, something which he can do or which can be done for him which will *put everything right* at once. Hence come magic and witch-doctors and shamans and sorcerers and miracle-workers: spells and oracles and trances and purgations. Every society at one time or another has been conscious of its subjection to mysterious forces of evil. Every society has acclaimed the discovery of methods by which the course of evil and misfortune can be stayed and the brooding doom or curse removed. In cases of misfortunes or accidents which come to individuals, the remedy proposed may be confined to the man and his own interests (though in fact no misdemeanour nor any remedial activity ever concerns an individual alone). But in cases where the general good has been disturbed or threatened, where there is a widespread feeling of distress and foreboding, piacular rites and ceremonies must be performed on behalf of the total population. Just as 'custom' has somehow been infringed, so 'custom' prescribes the particular means by which equilibrium can be restored.

The most notable aspect of these communal acts of reparation or purification is their *painful* quality. By a kind of empathy misfortune and malaise must be removed by means of a deliberate acceptance of painful and costly disciplines. These are expressed both through word and through deed, the verbal exercises consisting of ejaculations, groans, laments, sorrowing litanies, penitential psalms, confessions: the ritual actions consisting of self-woundings, lacerations, beatings, fastings, offerings of treasured possessions, sacrifices, even in certain cases (Jonah is a typical example) a voluntary self-immolation. Innumerable instances have been collected from the records of tribal life of the ways in which the community is purified. Though I have spoken of 'accident', nothing in the natural or social orders is really believed to happen by chance. When matters have gone awry the appropriate means must be employed in order that life may again flow smoothly once the accursed offence has been undone.

Inevitably man's expanding knowledge of the ordered processes of his universe and of the forces promoting peaceful relationships in society has gradually affected his views of the nature of appropriate piacular exercises. Some are seen to be plainly irrelevant and ineffective: others come to be regarded as offensive and excessively cruel. Practices regarded as necessary for the purging of the community are a matter of life and death and cannot therefore easily be changed. But movement to another environment and contact with other peoples are probably the two most powerful instruments effecting change and this holds true of piacular rites as of all other human customs. And although it has to be admitted that change can be for the worse—practices may be adopted which debase and degrade—yet recorded history also reveals changes towards deeper sensitivity and higher rationality which must, by any normal standards, be regarded as for the better. In the general field of piacular and purification ceremonies I shall suggest that the most elevated models of pre-Christian history are to be found in Greek tragedy and in the liturgical worship of post-exilic Judaism. I propose to look at each of these remarkable developments in turn.

B

Few subjects during the past century have excited wider interest than the origins and nature of Greek tragedy. The extant plays have been edited and re-edited, the manner of their performance has been reconstructed with painstaking attention to detail, the question of their meaning has been debated endlessly. Of the immense importance of the tragic *form* in human affairs and of the genius of the leading Greek dramatists who used it so brilliantly there can be little doubt. But uncertainties still exist about the roots and early growth of this particular form of communal activity and opinions still differ about its appropriateness (or otherwise) as a vehicle for the expression of Christian truth. To the question 'Can there be explicitly *Christian* tragedy?' no general acceptable answer has yet been given.

So far as the origin of the Greek tragic form is concerned we know that long before the sixth century B.C. religious ceremonies included forms of choric dancing and that organized groups of women performed at the great festivals. It is altogether possible that the dance was, at least in some of its manifestations, related to the purification-motif, to which I have already referred. Through corporate mime and song, expressing mourning or lamentation or supplication, the chorus acted on behalf of the whole people to cleanse the land of its accumulated impurities, and to renew its life.[2] Then, some time during the seventh century B.C., a new body of lyric poetry came into existence, written specially for performance by a chorus, and it was natural for the Athenian festivals in honour of the god Dionysus to include these choral lyrics in their repertoire. A further and most important stage was reached in the sixth century when a solo performer called the *hypokrites* (this was to become the regular Greek word for 'actor') was brought in to recite a prologue and make set speeches in a kind of contrapuntal duologue with the chorus.

By the beginning of the fifth century it was customary for a series of dramas to be performed at the festival, three poets being chosen to compete for the prizes by presenting a group of three 'tragedies' together with a shorter satyr play. The 'tragedy' had a well-defined form which served to expose vividly and movingly the essential characteristic of every true 'tragedy', namely a conflict which allowed of no easy resolution. Even before the period of supreme genius associated with the names of Aeschylus, Sophocles and Euripides, the Dionysiac festival recognized the contraries and imperfections of human existence which needed to be removed by some kind of representative expiation. But with the introduction of dialogue and the appeal to legendary episodes, it became possible to build up dramatic tension and to engage spectators in a more

2. 'If I understand early Dionysiac ritual aright, its social function was essentially cathartic, in the psychological sense: it purged the individual of those infectious irrational impulses which when dammed up, had given rise, as they have done in other cultures, to outbreaks of dancing mania and similar manifestations of collective hysteria; it relieved them by providing them with a ritual outlet. If that is so, Dionysus was in the Archaic Age as much a social necessity as Apollo; each ministered in his own way to the anxieties characteristic of a guilt-culture. Apollo promised security: "Understand your station as man; do as the Father tells you; and you will be safe to-morrow." Dionysus offered freedom: "Forget the difference and you will find the identity; join the θίασος and you will be happy today." . . . Apollo moved only in the best society—but Dionysus was at all periods δημοτικός a god of the people.'
At all times Dionysus was hailed as *The Liberator*—'the god who by very simple means, or by other means not so simple, enables you for a short time to *stop being yourself*, and thereby sets you free. That was, I think, the main secret of his appeal to the Archaic Age: not only because life in that age was often a thing to escape from, but more specifically because the individual, as the modern world knows him, began in that age to emerge for the first time from the solidarity of the family and found the unfamiliar burden of individual responsibility hard to bear. Dionysus could lift it from him.' E. R. Dodds: *The Greeks and the Irrational*, p. 76 f.

sympathetic identification with the tragic theme than had ever been possible before. The plays retained their strong religious reference—they were not simply for entertainment. Yet 'tragic' drama as developed in the fifth and fourth centuries B.C. proved to be an art-form which in no way depended for its validity upon the truth of the particular religious mythologies then associated with it. It appealed in an unparalleled way to certain perennial strugglings and questionings of the human spirit and became a unique instrument for the training of the spiritual sensitivity and understanding of mankind.

As I have already briefly suggested 'tragic' drama necessarily involved the display of *conflict*. That Zeus ruled over all—gods and men and natural powers—was unquestioned. That He maintained a general framework of ordered providence without which no stable and decent existence would be possible was also taken for granted. But then it was all too obvious that man's world contained strife and enmity, jealousy and intrigue, excess in personal ambition, neglect of social duties, conflicts between self-assertion and self-effacement, between past and present, between the one and the many, between ordered stability and dynamic change, between one 'good' and another. To project on to a stage before the view of an expectant company vivid examples of men and women torn between these antithetical forces was the central aim of the Greek tragedians. Perhaps no aspect of life stirs our emotions more deeply than the sight of heroic struggle. If then 'Art is in essence the expression or embodiment, in a permanent form, of some emotion which seems to him who has felt it to deserve perpetuation',[3] it is not surprising that the greatest works of art known to man have in some way expressed conflict: through music, through sculpture, through poetry but supremely through drama. And the creator of tragic drama has reached the heights when he has succeeded in portraying coherence within the total order of things together with some affirmation of the universality of conflict in actual human experience.

Perhaps in no Greek tragedy does such a conflict reveal itself more intensely, more poignantly, than in the Antigone of Sophocles. Here there are two major figures, Creon and Antigone. It would have been easy to portray the man Creon as hard, inflexible, obstinate, the woman Antigone as noble, courageous, utterly self-sacrificing. But although this could have produced conflict of a kind, Sophocles was far too clever a playwright to offer anything so simple. Rather the crux is that Creon is faithful to one set of values

3. A. H. B. Allen: *Philosophy*, 1942, p. 151.

and obligations, Antigone to another. Each acts in good faith, each pays a terrible price. Man's effort to obey the will of the gods leads him into dilemmas of overwhelming complexity. Again it is the supreme achievement of the dramatist to portray the crossing and recrossing of natural affections, religious duties, communal responsibilities, unsettled issues from the past, and to do this through a form which, replete with tension and strain, yet leads to a final sense of harmony and reconciliation.

The plot is well known. On the one side Creon, the king, is completely sincere in his devotion to state and people. A traitor has attacked the city of Thebes. He has met his just fate in death. But his crime must be fully exposed and his sin against the sacredness of the state expiated. Therefore the order is given that his body is to remain unhonoured and unburied upon the plain where it fell. Such an order appears to be right for the upholding not only of state but also of divine justice. But there are other obligations and loyalties. Antigone, sister of the dead man, believes passionately that it is her duty to defy the order and to perform the customary rites of burial. In so doing she is obeying a law which at least to her is more sacred than that by which the state itself is to be preserved. She knows that the penalty will be her own death but this she is prepared to pay if her brother may thereby gain eternal bliss. So the conflict is joined. Yet even this is not the end for a still deeper conflict, perennial within human relationships, emerges. Haemon, son of Creon, is Antigone's lover. How can he be true to his father whom he admires and respects and at the same time be true to the woman whom he loves not only for herself but for the supreme courage which she displays? Through this dreadful struggle of loyalties Haemon will meet his own death and the cup of misery will seem to be full—though again in a quite strange and illogical way, the portrayal of the tragedy will bring to the audience a deep sense of the reconciliation of life's mysteries rather than, as might have been expected, a deepening perplexity and an ultimate despair.

That conflict is of the very essence of tragic drama is generally agreed. That this conflict is presented in Greek tragedy within the context of the over arching providence of the gods is also agreed. That the divine ordinances governing the many aspects of human behaviour must be obeyed to the limits of man's ability and knowledge can hardly be questioned. That these constraints seem often to be contrary to one another is obvious. What remains, however, as the finally unsolved problem is why the stage presentation of these conflicts with the dire effects which they produce upon man's life in society, why the dramatic exposure of situations which harrow the emotions and strain the sympathies of the spectators, not only brought a deep satisfaction to those who first witnessed them but have continued to hold their place through succeeding centuries as amongst the noblest creations of the human imagination.

These questions, of intense interest in themselves, have gained a further significance because of the fact that they were discussed at depth by one who lived within a century or so of the production of the greatest Greek tragedies. In a justly famous passage of the Poetics, Aristotle essays to define tragedy, pointing out in particular the functions of plot, hero, chorus, style and poetic form. His central theme is tragedy as the imitation of *a complete action*, an action which is weighty in its significance and involves persons and their relationships with one another: an action, above all, which inspires *pity* and *fear*. The tragic drama has the signal effect, according to Aristotle, of properly purging these emotions and arousing a certain *pleasure* in the audience. Every word and phrase in the definition has been subjected to the most intense scrutiny and it is clear that no single theory of tragedy, no single interpretation of the tragic experience can be derived from it. Yet certain points of abiding interest and value deserve to be noted.

The two ideas which have perhaps caused greatest uncertainty and given rise to the widest variations in interpretation are those of imitation (*mimesis*) and purgation (*katharsis*). Aristotle insists that *tragedy is an imitation of an action*. Clearly *action* must be interpreted, not in narrow terms as a single act, an individual doing this thing or that thing, but rather as a comprehensive and continuous series of actions, what Aristotle calls a 'mode of action', a living movement involving a succession of actions from a beginning to an end. Everything must be directed to one end—the imitation of a *total action*. Good and evil will be mysteriously intertwined. No single character will reveal an integrated wholeness. But the total movement of the play will be such as to reveal a completeness, a unified design, and through the revelation of a certain inevitability of causation the audience will be moved to pity and fear.

Virtually all are agreed that for Aristotle *mimesis* (imitation) did not mean a mere copy on the stage of events which happen in real life. Art is not concerned with direct representation. Rather its aim is to make an abstraction from the manifold complexity of the universe to which we ourselves belong. And tragedy seeks so to construct its plot as to embody a complete series of actions, a series which enables us to see the working of universal laws moving inexorably towards their fulfilment. Thus tragedy is not just an attempt to copy a cluster of events from history or from contemporary life but rather a purposeful abstraction of a series of events and actions capable of throwing a vivid light on the majestic ordering of the Universe. This series may be derived from a relatively well-known myth or epic, itself a distillation of the insights and experiences of a man of genius. But the all important function of the tragic playwright is to combine words and actions in such a unity of form that they may give ultimate meaning to the universal drama whose plot seems so often confused and meaningless.

The second idea (*katharsis*) has also given rise to endless speculation. Did Aristotle mean that the viewing of tragic drama could purge away from man's psyche the actual emotions of pity and terror? Or did he mean that these emotions themselves would be purified? How far are the medical associations of the word katharsis to be stressed? What precisely are the connotations of the words pity and fear? These are tantalizing questions and Mr. T. R. Henn lists as many as nine different theories which have been advanced to interpret the cathartic process.[4] I cannot attempt to estimate the relative merits of these theories but must focus attention rather on those elements which are related to our general theme.

In the varying interpretations of the effect of tragic-drama on the audience two main emphases appear. First, stress is laid on the two elements, pity and fear, fear and pity, in tension, polarizing one another, pity directed towards the sufferer, terror towards the cause of the suffering, pity attracting towards, fear repelling from: the power of true tragedy lies in the strength of the tension between these opposing forces which it succeeds in generating. Secondly, stress is laid on the psychological effects which are known to happen as certain stimulants are applied either to individuals or to groups. What inferences can be drawn from this knowledge about the power of the tragic form to produce beneficial results in the community at large?

It is easy to construct modern theories and use them to explain Aristotle's comments on Greek tragedy. The difficulty is to extract from the past insights and explanations which can be of abiding value as we seek to come to terms with the tragic elements of human existence today. Certainly in placing his finger on pity and terror Aristotle selected two of the most powerful and at the same time two of the most ambiguous emotions in human experience. We see or hear of painful suffering. We are moved to feel pity for the sufferer. Such pity may issue in deepened sensitivity and sacrificial action: it may equally lead to an indulgence in sentimentality and an

4. T. R. Henn: *The Harvest of Tragedy*, pp. 14–16.

inoculation *against* effective action. We are moved also to feel a sense of fear lest the forces which must have operated to bring about the sufferer's plight may strike us and involve us in a similar predicament. Such a fear may lead to sensible protective action: it may lead to panic stricken flight from reality. If it is indeed the function of tragedy, effectively presented, to purge these emotions of their evil possibilities and to make them strong and creative in their relationship with one another, then clearly it has an overwhelmingly important part to play in the raising of human character to a higher plane.

Turning to the second emphasis—the effects of tragedy upon those who watch the performance not simply as remote spectators but who allow themselves to be caught up into the mood and the experience of the play itself—I have found the chapter entitled 'From Shame-Culture to Guilt-Culture' in Professor E. R. Dodds's book *The Greeks and the Irrational* specially illuminating. The term Shame-Culture he has applied to attitudes current in the Homeric Age when that which was most desired was public esteem, that which was most feared was any kind of dishonourable action causing 'loss of face'. But this he claims, gradually changed as men moved into the Archaic Age which was essentially a guilt-culture, burdened by the fear of pollution (miasma) and obsessed with a craving for purification (catharsis).

To say this is not to suggest that any hard-and-fast distinction can be made between one age and another. But it is at least possible to detect in a particular period a heightened sense of pollution as being both infectious and hereditary and needing to be removed by the due performance of recognized rites. And it is also possible to see gradual changes in social assumptions causing changes in religious attitudes. It is this which leads Dodds to see in the later part of the Archaic Age an association between the deepening sense of guilt and the loosening of the sense of family solidarity. It is a well-known psychological theory that any loosening in the ties of parental authority (normally that of the father) brings ambiguous and painful reactions. On the one hand the new generation feels a certain exhilaration in the experiences of greater freedom: on the other hand there cannot help being a certain unease, even a deep anxiety, when the most sacred of human obligations has been in any way disregarded. Repression of desires only exacerbates the situation. And it can therefore be urged that in the later part of the Archaic Age the fear of pollution and the resultant curse was intensifying into a terror of active divine retribution. How could man be cleansed from pollution and the inherited curse and his own distressing psychological feelings, all of which seemed to be linked to one another in a never-ending chain?

The ancient rituals had succeeded in giving the assurance that an adequate catharsis had been effected through their performance. Infringements of custom and of the law of nature could be removed by a due participation in the prescribed Dionysiac forms. But with the growing sense of conflict between youth and age, between son and father, between the striving for self-realization and the clinging to parental authority, something was needed which could speak more subtly and more imaginatively to the psychological realities of the situation. May it not have been this in part which was responsible for the powerful appeal of the great tragedies of Aeschylus, Sophocles and perhaps to a less extent, Euripides? May not Aristotle's emphasis on purgation have been more psychological than ritual, the brilliant recognition of the fact that man may be released from painful and unwanted feelings through contemplating their projection in a notable work of art?[5] Such a tragedy as *Antigone* brings out forcefully the struggles within the family, the conflict between son and father, the inherited curse, yet all within the context of the overarching rule of Divine providence. Pity and terror must certainly seize the hearts of those who participate in the performance of such a drama. Yet through the superb genius of Sophocles the contemplation of the tragic events leaves no final sense of despair. In and through the suffering of Haemon and Antigone the curse is annulled, corruption is removed, the total human situation is repaired and confidence is retored. So deep is the sense of reconciliation and of the 'rightness' of the final outcome that it becomes possible to speak in terms of 'pleasure' arising out of an experience marked by an almost unutterable poignancy and stress.

C

The liturgical worship of post-exile Judaism was in no way a completely new development. The offering of sacrifice, the celebration of the passover, the recitation of psalms, the public reading of the law—these all existed as part of the cultus before the Exile. But the effect of the Exile, it appears, was to create certain changes of emphasis or proportion in the cultus and in particular to give greater prominence to forms of a penitential and expiatory nature. The whole experience had resulted in a deep emotional shock for those who had endured it and, not unnaturally, the problems of

5. Dodds: op. cit., pp. 48 ff.

suffering and deprivation became more acute in the national consciousness than ever before. That God had been offended, that His people had been guilty of impiety, seemed evident. How then could the guilt be expiated? How could a free and full communion between God and His people be re-established?

It is evident that at earlier stages in Israel's history methods of removing guilt contracted through the breach of some taboo (particularly at times when a 'holy' war was in progress) were direct and ruthless. Even though a man might be father of a family, even though he might be the son of the king himself, even though the 'accursed' action had been committed inadvertently—the consequences must be borne. By this action he had put the existence of the whole community in jeopardy and no one could feel secure until the equilibrium, as it were, had been restored. And the normal method of restoration was the execution of summary justice by taking the life of the offender himself.

But at some stage modifications of the extreme penalty were introduced. Substitution was allowed in the form of an animal or treasured possession being devoted to the deity in the place of man himself. And the principle operating for the individual could be extended to the community. If during the period before the Exile there had been neglect of religious obligations, if during the Exile there had been compromises with paganism in varying shapes and forms, expiation must be made. But it was conceivable that this could be done by making provision for sacrificial offerings to be designated as 'for sin' or 'to remove guilt' in their intention: for laments and penitential hymns to be associated with these particular offerings: and (this seems to have been an altogether new development) for one appointed day of the year to be set apart as the occasion for a comprehensive ceremony of purification by the leading religious representative of the people. On the day which came to be known as the Day of Atonement sacrifices were offered, blood-rituals were performed, a scapegoat ceremony was enacted and lamentations were recited. Through a kind of national purgation the ritual and social health of the community could be restored and a new era of reconciled life could be inaugurated.[6]

6. Commenting on the increased importance of the festival of Ingathering or Booths in the post-exile period Professor A. S. Herbert shows that it was not only a celebration of harvest-home but also the inauguration of a new agricultural year. And the turning of a year was fraught with deep consequences. 'A year, like a day, is a real entity, not merely a chronological point of reference, to the mind of the ancient world. Whatever is to come to man is contained in it already. So man approached the turning of the year with the same foreboding that a person would have in leaving the known settlement for the unknown desert. . . . Appropriately enough at this "turning of the Year" the Day of

To bring about the ritual purification of the common life (and thereby restore the sense of confidence and well-being) it was necessary to use certain forms of words and to carry through certain forms of action. So far as words were concerned, prohibitions and the curses attendant on their infringement were recited by men holding divine authority. Such a recital in itself had a cleansing effect, it was believed, upon the manners of the community and the appropriate response was to be found in laments for wrong-doing and in liturgical prayers for the removal of defilement. Probably in ancient times curses and lamentations had been regarded as operating directly to purge and to heal. Words possessed a mysterious inherent power which made them effective in themselves to break down and build up. But in their use in the temple and synagogue worship of Israel 'the laments express man's submission to God, to whom in his lament he confides his troubles and before whom he utters his petitions in prayer. . . . The cardinal problem of the psalms of lamentation is thereby shifted to the inner life of man, and the burden of external threats frequently recedes into the background in face of the heavier burden of mental or spiritual distress. The point of most of the psalms of lamentation, more or less distinctly stated, is man's separation from God and his yearning for the restoration of his lost contact with God's living power, which he hopes to find again in the evidence of God's presence and in the grace and help which God may grant him.'[7] Often the lament is expressed through the voice of the individual but the individual is never separated from the community. The psalms formed part of the communal liturgy which was itself part of God's provision for the cleansing and renewing of the life of His people.

The actions prescribed as the means of purification may be classified under two main categories:

(1) OCCASIONAL SACRIFICIAL OFFERINGS

Though certain kinds of sacrifice may have been expiatory in character in pre-Exile times it was only in the later developments of Israel's worship that this type gained full expression and emphasis. It is in the Levitical regulations that we find provision made for

Atonement occurs, preceding the Feast of Tabernacles. By the rites of this Day, the life of Israel was freed from everything that inhibited a healthy relationship with God and the communication of the divine blessing with its attendant peace.' A. S. Herbert: *Worship in Ancient Israel*, p. 44 f.

Though there is obviously no direct parallel it is interesting to notice the similarities between the annual Dionysiac festival with its combination of tragic drama and satyr-plays and the annual Hebrew celebration allowing revelry in the fields after the Day of Atonement purgation.

7. A. Weiser: *The Psalms*, p. 82.

'sin-offerings' and 'guilt-offerings'. The former type dealt with 'unwitting' sins, i.e. unintentional infringements of the Divinely ordained customs of the community. There was no festal meal but the whole concentration of the action was upon the blood-ritual. The blood of the victim offered was poured or smeared on the altar and its accessories. Varying attempts have been made to explain the rationale of blood ceremonies, so common in the ancient world, but it is doubtful if any such can be fully satisfactory. Deep in the human consciousness lies the mysterious sense that blood and life are intimately related to one another. If blood is allowed to flow freely, life quickly ebbs away. Blood therefore is sacred, precious, never to be regarded lightly. When blood is applied by a priest to the most holy place of communion between God and man, any defect or defilement is deemed to be removed and the free communion or interflow of life with life is restored. The 'how' of this operation remains a mystery. That the sin-offering was regarded as a means of 'atonement' for inadvertent offences is beyond doubt.

The 'guilt-offering' seems to have been more specifically related to *conscious* offences. If a regulation about the handling of holy things had been transgressed, if some practice of fraud or theft had disturbed the community life, then a 'guilt-offering' provided the necessary reparation to God in addition to the restoration of whatever loss might have been sustained by the neighbour. In these offences the idea of *quid pro quo* is much more prominent. But the sacrifice of a ram and the manipulation of its blood were still necessary if the full health of community-life was to be regained.

(2) THE CEREMONIES OF THE DAY OF ATONEMENT

(*a*) *The High-Priestly offering:* 'Sin-offerings' were occasional and related to particular offences of individuals. The High-Priest's offering on the Day of Atonement was annual and related to the accumulated guilt of the whole community. At the beginning of a new year, all that had been detrimental to the life of free communion between God and man in the previous year must be expiated and cleansed away. Corporate neglect and defection must be atoned for by the symbolic representative of the whole nation and the covenant thereby renewed.

The actual ritual was unique in form and striking in its symbolism. The prescribed 'sin-offering' was designed to include both the high-priest himself and the people as a whole. They on their part were required to 'humble their spirits' (i.e. fast) and to refrain from work while the ceremonies were in progress. He on his part was required to go solemnly into the most holy place where the ark of the covenant rested, surmounted by a gold covering.[8] This meant passing through the veil which separated the holy of holies from the rest of the temple and when he was inside he performed a blood-ritual by sprinkling the covering of the ark. In this way he made atonement 'for himself and for his house and for all the assembly of Israel' (Leviticus 16: 17).[9]

(b) *The Scapegoat ritual:* It is well known that the practice of transferring sins to a substitute bearer—human or animal—was common and widespread in the ancient world. Because diseases, misfortunes, ritual faults and misdemeanours tended to accumulate in the life of any community, it seemed necessary to carry through periodically some dramatic act of expurgation. The normal way of doing this was to enact a ceremony in which a victim was made to take upon itself some kind of burden and carry it about in public before being sent away into banishment or to death. And that such ceremonies were practised in Israel is clear from the directions given for the purging of a leper in Leviticus 14: 4–7.

But the supremely important example to be found in ancient Hebrew practice is described vividly in Leviticus 16. In addition to a bullock and a ram two kids of the goats had to be taken by the High Priest as sin offering on the Day of Atonement. One of these was offered in the usual way. 'But the goat, on which the lot fell to be the scapegoat, shall be presented alive before the Lord, to make an atonement with him and to let him go for a scapegoat into the wilderness. . . . And Aaron shall lay both his hands upon the head of the live goat and confess over him all the iniquities of the children of Israel, and all their transgressions in all their sins, putting them upon the head of the goat and shall send him away by the hand of a fit man into the wilderness: and the goat shall bear upon him all their iniquities unto a land not inhabited' (Leviticus 16: 10, 21, 22).

The significance of this dramatic ritual is not difficult to discern. To confess guilt by open and public acknowledgment before God is not enough. The load must be symbolically transferred (by God's

8. The Hebrew *Yom Kippur* (Day of Atonement) is directly related to the verb kapporeth (to cover). In the LXX the name for the covering is *hilasterion* while the verb translated to atone is *exilaskesthai*. This last named verb in the Greek has as its essential conception 'that of altering that in the character of an object which necessarily excludes the action of the grace of God, so that God, being what He is, cannot (as we speak) look on it with favour'. B. F. Westcott: *Hebrews*, p. 58.

9. 'If Passover and the agricultural festivals celebrated Yahweh's gracious initiative in delivering his people from enslavement in Egypt, the Day of Atonement symbolised and sealed in the life of the people his continuing gracious initiative ever bent on renewing and restoring his covenant bond with his people.' R. Davidson: *The Old Testament*, p. 121

provision it is true) on to a living animal and taken away to the place of barrenness and terror where it can no longer harm the living and can be swallowed up in the realm of evil spirits. So the ritual of the Day of Atonement combined two ceremonial patterns (derived it would seem from different sources) in an altogether striking way. On the one side the ritual in the most holy place dramatized the restoration of communion through the direct application of the blood of the sin-offering to the symbols of the Divine presence: on the other side the ritual of the scapegoat dramatized the removal of accumulated guilt through a symbolic transference to the goat doomed to destruction. Since the destruction of the Temple the Day has been celebrated by fasting, confessions, prayers and the solemn reading of the record of the Levitical High-priestly ceremonies. The supreme concern is for a thorough and comprehensive catharsis. Here again we have a pattern of symbolic behaviour singularly appropriate to serve as a 'range of comparison' as we pursue our quest for the meaning of the actions and words of Him Who in the New Testament is called High Priest before God, expiating the sins of the people.

D

I have attempted to describe two remarkable 'models' which existed in the pre-Christian era and which in their highest and most developed forms were to provide structures of comparison for the interpretation of the central mystery of the Christian faith. In both traditions the basic motif was cleansing with a consequent restoration to favour and fellowship. That misconduct leads to defilement, that a misuse of 'holy' things results in a highly dangerous situation, that a Divine reaction to impious behaviour can affect a whole community and generations yet unborn—these were unquestioned axioms in the ancient world. If then guilt and defilement had been contracted, nothing could be more important than to learn what were the divinely ordained provisions for the removal of the taint and corruption. We have seen something of the character of the answers given through Greek tragic drama and Hebraic liturgical rites. We turn now to the New Testament itself.

(1) First let us look at the New Testament records against the background of the Greek tragic form. Is there any suggestion of the tragic in the New Testament Passion-stories for example? Do the Epistles in any way portray Jesus as a tragic-hero through whose suffering and death the entail of sin and corruption has been removed? Are we conscious as we read the New Testament

of being in the midst of tremendous conflicts of loyalties, of struggles between what appear to be equally compelling obligations? Is it in any way helpful to say that 'the New Testament shows Jesus passing through the tragic without presenting him tragically'?[10]

These questions are by no means easy to answer. No one can seriously doubt that the triumphant note of death transcended echoes and re-echoes through the New Testament writings. If there is one doxology which more than any other gathers into itself the deepest convictions of the early Christians it is that of 1 Peter 1: 3:

> 'Blessed be the God and Father of our Lord Jesus Christ who according to his abundant mercy hath begotten us again to a living hope by the resurrection of Jesus Christ from the dead.'

It is impossible for the Christian to contemplate a tragic *end*. And it is not surprising that many have felt that if tragedy is the wrong term to employ as a description of the total revelation in Christ then there is no place for tragedy strictly speaking in any part of that revelation.

Yet in the history of mankind the 'tragic stance', as Tinsley so rightly says, 'is a gesture against a meaninglessness which ought not to exist' and constitutes therefore one of the noblest features of the human situation. It would be strange, to say the least, if the Son of God had no relation to this tragic stance in His incarnate life. Again although the victory of all the ages was, in the Christian view, already won on Calvary the actual witness to that victory was to be expressed through good report and evil report, through honour and dishonour, through prosperity and suffering, through life and death. Both in Jesus' incarnate existence and in the earthly career of His disciples the tragic dimension could hardly fail to find some place. If compassion was in any way the keynote of Jesus' ministry and if this quality also manifested itself in the lives of those who became His followers, then there could not fail to be *some* entry into this aspect of the tragic experience which has been brought out so vividly, for example, in the Greek theatre. To describe the total career of Jesus as tragedy is obviously impossible but to eliminate tragedy altogether from the Christian testimony is to rob it of one of its profoundest patterns of interpretation.

If we examine the New Testament documents in detail, we find that one *form* stands out prominently as perhaps the earliest and certainly one of the most impressive vehicles of early Christian

10. E. J. Tinsley: *Christian Theology and Frontiers of Tragedy*, p. 11.

testimony. It is the story of the Passion of Jesus. If the very heart of early Christian preaching was the declaration that 'Christ died for our sins according to the scriptures' (1 Corinthians 15: 3) then it was obviously desirable to be able to present some expanded account of *how* He died, what led up to this awful event, who were responsible for inflicting such a shameful death upon Him, how He reacted to the sufferings and indignities which were heaped upon Him. 'The story of the Passion must be told in such a fashion that the stark reality of it be felt and the full redemptive meaning of it be realized.'[11] It was the supreme achievement of each of the four Evangelists to have constructed such a story, based in all probability upon an already existing skeleton record, differing in details of selection and emphasis but each in its own way an overwhelmingly moving tragic composition. It could be claimed that in the remainder of the New Testament the death and the resurrection of Christ are given a rough equality of emphasis while the passion itself is scarcely mentioned. In the Gospels, however, the passion dominates the narrative. The inevitable climax in death is graphically portrayed: the resurrection is briefly recorded. But it seems that the recital of the narrative of the faithful and courageous witness of the Son of Man even unto death was what men wanted most to hear.

It is highly probable that the chief occasion for the reading of the Passion narrative was the time when all came together for the breaking of the bread. Not only did the bands of Christian disciples perform the traditional actions associated with the bread and the cup: they set them within the wider context of the betrayal and the denial and the scourging and the trial and the crucifixion of their Lord. And it is surely not inappropriate to draw a comparison between the Greek tragedians composing dramas for the Dionysiac festival on the basis of familiar mythic themes from antiquity and the evangelists composing their passion-narratives for recital at the eucharistic celebration on the basis of the general tradition of what happened on the night when the Lord Jesus was betrayed. They introduced references from the Old Testament, stories about individual characters, sayings of the Lord which had been remembered—did all this in such a way as to reveal the inevitability and inexorability of the progress of the events recorded. All was according to the determinate counsel and foreknowledge of God. The suffering was the fulfilment of the sufferings of God's servants recorded in the Old Testament. The death was the fulfilment of the exodus of the people of God from Egypt. Jesus appeared to be the victim of circumstances. In reality He was advancing steadily

11. J. Knox: *The Death of Christ*, p. 19. Quoted D. E. Nineham. St. Mark, p. 365

towards His crowning triumph in perfect conformity with the will of God.

I suggest that it is from the Gospel of Mark that we derive the closest approximation to a 'tragic' presentation. 'The Markan Passion,' Tinsley writes, 'is most impressively free from tendencies to allow the resurrection faith to colour the narrative. . . . In an austere narrative the evangelist shows Jesus frightened in Gethsemane, shrinking from death as an end; at the trial he remains enigmatically silent, he is deserted by his disciples, those who are crucified with him jeer, the only word from the Cross is the cry of dereliction "My God, my God, why hast thou deserted me?" and he dies with a groan. And if the Gospel originally ended at 16:8 it finished with a very brief and cryptic reference to the Resurrection and ended on a note of bewilderment (ἐφοβοῦντο γαρ).'[12] To this list we might well add the grim account which Mark supplies of the treacherous behaviour of Judas and the sad defection of Peter, the perversity of the crowd in choosing Barabbas and the ironic truth of the chief priests' mocking words. The central figure of the drama is harried and tormented almost beyond endurance and yet contrives to retain a mysterious authority over outward events. The real stuggle and agony are inward as he grapples with the inexorability of the Divine Will. 'Remove this cup from me; yet not what I will, but what thou wilt.'

And indeed the altogether dominant impression which the narrative leaves upon the reader is that the pitiable and fearful succession of events which on the human level constituted the Passion of the Divine Son, were in no sense simply arbitrary and meaningless. They were held firmly and securely within the context of a Divine purpose of redemption. 'He saved others'—this mocking word expressed in ironic fashion ultimate truth. How exactly this could be is never defined. That it was through the distress and bitter suffering of God's chosen servant there could be no doubt. That He endured to the end and thereby brought salvation to many was also certain. Whatever the explanation might be in the ultimate logic of events, the immediate result in experience was that men and women, through hearing the recital of those tragic events and through pledging their own loyalty to the tragic sufferer himself, found themselves purged from base and selfish desires and renewed for the struggles which they themselves were being called to undertake in the world. While fully confident about the reality of the resurrection they knew that only through much tribulation could they themselves enter into that final Kingdom of God.

12. Op. cit., p. 11.

Though Matthew and Luke follow Mark in recording the story of the Passion in much detail, they make certain significant changes of emphasis which tend to lessen the feeling of tragedy. They give greater prominence to the promise and realization of the resurrection: to Jesus' confidence in the triumph of His Kingdom: to His control of events even when the powers of darkness seemed victorious. A certain regal dignity shines through the Matthean narrative: a noble compassion for other sufferers through the Lucan. The main outline of the forward march of events remains unchanged but we do not feel the clash of outward forces and the intensity of the inner struggle in quite the same way as we do in the Markan account. For Matthew Jesus is the victim of the cunning and envy of the Jewish authorities and yet all that happens is according to the prevision of Scripture: by His death He inaugurates a new covenant and assumes authority over all peoples. For Luke Jesus is the martyr who accepts indignity and suffering without complaint: His is the exemplary death of a righteous man.

The whole plan of the Fourth Gospel is different from that of the Synoptics, though the section of the Passion narrative which stretches from the arrest in the garden to the death on the cross follows the same general pattern with many variations in detail.[13] In an earlier section which records the progress of events from the raising of Lazarus to the farewell discourses in the Upper Room there are many dramatic scenes: the Council plotting to destroy Jesus with the High Priest saying far more than he knew when he urged that one man must die for the people: the outpouring of devotion in the Bethany home with Mary doing far more than she knew when she anointed Jesus' body for burial: the entry into Jerusalem with the crowd shouting far more than they knew when they acclaimed Him as King of Israel. Further there is the tiny drama of the Greeks requesting to see Jesus: the ideological conflict between 'he that saves his life shall lose it' and 'he that loses his life in this world shall keep it unto life eternal': the inner conflict between the desire

13. 'In all four gospels the narrative (i.e. the Passion narrative) falls naturally into five stages, which may be presented as acts in a drama:

Act I. *The Leave-taking:* Incidents of the Last Supper (including, in the Synoptics, the preparation for it, and in John the Farewell Discourses).

Act II. *The Arrest:* Retirement to a place on or near the Mount of Olives; Betrayal and arrest.

Act III. *The Trial:* Scene I—Examination before the High Priest; Scene 2—Trial before the Roman Governor.

Act IV. *The Execution.*

Act V. *The Reunion:* Scene 1—The burial; Scene 2—The discovery of the empty tomb; Scene 3—The appearance of the risen Christ.'

(I have omitted the details of successive stages in the Trial and the Execution).

C. H. Dodd: *Historical Tradition in the Fourth Gospel*, p. 29.

to be 'saved from this hour' and the dedication to 'glorify thy name': the ultimate spiritual conflict between the prince of this world and the Son of Man about to be 'lifted up'. And there is the second tiny drama of the disciples being cleansed and consecrated to their true vocation through an acted parable: he rose from table, laid aside his garments, took a towel, girded himself, poured water into a basin, washed his disciples' feet, wiped them with a towel, took his garments again and sat down: within the drama we see the tension between the generosity of God and the self-sufficiency of man, between the grace which goes out to the limit of human need and the sin which goes out to the limit of rejecting the divine approach.

Frequently in his two notable books on the Fourth Gospel[14] Dr. C. H. Dodd refers to the author's 'dramatic power' and to what he calls his 'dramatic technique'.[15] Speaking of the trial-scene, for example, he says:

> 'The proceedings in the Roman court are depicted on a large canvas, with an elaboration of detail, and a dramatic power and psychological subtlety, far beyond anything in the other gospels. The portrait of Pilate is vivid and convincing, and, not less so, the picture of the wily pertinacity of the priests, willing to exploit their status of political subjection to throw responsibility upon the foreigner, and yet knowing well how to play upon his weakness to get their own way.'

Evidences of this dramatic power (to some of which I have already drawn attention) can be found in all parts of the Gospel.

But a particular interest attaches to the use of what may be described as 'dramatic technique'. Dodd mentions two examples of this. First there is more than one place in the Gospel where the author seems to employ the device of two stages, a front and a back, when presenting an important series of incidents. A striking instance is that of the encounter with the woman of Samaria and the citizens of her town. 'The action takes place on two stages—the return of the disciples and the departure of the woman divide the dramatis personae into two groups. On the first stage Jesus converses with His disciples. Meanwhile on the back stage the woman converses with her fellow-townsmen and induces them to accompany her to the place where she left Jesus. The two groups then converge and move together to the town where Jesus makes a short stay. The scene is thus at an end, but a final sentence uttered by the Samaritans like the concluding chorus of a Greek play, sums up

14. *The Interpretation of the Fourth Gospel* and *Historical Tradition in the Fourth Gospel.*
15. Especially *Historical Tradition*, p. 96.

the meaning of the whole.'[16] Secondly there are various instances of the use of the *double entendre* and this can have a highly dramatic effect. A word or a sentence may have two quite opposing interpretations—one joyful and one sorrowful, one pleasing and one sinister. The most obvious example is the constant appearance of the verb translated 'to lift up'. Jesus' lifting-up will from one point of view be torture and shame: from another point of view it will be vindication and glory.

There is, however, a possible third aspect of the 'dramatic technique' to which Dodd does not, I think, draw attention. It is the extraordinary way in which the evangelist, as in Greek tragedy, contrives to give the reader (originally the *hearers* of the passion-narrative) the sense of an overwhelmingly mysterious and all-powerful Divine Actor Who is directing events forward to their final *dénouement*. On the stage before us the central figure plays his characteristic part at Jordan, in Nazareth, in Samaria, in Jerusalem. The scenes have a naturalness and spontaneity which make them altogether attractive in themselves. Jesus relates himself to the needs of this man here, that woman there, and thereby His human character is vividly sketched. But at the same time He reveals a constant awareness of a majestic plan or purpose which must be inexorably fulfilled. It is a purpose which in many ways runs counter to His own human feelings and instinctive desires; certainly it cuts clean across the ambitions of the society to which He himself belongs. The struggle grows in intensity. The dramatic *form* is directly related to the theological *content*. Only through the revelation on the historic stage of one in whom the Divine judgment on the sin of the world could work itself out to the ultimate limit, only through the action of one who was ready to take the curse upon himself and in so doing to absorb it to its limits, only, that is to say, through death accepted in the face of all its horror and seeming finality, only thus could the accursed entail of the sin of the world be broken and men be redeemed from their blindness to the Divine light, their deafness to the Divine word.

So the drama of the ages is played out on the stage of a small province of the Roman Empire in the first century of our era. We see the clash of forces, we hear the battle of words. The ultimate result on the human plane is never really in doubt. Yet the central figure goes forward, not without struggle, but with the assurance that He is fulfilling a Divine purpose however mysterious it may seem to human eyes. The cry from the Cross recorded only by the Fourth Evangelist sums up the tragedy and leaves us, the onlookers,

16. *Interpretation*, p. 315.

still free to make our final response. 'It is finished'—and to some this must stand as the final verdict on the meaningless suffering of an innocent man. 'It is finished'—and to others this stands as the final vindication of the ways of God Who through taking suffering into His own being bears away the sin of the world.

(2) Secondly, let us look at the New Testament records against the background of Hebrew liturgical practice. What evidence is there that Jesus' work in death and resurrection was regarded as a purificatory sacrifice? How far do we find language and imagery fulfilling or even suggesting the piacular rites of the Old Testament? Are we justified in thinking that the early Christian imagination saw Jesus as taking the place of the victim or victims associated with the Day of Atonement ritual? Was there a deliberate extension of that which had been prescribed as a means of atonement for the people of Israel to the new sacrifice—the means of atonement for the total human race?

These again are not easy questions to answer. A word here, a phrase there, which may seem to point back to Old Testament ritual practices, may in fact be little more than expressions commonly in use and bearing no particular load of studied comparison. Yet there is enough in the New Testament of deliberate appeal to the ceremonies of the post-exilic Temple to convince us that at least in some quarters this was a favourite means of interpreting the meaning of what by ordinary human standards was an inexplicable mystery—namely that God's Messiah should have become a victim for slaughter and that His blood should have been publicly shed. In the books which contain the largest number of references to Jewish liturgical practices—the Epistle to the Hebrews and the Johannine writings—we find such striking statements as the following:

'For if the sprinkling of defiled persons with the blood of goats and bulls and with the ashes of a heifer sanctifies for the purification of the flesh, how much more shall the blood of Christ, who through the eternal Spirit offered himself without blemish to God, purify your conscience from dead works to serve the living God.' (Hebrews 9: 13–14).

'If we walk in the light as he is in the light we have fellowship with one another and the blood of Jesus His Son cleanses us from all sin. . . . If any one does sin, we have an advocate with the Father, Jesus Christ the righteous; and he is the expiation for our sins and not for ours only but also for the sins of the whole world.' (1 John 1: 7; 2: 1–2).
'Behold the Lamb of God Who takes away the sin of the world.' (John 1: 29).

These statements are exceedingly impressive. On the other hand the Synoptic Gospels and the Pauline Epistles contain little that could be called sacrificial imagery. In the Gospels the only significant passage seems to be that which bears witness to the rending of the veil of the Temple. Nothing is more certainly attested than that Jesus made some reference to the destruction of the Temple and to the establishment of a new shrine for worship. And the rent veil seemed to symbolize for the Evangelists the access into the immediate presence of God actually made possible by the Saviour's death. But this is only inferred—there is no expanded commentary on the significance of the startling event. The season of Jesus' death was not that of the Day of Atonement and there is no reason to think that its ceremonies were specifically in their minds.

With Paul the situation is very similar. He shows little interest in liturgical provisions or practices. If the Epistles to the Colossians and to the Ephesians can be regarded as his own compositions, then it is true that they contain interesting references to lustration and initiatory rites of a general kind. In 1 Corinthians there is the brief passage linking the career of Jesus with the Passover cultus and there is a side glance at pagan sacrificial meals. But none of this is concerned with sacrifice as piacular or expiatory. In only one instance is there a possible use of the imagery of the Day of Atonement, and this is in the classic declaration of Romans 3: 23 ff. But I intend to submit this to a full examination in Chapter V.

In the Epistle to the Hebrews the imagery is quite explicitly that of the Jewish cultus. In a manner unparalleled elsewhere Jesus is spoken of as High Priest, though of a different order from that of the regular Levitical priesthood. Clearly the political activities of the High Priest in later Judaism are of no significance in this context. The whole concentration of interest is upon his focal exercise of priestly responsibility once a year when after due preparation he took the blood of the appointed victim into the most holy place and there so manipulated it as 'to make atonement for the sins of the people'. In harmony with this general pattern, yet in certain respects in complete contradistinction to it, Christ the High Priest of a new order entered into heaven itself, once and for all, bearing his own life-blood to make an adequate reconciliation for the sins of the whole world and for peoples of all ages. The 'how' of the purifying act is not a question for enquiry. The all-important matter is that we have such a High Priest who is set over the household of God: He has pioneered the way of liberation: now we are free to enter ourselves into the inmost sanctuary of God by a new and living way. The all-inclusive act of purification has been made at the mid-point of the world's history. There is no need for any further sacrifice. With eyes set upon Jesus and with a complete confidence in what He has achieved we can boldly approach the throne of God and find grace to help in every time of need.

Turning to the Johannine writings we find in the First Epistle of John a reiterated plea for purity of heart and conscience. It seems evident that in the community to which the letter was addressed standards of conduct were being accepted which were far removed from the truth and the love which had been revealed in Jesus Christ. His life had been made visible once and for all. Through Him the light of God had pierced the world's darkness. Henceforward it is possible for men to walk in the light as He is in the light with the assurance that the blood of Jesus will cleanse from every sin. On the human side there needs to be a rigorous honesty and a readiness to confess that sins have been committed. On the Divine side there is One Who is ever pleading the cause of mankind and making available the expiation which He has wrought. How far the author of this letter was referring deliberately to liturgical practices and in particular to ceremonies of purification it is impossible to say. The language certainly suggests sacrifice such as was enacted on the Day of Atonement with its attendant fastings and confessions. Certainly the exhortation is to become pure as He is pure, this having become possible because of the complete purification which He has effected through the blood of His sacrifice. In that sacrifice the ultimate meaning of love has been manifested and if God so loved us, we ought also to love one another.

E

The Christian Church went forward from the apostolic age possessing two treasures of supreme value—its own distinctive documents at the heart of which was the Passion Story, and the Hebrew Scriptures at the heart of which was the record of a covenant sealed and renewed by sacrifice. Each of these had powerful dramatic qualities: each was related to what may be called a symbolic or sacramental pattern of social behaviour. It is no cause for surprise therefore that in a comparatively short time the sacramental life of the Christian society became regularized and to some extent formalized. Deep human needs which had found a certain satisfaction within the experience either of Greek tragic drama of Hebrew liturgical practice were to find an alternative opened to them through the possibility of participating in the Christian mysteries. In particular man's abiding need for some assurance of *catharsis* leading to communion could be met through the acceptance of baptism and through the subsequent sharing in the Eucharist.

Although, as I have already suggested, there are markedly tragic elements in the passion stories of the four evangelists, it could not be claimed that the writers of the New Testament borrowed in any direct way from the Greek tragic tradition. In point of fact the theatre generally was in a sadly weakened condition in the first century of the Christian era and little attempt was made to deal with the great issues of human life within its context. The whole emphasis, whether in the great cities of the Eastern Mediterranean or in Rome itself, was on spectacles, comedies, above all on farce. Mimes, pantomimes, riotous histrionic performances were enormously popular and no emperor dared deny the people their indulgence in the *ludi* and the *spectaculi*. And whereas, during the first three centuries of the Christian era, members of the Church had little desire to share in these pagan exercises, the coming of the Edict of Toleration meant the relaxing of tension between the Church and the world and a consequent disposition on the part of individual Christians to enjoy the fun of the theatre as much as their non-Christian neighbours. Those in authority in the Church constantly rebuked any compromise of this kind but in a curious way it seems to have been the barbarian invasions rather than Christian opposition which finally brought about the downfall of the theatres of the ancient world.

In a striking passage Sir Edmund Chambers summarizes the relationship between the Church and the theatre before the outburst of new drama in Europe in the eleventh and twelfth centuries. He points out that the tragedy and comedy of ancient Greece were already a closed account before the Christian era began:

'The plays of Seneca were probably intended for readers only. In the theatre of Pompey legendary stories were sung to the dancing of a *pantomimies*, and *mimi*, long branded with infamy, performed satirical and shameless farces. They did not spare the new religion, and in return the theatrical performances became the subject of many condemnations by ecclesiastical writers from the *De Spectaculis* of Tertullian onwards and in more formal pronouncements by early councils of the western Church. If Augustine and others still retain some interest in the classical playwrights, it is as literature only, not as living drama. The degenerate theatre finally disappeared during the barbaric invasions of the sixth century, and the dispossessed histriones, as they were then called, were driven afoot, to merge with the descendants of the storytelling Teutonic poets, in the miscellaneous body of entertainers who haunted the towns and thoroughfares of the Middle Ages.'[17]

17. E. K. Chambers: *English Literature at the Close of the Middle Ages*, 1. Cp. *The Mediaeval Stage*, Vol. 1. Chap. 1.

With the secular theatre contributing virtually nothing in the first millennium of the Christian era to the interpretation of the tragic elements in human life, it became the exclusive responsibility of the Church to provide opportunities for dramatic participation in sacramental ceremonies bearing a transcendent significance. Their meaning was by no means confined to the removal of stains of defilement, to the purgation of accumulated social guilt, or to the catharis of the emotions of fear and pity but that these notes entered into the developing liturgical tradition of the Church can hardly be doubted. In baptism there was the obvious symbolism of the cleansing effected by water, especially running water, but in addition there were ceremonies of exorcism involving the use of breath and fire and the symbolic use of light to drive away darkness. In its fully developed form baptism was a highly dramatic communal action which had the effect not only of incorporating a new member into the body of the Church but also of renewing the purification of those already within it. The preparation for worship sketched in the Epistle to the Hebrews ('with our hearts sprinkled clean from an evil conscience and our bodies washed with pure water'— Hebrews 10: 22) was constantly re-enacted whenever the baptismal ceremony was performed and especially when, as on Easter Saturday, it was made an outstanding occasion in the life of the community.

But although participation in a baptismal ceremony could renew the worshippers in their identification with the Saviour, whose death and resurrection were symbolically represented to the eyes of faith whenever the baptizand was plunged beneath the water, something more was needed to give fullness of assurance to those who were conscious of individual and corporate sins committed after baptism had actually taken place. To meet this need a more comprehensive liturgy gradually took shape, centred indeed in the solemn mystery of the Eucharist but including also penitential litanies and certain forms of bodily mortification of which fasting was the most common. By penitential prayer and disciplined fasting (acts which might be individual but were more normally social performances) Christians identified themselves with their Redeemer through whose sufferings the sin of the world had been purged away.

It was, however, supremely in the Eucharist itself that they experienced the sense of being identified afresh with Christ in His saving death and resurrection. In the West, as we shall see, the central eucharistic action came to be interpreted principally in terms of a sacrifice of propitiation and satisfaction. But in the East the liturgy was much more a re-enactment of the total passion story and this fulfilled, at least to a degree, the Day of Atonement ceremonies with which the Church was familiar through its possession of the Old Testament scriptures. Just as the Jewish High Priest went into the most holy place to perform the blood ceremony and thereby make atonement for the whole people so the Christian priest went behind the veil to perform the most solemn sacrificial actions and thereby to renew the life of his people by uniting their sacrifice with that of the Son of God. To a remarkable extent the form of service which had been established in the East by the time of St. Chrysostom has remained unchanged down to the present day. It is true that no single form of words has ever attained the seemingly impregnable position of the Canon of the Roman Mass but whichever of the three main forms of liturgical wording is used[18] the general shape and in particular the carefully regulated symbolic actions remain the same.

The very structure and furnishing of the Church are highly symbolic: in particular the iconostasis separates the sanctuary, symbolic of the very dwelling place of God Himself and scene of the eternal sacrifice, from the nave in which the people assemble with the choir and the deacon who directs the service. Throughout the Liturgy there are processions in and out of the sanctuary, veilings and unveilings of the Royal Door which gives access to it and openings and closings of the Door itself. All of this has symbolic significance to the worshipper, being associated with the ultimate mystery of the Divine Presence which is felt intensely but never expressed in words.

The Liturgy consists of biddings, dialogues, prayers, hymns and above all ceremonial actions. The total drama to be re-enacted is that of the entrance of God into human flesh, the life, passion, death, resurrection and ascension of God Incarnate, the restoration of the glory of God's eternal Kingdom. There are highly dramatic moments—for example the warning cry of the deacon 'The doors, the doors!' before the doors of the Iconostasis are shut and the priest proclaims 'Christ is in our midst'—but the whole service is a liturgical drama in which the members of the assembled congregation are in part spectators but in part actors: in ideal they are certainly participators and the essential character of their participation may be described as 'through cleansing to communion'. Again and again as the service progresses all who worship grow conscious of weakness and sinfulness and of a consequent unworthiness to take

18. The Liturgy of St. Basil, the Liturgy of St. Chrysostom and the Liturgy of the Pre-Sanctified. The Liturgy of St. Chrysostom is now in common use the other two being reserved for special occasions.

part in so divine a mystery: again and again there comes the plea for purification and forgiveness and the renewal of communion with all the saints and angels and blessed dead in the love of the eternal Trinity. It is in the Cross that the all-sufficient means of purification has been revealed to men. So the bidding rings out: 'The expiation and forgiveness of our sins let us ask of the Lord, the great and powerful strength of thy Holy Cross for the help of our lives let us ask of the Lord'.

Yet whereas the total movement of the Liturgy has a dialectical pattern, swinging backwards and forwards from humiliation and abasement to transfiguration and exaltation, there is for every worshipper the most solemn moment of all when through the reception into his own body of the holy mysteries he is overcome with the sense on the one hand of trembling and awe, on the other hand of confidence and joy as he partakes of the holy Body and Blood of the Son of God. Something of the priest's feeling may be felt as we read the words of his prayer immediately before communicating:

'I am not worthy, Lord, that thou shouldest come unto me, but as thou wast content to lodge in the stall of brute beasts and in the house of Simon the leper, and didst receive the harlot a sinner like unto me, vouchsafe in like manner to enter into the stable of my brutish soul, my defiled body dead in sin and spiritually leprous, and as Thou didst not disdain the mouth of the harlot when she kissed thy unpolluted feet, disdain not me a sinner, O Lord my God, but make me worthy to partake of Thy most Holy Body and Blood.'

So the priest; now, having communicated first himself and then the deacon, he stands forth purified of all his transgressions by virtue of His communion with the Crucified and is thereby worthy to communicate others. The description of this further dramatic movement in which the members of the faithful who are present come forward to renew their own communion in the Body of Christ I shall quote from the remarkable account of the Divine Liturgy of the Russian Orthodox Church written more than a century ago by the famous author of *Dead Souls*, Nikolai Gogol. In the background we see the prophet Isaiah in the Jerusalem temple. It is his essential experience which is re-enacted in the body of every devout worshipper who comes in faith to the table of the Lord. These are Gogol's words:

'Having made this confession, each one approaches, not as to a priest but as to a flaming seraph—ready with open lips to receive from the sacred spoon the live coal of the Holy Body and Blood of the Lord, which is to burn away like dead brushwood all the black dross of his transgressions, driving eternal night from his soul and transforming him into a shining seraph. And when raising the sacred spoon to his mouth and pronouncing his name, the priest says: The servant of God (naming the communicant) partaketh of the precious and holy Body and Blood of our Lord and God and Saviour Jesus Christ, for the remission of his sins and unto life everlasting, he receives the Body and Blood of the Lord, and in them he meets God, coming face to face with Him. In this moment time does not exist. . . . With the sacred *aer* his mouth is wiped, accompanied by the words of the seraph to the prophet Isaiah "Lo this hath touched thy lips. Thy iniquity is taken away and thy sin purged".'[19]

I have only been able to touch briefly on the distinctive character of the Eastern Liturgy. But it has perhaps become evident that there has never been in the East that sharp distinction between the 'sacred' and the 'profane' such as has been so greatly emphasized in the West. This means that the Liturgy is in no way a cult designed to establish contact between the worshippers (who belong to the 'profane' world) and God who belongs to the 'sacred'. Rather it is the repeated actualization in the symbolic earthly sanctuary of that which is forever being enacted in heaven: it is, in fact, the very expression in dramatic form of the life of the Church which is hid with Christ in God. Hence every time the Liturgy is performed, Atonement is re-enacted. The individual worshipper is caught up into the total reconciling activity of God and realizes sacramentally what he will one day realize fully in the eternal Kingdom of God. However much the vicissitudes of history may have dimmed this vision and detracted from this ideal it remains true that for Orthodoxy atonement is not penal but sacramental, not confined to a moment of time but expressed through God's eternal drama of sacrifice.[20] Doubtless it would be possible to suggest psychological parallels between the experience of worshippers participating in the Liturgy and that of spectators participating in Greek tragedy. But for the Orthodox there is no radical break between psychology and theology. If the worshipper experiences a catharsis of the emotions through pity and terror this is all the work of the Divine Spirit Who is ever operating in and through the Divine Sacrifice to restore men to the fullness of communion with God in Christ. This is the essence of atonement. This is one Christian interpretation of the meaning of reconciliation. And wherever, in other parts of Christendom, worshipping activities have been in the form and in the spirit of the Orthodox Liturgy there atonement has been actually

19. N. V. Gogol: *The Divine Liturgy of the Russian Orthodox Church.* (Translated 1960. Darton, Longman and Todd.)
20. See Alexander Schmemann in *Worship in Scripture and Tradition*, edited by Massey H. Shepherd, Jr., p. 172 ff.

realized: in the words of the Epistle to the Hebrews worshippers have in very truth 'drawn near to God'.

I turn now to the West. The tenth century dawned with the symbolic life of Western Europe concentrated in its cathedrals, abbeys and parish churches. The secular theatre scarcely existed any longer and there seemed little hope of its revival. Yet a movement was afoot which was to lead to a revival of drama outside the confines of church buildings, though its themes remained closely related to the story of man's salvation through Christ.

This new development came about very naturally and understandably. In earlier centuries it had always been the custom to commemorate special days by celebrating the Eucharist but in course of time the performance came to be as it were embellished by adding small ceremonial actions related to the particular festival. The Christmas crib, the Palm Sunday procession, Pentecost, above all Passiontide itself, immediately suggested mimetic actions which could bring a sense of deeper participation in the meaning of the day. But in the tenth century there was a new departure. Besides mimetic actions with symbolic objects we find the beginnings of dialogue, with question and answer, sung or said, related to the theme of a particular day. The earliest known to us and the most famous was associated with Easter Day. Definite directions were given for the imitation of the scene in which the angel sits on the tomb and the three women come to anoint the body. As dialogue the following was to be recited:

Q. Whom do you seek in the sepulchre, O Christians?
A. Jesus of Nazareth, who was crucified, O heavenly ones.
Q. He is not here; he has risen even as he said before.
   Go, proclaim that he has risen from the grave.

'The *Quem Quaerites*', Mr. Robert Speaight comments, 'enacted throughout Europe in the privacy of monastic choirs in the small hours of Easter morning, may stand as the first Christian play. The reading of the Passion, now a regular part of the Good Friday liturgy, is its lineal successor.'[21]

From such small beginnings a new and highly important dramatic form emerged—the liturgical play. Between the eleventh and the fifteenth centuries we see a process of development by which the mime and dialogue expanded into a play or cycle of plays and, whereas at first the place of acting was in the church itself, gradually a movement was made to perform in the churchyard or in the market place or to move from station to station on a cart or

21. *The Christian Theatre*, p. 10.

'pageant'. The miracle plays so-called (though they were concerned not with miracles in our modern sense but with the mysteries of the Christian faith) and the moralities constitute one of the most interesting and most highly treasured legacies of the Middle Ages. Appearing first within the church-building, developing within the total church-culture of medieval towns, they were to form the transition to the rebirth of a theatre which was independent of churchly control and was ultimately to be separated from the life of the church altogether. This is a long and complicated story but for our purpose it is significant to note that during the period between the eleventh century and the Reformation the chief means by which the story of man's salvation could touch the *feelings* of the general populace in Western Europe was through these liturgical plays.[22] Gradually laymen were given parts to act and the guilds became virtually responsible for staging and financing the performances. Soon the vernacular was brought into use (by the fourteenth century) and earthy scenes and very human motifs were incorporated into the heavenly plots. Through the plays the great drama of man's redemption was enacted again and again and those who participated whether as actors or spectators gained at least some sense of having been reconciled to God through the blood of the Cross.

Of all the plays performed no genre is of more interest for our own enquiry than the Passion Plays. I have already referred to the tendency in early medieval times to introduce symbolic actions into the Mass whenever the occasion made dramatic illustration appropriate. Of these occasions none was more solemn and none more open to elaboration than Holy Week itself. It was the custom to read the gospel narratives on successive days and at some period 'reading' took on the form of regular oratorio. 'A tenor voice rendered the narrative of the evangelist, a treble the sayings of Jews and disciples, a bass those of Christ Himself. To particular episodes of these Passions special dramatic action was appropriated. On Wednesday at the words *Velum templi scissum est*, the Lenten veil, which since the first Sunday in Lent had hidden the sanctuary from the sight of the people, was dropped to the ground. On Good Friday the words *Partiti sunt vestimenta* were a signal for a similar bit of by-play with a linen cloth which lay upon the altar. Maundy Thursday had its commemorative ceremony of the washing of feet: while the *Tenebrae* or solemn extinction, one after another, of lights at the Matins of the last three days of the week, was held to sym-

---

22. The preaching of the friars was also important but I doubt if its influence was as profound as that of the plays.

bolize the grief of the apostles and others whom those lights represented.'[23]

Symbolic actions of these kinds could easily develop into full-scale drama. And so far as the Passion Play itself was concerned this seems to have resulted through the elaboration of the laments which had come to be associated with Mary, the mother of the Lord. The early dramatic scene at the tomb gave scope for laments to be put into the mouths of the three Maries when they failed to find the Lord whom they had come to anoint. Then, as a natural extension, the scene at Calvary with Mary and John watching together at the foot of the Cross included other laments in which Mary speaks to Christ, to the women of Jerusalem and to John himself. The progress from Gethsemane to the Crucifixion, beginning in dumb show, gradually added spoken parts and ultimately a Passion Play had come into being as a virtually independent structure. The Resurrection play, the Passion play, plays involving other Biblical characters, were acted on varying occasions not necessarily associated with their particular provenance and ultimately, in the notable cycle performed in England on *Corpus Christi*, the total drama of salvation with the Passion at its centre was displayed before men's eyes. And the intrinsic dramatic character of the records of the Passion must have made this performance the most impressive of all. The famous play staged every ten years at Oberammergau brings the spirit of medievalism into our own time and reveals the undying appeal of the story of the Cross.

F

Of the immense popularity of the Mysteries and the Moralities in the period between roughly A.D. 1200 and 1500 there can be no doubt. Yet the sixteenth century saw an astonishing change. This particular phase of dramatic development suddenly came to an end. Partly through the renewal of the knowledge of classical literature and pagan drama, partly through the antagonism of the Reformers to images and ceremonial actions, partly through a sheer waning of interest in heavenly things as exciting new possibilities of earthly achievements came over the horizon, the great cycles gradually fell into desuetude, being irregularly performed and ultimately surviving only in country places distant from the metropolis. The 'pageants' were allowed to decay and the companies of actors dispersed. Another form of drama was about to appear, a form which did not reject the values and insights of the Christian tradition but which

23. E. K. Chambers: *The Mediaeval Stage*, II, pp. 5–6.

was in no way dependent on the authority or the cultus of the Christian Church.

The first great playwright of the new era in England was Marlowe. His Dr. Faustus still remains within the tradition of the mystery and morality plays but, drawing upon a legend first appearing in the sixth century A.D. of a man selling his soul to the Devil, it focusses interest upon a particular individual who possesses an overriding ambition to attain eminence and thereby gain power: it is, in fact a tragedy of *man*, exceptional man perhaps, but still a man whose motives and conflicts can be portrayed in dramatic form. In Marlowe the new humanism of the Renaissance is already partially revealed. In Shakespeare we find ourselves in a new world of human interests, struggles, delights, tragedies, set, it is true, within the context of an ultimate divine order and still related to abiding standards of good and evil. While Scripture and Prayer Book recalled men to the divinely ordained way of salvation, the plays outside the Church shed a brilliant new light on human nature itself, its ambitions, its follies, its loves, its hates, its bitter estrangements, its tender reconciliations. Henceforward the theatre went its own way, occasionally patronized by the Church but normally regarded as a secular institution. The interesting question for our purpose is whether Shakespeare and his successors, through the medium of the tragic-form, have communicated to their audiences an experience which can justly be called a social catharsis or purgation and whether this is in any way related to the Christian interpretation of atonement.

In any approach to this question Shakespeare is obviously the key figure. Standing nearest in time to the Biblical drama of the Middle Ages he yet breaks through to a completely new expression of the tragic-form in terms of events recorded in secular literature or imagined by minds outside the direct Christian tradition. Moreover he presents in a superlative way the artist's vision of *man*, lifted up and cast-down, living intensely and dying heroically, doing good and doing evil, all within the context of an unseen divine order but with scarcely any reference to direct divine action in history. There is little doubt that Shakespeare assumed the truth of the essential Christian gospel. But his overmastering concern was to construct works of art out of the raw material of human greatnesses and weaknesses, of human actions large-hearted and ignoble. On this stage we see the horror and the glory of human life and no works of English literature have surpassed the splendour of his tragic dramas. As George Steiner has finely said: 'The playhouse of Shakespeare and his contemporaries was *el gran teatro del mundo*. No variety of feeling, no element from the crucible of experience was alien to its purpose.'[24]

Yet to estimate the significance of these tragedies as guides towards a total interpretation of human existence is by no means easy. Some have regarded them as no less and no more than a magnificent exposure of the varieties of human character, the plot being largely irrelevant. We can learn much about psychological motives and moral experience but we have no right to ask for more. Others, of whom A. C. Bradley is an outstanding example, have gained a sense of 'law and beauty' from the whole working out of the tragic drama. At the end of the play we feel 'not depression and much less despair, but a consciousness of greatness in pain, and of solemnity in the mystery we cannot fathom'.[25]

More recently the emphasis has swung away from any attempt to unravel Shakespeare's total philosophy of life towards the analysis of his activity as superb craftsman, taking up the ideas and beliefs of his age and weaving them into the great works of art which his tragedies so obviously are. In another direction a number of critics have turned to the Christian tradition of theology and ritual and have sought to show that Christian symbols and patterns are deeply imbedded in his language and in the structure of his plots.[26] In other words there is less readiness to see in his plays any reflection of a total philosophy of life, more readiness to recognize continuity with the liturgical plays of the Middle Ages, their Biblical imagery and their concern for man's salvation. If this is in any way true it means that Shakespeare's plays could be regarded as an expression of the gospel of man's salvation in dominantly secular terms. G. Wilson Knight's claim that 'each of Shakespeare's tragic heroes is a miniature Christ' could be interpreted to mean that what had ceased to be possible *directly*—moving the depths of man's feeling and imagination by, for example, the presentation of the cycle of the *Corpus Christi* plays—was now being attempted *indirectly* by presenting in the theatre a succession of Christ-figures, each of whom, through his death, was to bring about the catharsis of human emotions described by Aristotle so long ago. It is indeed doubtful in the extreme whether Shakespeare had any such *conscious* intention in mind as he created his tragic-heroes. The very existence of the 'fatal flaw' in the central character and the final emphasis on death rather than on resurrection make it difficult to draw any

24. *The Death of Tragedy*, p. 20.
25. A. C. Bradley: *Shakespearean Tragedy*, p. 279.
26. In this whole section I am indebted to R. W. Battenhouse for his essay on Shakespeare in the volume *The Tragic Vision and the Christian Faith*, edited by Nathan A. Scott, Jr.

close parallel between say Christ and Hamlet. Yet insofar as the career of the tragic-hero moves us to sympathy and pity, to terror and awe, and thereby purges us of the base ingredients which so constantly infect and spoil the life of society, it is at least in the pattern of the Christ Who through conflict and suffering and resistance unto blood purges our conscience from dead works to serve the living God.

Whether or not Shakespeare's tragedies are examples of 'tragic vision illuminated by biblical faith and of biblical faith transforming the tragic vision of life',[27] Milton's Samson Agonistes can certainly be regarded in this way. It is closer to the form of Greek tragedy than are Shakespeare's plays: at the same time it is more explicitly Biblical. It is perhaps the most magnificent attempt in the whole history of drama to hold together the essential faith of the Old Testament that God purifies His servants through suffering and vindicates them even through their death and the essential conviction of Greek Tragedy that the vision of suffering can bring purification to the beholders while the vision of death can ennoble and transform. In the illuminating words of George Steiner:

> 'The organization of the play is nearly static in the manner of the Aeschylean Prometheus; yet there moves through it a great progress toward resolution. Like all Christian tragedy, a notion in itself paradoxical, Samson Agonistes is in part a *commedia*. The reality of Samson's death is drastic and irrefutable; but it does not carry the major or the final meaning of the play. As in *Oedipus at Colonus*, the work ends on a note of solemn transfiguration, even of joy. The action proceeds from night-blindness of eye and of spirit to a blindness caused by exceeding light.'[28]

Steiner refers to the *paradox* of the term *Christian tragedy*. Not only is the term a paradox. Its two elements are in many ways so disparate that their conjunction may appear to be sheer contradiction. How, it is said, can the Gospel whose essential note was from the beginning the triumph of the resurrection, the victory over death, be associated with *tragedy*? How can tragedy, which by its general character as a play must have a beginning, a middle and an end and by its particular character as a tragedy must end in death and seeming disaster, how can this by any stretch of terminology be called Christian? It may be possible to see a great Old Testament character such as Samson as a tragic-hero. After all, the Hebrews for a great part of their historical existence had no hope of life beyond the grave and the over-ruling moral law of the God of Israel is not very different in conception from the over-

27. T. S. K. Scott-Craig: op. cit., p. 100.
28. Op. cit., p. 31.

arching fate of the Greek tragedians. We are quieted by a death so noble and left with 'peace and consolation . . . and calm of mind, all passion spent'. But can this be true of Christ or indeed of those who have followed Him in the way of suffering and death? Is such a final resolution as Samson Agonistes gives us in any way to be compared with the final reconciliation wrought by Christ?

These questions have given rise to an almost impassioned debate. Some regard 'Christian tragedy' as an impossible contradiction in terms: some as a striking paradox: some as 'pointer to the true interpretation of the Atonement'. Probably no writer has investigated the problem more carefully than has Mr. T. R. Henn in his book *The Harvest of Tragedy*, though since 1956, when this volume appeared, there have been many more contributions to the debate.[29] The obvious difficulty about using the term *Christian tragedy* is the conviction, central in the Christian Gospel from the very beginning, that the Christ who died in weakness has been raised in power, that His sufferings were the prelude to glory, that because of His obedience to death, even the death of the Cross, God has highly exalted Him and given Him the name above every name. How can there be the true tagic feeling, even when contemplating the agony of Gethsemane, if we already know that after the briefest interval the heroic protagonist will be standing above the storm and strife and speaking words of comfort and peace to His disciples? How can we imagine that one who was truly divine could share the tragic vision and see death as the limit to all human possibilities?

These questions present such obvious difficulties that as great a thinker as Reinhold Niebuhr has chosen the title *Beyond Tragedy* to describe a Christian interpretation of history. C. S. Lewis has affirmed that in Christian theology 'the whole cosmic story, though full of tragic elements, yet fails of being a tragedy'. Mr. Philip Toynbee, in his review of Richard Sewall's *The Vision of Tragedy* declared that 'Christianity is not a tragic religion and the Crucifixion was not a tragic event. The greatest message of Christianity is redemption and the most execrated Christian sin is the sin of pride.'[30] And it was Lessing, long ago, who wrote 'The first tragedy that deserves the name Christian has beyond doubt still to be written.'

29. Mr. Henn includes a most comprehensive bibliography. An inaugural lecture (1963) by Professor E. J. Tinsley, *Christian Theology and the Frontiers of Tragedy* refers to certain works published since 1956. Nathan A. Scott's *The Tragic Vision and the Christian Faith* (1957) has an excellent bibliography. Mention may also be made of Richard Sewall: *The Vision of Tragedy* (1959); Murray Krieger: *The Tragic Vision* (1960); D. D. Raphael: *The Paradox of Tragedy* (1960); and Leo Aylen: *Greek Tragedy and the Modern World* (1964).

30. The reference to pride arises out of Mr. Sewall's claim that *hubris* is the distinctive mark of every tragic-hero.

Yet so overpowering has been the appeal of Christ Crucified to the depths of human sensibilities, so aesthetically satisfying has been the story of the Passion, whether in poetic or dramatic form, that men in every age have clung to the idea of expressing the essence of Christianity in tragic form even though this may not constitute the whole Gospel. It is interesting for example to find Mr. Toynbee continuing his review by commenting that Christianity's chosen symbol 'has not been of Christ Resurrected, which annuls the potential tragedy, but of Christ Crucified, which remains obstinately tragic in men's minds in spite of their official faith **that this was not the last act of the drama'. In concentrating upon** this symbol, he argues, Christianity has adopted tragic elements which cannot be reconciled with its fundamental concept of Atonement and yet which are in fact profoundly true to life and indispensable for the adequate interpretation.

Mr. Middleton Murry was prepared to go even further. Here was an extremely gifted literary critic, of the finest sensibility, who in his personal life had passed through distress and suffering beyond the range of most of his fellows. In the depths of his tribulation it was the figure of Jesus in the Gospel story that brought him comfort and resolution and courage to endure. It is not altogether surprising therefore that in an essay on Tragedy which brings to a conclusion his interpretation of the life and thought of two great figures— D. H. Lawrence and Albert Schweitzer—he should have urged that whereas there has always been an opposition between official Christianity and the tragic interpretation of Life, it is the Resurrection-dogma which must be abandoned in order that a gospel of redemption through tragedy may live.

'The nearest I come to an understanding and acceptance of the Christian conception of God,' he writes, 'is in a contemplation of the life and death of Jesus. This plunges me into despair and lifts me out of despair in the same timeless moment. It is the defeat of love; yet it is the triumph of love. Though I am totally unable to believe in the physical resurrection of Jesus as an historical fact, he lives in my imagination. In this sense, the resurrection of Jesus is a spiritual reality for me. And a spiritual reality, in this sense, is more than any other kind of reality to me. It enters my life and changes it. . . . The tragedy of Jesus enables us to understand more clearly the nature of tragedy for it is, so to speak, the pure case, the ne plus ultra, of tragedy: the tragedy of the man who died in order to establish love at the heart of the universe, as God.

'I believe', he continues, 'that those who are overwhelmed by their sense of the pathos of the Christian civilization: its failure, its disruption, its self-betrayal, of which they share the guilt, may find relief and purification and peace by learning to regard the history of Jesus as the archetypal tragedy and by entering into the spiritual experience that comes from it. This reawakening of the tragic consciousness would involve no escape from reality, no violation of integrity. On the contrary it would proceed from a more resolute acceptance of the truth concerning the human condition.'[31]

We may sympathize with Mr. Murry and still regard his proposed solution as too radical. That the expression of tragedy in artistic form has been one of the greatest of all human achievements is generally agreed. That a large proportion of the Gospel story is capable of being expressed as tragedy is also obviously true. The crucial question is whether a deliberate concentration of attention upon the tragic elements of the Gospel to the temporary exclusion of the Resurrection-faith is either possible or desirable. Can there be a temporary suspension of belief in the Resurrection in order that the full impact of the Passion and Crucifixion of Jesus may be experienced? Can the limitations of knowledge which the Incarnation may rightly be claimed to have involved, be held to have included the conviction that He would rise again? That is to say, did the Son of God, in emptying himself (Philippians 2: 5), expose himself to the full experience of the tragic-hero and thereby to the possibility of being represented in artistic form as the archetypal tragic figure?

If it be held that one form and one form only of interpretation of the Atonement is required by the New Testament witness to Christ then there can be no doubt about the answers which must be given to the questions I have proposed. If on the other hand the total thesis of this book is accepted, the thesis namely that there are numerous ranges of comparison by which the meaning of the Death of Christ may be presented to men, then it becomes possible to accept the tragic interpretation as one of these modes of comparison, recognizing fully that it is not complete in itself and that the artistic experience, important as it is, does not constitute the whole of human life. For Jesus, as He is presented to us in the records of the four evangelists, is undoubtedly a tragic figure in the sense generally attached to the word tragic. Taking, for example, Allardyce Nicoll's analysis of tragic drama,[32] we see the fulfilment in the Gospel story of all five of the principles which he regards as recurrent and essential.

(1) Death is central—a constant preoccupation. Nothing could be truer of Mark's Gospel.

31. J. M. Murry: *Love, Freedom and Society*, pp. 232, 244, 251.
32. A. Nicoll: *The Theatre and Dramatic Theory*, p. 105.

(2) Normally tragic drama has a historical foundation. The event actually happened though often in the remote past.

(3) There is a certain sense of grandeur attaching to the persons represented and above all to the central figure who is a person of symbolic greatness.

(4) The fourth is perhaps the most striking of all. 'In tragedy,' Nicoll writes, 'we are confronted by infinity and the finite, by the unseen pressure of unfathomable forces and by men. . . . Yet central upon the stage stands a man of such magnitude that we feel the infinite is almost being matched by the finite'. Contemplating all that ensues in the development of the tragic action the audience becomes aware of finite and infinite being brought together (atonement? reconciliation?).

(5) All tragedy possesses a certain ritualistic tone, a sense of form. Who can read the Fourth Gospel in particular without the sense of a mounting tension, a measured forward progress, a sacramental quality in the movement of events?

To these principles we may add the constant revelation of *conflict* —of loyalties, of attachments, of motives, of yearnings in the hero's own soul: a striking motif of tragedy emphasized by Karl Deutsch in his introduction to Jasper's *Tragedy is not Enough*—the 'tragedy occurs wherever awareness exceeds power: and particularly where awareness of a major need exceeds the power to satisfy it. The thirst that cannot as yet be quenched, the compassion with human suffering that cannot as yet be alleviated'; and, using another striking phrase of Deutsch, the potential heartbreak which comes from the fact that 'our eyes can see further than our hands can reach'.[33] The very limitations which are involved in any doctrine of Kenosis make the very stuff of Tragedy. In fact, by all the canons of this particular form of human experience, it can be claimed that Jesus in his suffering and death is the central figure of great tragedy, at Caesarea Philippi, on the hill overlooking Jerusalem, in Gethsemane, on Golgotha. And just as in the highest aesthetic experience of the Tragic, the Infinite and the finite, the Order which is all encompassing and the passion which somehow breaks through it, the perfection of Beauty and the awfulness of human suffering, are brought together into a temporary reconciliation, so we may claim that as man exposes himself, with openness and longing, to the story of the Passion and Crucifixion of Jesus in all its tragic splendour, he will experience aesthetically the Reconciliation which is eternal in its relevance and significance. In this particular area of

33. *Tragedy is not Enough*, pp. 17–18.

human apprehension the resurrection of the spirit seems more important than the resurrection of the body, spiritual grandeur more impelling than bodily revivification.

To speak of experiencing reconciliation aesthetically may seem to be narrowing the reference of the work of Christ to the comparatively few—those, it may be said, whose aesthetic sensibilities are unusually keen and who may be open to an emotional experience of this kind. Is it not the *moral* experience which is all-important? Is it not in the area of *moral* estrangement that men of every class and race find themselves sharing a common predicament and needing a common salvation? But this is surely not a matter of a strict either-or. Without in any way denying the urgency of the moral question we may at the same time recognize the universality of emotional experience and the need for the resolution of discords and for the drawing together of warring sentiments into some kind of satisfying unity. There may be wider varieties of aesthetic experience than of moral, the relation of the moral to the religious may seem more obvious than is the case with the aesthetic, but that both aesthetic and moral needs must be met within any doctrine of reconciliation which claims to be universal and comprehensive seems to me unquestionable.

What then are some of the emotional needs to which I refer? I have spoken a good deal of catharsis in the course of this chapter and this may have given an unduly negative emphasis to the experience of aesthetic reconciliation. But catharsis does not imply a simple wiping of the slate clean, a removal of an uncomfortable sense of having been soiled through involvement in unworthy and unpleasant aspects of the life of humanity. It does indeed imply (in the words of Karl Jaspers) 'cleansing us of all that in our everyday experience is petty, bewildering and trivial—all that narrows us and makes us blind' but this only in order that we may become more keenly receptive to reality, may respond to the claim of ultimate beauty and truth. As we become not merely spectators but involved participants in some tragic form we may feel the terror, we may experience the pity, but these emotions will be cleansed of their meanness and one-sidedness and brought nearer to that 'majestic sadness' which Racine regarded as the form of aesthetic reconciliation most to be desired.

In the various attempts which have been made to analyse this particular experience two notes constantly recur. On the one side there is the stress upon the recognition (which comes through participation in the tragic form) of a transcendent *orderliness*, however mysterious and inscrutable, which governs the universe.

This recognition leads to the feeling of awe but also to the feeling of exultation. Fear may be present but it is transformed into a kind of ecstasy. Beyond the horror and the disaster there are glimpses of transcendent glory. Through this recognition, the almost unbearable strain which comes from looking steadily at the sufferings of humanity, begins to be resolved into a feeling that the universe is not an anarchy of uncontrolled forces but an infinitely mysterious movement towards the goal of ultimate harmony. This on the one side. On the other side there is the emphasis upon the recognition (again through participation in the tragic form) of a heroic *defiance*, defiance of immediate circumstances, defiance of penultimate authorities, even defiance of every human definition of the transcendent universal order. Such defiance inevitably leads to suffering and agony of soul and the emotion aroused in the beholder is bound to be pity and compassion. Yet this pity too is transformed into a kind of ecstasy. Beyond the pain and the apparent waste there are glimpses of a sublimity which endures. Through this recognition, the strain which comes from looking steadily at what appears to be undeserved suffering begins to be resolved into a feeling that all suffering passes, the experience gained through suffering endures for ever.

Transcendent order exciting feelings of awe and exultation: heroic defiance exciting feelings of compassion and ecstasy. And the very inexorability of the order is mysteriously related to the inner freedom of the defiance within the full tragic experience.[34] Perhaps Allardyce Nicoll has, I think, come very near to expressing the essential pattern of tragic feeling when he writes:

> 'When we have witnessed an adequate performance of a great tragic drama, we do not leave the theatre cast down and in despair. There may be no "reconciliation" for the central hero, who stands as an image of mankind; Macbeth may go to his death a man utterly damned and Othello may be forced to take his own life; but, even so, our spirits are not made despondent. Even although we may be left with a feeling of waste, a great sense of emptiness, there comes a reconciliation for ourselves, if not for persons in the play; and the source of this reconciliation seems to arise from the fact that, amid the contrasting passions aroused by the tragic action, we are left with a profound impression of the universe, not as kindly or inimical or indifferent towards man, but rather as something inscrutable, obeying laws of its

34. Commenting on James Joyce's famous interpretation of Aristotle's definition in terms of 'whatsoever is grave and constant in human sufferings', Joseph Campbell writes: 'Tragedy transmutes suffering into rapture by altering the focus of the mind. Released from attachment to one's mortal part through a contemplation of the grave and constant in human sufferings . . . one is united, simultaneously, in tragic pity with the "human sufferer" and in tragic terror with "the secret cause".' (J. Campbell: *The Masks of God*, p. 50).

own beyond our imperfect understanding. It is the mystery of the world which tragedy presents to us—not the feeble and facile mystery beloved by a Maeterlinck, but a mystery strong and profound.'[35]

Against such a general background it is possible to express the Christian doctrine of reconciliation in tragic terms. Again and again the Biblical writers bear witness to the majestic ordering of human history by the Divine Providence. 'The definite plan and foreknowledge of God' (Acts 2:23) excites awe and exultation.

'O the depth of the riches and wisdom and knowledge of God! How unsearchable are His judgments and how inscrutable His ways!' (Romans 11:33).

On the other side there is a persistent witness to the heroic determination of God's Servant.

I gave my back to the smiters, and my cheeks to those who pulled out the beard;
I hid not my face from shame and spitting.
I have set my face like a flint,
And I know that I shall not be put to shame (Isaiah 50:6–7).

I have a baptism to be baptized with;
And how I am constrained until it is accomplished (Luke 12:50).

And they were on the road, going up to Jerusalem, and Jesus was walking ahead of them and they were amazed and those who followed were afraid. And He began to tell them . . . Behold we are going up to Jerusalem; and the Son of Man will be delivered to the chief priests and the scribes: and they will mock him and spit upon him and scourge him and kill him (Mark 10:32–34).

Shall I not drink the cup which the Father has given me? (John 18:11).

Such heroism aroused the compassion both of his own kins-women and of the bystanders who watched him as he went forth bearing his cross. But it also aroused a kind of ecstatic outburst when outsiders scarcely knowing what they were saying cried out:

'Here is the Man' ('the heavenly Man, the Son of Man'[36]) (John 19:5).
'Truly this man was the Son of God' (Mark 15:39).

and when the man who became his devoted follower summed up his own feelings in the characteristic paradox:

'Far be it from me to glory except in the cross of our Lord Jesus Christ by which the world has been crucified to me and I to the world' (Galatians 6:14).

Thus the two essential elements of the tragic vision confront one another, as it were, in a polar tension of ultimate dimensions in the

35. A. Nicoll: *The Theatre and Dramatic Theory*, p. 107.
36. C. H. Dodd: *Historical Tradition in the Fourth Gospel*, p. 98.

Biblical record of the suffering of God's chosen Servant. Here is the archetypal tragic drama of the ages. There is no formal or rational resolution of the polarity. But time and again when the Passion Story has been read or sung or re-enacted in drama or liturgy those participating in the recital have been *arrested* (the word used by James Joyce in his description of tragic experience), *purified* (in the pattern of Aristotle's *catharsis*), *transfigured* (a favourite word of St. Paul). In a mysterious way, every presentation of authentic tragic experience leads to a certain metamorphosis. In the presentation of the supreme Tragedy of the ages there can be the most wonderful transformation of all—the rebirth into the likeness of Him Who 'in the days of his flesh, offered up prayers and supplications, with loud cries and tears, to him who was able to save him from death, and was heard for his godly fear. Although he was a Son, he learned obedience through what he suffered; and being made perfect he became the source of eternal salvation to all who obey Him' (Hebrews 5: 7–9).

For in a real sense the tragic drama must be enacted again and again in and through the experience of individual Christians and of the corporate society which is called the Body of Christ. So St. Paul could speak of completing in his flesh 'what is lacking in Christ's afflictions for the sake of his body, that is, the church' (Colossians 1: 24). St. Augustine could declare that 'Christ continues still to suffer in His members, that is, in us—The full measure of the Passion will not be complete until the end of the world'. Pascal in still more striking language could say that 'Jesus will be in agony until the end of the world' while in our own day Ignazio Silone has called us to remember that 'in the sacred history of man on earth it is still, alas, Good Friday'. Here is the authentic voice of *Christian* tragedy. Here is one pathway of interpretation of the Christian doctrine of atonement which, it may be claimed, leads to an ever increasing illumination upon the dark and seemingly meaningless elements in the experience of mankind.

CHAPTER V

THE DECISIVE JUDGMENT

Second Parable

Every human society, in the course of its historical development, constructs a system of laws to preserve the harmony and security of the community. Yet such a system is only necessary because of the clash of individual or group interests within the social whole and because of the constant danger of social disintegration through some form of excess, positive or negative, on the part of its members. Experience has shown, however, that no system is able to curb 'the unruly wills and affections of sinful men' completely. Breaches of law constantly occur and means have to be devised to uphold the sanctity of the system and to repair its broken-ness. Normally this takes the form of penalty imposed upon the offender—corporal punishment, fine, imprisonment, even death. Through such a system of sanctions, it is believed, order is restored and the authority of the law is vindicated.

On a wider universal scale there is need for some means by which an all-inclusive reckoning can be made and a critical vindication of the majesty of the total system of law can be provided. It is the Christian claim that such a comprehensive reparation has in fact been made by the Son of Man, the representative man, the one who acts inclusively on behalf of an anarchic and disordered world. Living within a particular social order and submitting himself to its laws, He shouldered the vast weight of lawlessness inherited from the past and accepted in his own body the crushing judgment which involvement in the human situation entails. He died once for all (the ultimate penalty), the just for the unjust, that He might restore His fellow members within the total human society to a full relationship with God. By Himself submitting to judgment, He has brought justification to the many.

A

At the beginning of Chapter IV, I drew attention to a rough distinction between what I called on the one hand 'custom' and on the other 'formal law'. Custom is concerned with places and objects, times and seasons, animals and people, which it is wise either to avoid or to treat with particular caution. Mystery is involved. Often there is foreboding and apprehension. A man ignores taboo at his peril.

Yet from time to time there cannot fail to be breaches of taboo. Through negligence or ignorance on the part of certain members of the community the life of the whole body corporate may be endangered. Even more serious, through the foolish assumption on the part of some ill-intentioned person that he could 'get away with it', plague or famine or pestilence may bring untold distress to the land. Then it may appear that the whole society—its living members, its land, its possessions—has become *defiled*. At all costs the source of uncleanness must be expunged. By direct action or by ritual representation the cause of offence is purged away—expelled into a waste place or into the uninhabited desert or into the fire or into the fearsome abode of the departed. We have looked at some of the more refined ways in which the fundamental motif of purification has been worked out. 'Custom' and the expiation of the breach of 'custom' belong to the pattern of human life-in-society wherever found.

But besides the obligations associated with taboo and long-established custom, there have been other obligations formulated more explicitly and precisely in *traditional law*. As soon, it would appear, as man tried to establish any kind of communal existence it became necessary to establish certain rules of behaviour for the ordering of the living society. Gods and ancestors might also be involved but the ordering of inter-human relationships in response to the demands of a particular habitat normally provided patterns whose reference could be extended to relationships with super-natural beings. For an impressive picture of the place of formulated law in the life of a primitive society I turn to an enquiry already mentioned in Chapter IV—Dr. Pospisil's careful examination of the system of law governing the social relations of the Kapauku Papuans.

In this system—and probably within all similar systems—four basic elements are involved. In the first place, by an almost automatic process, a particular individual assumes authority within a society and his authority is recognized by all who desire to remain together within this social complex. Experimental psychologists assure us today that even amongst animals a certain authority is accorded to a particular member of the herd. Superior age, superior strength, superior natural gifts—these are obvious qualifications for headship. In the case of man, however, other factors operate—

continuity within family or class, superiority in wealth or wisdom. But by whatever processes the authority of an individual comes to be established, it is this authority which makes formal law possible. The authority gives decisions, these decisions are accepted and obeyed, the precedent thus established is preserved and extended and gradually a body of laws comes into existence.

The second attribute grows immediately out of the first. If the authority makes a purely *ad hoc* decision to meet some isolated circumstance this is not regarded as law. But wherever there is an intention of universal and permanent application within the affairs of the society, there law is established. Man always gains security by being able to appeal to precedent and to a certain width of social acceptance. Intention to repeat in substantially the same form is therefore a second basic attribute of given law.

The third is of crucial importance. It is best designated, perhaps, by the Latin term *obligatio*—a term which contains within itself the image of binding. Those who are content to live within the protection of the law are entitled to certain rights: they are also subject to certain duties. The harmonious ordering of any society depends upon an open knowledge of what the group as a whole expects from the individual, of what the individual can rightly expect from the other members of the group. Adjustments and adaptations have constantly been made in the course of man's historical progress but every society which has attained stability has done so by communicating to its members as clearly as possible the terms of the *obligatio* within which all are bound.

The fourth attribute Dr. Pospisil describes as *sanction*. This term includes all the means by which the obligatio is upheld and maintained. There may, for example, be the infliction of physical pain or the withdrawal of privilege if rules have been contravened. 'In Kapauka society, the psychological sanction of public reprimand and the resulting ostracism is, except for capital punishment, more feared than any type of physical sanction.' Obviously the assumption behind the imposing of sanction is that it will ideally prevent the breaking of the law or, in the event of the law having been broken, will serve to repair the breach and strengthen the fabric for the future. It is in this area that the most urgent questions relating to law are being asked today and these will demand our consideration at a later stage.

If it be granted that these four attributes belong to all formulated legal systems—an authority capable of promulgating and applying law, an intention towards universalizing law, an *obligatio* defining rights and duties within law and a sanction regulating penalties following breaches of the law—it follows that each must gain proper recognition when the attempt is made to set forth the process of Atonement in forensic or judicial terms.

B

From these general reflections I turn to the particular legal systems which had gained a widely acknowledged authority in the world to which the Christ came. They were in fact two of the most notable systems to appear within the whole social development of mankind. On the one hand a small collection of nomadic tribes, cradled in the fertile crescent of the Eastern Mediterranean, had maintained its essential identity in the face of all manner of hostile attacks and communal disasters, largely as the result of its recognition of the place of the Divine Law in its social life. The Law of God enshrined in the Old Testament Scriptures and elaborated in subsidiary writings constituted one of the major systems with which the emerging Christian movement had to come to terms.

On the other hand a collection of agricultural clans, cradled in the Italian peninsula, had risen to the heights of imperial power, and Rome was now mistress of the Mediterranean world. Throughout this period of development the Romans had displayed a particular genius for organization and this expressed itself above all in the growth of their legal system. Roman Law was the second major system with which Christianity would sooner or later have to come to terms. In order to gain some appreciation of the framework of legal ideas within which early Christian teachers necessarily operated as they sought to expound their faith I propose to describe briefly the outstanding characteristics of these two systems.

To discover the basic motif of the Jews' legal system we need to penetrate far back in history to their early existence as nomads in the semi-desert areas between the Nile and the Euphrates. Nomads have no desire to possess lands on which they can build houses and establish farms. They claim indeed a proprietary right of possession in regard to wells and pastures but arrangements to share or exchange these with other clans can easily be made. Their chief dependence is on the flocks and herds under their care and the pattern of their communal life is largely determined by the need to move from one oasis to another. To ensure reasonable mobility the unit of society (a family or group of families) needs to remain quite small. On the other hand to ensure protection and safety one tribe needs to be able to rely upon or call upon the help of another in times of emergency. Hence the fundamental necessity for pacts or promises or agreements if life and possessions are to be preserved and some degree of security enjoyed. The significant, even exciting events in nomadic existence are the *meetings*, the encounters with kinsmen, the renewals of friendship with other tribes, the enjoyment of hospitality and the sharing in common feasts.

Authority amongst nomads, then and now, finds its focus in the sheikh, or leader, the man distinguished by his personality, his physical strength, his courage, his skill. The hereditary principle does not necessarily operate for the tribe usually includes a number of families and if a particular individual is seen to possess the necessary qualities to an outstanding degree he is readily acclaimed as leader of the group. His responsibilities then include the giving of judgment where matters of internal dispute arise, the planning and directing of military operations and above all the making of covenants on behalf of himself and his followers. These covenants or agreements may be with the leaders of other tribal units. Still more important, they may be with a tribal deity. Through a covenant something is given, something is received. Normally one party involved in the covenant is stronger or richer than the other and pledges his protection and his responsibility to provide for special needs: the weaker pledges on his part the use of his own resources for the sake of the other's good, and promises faithful co-operation whenever called upon to do so. Thus when a tribe enters into a covenant with a particular deity it believes that it will be assured of his protection and favour: the members of the tribe on their part pledge their faithful service and allegiance to this god above.

Where a people exists without settled home, without cultivated land, with only the minimum of goods and chattels the all-important possession is *life* itself. To be robbed or deprived of life is the ultimate disaster. To enhance or to reinforce life is the ultimate blessing. And of all manifestations of life none is more sacred or more treasured than blood. All the members of a tribe share the same blood. Blood-revenge, blood-ceremonials, blood-covenants are of intense significance in nomadic life. When blood is taken, blood must be restored. When blood is shared as in a covenant, the two parties involved are bound together in a common life. It is true that any deprivation of life, e.g. the loss of a limb through violence, must be made good by an exact restitution of life for life. But this is above all true of blood. Only when blood has been restored can conditions of peace be re-established.

For men of the desert, living as they do under constant threat either from natural forces—the storm, the burning sun, hunger and thirst—or from human rivals and enemies, the most dastardly of all sins is that of treachery or unfaithfulness. Failure to come to the aid of fellow-tribesmen in distress, betrayal of those with whom a covenant has been made, neglect to fulfil obligations accepted within the covenant-arrangement, all these are offences of the gravest kind. They cannot be allowed to pass unnoticed. Full and adequate reparation must be made if the harmony of souls within the relationship is to be restored. An eye for an eye, a tooth for a tooth, ultimately a life for a life—the exchange of gifts with all its implications is fundamental in the lives of desert-dwellers and only when that which has been taken away through treachery or unfaithfulness has been restored can justice be satisfied.[1]

Israelite law came at length to be a massive and complicated system. Which of its characteristics were to prove of greatest influence in the later Christian interpretation of atonement? First and foremost God Himself was always conceived as the all-powerful and all-righteous Judge. He did indeed empower His anointed king, His prophets, His judges and His priests to execute judgment and justice on His behalf among the people. But the great issues of the Covenant, of reward for faithfulness to its requirements and retribution for apostasy, of judgment where human wisdom failed and of deliverance where human power was inadequate—these issues remained in the hands and under the direction of God Himself. He, in other words, always remained the final authority.

Further as the vision and historical experience of Israel expanded, as the great empires of the ancient world with their city-building and campaigning came into view, the reference of law was extended and the conviction deepened that ultimately all the nations of the earth must be brought under the suzerainty of the law of Yahweh. The Law had been given to Israel but it was not only designed for Israel. The Law embodied God's will for all peoples in all places and all who disobeyed it would be subjected to His judgment.

Thirdly there is the question of the actual formulation of the Law. Amidst all the developments and elaborations of Israelite law what parts (if any) were to be given special reverence? The Decalogue? The Code of the Covenant as it was re-enacted when the tribes settled in Canaan? The Pentateuch as a whole? Or was there a far simpler crystallization of essential law which could serve to determine man's ultimate relationship to God? According

---

1. Two significant legal institutions, however, eased this demand for exact retribution. (a) A go'el (Leviticus 25 : 47–49) might pay the price on behalf of a neighbour in distress. (b) A surety (Genesis 44 : 32–34) might bear the penalty on behalf of another whose lot seemed hopeless.

to the Gospel-story it was not only Jesus Himself but also a well-informed scribe who judged that the whole Law was summed up in the two requirements of whole-hearted allegiance to God Himself and unqualified devotion to the neighbour. The striking thing about this summary is that it corresponds almost exactly to the ancient terms of the Covenant-relationship in which man was responsible to God and to his neighbours and to those who were within the Covenant. The ultimate sins were apostasy from the living God and breaking faith (by failing to maintain a just system of exchange) with the neighbour. In other words sin was conceived pre-eminently in terms of failure to keep one's promise, to fulfil one's rightful obligations, to honour the Covenant.

How then was the guilt of the sinner to be established? From ancient times customs such as the trial by ordeal or the trial by lot still survived. But in normal experience the judge examined the evidence of witnesses, related it to the requirements of the covenant and decided if the accused was guilty or not. So far as the nation itself was concerned, it was the prophets who bore witness against the wrongs which they saw in its corporate life. But more and more it tended to be assumed that prosperity was the index of guiltlessness, misfortune the index of faithlessness. According as Yahweh bestowed His favour in outward circumstances, so must the state of the inner soul of the nation in reality be.

For at all times in Israel's history the *lex talionis* remained a fundamental assumption within the realm of social morality. Faithfulness to the covenant would bring its own reward in conditions of harmony and well-being: disloyalty or disobedience to the covenant would inevitably bring a retribution equivalent to the injury which had been done. As we have seen, ways were found in the actual administration of law of allowing a compensatory payment to be made or a substitutionary punishment to be borne in the fulfilment of justice. The strict eye for eye, tooth for tooth was occasionally relaxed. Yet the basic principle remained unchanged both in the relations between man and man and between man and God. Every transgression must receive its just retribution: every act of faithfulness its due reward.

In the main, then, law in Israel was based upon a covenant of mutual obligation. Sin was essentially a transgression of this covenant and reparation was essentially a payment of the equivalent of that which had been withheld or an endurance of the equivalent of that which had been inflicted. Yet even in Israel certain voices challenged the strict law of equivalence and claimed that by other means atonement could be made. The question which lay behind every such attempt to reinterpret the strict law of retaliation according to which every action received its due retribution or reward was this: Why do the wicked often seem to prosper, why do the innocent often seem to suffer? Granted that no man or nation is entirely innocent, why does there often seem to be a disparity between the measure of the offence and that of the penalty? Such questions naturally became acute in times of national disaster. Later in Israel's history they became urgent in relation to the individual and his apparently undeserved sufferings. But it is not easy to gauge the effect upon *general* attitudes and ideas of certain important documents which gained a place within the Old Testament Canon.

Foremost amongst these are the so-called Servant Songs of Isaiah. It is now normally assumed that the poet is wrestling with the theme of the sufferings of his own people among the nations of the world. War, pillage, exile, captivity—all have taken their toll. Surely the nation has received the full punishment for its own sins. Yet God is righteous and will not allow any virtue, either of active good or of patient suffering, to remain unrequited. May it not be therefore that Israel, through her extremes of suffering, is bearing the chastisement due to others and making a sacrificial offering for the sins of other peoples? Again the patriarch Job, a representative figure, does not only bear the punishment for his own offences but, through his own integrity, brings succour to his persecutors. Through the soul-wrestlings of psalmists and prophets the rigid law of retribution was questioned and the possibility of some kind of vicarious atonement envisaged.

Another idea of still greater significance began to attain prominence in the period of troubles which began in the second century B.C. and it is this which deserves special attention in that it may have influenced early Christian interpretations of atonement in terms of justice and reparation. As is so often the case when estimating how far Jewish ideas may have formed the background of early Christian thought, great care has to be taken in dating the documents from which evidences are taken. But when full allowances have been made in this respect, it still seems clear that certain notions of transferred merits and substitutionary atonement were current in Jewish circles in the immediate pre-Christian period.

The main source of these ideas seems to have been the impact of the Maccabean persecutions and the heroism of the martyrs who suffered on account of their faithfulness to the religion of their fathers. As a modern historian has expressed it Judaism, in the period of the Maccabees, became a religion of martyrdom. The appalling sufferings inflicted upon those who remained true to their convictions evidently stirred the popular imagination to the depths. And the teachers of the people found in the martyr-stories an occasion to develop thoughts about the meaning of suffering which are of profound significance for every time and place. To bring out the force of this particular contribution I shall quote at some length from H. Wheeler Robinson's sympathetic account in his lectures entitled *The Cross of the Servant*. Defining the general idea as that which saw in the willing acceptance of these unexampled sufferings the offering of a pure priestly devotion to God he goes on to say that 'there is no more impressive example of this attitude than that of the interpreters of the Maccabean martyrdoms. The first Jewish answer to the persecution of Antiochus Epiphanes in the second century before Christ was not the armed revolt of Mattathias and his heroic sons, but the passive endurances of suffering by such men as the aged Eleazar and the seven brethren. They are represented as consciously accepting the sufferings unjustly inflicted by their persecutors as a just recompense for the sins of Israel and as they hope, the final instalment of that recompense due to God: "We are suffering for our own sins and though our living Lord is angry for a little, in order to rebuke and chasten us, he will again be reconciled to his own servants. . . . I, like my brothers, give up body and soul for our father's laws, calling on God to show favour to our nation soon . . . and to let the Almighty's wrath, justly fallen on the whole of our nation, end in me and in my brothers" ' (2 Maccabees 7: 33, 37, 38).

The martyrs do not complain that they, being personally innocent, are involved in the sufferings of guilty Israel; they accept Israel's corporate existence as involving themselves and glory in the opportunity of this service to their brethren. This attitude becomes more clearly articulate in the homiletical treatment of the martyrdoms which forms the so-called Fourth Book of Maccabees:

> Be gracious to thy people, being satisfied with our penalty on their behalf. Make my blood their purification and take my life as the substitute for theirs.
> Because of them the enemy had no more power over our people and the tyrant was punished, and the fatherland purified, inasmuch as they have become a substitute for (the life forfeited by) the sin of the people, and through the blood of those pious men and their propitiatory death, the divine Providence rescued Israel that before was afflicted (4 Maccabees 6: 28, 29; 17: 21, 22).[2]

2. *The Cross in the Old Testament*, p. 94 f. For further references in the Old Testament and the Apocrypha to the martyrs and their sufferings see E. Stauffer, *New Testament Theology*, pp. 331–4.

In these pasages, Robinson urges, the crucial point is the principle of substitution by which one life was to be allowed to replace another, not through some kind of external and arbitrary transaction, but on the ground of the solidarity of the people: the sufferings of the righteous do not redound to their own credit, they are for the benefit and healing of the whole community.

This idea, developed in days of persecution, can be dangerous if extended too widely for it can easily imply that a treasury of merits is available for those who care to reckon on it. W. D. Davies in his discussion of the Doctrine of Merits as it appears in Rabbinical Literature[3] shows that opinions amongst the Rabbis were divided and that whereas some were inclined to glorify the fathers for their merits which procured redemption and absolution for their descendants, others warned their contemporaries in the manner of John the Baptist not to presume on the good deeds of Abraham as if these alone would suffice for their own justification. The question of dating again presents difficulties and it is not certain how far ideas which definitely appear in the second century A.D. were already current at the beginning of the Christian era. But that the general notion of the possibility of receiving benefit through the noble deeds of the Jewish Fathers or through the self-sacrifice of the Jewish martyrs by a kind of transference of merit was in the air as early as the first century B.C. seems relatively certain. After a thorough-going examination of the dates of the extant documents John Downing can conclude that 'at the time of Jesus, people thought in terms of human beings making atonement for others by means of their sufferings and death'.[4] And of all those who proved themselves worthy to make such an atonement none occupied a higher place in the esteem of their contemporaries than did the martyrs, the representative men who had voluntarily given up their lives even unto the death on behalf of God and His truth.

Let me now try to sum up the contribution of Hebrew law to

3. *Paul and Rabbinic Judaism*, p. 268 ff. Cp. R. Bultmann in *Theology of the N.T.I.*, p. 12, 'A statute, unlike an ethical demand, can never embrace every specific situation of life; instead there inevitably remain many cases unprovided for, cases for which there is no command or prohibition; that leaves room not only for every desire and passion that may arise but also—and that again is characteristic of Judaism—for works of supererogation. In principle, when a man's duties are conceived of as the committing or omitting of specific acts under legal requirements, he can completely discharge them and have room left over for extra deeds of merit. So there developed in Judaism the notion of "good works" that go beyond the required fulfilment of the Law (such as almsgiving, various acts of charity, voluntary fasting, and the like) establishing literal merits and hence also capable of atoning for transgression of the Law.'

4. *J.T.S.*, XIV, p. 284.

the complex of categories available for the interpretation of atonement in Christian terms. As we have seen, the basic concept retained throughout the history of the Hebrew people was that of strict retaliation. Every sinful act must receive due retribution: every righteous act must receive a just reward. The whole complex of relationships between individuals and tribes is structured according to this principle. An eye for an eye, a life for a life, blood for blood.[5] Even in a document as late as the Wisdom of Solomon, although chapters 1–10 seem to modify the age-old teaching, the second portion of the book (chapters 11–19) returns to it with renewed emphasis.[6] The punishments which God exacts, it is taught, are extraordinarily appropriate, and the misfortunes which befall men are in no wise arbitrary. For 'by measure and number and weight Thou (O God) didst order all things' (11: 20). The river Nile turned by God to clotted blood was His vengeance upon the Egyptians for their slaughter of the Israelite babes, for 'by what things a man sins by these he is punished' (11: 16).[7] According to such a doctrine the only way by which atonement can be made is by restoring the exact equivalent for whatever has been taken away, the imposition of an exact degree of pain and distress for whatever hurt has been inflicted.

Yet it is equally clear that in all kinds of ways attempts were being made to reinterpet this principle of strict equivalence under the pressure of circumstances. First there was the question of what seemed to be the excessive suffering of the people as a whole. Granted that the nation had sinned and deserved to be carried into exile: surely their oppressors were greater sinners and surely there must come a time when the length and rigour of the punishment had more than compensated for the offence. Secondly there was the problem of the sufferings of those who seemed to be finest of the nation's heroes, particularly the martyrs. Granted that even they were not sinless: yet surely their sufferings were of a different order of magnitude compared with what might have been anticipated as a just equivalent. To safeguard the main principle and yet to cover those apparent exceptions appeal was made to two subsidiary ideas:

5. 'The necessity of vengeance for blood shed is a theme running right through the Old Testament. Job asks that the earth may not cover his blood (16: 18) because he feels he has been condemned unjustly and that it will cry for vengeance. Ezekiel tells the people of Jerusalem that their blood will soak into the earth and be forgotten; whereas the blood they have shed will be on the rock so that it will have to be avenged (24: 7).' (J. Downing in *J.T.S.*, XIV, p. 283.)

6. It may be by a different author.

7. O. S. Rankin: *Israel's Wisdom Literature*, p. 112.

(a) The balancing of accounts might not be made within a single generation, nor even within the third and fourth generation. The final reparation might take place within a totally different order of things—a new heaven and a new earth in which the righteous would enjoy a final reward and from which the unrighteous would be for ever excluded.

(b) The balancing might not be made within the strict context of the nation's or the individual's own welfare. Seeing that all souls are bound together within the one bundle of life, the merits of one might be transferred to another, the suffering due to one might be borne by another.

> But surely our sicknesses *he* bore
>   And our pains—he carried them:
> Whilst *we* thought him stricken,
>   Smitten and afflicted by God.
> But *he* was pierced through our rebellions
>   Crushed through our iniquities;
> The chastisement bringing us welfare was on him,
>   And by the stripes he bore there was healing for us.[8]

Once such a possibility had been accepted into the general stock of Israel's moral ideas, a change had been made which was to affect the interpretation of atonement in the whole subsequent history of mankind.

C

I turn to the legal system of Rome. Commenting on the greatness of Roman law as an historical phenomenon Fritz Schulz has written, 'Roman law is the purest expression of the Roman nature and the most powerful witness to the greatness and glory of Rome'.[9] And as he contemplated its influence upon the history of Europe John Buchan wrote: 'The Romans as a race had legal genius and their juristic conceptions, elaborated early in the Republic and codified by the great jurisprudents of the later empire were the foundation of the law of the mediaeval and modern worlds'.[10] That Roman law has greatly affected the development of Christian thinking on the atonement there can be little doubt. I intend therefore to glance briefly at its early history and fundamental motifs before coming to a description of the imperial legal system within which the early Church, especially in its missionary outreach, had to operate.

8. Wheeler Robinson's translation.
9. F. Schulz: *Principles of Roman Law*, p. 253.
10. J. Buchan: *Augustus*, p. 226.

In contrast to the Hebrews who were first and last a pilgrim people, nurtured in desert encampments and accustomed to constant journeyings with their flocks and herds, the Romans were a settled people, nurtured in the fields and farmsteads of the Italian peninsula and ever concerned to build up a more stable and more extensive civilization. The whole social structure was based on an agricultural economy though in course of time commercial interests increased as trade with the other peoples of the Mediterranean world developed. And in this agricultural economy the basic and all-important unit was the household under the *pater familias* who at all times exercised an unusual authority.

To gain a general picture of this household we can best envisage a rectangular strip of land with a home (a kind of wigwam) established on it. At the centre of the home was the hearth and around this all the activities of family life revolved. Included in the family were not only the parents and their children but also servants, retainers, the household gods and the possessions in kind. The *pater familias*, inspired and empowered by the divine Genius of the family, held absolute and final authority not only in disciplining the community but even in final matters of life and death. He was not normally a tyrant but gained authority as judge partly because of his knowledge of tradition, partly because of an ingrained respect on the part of the Roman for the powers governing his universe, human and divine. 'Over all the human beings whose place was in this little social world various degrees of power were wielded by the father at its head; and though there were certain limitations in its exercise which it was customary for him to observe, in reality to all alike he came near to being absolute master.'[11]

A farm of this kind was in most respects a self-contained unit. By tilling the soil a reasonable food supply could be assured and simple processes of exchange could deal with surpluses or deficiencies. Yet there were tracts of land which were uncultivable and could best be used for common grazing: there were rights of way needed for access to water or upland pastures: there were calls to expand with growing populations: there were disputes over boundaries: in all these ways the smallholder was to find that he could not lead a completely isolated existence. And as soon as decisions had to be made about property rights, ownership of chattels and boundary demarcations it became obvious that something more than the authority of a single *pater familias* was required. Recourse might be had to the strong arm of one man enforcing his rights against another but such a system, especially where land is concerned,

11. Hugh Last in *The Legacy of Rome*, p. 214.

ultimately becomes ruinous. Instead the principle of arbitration was accepted, the recognition, that is, of one empowered to judge between the claims of rivals and in some sense therefore to stand above them and decide.

The picture now begins to appear of Roman law as a living organism, intimately related to the land, its needs, its cycles, its productivity: intimately related also to the family group, its divisions of status and responsibility, its duties to higher powers, human or divine. It is essentially, as Schulz has pointed out, a Law of Nature.[12] 'The Roman jurists' aim is to find—within the specified framework— the rule arising out of the nature of the thing itself, out of conditions as they are.' In matters of possession and ownership, sale and hire, contract and liability, 'it may be observed that legal writers are not satisfied with describing the positive Roman law in force at the time but that they are at pains to evolve a law of Nature. This is the determining cause for the peculiar manner in which legal science is presented; it does not actually prove the rules stated, but derives them direct from the contemplation of life.' In fact the rules and prescriptions are never regarded as products of the human mind, gradually established through experiments and experience; rather they are regarded as objective realities with which the human mind becomes increasingly acquainted through long association. Thus they take on the character of axioms or theorems in a mathematical system. They belong to the very constitution of the order of Nature and man's ongoing task is to acquaint himself more fully with them and to apply them within the changing circumstances of his social life.

The obvious implication of such a view is that Law itself is the final authority. Law governs the fertility and the sowing and the harvesting and the division and the appropriation of land: Law governs the times and seasons, day and night, summer and winter, days of fasting and days of feasting, days of favour and days of ill-fortune: Law governs relationships between humans, between men and animals, between men and the gods: Law governs actions and arrangements of all kinds. The father, the magistrate, the emperor interprets and administers this Law—he certainly does not create it. For the time being he exercises authority in saying what should be done in a particular instance but the Law is before him and above him and will be after him. It is a system of eternal principles inherent in the natural order, waiting to be formulated openly, with a kind of scientific detachment, in relation to every particular case.

12. Op. cit., p. 35.

As far as human beings themselves are concerned all are subject to a comprehensive *obligatio* which binds them together within one organic whole. This implies for every one a duty 'to convey something or do something or provide something' (Paulus, third century A.D.): the context is fundamentally that of an agricultural community organized within a co-operative whole. The obligations are unquestioned for unless they are fulfilled disintegration takes place and the land returns to waste. Yet the obligations have to be more clearly defined as the community grows and as disputes or questions arise. And provision above all has to be made for the settling of disputes and the punishment of wrongdoing. At an early stage man found that direct vengeance within a closed and united context was dangerous to and wasteful of the life of the whole community.[13] Hence arose the concern for indirect satisfaction through some form of compensation or composition. A money payment or a transfer of possessions might be agreed. If this transfer was not made immediately a hostage might be held or a surety appointed to guarantee that the wrong would be righted. Every failure to fulfil the necessary *obligatio* carried an appropriate penalty which had to be publicly declared: then the penalty would be inflicted and satisfaction obtained either directly or through compensation or through a substitute or through a surety guaranteeing future redress. Wrongdoing is essentially failure to fulfil obligations within the one organic society. Reparation is made by means of an appropriate act either of offering compensation or of enduring pain.

Roman punishments included banishment from the life of the community either to some distant territory or to the realm of death itself: beating: degradation of status: restraint of freedom: deprivation of lands, possessions or wealth. Every offence carried an exact and appropriate penalty and only when this had been imposed could peace be restored to the life of the whole society. The penalty must not be diminished but neither must it be exceeded. There was no savagery or wantonness allowed in establishing order under Roman Law. And in one respect punishments of all kinds could be mitigated and made easier to bear. This was through the existence in Roman society of the institution of friendship (*amicitia*), a voluntary association between man and man or between family and family through which one person would go to extraordinary lengths in accepting responsibility on behalf of another.

13. It has been another matter with strangers. Not yet has the world discovered itself to be a single organic community within which direct internecine vengeance is utterly wasteful and self-defeating.

Once a bond of friendship had been established, a man felt himself bound at whatever cost to support his partner in time of need. 'When it is noted how frequent *cautiones* were under Roman law, for the most part necessitating the personal guarantee of a third party, the modern observer is inclined to wonder how it was possible to obtain so many people willing to stand surety. For the Romans this presented no problem: to go bail for a friend was as much part of the *officium* as it was a matter of course for the friend in Schiller's poem. The giving of sureties and pledges too, which was obligatory for contracts with the censors, presupposed friends and patrons ready to spring into the breach and undertake the charge. Lastly, the institution of the *consilium* (a group of men consulted by the magistrate when making judgments) which permeates all Roman life, is inconceivable without a large group of friends and patrons whom one is allowed to burden with serious matters of business, who even expect to be consulted. The authority of this *consilium* is thus explained; certainly it was possible to ignore the advice given, but that would have entailed offending one's friends. They would withdraw and in the end one would be left alone.'[14] But to be left alone was unthinkable within a closely integrated society. If one member suffered, others suffered with him: if one prospered, others shared his prosperity. Law itself was a vast interlocking system of principles of obligation. The ideal society would be one in which all showed forth these principles in disciplined public action.

What applied to the relations between man and man applied also (though with less possibilities of elaboration) to relations between men and the gods. Essentially men had obligations to fulfil towards their divine patrons and reparations to make where there had been negligence or mistake. The medium by which these responsibilities were carried out was that of sacrifice accompanied by prayer—and sacrifices were of various categories. There was the *lustratio*, a ceremony designed to protect the home or the family or the city from any evil influence, in which circumambulations preceded the offering of the victims. More commonly the *sacrificium* was enacted, devoting portions of the animals to the gods by a holocaust on the altar and portions to the worshippers for their consumption. Prayers were appointed for recitation and any slip or mistake had to be atoned for by another offering. The chief means of atonement for offences was the *piaculum*, a compensation which belonged to the god by right and normally included blood. All these sacrifices were strictly objective public acts whose details were prescribed by traditional religious law and whose efficacy

14. Schulz: op. cit., p. 237.

depended in no way upon the participation of the people at large. Authorized representatives offered the appropriate sacrifices while others simply refrained from work. The offering was according to the Law of Nature and the effects were believed to accrue automatically by the same Law. All was concerned with the maintenance of harmonious interchange in the total society. Sacrifice was the appointed means to that end.

D

I have dwelt at length on certain basic features of these two great ancient systems of law, the Hebrew and the Roman, in order to indicate differences between them and in order to raise the question how far New Testament interpretations of atonement are dependent upon them. I want now to record my own conviction that there is no evidence that New Testament writers took over *Roman* legal concepts when seeking to draw out the meaning of the Cross and Resurrection. The Roman power was an occupying power in Palestine and its prescriptions were only grudgingly fulfilled. There was no inclination whatsoever to view its prescriptions as constituting a model for the Divine ordering of mankind. Even when Christianity gained a foothold in the Roman colonies of the Mediterranean world and in the imperial city itself, Christians still regarded themselves as living under an alien régime, a régime indeed which might provide a framework of ordered social life but which might also become a cruel and oppressive persecutor of the faithful.

It is true that a succession of passages in the New Testament enjoin obedience to the Roman authority in matters which do not touch the religious conscience. The chief of these would seem to have been rioting and turbulent behaviour on the one hand, refusal to pay taxes on the other. Jesus' counsel to render to Caesar that which is demanded as tribute is echoed in Romans 13, a chapter which in its general tenor occupies a unique place amongst the writings of the New Testament. But apart from these passages there are only brief references in 1 Peter and the Pastorals to submission to Roman authority and it can be assumed with some confidence that the Roman system as such played little part in the Christian imagination. If it was simply a matter of maintaining public peace and supporting essential public services the Christian was advised to perform what was asked of him without cavilling. If, however, larger claims should be made, involving the offering of allegiance of a religious kind, then the battle must be joined and resistance must, if necessary, be to the death.

It is interesting that even in such a chapter as Romans 13 where Paul gives his most extended treatment of the Christian's duties to the state, he moves straight on to another system of law which was supremely important for him and never far from his thoughts. This was the Mosaic Law in which he had been reared, and whose splendour he continued to recognize. This system had borne witness to God and His righteous demands. But had the Righteousness of God been finally revealed in and through the Law? It is the dominant purpose of Paul in chapters 1–3 of the Epistle to the Romans to answer this question.

In brief his answer runs along these lines: The Jews, God's Covenant people, possess a Law which is the fullest revelation of His will hitherto made known to men. Its precepts and prohibitions provide the Jew with an altogether comprehensive code to indicate what he must and must not do. If he were able to keep these injunctions in their entirety, he would live by the law and be capable of responding to God's righteous demands through the law. But in point of fact no one has proved able to obey the Mosaic law in its entirety. Instead the very opposite is true. All have broken the law and stand under judgment, guilty in the sight of God.

What then of the Gentiles who have no knowledge of the Mosaic Law? Paul will not admit that they are 'without law'. 'For what can be known about God is plain to them, because God has shown it to them. Ever since the creation of the world his invisible nature, namely, his eternal power and deity, has been clearly perceived in the things that have been made' (Romans 1: 19–20). Here was a law, not indeed as clear and explicit as the Mosaic law, but still sufficient to leave men without excuse. Fundamentally it summoned men to honour and give thanks to the Creator, acknowledging Him as the governor of the universe and following in their lives the pattern of his revealed will. But again no man anywhere had given the full obedience thus demanded. An individual might have instinctively obeyed some of the requirements but this could not save him from the ultimate verdict of guilty. All men, Jew and Gentile alike, have broken the law of God. All have disobeyed His revealed will, all are unrighteous, all stand under His judgment. Whatever may be said about the processes of Paul's thinking there can be no doubt about his final conclusion. 'All the words of the law are addressed . . . to those who are within the pale of the law, so that no one may have anything to say in self-defence but the whole world may be exposed to the judgment of God' (Romans 3: 19, N.E.B.).

If then all stand under condemnation as having refused obedience and allegiance to God, what punishment must they expect to receive? What is the end of apostacy and lawlessness? There can be only one answer—death. 'Death spread to all men because all men sinned' (Romans 5: 12). That which had been ordained when man was first created—'you shall not eat for in the day that you eat of it you shall die' (Genesis 2: 17) has inevitably found its fulfilment in every member of the human race.[15] All have sinned, all share the condemnation of death: a death moreover, which 'is conceived not merely biologically but theologically or, if the expression may be allowed, *sacramentally*: that is, biological death is the sign or symbol of the extinction of man's spiritual life in God'.[16] However complex the argument of Romans 3–7 may at times appear, this recurring theme never loses its emphasis. All mankind is guilty in the presence of the righteous God Who made known His nature and His will both through the things that have been made and through the law that was given through Moses. And being guilty, having rejected the righteousness of God, having broken the covenant to which the law bears witness, all are doomed to be rejected by God and to be condemned to final death.

Such was man's situation before the coming of the Messiah. There was no way of redemption, no way of justification through any recognized legal process. The only hope was that God might act in some altogether new way, vindicating his own righteousness and at the same time delivering sinful mankind. In a passage of supreme importance Paul affirms that such a manifestation of God's righteousness has, in fact, taken place. A new era has dawned. The law and its requirements have been superseded. The past and its failures have been overlooked. The future is to be constituted according to a different principle, the principle of faith. Death is to be swallowed up in life.

But such a complete change could not have taken place arbitrarily. God is righteous and whatever action He takes will be a demonstration of His righteousness. Quite clearly the new action which has changed the whole situation is His act of redemption or liberation through Christ Jesus (Romans 3: 24). We have seen at an earlier stage that the concept of redemption was fundamental in the Old Testament. To redeem from slavery was the greatest boon that could be conferred on any man. The redemption from the slavery of Egypt was the greatest event in the whole historical experience of Israel. The future redemption, whether from the

---

15. Cp. 'They know God's decree that those who do such things deserve to die' (1: 32).

16. W. Manson in *New Testament Essays*, p. 189.

servitude of Babylon or from the oppression of more intangible enemies—sin and death—was the radiant hope to which men looked forward. He who had redeemed His people in the past would redeem them again by a still mightier deliverance.

This then at least is certain in the difficult passage Romans 3: 21–25. Paul was convinced that the great redemption upon which the ancient scriptures so often focussed attention had indeed taken place. All men (as he has shown) are shut up under the law and under the due retribution of their sinful deeds. Yet the great redemption has been effected. The prison doors have been flung open. The way of liberation has been revealed. The only requirement on man's side is faith—faith to accept what God has done and to walk out into newness of life. As he is to emphasize again and again in the succeeding chapters, faith is the all-sufficient way by which man can honour God. Abraham believed God, the psalmist believed God: though the cross may appear to be a stumbling block, even foolishness, yet to those who will accept God's action in Christ as the way of redemption and will glorify God by so doing, faith will certainly be counted to them as justification. Being justified by faith they will enjoy peace with God through our Lord Jesus Christ.

But a crucial verse still remains unexplained. What is the significance of 'blood' and 'expiation' in Romans 3: 25? Many answers have been given to this question and a particularly illuminating summary of the chief possibilities may be found in Dr. W. D. Davies's book *Paul and Rabbinic Judaism* (p. 230 ff). The fundamental problem is to determine the most likely background of imagery to which St. Paul was appealing in using these two keywords. His early epistles contain only two references to the blood of Christ—here and in Romans 5: 8–9, and the latter of these may well be a general continuation of the theme set forth in the former.[17] The Greek word now usually translated 'expiation' (*hilasterion*) occurs nowhere else in St. Paul's writings. We cannot therefore appeal to any wider usage of the apostle in this connection. Nor does the general context give any clear guidance. The reference to the new redemption tempts us to think of the blood which was smeared on the houses of the Israelites at the time of the redemption from Egypt or—less obviously—of the blood by which the covenant at Sinai was sealed after the deliverance had taken place. But in neither of these contexts would the reference to 'expiation' seem appropriate.

We are therefore driven back to the one notable place in the

17. I exclude the reference to blood in the eucharistic sections of 1 Corinthians.

Old Testament where 'blood' and 'expiation' are found in close conjunction, the LXX using the two words which here occur in such close relation to one another. This is the account of the great Day of Atonement ceremonies contained in Leviticus 16. At one point in the first Epistle to the Corinthians St. Paul suddenly turns to the imagery of the Passover festival and declares that Christ, the lamb of the new Passover, has been sacrificed for us. It therefore seems entirely possible that he should have suddenly turned here to the imagery of the Day of Atonement, declaring thereby that Christ was made the victim in the new Day of Atonement and that through the shedding and the applying of His blood the new and all-inclusive expiation has been made. Such an interpretation prevents the construction of any neat consistency of imagery for a 'redemption' from bondage does not easily combine with a 'purification' from all uncleanness. Yet a mixture of imagery does not impair the central 'drive' of this vitally important section. Throughout, the dominant motif is to be found in the complete denial that anything that man could do would suffice to save him from the predicament in which all, Jew and Gentile alike, are involved. All without exception are unrighteous, alienated, that is, from the favour of a righteous God. All are helpless to justify themselves, to restore themselves, that is, to a right relation with God. Nevertheless—and here we are at the heart of Paul's Gospel— what man could in no wise do, God actually did out of his own gracious initiative. He it was who came to the rescue with a new redemption effected through His Messiah, Jesus. He it was who openly set forth a new means of removing sin, namely the blood of the Messiah crucified. The ransom, the cleansing could now be appropriated by faith. And by faith all could be justified and enjoy peace with God through our Lord Jesus Christ.

But what are the implications of such a claim for the interpretation of atonement in forensic or legalistic terms? First and foremost it implies that the Rabbinic system of Law is rejected as in any way appropriate for the purpose. Nothing could be more definite than the first part of chapter 3 of the Epistle to the Romans. By obedience to the precepts of the Mosaic law as set forth by the Rabbis no flesh can be justified. The whole concept of a total system of rules calling for a total detailed obedience is regarded as having been superseded. It only led men to the final impasse of standing guilty before God with no hope of acquittal. But now, altogether apart from this kind of law, God has intervened to deal with the situation. His act may be described in terms of redemption, that is release from the complete state of enslavement in which mankind was held. There is no necessary thought of a ransom price. Just as Israel was brought out of Egypt by the hand of God acting through His servant Moses so the new Israel has been brought out of its bondage under the Law by the hand of God acting through His servant Jesus. Or again His act may be described in terms of expiation, that is release from the defilement of guilt which mankind had incurred. There is no necessary thought of a sin-offering. Just as the blood of the victim was applied by the High Priest to remove all hindrances to full communion between God and His people, so the blood of the Messiah was given by God as the way of expiating the sins of all the people.

However this double imagery may be interpreted in its details, the ultimate result is clear—it is described as *justification*, a new state of affairs in which God remains just, with His righteousness unimpugned, while man is restored to an unhindered covenant relationship with God made possible by what Jesus has done. Here the most natural link is with the prophetic covenant imagery discussed earlier in this chapter. Man is in a hopeless predicament, for the terms of the covenant have been broken and he is in no position to attempt to put things right. But God, the strong partner in the covenant, takes in hand to restore man and to vindicate him openly. By His act in Christ He demonstrates His own righteousness for He upholds the sanctity of the covenant: at the same time He puts man in the right, He justifies him, simply on the basis of his faith in Jesus. The imagery can be called 'legal' only in so far as 'legal' is held to imply the law expressed in covenant commitments. It is the kind of law which is not concerned with exacting strict equivalents of retribution but rather with graciously restoring to a rightful place in the covenant at a cost which is borne by the initiator himself. In fact I do not find in Paul any doctrine of atonement expressed by modes of comparison drawn either from Roman law or from late Pharisaic and Rabbinic Law. In the developed system of the Rabbis the means of atonement included penitence, fasting, the merits of the fathers, private and public sacrifice and much more. In other words it was by the offering of religious devotions believed to be acceptable to God and in some way compensating for wrong done. But Paul's movement of thought is in exactly the opposite direction. It is God Who comes forth to re-establish the broken relationship by fulfilling His own gracious commitment to men even to the limit of blood and by inviting all who will to accept by faith the atonement which He has made.

The development of Paul's thought in the subsequent chapters of the Epistle to the Romans is along the same lines. References to the blood of Christ (5:9) and to the sin-offering (8:3) are almost certainly to be set within a ritual rather than a legal context. And the contrast between the disobedience of Adam and the obedience of Christ, though set against a background of law and trespass and condemnation, is to be interpreted in terms of the abounding grace of God and the supreme act of righteousness of the incarnate Son rather than in terms of a strict payment for acts of lawlessness. The atmosphere of Romans 5–8 is not that of a law court nor of an adjudication of penalties. Rather it is of an utterly new beginning in human affairs made possible by a refusal to be bound by the strict injunctions of any legal system. The whole emphasis is on man's helplessness, man's alienation, man's hopelessness. It is into this situation that God comes, revealing His love, offering His abundant grace, breaking the bonds of sin and death, establishing righteousness amongst men and opening the path to eternal life. The atmosphere is that of a great deliverance, a dramatic reversal, a glorious vindication. It is not that of penalties being measured out, inflicted, possibly transferred, possibly endured. Certainly the Cross was the supreme vindication of God's righteousness but it was the righteousness of a covenant relationship rather than of a Roman or even of a Palestinian law court.

It is indeed true that in the account of the Year of Jubilee ceremonies in Leviticus 25 the imagery of expiation by blood and that of redemption from bondage are closely intertwined. According to the regulation of Leviticus 25:9 a great proclamation is to be made on the Day of Atonement which falls in the Jubilee Year. Normally the ceremonies of the Day implied the removal of all sins accumulated during the year immediately past. But on this special day in the fiftieth year, everything was to be restored to the *status quo ante*, reckoning back for half a century. All binding commitments which had been imposed during that period, whether upon humans or upon land, were to be remitted. An epoch-making ransom was to be effected. The proclamation was to bring good news both of expiation and release. And the release was to be granted with graciousness and generosity. No hard bargains were to be struck. Ransoms could be paid but no excessive price was to be imposed. The whole atmosphere was to be that of joyful release.

Doubtless the provisions of Leviticus 25 were never fulfilled *au pied de la lettre*. It was a splendid ideal hardly realizable in the harsh conditions of mundane existence. But this did not prevent Jewish interpreters from dwelling upon the picture as a condition to be attained on a still vaster scale in the day of Yahweh's own redemption. In particular the sufferings of martyrs were regarded not only as a sacrifice effecting expiation but also as the means by which the great redemption could be inaugurated. In a vivid reference to the death of the seven martyrs recorded in 4 Maccabees, Ethelbert Stauffer has written: 'Through these martyrs God begins a new epoch in the history of Israel. The Yom Kippur of Leviticus 16 is valid for a year (retrospectively). The great day of atonement of Leviticus 25 is valid for half a century. The death of the seven martyrs is valid for a whole epoch—an epochal day of atonement'.[18] What more natural than that in the early Christian imagination the blood and death of Jesus should have come to be regarded as the supreme, all-inclusive act of expiation by which God had removed the sins of the whole world, the supreme, all-embracing act of redemption by which God had wrought deliverance for a universe enslaved.

Before leaving the subject of the legal framework of Paul's thought about sin and atonement, a brief reference may be made to its eschatological dimension. Paul never loses sight of the Day, the Day of wrath (Romans 2: 5), the Day when God will judge the secret things of men by Jesus Christ (Romans 2: 16). Then 'He will render to every man according to his works: to those who by patience in well-doing seek for glory and honour and immortality, he will give eternal life; but for those who are factious and do not obey the truth, but obey wickedness, there will be wrath and fury' (Romans 2: 6–8). 'Each man's work will become manifest; for the Day will disclose it, because it will be revealed with fire, and the fire will test what sort of work each one has done' (1 Corinthians 3: 13). 'For we must all appear before the judgement seat of Christ, so that each one may receive good or evil, according to what he has done in the body' (2 Corinthians 5: 10).

And indeed this general framework of man's moral history is accepted by writers of Old and New Testaments alike. They may differ in details about the interpretation of the framework—how near or how distant the day of retribution is likely to be, how far judgment will be social and how far individual, how extensive are the possibilities of being absolved from wrongdoing in the period before the final reckoning is made. But that there is a general moral order which is governed by a Righteous Judge who will at some time, in some way, render to every man according to his deeds is never seriously questioned. They were at one in their conviction that the work of Christ was *God's* action, that the division which He evoked was the fore-enacting of *God's* final partition, that His vindication was in very truth their own vindication by *God Himself*,

18. *New Testament Theology*, p. 291.

their justification already before the time came to stand at the final bar of judgment. There are variations of emphasis and of metaphorical description but the notable words of Paul would have been acceptable to all:

'Who shall bring any charge against God's elect? It is God who justifies; who is to condemn? Is it Christ Jesus, who died, yes, who was raised from the dead, who is at the right hand of God, who indeed intercedes for us? I am sure that neither death nor life nor things present nor things to come will be able to separate us from the love of God in Christ Jesus our Lord' (Romans 8:34 ff.).

E

So far our enquiry about the possibility of interpreting the atoning work of Christ in terms of forensic comparisons ready to hand has yielded three main results:

(1) There is no evidence that categories drawn from Roman law were employed in New Testament times though Paul may have been dependent (consciously or unconsciously) upon the Stoic doctrine of the law of nature and the inner law of conscience in building up his argument that the whole world stands guilty before God.

(2) The writers of the New Testament were undoubtedly familiar with the legal conceptions of orthodox Judaism and none more so than Paul himself. They appeal to certain fundamental axioms which would have been accepted by all, e.g. that God judges all men according to their deeds, that a critical day of judgment will ultimately be enacted for all mankind, that death is the natural and inevitable penalty for deliberate disobedience to explicit commands. But they do not accept the varying means of atonement by which, in current Judaism, the sinner could make reparation, though to a degree the work of Christ may have been compared to that of the righteous martyrs of Judaism whose merits, it was held, were effective on behalf of their fellow men.

(3) The most important conception of law belonging to the background of the New Testament interpretation of atonement is that which is derived from what may best be called the prophetic tradition. It appeals to God's covenant with His people, His gracious commitment to them, His concern for them even when they have been unfaithful. It refuses to be bound by the inexorable law of exact retribution, of the payment of a *quid pro quo*. Instead it makes room for God's new action which is agreeable to the covenant and yet brings new possibilities into it. God's righteousness is revealed in a critical renewal of the covenant and by a restoration of the

guilty to a place of favour within the covenant. He is revealed as righteous by His very act of restoring to covenant status ('justifying') all who believe in Jesus, the mediator of the new covenant.

All this means, I believe, that no unified theory of atonement in terms of legal comparisons can be derived from the New Testament. That legal conceptions were in the writers' minds I do not doubt. That it was natural to appeal to the accepted axioms of their time I readily allow. But that they took over ready-made either the Stoic law of nature or the Rabbinic law embodied in the Torah and deliberately used it as the framework of atonement-interpretation seems to me unlikely and in fact unproven. The all-important concepts are covenant, righteousness, justify, grace. The only notable complex of imagery derived from late Judaism in connection with the problem of sin and its deserts is that of the Day of Atonement ceremonies.

It is when we leave behind the Palestinian environment, however, and move out into the Graeco-Roman world that we encounter the possibility of interpreting the work of Christ far more precisely in legal terms. The great system of Roman law was largely responsible for holding that world together and wherever there was an important city, men trained in the law could be found amongst its citizens. Sooner or later a man would be brought to Christian faith who would use his *legal* knowledge and training to clarify and confirm the doctrine and discipline of the Church. Such a one was Tertullian, an able Carthaginian lawyer, who embraced Christianity and soon set to work to interpret its teaching in terms of his own familiar categories. As A. C. McGiffert once wrote: 'He (i.e. Tertullian) looked at everything with the eyes of a lawyer. Religion and morals, the gospel itself, bore a legal aspect to him, and he gave the language and the theology of western Catholicism a legal cast which they have never lost.'[19]

By quoting this judgment I do not intend thereby to condemn Tertullian and his successors. Law is an essential feature of ordered social life and Christian doctrine, if it is to be fully relevant to human needs, must include references to legal structures and categories. Moreover history shows that men and women of all classes have an abiding interest in legal procedures. All members of a society are subject to the laws of that society and whenever life or property is threatened, whenever limits of freedom or of obligation are under dispute, an appeal is naturally made to the guardians of the law for its provisions to be brought into effect. The danger always

19. *A History of Christian Thought*, Vol. II, p. 7.

arises when the appeal and the response are framed in such rigid legal terms that personal considerations are overriden in favour of a neat and immediate solution. And once the solution has been recorded in writing it stands intact, inflexible, until challenged by one who is brave enough to face the consequences of a revolutionary action.

Tertullian did not attempt to construct a doctrine of atonement in terms of his own particular interests for it was not an age for systematic theological exposition. Rather was it a period, especially in the West, of applying the Christian revelation to the urgent practical problems with which the Church had to deal. In Tertullian's time no problem was more poignant, even agonizing, than that of how to deal with the weaker members of the fellowship who fell victim to open and grievous sins. Initially the assumption had been made that whoever had been baptized, had thereby been cleansed from all the evil associations of the past and made a new creature in Christ. Ideally this new creature ought now to go forward joyfully, living a pure and blameless life. But it was all too obvious that this did not necessarily follow. Under stress of threats and persecution a man might be guilty of apostacy—giving honour to an idol and renouncing his true Lord. Or again under the strain of provocation he might cause injury, even death: allured by the flesh he might be guilty of adultery and fornication. Such offences could not be overlooked. Could a single failure be condoned? Possibly, if due penance was imposed. But beyond that most were unwilling to go. Some allowed special treatment for those who had committed minor sins. Yet the general temper was hard and rigorous, especially in North Africa. There fiercely puritanical groups were prepared even to go into schism rather than remain in communion with those who, they believed, were lax in their treatment of sin and soft in imposing penance.

The general atmosphere of the period has been vividly described by Dr. Leonard Prestige in his Bampton Lectures:

'Christians, convicted of grave sins,' he writes, 'were put to open penance. Having confessed their sin to the bishop, they were formally enrolled in the order of penitents for a specified period, often extending over many years. Debarred from communion and excluded from the common worship, they submitted themselves to episcopal exhortation and moral castigation, and sought the benefit of the bishop's prayers and the laying on of his hands. They wore sackcloth and lay in ashes; they shed tears and uttered supplications for mercy. . . . They fasted, they gave alms; if unmarried they became celibate, if married, they separated from their wives. They were forced to abstain from most kinds of public activity, and to live a life of rigorous asceticism. In due course their entreaties were favourably heard, and their repentance was accepted. They were solemnly restored to the membership and communion of the Church. But not even then were their disabilities concluded. They remained subject to special ascetic discipline for the remainder of their lives; they could neither marry nor be ordained. And a person who had once been admitted to penance and received absolution, and subsequently lapsed, could never undergo penance for a second time. He could be recommended to live hard and tearfully in the hope that God might possibly forgive him after death; but the Church on earth refused to undertake more on his behalf; no second absolution was possible. So long as Christians occupied the position of heroic legionaries, fighting for their lives with in-adequate protection under burning skies against a world of savage adversaries, the contrast between the Church and secular society was too absolute to permit an act of moral treachery to be regarded with-out the most extreme horror. That a genuine soldier of Christ could commit such an act of treachery twice was positively inconceivable.'[20]

This was the kind of background against which the writings of Tertullian must be set. He was a lawyer and in law the man found guilty must bear the appropriate punishment. Feelings of pity and compassion must not affect the verdict. As Prestige suggests, it was a time of crisis and there was need for a quasi-military discipline. The defaulter must be dealt with summarily. 'Every sin', says Tertullian, 'is discharged either by pardon or penalty, pardon as the result of chastisement, penalty as the result of condemnation.' In one way or another *satisfaction* must be made. Here Tertullian takes over a keyword from Roman law, a word bearing the funda-mental idea that wherever the harmonious ordered working of the whole society has been disturbed by a failure to comply with its essential laws (either by some excess or by some deficiency) an adequate reparation must be offered not only in the sense of doing now what was originally commanded but also of offering now an extra which can be accepted as sufficient payment for the delin-quency. In one place Tertullian says that satisfaction is made by confession of sin: in another that it is through meritorious works such as fasting, bodily mortification and penitential prayers. The sinner must be seen to be offering publicly due reparation for his failure. Only so can general harmony be restored.

The question of post-baptismal sin continued to be urgent in the life of the Church. For this reason the prescriptions of Tertullian retained their importance and the vocabulary he employed esta-blished itself firmly in Latin-speaking Christendom. And although

20. *Fathers and Heretics*, p. 67 ff.

for the moment little attempt was made to compare the altogether excellent saving act of Christ with the satisfaction offered by penitents, in time the comparison was almost certain to be made. In a famous and trenchant passage Dr. James Denney has traced the likely course of this development. A way had been defined by which satisfaction could be made for certain post-baptismal sins. This is first and foremost the task of the sinner himself. Yet 'Tertullian represents the Church as shedding tears with the penitents . . . joining with them, in fact, in making satisfaction; and it is in this sympathetic entrance into the experience of the penitents, in this taking the sins of others on itself, that he identifies the Church with Christ. . . . The formula was bound to come, and for better or worse it did come, that Christ by His death made satisfaction for sins.'[21]

Thus it was the conjunction of legal comparisons drawn from a study of Roman law with an urgent practical need arising from the pressure of the pagan world which led to the full acceptance of the important notions of merit and satisfaction into the vocabulary of Christian theology. The idea of merit was not indeed entirely new: something akin was already present as we have seen in the writings of late Judaism. But now it was introduced in a more formal and even quantitative sense. If to make satisfaction certain meritorious works had to be performed then in certain instances it was possible to imagine that the necessary merit could be made available by whomsoever the works were performed (so long as there existed some organic relationship between those who acted and those for whose benefit the acts were performed). And in the case of the satisfaction itself this could be interpreted either positively in the sense of offering a gift or an action known to be well pleasing to God or negatively in the sense of suffering a deprivation or some form of bodily suffering as punishment for the injury that had been caused. From Tertullian's time onwards satisfaction was to become an extraordinarily significant word in the vocabulary of Atonement doctrine. Under careful safeguards it has proved useful to indicate the seriousness of sin as a disturbance of the just order of God for which reparation must be made. But on balance its use has probably been more harmful than beneficial in that it has represented the relations between God and man too strictly in legalistic and even quantitative terms. There is something simple and practical in conceiving God as One who is prepared to accept a compensation when damage has been done to His righteous order. But this simplicity can be purchased at too great a price when it leads to ideas of commercial transactions or court fines as being adequate

21. *The Christian Doctrine of Reconciliation*, p. 50.

metaphors to encompass the great act of God by which He reconciled the world to Himself in Christ.

F

The ideas and language which Tertullian employed in dealing with an urgent practical problem in the life of the Church were to be taken up and used in a brilliantly logical and systematic way by Anselm in his attempt to provide a convincing demonstration that the Incarnation was not only a fact but also a necessary fact, the only possible means by which sinful man could have been saved. It was a time of eager intellectual enquiry amongst younger Christians in particular and challenges from unbelievers were not lacking. With great daring Anselm determined to construct a logical answer to the question which was apparently being asked by believer and unbeliever alike: for what reason or necessity did God take upon Himself the humiliation and weakness of human nature in order to restore it?

As has often been pointed out the first and in many ways the most remarkable stage of Anselm's argument was the firm rejection of the Devil and his role in the drama of man's redemption. In an earlier chapter I have drawn attention to the popularity in the Middle Ages of pictures, whether visual or auditory, of Christ in conflict with the Devil, of the harrowing of the Devil's domain by the mighty Victor, of the Devil's rights which had to be recognized and justly met. To leave all these aside and to concentrate attention upon God dealing directly with man was in one sense to exalt man—no longer was he visualized as the helpless vassal of the Devil but as one who had failed by his own weakness to achieve his true destiny—and in another sense to sharpen the problem of redemption so far as God was concerned. It was conceivable that God could have acted in such a way as to bring about the complete destruction of the devil in order to release man. But it was not conceivable that God could have destroyed man in order to release him. If the devil and his rights were ignored the focus of all attention must be God and his direct relations with man, what God had required of man, what man had failed to render, how the broken situation could be repaired.

But now the all-important question arises: How did Anselm envisage the basic relationship between God and man? In particular how was the authority of God imagined? In his great book on Anselm[22] Professor Richard Southern has drawn a vivid and

22. *St. Anselm and his biographer.*

convincing picture of the two institutions which provided the framework for his thinking. On the one hand there was the monastery, the institution in which Anselm had found supreme happiness and within whose ordered obedience he would have preferred to stay to the end of his life. On the other hand there was the feudal world of northern Europe within which the monasteries were set and to which in all kinds of ways they were related. But this was not a settled and quiescent world. 'The Cur Deus Homo was the product of a feudal and monastic world on the eve of a great transformation. With all its originality and personal intensity of vision it bears the marks of this rigorous and—if the word can be used without blame—repressive régime. Anselm's favourite image of the relations between God and Man was that of a lord and his vassals. The status of these dependants varies. Sometimes they are knights, sometimes freemen, sometimes serfs, but the emphasis is always on subordination to the lord's will. It is characteristic of all these classes that they must render a full service to their lord or lose their inheritance. This is the state of mankind. It had happened once at the very beginning of history that the great diffidation had taken place which condemned all the successors of Adam to the loss of their inheritance. At great cost the lord had paid the service in full. He had not only paid the original service; he had made it possible for future deficiencies to be paid—but only under certain conditions, in appearance simple, but in practice so arduous that only a few would in fact fulfil them. The simplicity of the conditions lay in the demand for no more than faith, submission and repentance; the difficulty lay chiefly in the need for a rigorous submission of flesh to spirit, of spirit to law and of law to God.'[23]

To appreciate the background of Anselm's thinking, it is particularly important to notice the kind of illustrations which he used in his addresses and ordinary conversations. They are essentially hierarchical in pattern after the model of ancient Roman institutions. No simile is more significant than that of the castle. In the centre of a particular area, on an elevation which raises it high above its surroundings, stands the castle (it might equally have been the abbey or cathedral). Within the castle the final resort for safety is the keep. But outside there is a series of concentric circles, each at a lower level, both of position and of safety, representing symbolically varying categories of humanity in their relation to God. The keep corresponds to the angels, the rest of the castle to the religious, the city inside the walls to the faithful laity, the country outside the walls to unbelievers. Even within these categories there can be subdivisions

23. Southern: op. cit., p. 108 f.

representing higher or lower ranks. No model of the Middle Ages is more characteristic than that of the cone or pyramid. It seemed to be the ideal structure for the ensuring of safety and order and proportion and at the same time ever served to direct men's eyes upwards to God, the source of all life and the summit of all authority. Moreover the distance of any category from the peak of the cone is likely to correspond inversely to the magnitude of its offering of service: those nearest give with the maximum of intensity, those farthest away scarcely offer anything at all.

And the concept of *offering* is all-important, though it is of course resultant upon gifts already received. Every good and perfect gift has come down from above. Angels and men have received bounties from God according to their capacities to receive and use. And they in turn are obligated to provide whatever is necessary for those beneath them in the scale of existence. But with the prevenience of grace assumed, it follows that a regular and appropriate service must be offered by every rank if the smooth and harmonious working of the social whole is to be assured. Hence the emphasis is on every man in his own order offering his debt of service to his overlord. Extending this conception to its limits we are brought to the comprehensive vision of God as the universal overlord, waiting to receive from his ranks of servants the offering which is in each case appropriate and which is his just due. The crucial idea governing the whole structure is that of *honour* and it is impossible to assess the argument of the *Cur Deus Homo* rightly except against the background of this idea.

Perhaps the key chapter is the eleventh in Book One. It begins with Anselm asking what it is to sin and what to make satisfaction for sin. This leads him at once to his famous definition: Is sin anything else than not rendering to God what is his due? But what is man's due? It is summed up in the one word *honour*, and for a convincing exposition of this term I turn again to Professor Southern:

'In the language of feudal tenure a man's honour was his estate. Normally this was a unit of land, but the term honour also embraced his title and status. The fundamental crime against a lord and against the social order, was to attempt to diminish the lord's honour. The seriousness of the crime was quite independent of the rebel's power to give effect to his evil intentions; it was his disloyalty, the loosening of the social bond which outlawed him. At the time when Anselm was writing, the word "honour" was at the height of its development as a term of social importance. It was the maintenance of a king's "honour" which preserved his kingdom, of a baron's honour which preserved his barony and so on down the scale. . . . Anselm's references to God's honour are to be interpreted in the light of contemporary usage. God's honour is the whole complex of service and worship which the whole creation, animate and inanimate, in heaven and earth owes to the Creator. Regarded in this way God's honour is simply another word for the universe in its due relationship of service: by withholding his service Man is guilty of attempting to withdraw some part of God's "honour". He fails; but he puts himself outside the law and excludes himself from the order and beauty of the universe. This is his punishment. But his disobedience also requires a counter assertion of God's real possession of his honour; he takes seisin once more of that part of His honour forfeited by the sinner and hands it to another. And so, in the end, the whole *servitium debitum* of the universe will be established throughout eternity, and God's "honour" will be displayed in the order and beauty of the whole.'[24]

Anselm's diagnosis of the human situation is fundamental to his argument. Man's failure to give due honour to God constitutes a weight, a debt, a doom. If he is to be saved from irretrievable disaster he must in some way make satisfaction. Yet it is obvious that this is quite outside his competence. How then can God's original purpose for man be fulfilled? Only if a new man can be found, a man who by perfect obedience can satisfy God's honour himself and by some work of complete supererogation can provide the means of paying the existing debt of his fellows. Such a one was the God-Man. By His unswerving obedience throughout His earthly life He perfectly fulfilled His own obligations as man: by His willing acceptance of death He established such a treasury of merit as would avail to pay the debts of all mankind if they would simply look to Him, accept His grace and be saved.

The picture of atonement painted in the *Cur Deus Homo* is impressive if set in the midst of medieval feudalistic conceptions of authority, of sanctions and of reparation. It belongs to what may be called the style of the Roman legal tradition even though the great revival of interest in Roman law had scarcely begun when Anselm himself was a student. Yet the general ideas of Roman justice were abroad in Europe and the structure of feudal life with the emphasis upon the land and its produce, upon a hierarchy of functions necessary for the organization of a land-based society and upon methods by which any disturbance of the smooth working of the social organism could be dealt with, was in many ways parallel to the structure of life in ancient Rome. The essential conceptions were

24. Op. cit., p. 112 f.

obedience, obligations, merits, satisfaction. These provided a useful mode of comparison for the Christian interpretation of Atonement for it was a time of social change and men needed an orderly framework within which to live and move and have their being. Anselm's exposition certainly provided such a framework though there is no evidence that his argument was widely accepted. It was a remarkable piece of logical reasoning and it carries conviction so long as the initial postulates are accepted.

The model of God as supreme overlord, holding the universe and all estates of men under his control, establishing an order within which everyone is obligated to offer appropriate service to his superior in the social scale, is confirmed and validated by large sections of human experience in history. Similarly the model of one who from within humanity offers a supreme service on behalf of humanity, who accepts even the final penalty of death (in his case entirely undeserved) in order to release his brethren from a crippling indebtedness, has appealed to many as a reflection of that which in an imperfect way has been played out in their own social relationships. But if Anselm's model be regarded as an exact reflexion of God's ordering of His world, if the legal processes which he takes for granted be accepted as valid for all time, if the *Cur Deus Homo* be given the status of a definitive theory of atonement or a logical proof of the necessity for the Incarnation, then the result for Christian theology can be disastrous. Neither Roman law nor feudal law, impressive as each is as a means of regulating a hierarchical society, can claim timeless validity as the structure necessary to express the relations between God and man. Anselm's dialectic was doubtless satisfying to the educated monk of his own day and its relatively simple categories of debt, merit, satisfaction, payment, transfer of assets, have elicited a response in the imaginations of Protestants who from the seventeenth century onwards became increasingly familiar with the structures of capitalism. But neither to the philosopher nor to the man of the world is it likely to make any strong appeal today. New concepts of law are being entertained and if atonement is to mean anything in the context of the ordering of society, these new ideas must be seriously considered and imaginatively employed.

G

Anselm believed that he could demonstrate by an appeal to reason alone that the incarnation and atonement of Christ must necessarily have taken the form that they did. He made little reference to the Bible or even to the tradition of the Church. Starting from what seemed to be first principles his aim was to make the process of atonement vivid and convincing by presenting it in terms of the social bonds which held together both the monastic and the secular life of his age. When we reach the next most famous figure in the history of the legal interpretation of atonement, we find ourselves in a very different atmosphere. Calvin had been thoroughly trained in the science of law as it was being taught in France in the sixteenth century. That this training gave a sharpness, a precision, an orderliness to his mind is abundantly clear. But when it came to expounding Christian doctrine, there was no question of his arguing a case in order to convince believers and unbelievers by the methods of law and logic. Rather it was Calvin's constant ambition to present the evidence of the Scriptures in so comprehensive and so orderly a way that the doctrines of the faith would strengthen the conviction and purpose of God's elect and would stand as a bulwark against all false teaching and aggressive unbelief. Where necessary he was prepared to appeal to the Fathers of the Church and especially to St. Augustine. But his overwhelming concern, both in the Institutes and in the Commentaries, was to draw out from the Scriptures the authoritative doctrines which would instruct men in the true knowledge of God and thereby bring stability to the Church.

The general atmosphere of Calvin's writings is also strikingly different in that whereas the key-terms in Anselm (and the later scholastic theologians) were those belonging primarily to Roman civil law and to medieval feudal law—debt, liability, compensation, satisfaction, honour, price, payment, merit—in Calvin we find constant reference to punishment, death, the curse, wrath, substitution, surety, merit, imputation—in other words to criminal law reinterpreted in the light of the Biblical teaching on the Law, sin and death. In Anselm man's life is indeed forfeit and his position is hopeless because he has failed to render God His due and is utterly devoid of resources to meet His obligations. In Calvin man is guilty before God's bar of judgment and his position is hopeless because the only appropriate punishment for his disobedience is to suffer the pangs of eternal death. In Anselm the merit of Christ's work is available to pay for the sinner's indebtedness: in Calvin the merit is available to save him from bearing the punishment of his sins.

The obvious question which arises regarding Calvin's doctrine of atonement is whether the Latin legal terms with their associations in current penal theory have influenced his interpretation of the

Scriptural evidence or whether the Scriptural teaching on the Law and sin and punishment has influenced his interpretation of the Latin words. But it is impossible to answer this question with a direct Yes or No. As David Daube has so clearly shown in his book *Studies in Biblical Law* a social institution influences a theological construct but in turn the construct can modify the institution. It is easy to point out that substitution, surety, merit are not strictly Biblical words. Yet Calvin keeps them very closely related to Biblical statements. Similarly it may be said that the *lex talionis* of a nomadic people is far removed from the traditional structure of imperial law. Yet Calvin takes over the Biblical judgments and penalties and relates them to the treatment of criminals accepted as normal in the general social situation of sixteenth-century Europe. This means that there can be no finality about Calvin's picture either as an exposition of Biblical theology or as a comparison related to current legal practice. That his picture made an immense impression upon the imaginations of the members of the Reformed Churches there can be little doubt. Its suitability as a mode of comparison for today is a very different matter.

His picture is perhaps more economical in construction and more sharply defined than any other in the history of the theology of the Atonement. God has given man his Law: man has defied God by breaking the Law: he therefore stands condemned at the bar of judgment and no punishment is conceivable except eternal death: yet the Son of God has become man and has stood *in man's place* to bear the immeasurable weight of the Wrath, the Curse, the Condemnation of a righteous God: Christ in fact 'was made a substitute and a surety in the place of transgressors and even submitted as a criminal, to sustain and suffer all the punishment which would have been inflicted on them' (*Institutes*, 2:16:10); so man's guilt was obliterated: God has opened the way for man to accept his release, to be justified by faith, to become accepted in the Beloved. This picture, with minor variations, remained dominant in Reformed theology until well into the nineteenth century. It seems to provide a clear delineation of Biblical truth. It appears to be void of ambiguity and mystery. It links up with common human experiences of the law court, the trial and condemnation of offenders, the imposition of the death sentence, the occasional (and thereby the more dramatic) reprieve. Is this not the best mode of comparison available to bring the message of reconciliation vividly before the imaginations of sinful men?

The difficulties in the way of accepting Calvin's doctrine as it stands are mainly two. In the first place his approach to Scripture presents great difficulties in the light of the changes brought about by the study of history during the past century. The written word is accepted unquestioningly by Calvin as the source of all true knowledge of God. In this, the Bible, Law obviously plays a major part. If this Law is Divine Law then it demands explicit obedience unless any provision is made by God for changing circumstances. But is it conceivable that all the statutes contained in the Pentateuch are to be regarded as binding for all peoples at all times and in all places? To this crucial question Calvin gives an answer which already had a considerable history behind it. The Law of the Bible must be divided into three. First there is the moral law, condensed in the Ten Commandments of the Old Testament and the Two Commandments of the New, and this law is applicable to all men at all times. It is expressed explicitly in the Scriptures but it is implicit in the witness of the human conscience. Whatever his precise condition may be, man recognizes the 'rightness' of the moral law and that its condemnation of his own misdeeds is just.[25] This Law is of immense importance. It holds in check the unruly passions of sinful men, it strikes home to the conscience of the individual who is living in disobedience to God, it is a constant spur to the regenerate to conform more closely to God's will. Calvin quotes again and again from the Epistles of Paul to substantiate this view of God's moral law: it exposes, it condemns, it imposes a curse, it kills, it leaves man without excuse, it brings all men under judgment and shows them how desperately they need the salvation and mercy of God. There is no thought that this moral law could have been imperfect or partial or dependent upon historical circumstances in its Biblical expression. It stands majestic, eternal, unchangeable.

But there is also the judicial law. This law was given to the Jews for their civil government and imparted those formulas of equity and justice by which they could live together blamelessly and peaceably. But this law was open to change, even to abrogation, in other social conditions, so long as the underlying equity, by which it conformed to God's moral law of love, was preserved. Thirdly there is the ceremonial law, provided by God to train His people in service and reverence to God. Calvin's favourite image, in discussing this law, is of children being trained by types and pictures to raise their aspirations towards higher realities or to look forward to the fulfilment of that which in ceremonies is

25. 'It is a fact that the law of God which we call the moral law is nothing else than a testimony of natural law and of that conscience which God has engraved upon the minds of men.' (*Institutes*, 4:20:16.)

seen only in shadow. He states unequivocally that the ceremonial law has been abrogated *in use* but not *in effect*. 'Although the rites of the law have ceased to be observed, by their termination one may better recognize how useful they were before the coming of Christ, who in abrogating their use, has by his death sealed their force and effect' (*Institutes*, 2:7:16).

The important question is what exactly constitutes this continuing 'force and effect'. Calvin stresses the sanctity and sacramental character of the sacrificial system because above all it was pointing forwards to Christ. But to what particular aspect of Christ's nature or work? Undoubtedly to His atoning death. The fundamental principle in the sacrificial system, in Calvin's view, appears explicitly in the Epistle to the Hebrews: 'without shedding of blood is no remission'. To this text he constantly appeals. This *principle* cannot alter, whatever change may occur in the way by which the principle is demonstrated. Under the sacrificial system of the Old Testament blood had to be shed in order that sins might be expiated. Under the New Covenant the blood of the Mediator has been shed and thereby the sin of the world has been expiated and atonement has been made.

In all this there is no suggestion that the judicial and ceremonial laws, as set forth in the Pentateuch, were composite structures, the result of a long process of historical development, and comparable to those of other ancient tribal cultures (though Calvin allows that every nation has the right to make its own judicial laws so long as they conform to the eternal moral law of love). In his view Moses had been chosen by God to be the law giver to the elect people and had given them ceremonial and judicial laws suitable to their condition and expressive of the eternal principles of the Divine Will. Of these principles none was more important than that blood was the only means of remitting sins. This principle had the force of absolute law. Hence it became easy for Calvin to assume that what he regarded as the *principle* of sacrifice possessed an abiding sanction whatever changes might take place in its precise form of external manifestation. What was, in its historical origins and development, a cultic practice associated with many different aspects of tribal life, became in Calvin's exposition a once-for-all given principle, exhibited in child-language and preparatory symbolic form to the Jewish people but consummated and fulfilled in the sacrifice of the Cross. Thus sacrifice, an exceedingly common if not universal cultic rite, associated with occasions of thanksgiving, of communion, of new departure, of dedication, of expiation, a rite of great complexity ranging from crude orgy to refined spirituality, became narrowed and directed in Calvin's exposition to one specific end. It was a fundamental requirement of the Divine Law, he held, that sin should be removed only by the blood of sacrifice. Cult was taken up into Law. The shedding of blood in a cultic context was transferred to the shedding of blood in a punitive context. An extremely limited and unhistorical view of sacrifice was made the determinative legal symbol to interpret the significance of the death of Christ.

The interplay of legal and cultic language is revealed particularly clearly in a notable section of the *Institutes* which deals with Christ's priestly office (2:15:6). 'God's righteous curse bars our access to him, and God in his capacity as judge is angry towards us. Hence an expiation must intervene in order that Christ as priest may obtain God's favour for us and appease his wrath. Thus Christ to perform this office had to come forward with a sacrifice. For, under the law, also, the priest was forbidden to enter the sanctuary without blood, that believers might know, even though the priest as their advocate stood between them and God, that they could not propitiate God unless their sins were expiated. . . . We or our prayers have no access to God unless Christ, as our High Priest, having washed away our sins, sanctifies us and obtains for us that grace from which the uncleanness of our transgressions and vices debars us. . . . Although God under the law commanded animal sacrifices to be offered to himself, in Christ there was a new and different order, in which the same one was to be both priest and sacrifice. This was because no other satisfaction adequate for our sins and no man worthy to offer to God the only-begotten Son could be found.'

The framework is legal, the process is cultic. Removal of legal sanctions is equated with freedom of access in worship. The offering of a priestly sacrifice is regarded as the equivalent of presenting a satisfaction to an offended judge. The ordering of ceremonial for worship is given an absolute legal validity. And blood-shedding as a sacrificial symbol becomes associated with blood-shedding as the direct outcome of capital punishment. It would be unfair to blame Calvin for this. He was living in a day when a critical and historical approach to the Old Testament was unthinkable. It is remarkable that he should have insisted as firmly as he did upon the educative and preparatory function of the sacrificial rites as pointing the people of God forward to the fullness of the time. But his assigning of an absolute legal sanction to the cultic requirement that blood should be manipulated within the sacrificial ceremony proved to be a dead weight upon the thinking and the imagining of Reformed Christendom. Blood is a symbol possessing far-reaching implications and applications. To confine its reference to a death offered as appeasement or satisfaction or propitiation is sadly limiting. An over-simplified legal transaction of a negative kind overshadows the positive testimony (which Calvin expresses with depth of religious feeling) to the access of the believer in prayer and worship to the gracious presence of a merciful Father.

The second main difficulty which confronts us as we examine Calvin's doctrine of atonement is his use of terms which had a well-defined reference and validity within the legal context of his own day but which are inapplicable as they stand either to the social order of Israel in the Biblical period or to that of Europe or America in the twentieth century. Such terms as eternal law, surety and substitute, imputation and satisfaction, penalty and merit, are freely used with the assumption that their framework of reference remains inviolable amidst all processes of social change. But this is a very large assumption. Satisfaction and merit have a clear-cut quantitive reference within the context of Roman law. Is it certain that exact equivalents can be found within the social structure of Hebrew society, even in its later period, to say nothing of the early patriarchal era? Substitute and surety can be employed within the context of a well-established court of law with a judge imposing the death penalty and then accepting some surety on behalf of the condemned prisoner. But is this necessarily the framework within which the great declarations of Old and New Testaments ought to be set?

There are two Biblical passages to which Calvin makes a special appeal when he is expounding the nature of Christ's work. The first, naturally enough, is Isaiah 53. The second, less obvious to us today, but explainable because of the wide popular interest in the idea of the descent into hell, was 1 Peter 3:19-22 linked with Acts 2:24. From the first he singles out the phrase 'Upon him was the chastisement of our peace' for special attention: from the second it is 'the *pangs* of death' which is specially emphasized. Both are set within the context of Pilate's judgment court and the penalties which he was authorized to impose. 'To take away our condemnation, it was not enough for him to suffer any kind of death: to make satisfaction for our redemption a form of death had to be chosen in which he might free us both by transferring our condemnation to himself and by taking our guilt upon himself. If he had been murdered by thieves or slain in an insurrection by a raging mob, in such a death there would have been no evidence of satisfaction. But when he was arraigned before the judgment seat as a criminal, accused and pressed by testimony, and condemned by the mouth of the judge to die—we know by these proofs that he took the role of a guilty man and an evildoer.'[26] 'He therefore suffered under Pontius Pilate, and by the governor's official sentence was reckoned among criminals. Yet not so—for he was declared righteous by his judge at the same time, when Pilate affirmed that "he found no cause for complaint in him". This is our acquittal; the guilt that held us liable for punishment has been transferred to the head of the Son of God (Isaiah 53: 12). We must, above all, remember this substitution, lest we tremble and remain anxious throughout life— as if God's righteous vengeance, which the Son of God has taken upon himself, still hung over us' (Ib).

In this passage Calvin's chief point is that Christ had necessarily to be condemned in a judge's criminal court rather than suffer 'any kind of death'. In commenting on the passages referring to the dereliction of the Cross and the descent to hell his chief point is that a bodily death by itself would have been ineffectual. He had to suffer the *pangs* of death, the *fear* of death, the *anguish* of death, the *experience* of death as a sign of the wrath and vengeance of God. 'It was expedient for him to undergo the severity of God's vengeance, to appease his wrath and satisfy his just judgment.'[27] Christ 'was made a substitute and a surety in the place of transgressors, and even submitted as a criminal, to sustain and suffer all the punishment which would have been inflicted on them'.

That Calvin is wrestling seriously with ultimate realities in such passages as these is hardly open to question. That his words brought illumination and comfort to many who had felt the burden of their own guilt but found no assurance of God's favour and mercy through the medieval system of penances and indulgences also goes without saying. But that Calvin rightly discerned the background and the dynamic range of comparison either of Isaiah 53 or of the particular New Testament passages which he quotes in connection with the descent into hell is extremely doubtful. The poet who so poignantly and vividly described the sufferings of the righteous servant moved, it is true, within a generally accepted social philosophy of retribution and reward but the processes are not strictly legal and are certainly not to be interpreted in terms of developed Roman jurisprudence. The New Testament writers who bore witness to the anguish and dereliction of the Saviour were certainly not relating them to a court of criminal law and the writer of the first Epistle to Peter was celebrating the victory over death and hell rather than a submission to their pains and tortures.

26. *Institutes*, 2:16:5.
27. *Institutes*, 2:16:10.

It may well be argued that *every* system of law must find place for authority, sanctions, punishments, remissions. If there is to be any coherence, if individuals are to be assured of protection of life and property, some set of rules must be accepted by all who belong to the society. In these rules some attention must be given to the gravest offences which seem to call for the imposition of ultimate penalties. Some attention must also be given to the provision of ways and means by which the final penalty can be avoided. In all these aspects of social law there are likely to be general parallels and correspondences. But to assume that the framework is the same for all times and places and that its details represent on earth that which abides eternal in the heavens is to go far beyond what the evidence of history and experience allows. The magnificent vision of vicarious suffering depicted in Isaiah 53, the daring faith that the merits of heroic martyrs can somehow be transferred to their weaker brethren, the confident assurance that a total obedience in humanity even to the point of death is of vital significance to the moral situation of all mankind—these can be related to the patterns of imagination of any society. The details, if applied according to the strict legal system which obtains at any one time, can become offensive and repellent in another age and a hindrance rather than a help to a true understanding of the relations between God and man.

Much of Calvin's exposition is impressive and moving to the imagination when allowance has been made for his unquestioned acceptance of the late Jewish concentration upon God as Law-giver. Whatever else may be true of man, he declares, the all-important aspect of his situation is that he is unrighteous, disobedient, a law-breaker and therefore 'estranged from God through sin, an heir of wrath, subject to the curse of eternal death, excluded from all hope of salvation, beyond every blessing of God, the slave of Satan, captive under the yoke of sin, destined finally for a dreadful destruction and already involved in it' (2:16:2). 'But because the Lord wills not to lose what is his in us, out of his own kindness he still finds something to love. However much we may be sinners by our own fault, we nevertheless remain his creatures. However much we may have brought death upon ourselves, yet he has created us unto life' (2:16:3). So out of His pure grace God devises a way of salvation which is according to the justice of His essential nature as Law-giver and yet is adequate to our situation as guilty and condemned. Any man can learn that 'Christ interceded as his advocate, took upon himself and suffered the punishment that, from God's righteous judgment, threatened all sinners, that he purged with his blood those evils which had rendered sinners hateful to God: that by this expiation he made satisfaction and sacrifice duly to God the Father; that as intercessor he has appeased God's wrath; that on this foundation rests the peace of God with men; that by this bond his benevolence is maintained toward them' (2:16:2). When he learns all this, says Calvin, will not a man be moved as he realizes the greatness of the calamity from which he has been rescued? But what if he does not first realize the greatness of his calamity, what if his mind is not 'struck and overwhelmed by fear of God's wrath and by dread of eternal death'? Then much of Calvin's imagery and many of his legal similitudes cease to exercise their appeal. As in all life-situations a remedy must in some way be related to the diagnosis of the disease.

H

Calvin's general framework of law, guilt, condemnation, reconciliation remained normative within Reformed Christendom for roughly three centuries. It was essentially a simple structure which corresponded to the general experience of mankind. For Europe the sixteenth, seventeenth and eighteenth centuries constituted a time of ferment, wars, revolutionary tendencies, the struggle of minority groups for recognition and toleration. The one safeguard against complete anarchy was the existence of a system of law which was above individual caprice or even minority plots. Law could protect the few and the weak from the tyranny of the great: at the same time law could protect the ordered and the established from the wild upsurgings of fanatics. In a certain sense all men feared the consequences of disorder and antinomianism. That law was essential in human affairs, that law belonged to the Divine ordering of the universe was doubted by few.

Yet it was still possible to question how far Anselm or Calvin had rightly interpreted the Divine law. It was still possible to speculate about the relation between Biblical law and the classical expressions of law to be found in Aristotle or Seneca or the Code of Justinian. Socinus, for example, launched a vigorous attack on the Calvinistic scheme of things within the sixteenth century itself. He was a noted logician, well versed in Roman law, and refused to accept the interpretation of the workings of the Divine justice which had become virtually the orthodox doctrine of the Reformed Church. What Socinus mainly did was to emphasize the transcendence of God in so extreme a fashion as to leave no room for the Christ save as a voice proclaiming salvation. For salvation he says is not gained or won by Christ in virtue of His work. It is freely (gratuitously) given by God, it is a direct exercise of His will: He does not require payment or mediation or satisfaction but rather, because he is Lord of all, he is able to forgive freely and to exercise mercy and to 'abandon as much of his rights as he pleases'.

Perhaps the chief contribution of Socinus was a negative one. He showed unmistakably that the rigid schema of law, involving satisfaction through punishment, which had gained such wide acceptance in the Reformed Church, could in no way be regarded as the sole interpretation of atonement to be found in Scripture. Socinus lays the greatest emphasis upon the free forgiveness of God and upon His mercy which cannot possibly be in opposition to His justice. In effect he claims that the Divine justice is revealed in the very act of Divine mercy, not in some abstract insistence upon the payment of satisfaction. In any case he denies that one death could make satisfaction for many or that a death in the time-series could satisfy the demand for eternal death. His criticism is penetrating and gains strong support from the Old Testament. But where he entirely fails to convince is in his treatment of the New Testament. He can indeed select New Testament references to the free and untrammelled grace of God, issuing in forgiveness and release. But the massive New Testament witness to the fact that through the death and resurrection of Christ the whole human situation has been changed, to the faith that God was reconciling the world to Himself in Christ, he either misunderstands or ignores. Those who followed were quick to see that whatever the strength of his criticism might be his positive doctrine allowed no essential place for Christ and His work at all. Socinus rightly questioned the attempt to enclose the doctrine of atonement within a single rigid forensic framework. He did little towards constructing an alternative framework within which man's individual and social existence could gain stability and significance.

In sharp opposition to Socinus, the great international jurist Grotius propounded a new theory of atonement which corresponded to an expanding view of the Divine ordering of the world. Legal comparisons were still favoured but instead of the somewhat restricted context of a court of law arraigning and condemning a debtor or a criminal, we are invited to imagine a centre of government responsible for establishing justice and order over a wide area. God is conceived as head of a state or institution (Grotius uses the significant term Rector) and as such he is not concerned to exact satisfaction for every debt or to impose punishment for every small misdemeanour. Rather He gives Himself to the establishment of good government and above all to the maintenance of public order. Punishment must be inflicted not in order to satisfy the demands of affronted honour but in order to preserve the safety and welfare of the community at large by deterring evildoers. Moreover so long as punishment was duly imposed and was seen to be imposed it was not an absolute necessity that it should fall upon this or that individual in the community. So long as one could be found who, from within the community, would take upon himself the just and appropriate punishment, justice would be effected and the proper ordering of society would be vindicated.

However open to criticism Grotius's theory of transferred punishment may be, there is no doubt that his approach was fresh and original and an indication of the way in which developments in legal science can affect theological formulations. For the idea was gaining ground that a king could not administer law absolutely: he must at all times pay attention to the common good of the whole society. This idea affected Grotius's whole view of the way in which God dealt with the law and offences against it. Instead of a private, somewhat mysterious, transcendent law which God operates for such purposes as He deems best, we have now a public, open and intelligible law which God may indeed relax or manipulate in certain circumstances but which is altogether for the common good. We are moving away from the concept of the empire towards that of the republic and the ideas of law and penalties under the law are changing accordingly. It is not that the sanctity of law as such is being questioned. It is rather that the relation of the head to the body, of the king to his subjects, of the governor to the law is beginning to be viewed in a different way. And the overall effect is to lessen the power of the king or emperor to direct the law towards ends of his own choosing but instead to magnify the place of the law as that to which even the king must pay heed if the common good is to be sustained.

The important point is that changing conceptions of law have certainly affected theories of atonement in the course of the centuries. Imperial law, feudal law, Biblical law, common law, natural law each in its own subtle way has influenced the mind of the man who at a particular period seeks to set forth his understanding of atonement by means of legal comparisons. At one time, as in the scholastic period, it is imagined that a total philosophy of law can be constructed from first principles and that God's relations with man are bound to conform to this general schema. At another time, as in the period of the Reformation, it is imagined that a total body of law has been revealed through the Scriptures and that the relations between God and man are entirely governed by this code. In both cases law is accorded something approaching an absolute status for it is held to be the authoritative expression of the Divine will. In the first instance transgression of the law damages the total scheme of things: in the second instance revolt or disobedience is a direct affront to the Law-giver himself. Atonement then depends upon how the breach is to be repaired and the just requirements of the law vindicated.

The altogether significant change which has been gradually taking place in the past century has been the growing realization that laws are historically and socially conditioned and that the whole concept of natural law needs to be thought out afresh in the light of modern scientific developments. Perhaps the last great treatment of the atonement in terms of the concept of law as generally accepted in the English social tradition was that of Dr. R. W. Dale in 1875. The most significant phrase in his book is *the eternal Law of Righteousness*. This Law is, as it were, placed alongside the direct personal will and activity of God. God may act in new ways to deal with particular situations but the eternal law of righteousness remains firm and unchanging. No transgression of it can be overlooked. Every infringement deserves an appropriate penalty and this penalty must in some way cause the offender to suffer. Dale assumes—and his assumption would have gained very wide acceptance in the mid-nineteenth century—that the sequence crimesuffering, offence-punishment is axiomatic. It is he believes the essential principle of the eternal law of righteousness. Hence it follows that within the total outworking of universal history it ought to be the case that somehow, somewhere, a massive concentration of suffering corresponding to the enormity of the accumulation of mankind's offences ought to be inflicted.

'If God does not assert the principle that sin deserves punishment by punishing it, He must assert that principle in some other way. Some Divine act is required which shall have all the moral worth and significance of the act by which the penalties of sin would have been inflicted on the sinner.' And Dale goes on to affirm that this Divine act, of an intensity and energy equal to what would have been expressed in a universal punishment, took place when God in the person of his Son endured the awful suffering of Calvary's Cross.

Dale can appeal to what he regards as a fundamental principle of the eternal law of righteousness. Denney, some thirty years later, could appeal to what he regarded as fundamental principles of the Divine law as revealed in Holy Scripture. But meanwhile inexorable forces were at work in the world around them, gradually leading to a vastly different view of law and its place in human affairs. To interpret the Christian doctrine of atonement in terms of legal processes and penal analogies became increasingly dangerous for there was little assurance that the forensic reference would carry immediate conviction or would even correspond to the inner reality of the legal images contained in the Bible itself. The great advances in the study of history have served to call in question the whole concept of a Divinely-given code. How is it possible to imagine that a set of laws, formulated for a particular people at a particular moment in history, could have a universal reference for all times and all nations? Similar advances in scientific studies have undermined the concept of natural law. How is it possible to imagine that a single set of symbols, however abstract, can embrace within an unchanging formula the principles governing the process of the whole universe? That there have in the course of human history been epoch-making declarations of moral law on the one hand and expressions of natural law on the other hand is clear enough. How man's conduct in any particular period is to be related to them is by no means so obvious.

I

My main concern in this chapter has been to show that in the nature of the case no single theory of atonement can be constructed in terms of legal and forensic comparisons. The most ambitious attempts to do this have been made on the basis *either* of a system of law which it was believed could be derived from axioms accepted without question by every human mind *or* of a system which it was believed could be derived from the authority of the Biblical revelation. But as we have seen in the course of our examination of history, the axioms accepted by a particular society at a particular stage in human development differ considerably from those of another society at a different stage. And only by a severely selective process can a body of law derived from the Bible be regarded as universal in its relevance: even then it is so restricted in its content that it leaves vast numbers of human problems untouched.

The final question remains whether we ought today to abandon all further attempts to interpret the Christian doctrine of atonement by the aid of forensic comparisons. Are there still any basic concepts of law which commend themselves immediately to the human conscience and which can be used to throw light upon the primal affirmation that God was in Christ reconciling the world to himself, not imputing their trespasses to them? Is law any longer associated with a Divine authority, with supernatural sanctions, with penalties which must be accepted as just and right in a religious sense? It is of little use to construct a legal comparison if the very system from which the comparison is drawn is believed to be outmoded.

It is doubtful if there has ever been a time when law and its operations have been so widely questioned and criticized. The increasing acquaintance with the mores of other peoples and cultures has brought a corresponding sense of the relativity of legal prescriptions: a system of law in one country may be very different from that in another and any idea of international law or even of a general rule of law for a free society becomes difficult to conceive. Again the very rapidity of social change in the world at the present time makes it difficult to imagine how any stable structure of law can long survive just as it stands. Furthermore the idea of individual responsibility has been undergoing radical reconsideration in the light of all that modern psychology has told us about repressed desires and unconscious motives affecting conduct. And the concern for the individual has shown itself in new anxieties about the effect of punishment upon the one who has been found guilty: is it right for an imposed penalty to be purely retributive or ought it rather to be remedial and reformatory? How are the basic duties of the individual to society at large to be defined and what are appropriate punishments if and when these duties have been neglected? The subject of law reform is in the air. Congresses of lawyers meet, commissions are set up, educational policies are proposed, philosophical principles are advocated, conflicts within the law are dramatically exposed. From a day when law and its sanctions were regarded as ultimate and sacred we have passed to a time when everything is under scrutiny and the majesty of the law must be redefined if it is to guarantee a new stability within contemporary society.

Yet when all this has been said it still remains true that no cohesive society known to us has remained stable without some system of law. Indeed the very conception of community implies an orderly arrangement of duties and privileges and these can only be safeguarded if they receive some formal expression in verbal or written rules. The basic unit of society, the family, is so small and intimate that a minimum of rules is sufficient to hold it together. But the larger and more complex a society becomes, as for example in a great modern city, the more it needs detailed rules for the preservation of safety and the promotion of the common good. That there must be laws and sanctions governing the conduct of fallible, self-regarding and sometimes even violent individuals and groups, few would dispute. The question of almost infinite complexity is how the laws are to be established and how breaches of the laws are to be punished.

It is, of course, tempting for the Christian to affirm that love is the fulfilling of the law and that therefore to depend upon the law is to fall short of the Christian ideal. That the words and example of Jesus Himself, echoed and followed by the apostle Paul, set love in the forefront of Christian living goes without saying. But that this dispenses the Christian from any interest in or concern about law by no means follows. As it has been well said: 'Law, by which I mean society's effort to establish just relations among people, to resolve conflicting interests, to regulate social life, and love, by which I mean the sacrificial sharing of one's whole life with God and with one's fellow-men, stand in a complementary relationship to each other. Love needs law to give it structure; law needs love to give it direction and motivation.'[28] Or again, commenting on the words of Berdyaev that 'A person's fate cannot be made to rest solely upon other people's spiritual condition. This is where the significance of law comes in. No one can be made to depend upon his neighbour's moral qualities and inward perfection', John Bennett has said: 'Love should, therefore, seek the enactment of laws to protect the neighbour not only against cruel and willful injustice but against those acts that are the product of thoughtlessness that often accompanies general loving intentions.'

Yet while recognizing the need for laws to secure justice in social life generally, the Christian dare not appeal to concepts of law or systems of law which no longer command the respect and allegiance of competent jurists. Especially is this so in the context of atonement-theories. To employ uncritically structures of law drawn from pre-Christian times or from feudal times as frameworks of interpretation of the doctrine of atonement is fatal. That there may be basic principles which were embodied in ancient systems of law may be perfectly true. The altogether difficult task is to determine what were primary obligations, binding upon man in any kind of stable society, and what were secondary rules, valuable at a particular stage of social development but impossible to transfer to a later age. Are there, in fact, structures of human dependence and responsibility which belong to the existence of man in social relationships everywhere? And if so, how are these to be determined? It is, I suggest, only these that can be rightly borrowed by the Christian theologian for his task of building up a legal mode of comparison in atonement-

28. In an address by Professor Harold J. Berman of the Harvard Law School.

theory. The secondary rules in law of his own day may well lend themselves to be used for purposes of illustration and suggestion. But the main structure of his theory must, as far as possible, be within the realm of those primary obligations which have been regarded as essential wherever a stable and just order has been established in the world.

To discover what these principles of primary obligation are has been one of the main purposes of this chapter. Yet at the end I have to admit that no single and uniform pattern has revealed itself which could serve as a model for atonement-interpretation in every age. In the social life of Western Christendom two models it is clear have been enormously influential. The first is Roman Law, a system already firmly established in the Mediterranean world before the Christian Gospel began to be proclaimed in its cities. The second is Hebrew tribal Law, enshrined in the Bible and rediscovered when men came to look at the Bible with fresh eyes at a time of striking change in human affairs. Roman Law is essentially related to the settled city-state, Hebrew Law to mobile mercantile existence. The former draws its concepts from land-enclosures, from processes of organic growth, from the inter-relationship of higher and lower orders within one living whole. The latter draws its principles from the open country, from processes of personal exchange, from the inter-relationship of past and future within one common purpose. And although in the course of Christian history these two patterns have inter-acted and inter-twined yet they have never completely lost their separate identities. It is questionable then if a single synthetic legal model can ever do justice either to our inherited traditions of the Christian theology of atonement or to the realities of social life which are not (or should not be) encompassable within one type of legal system.

If we take the general model of Roman Law we find a massive emphasis upon the authority of the head (whether he be *pater familias* or ruler or king or emperor), on the delegation of certain aspects of authority to those on lower levels of the hierarchy, on the absolute necessity for those on lower levels to render due homage to their superiors in the social scale, on the gravity of the debt incurred if such a response is not made, on the need for adequate reparation if the total organism is to function again without let or hindrance. Further, just because of the sense of inter-dependence within the organic whole the concept of a substitute payment or satisfaction is natural and unquestioned. Laws then are concerned with duties to one's superiors (by age or by caste or by function) and above all to the supreme overlord, with penalties for neglect of or failure in those duties, with the means by which debts thereby incurred can be met and fully satisfied. In other words the general model is that of a human body in which there is a continuous interchange between the centre of the nervous system in the head and the members of the organism; in which signals of demand expect an adequate response; in which a breakdown or failure on the part of some elemental constituent of the body needs to be repaired and restored in order that the life-flow of the whole may be uninhibited. Such a model is imaginable, it corresponds to large sections of social life, it lies behind statutory codes in which demands for personal service, for payment of taxes, for respect for another's dignity and property are made; it provides the context for ideas of damages, delict, indebtedness, repayment, fine, satisfaction, compensation; it allows for the institution of bail, surety, sponsorship, outright payment by one on behalf of another. All kinds of variations are conceivable to meet changing circumstances. There is little reason, however, to think that so long as the individual maintains any kind of identity within the larger social whole such a conception will become altogether irrelevant or outmoded.

This means that the language of demand and satisfaction can still be used in the theology of atonement provided that it be not pressed too far in conformity with the detailed secondary legal prescriptions of any particular age. If God be conceived as the Sovereign Head of the total human society, as the One Who is continuously revealing the pattern of order by which His universe coheres and by which men can live together in harmony and mutual fulfilment, then it follows that man has a framework within which to live and a set of social duties to perform. If he seeks deliberately to disrupt this framework or fails to make his own particular contribution to the welfare of the social whole then he is a cause of damage and a debtor. He stands under judgment as owing reparation for injury done and for failure to pay. 'We have offended against thy holy laws. We have left undone those things which we ought to have done; And we have done those things which we ought not to have done; And there is no health (wholeness) in us.' The vast accumulation of injuries done and debts unpaid alienates man from God, for in no way can he hope to render a complete 'satisfaction' for his own debts, let alone the sins of the whole human race.

Yet it is possible to conceive of One Who, being completely identified with humanity in his biological and psychological existence, rendering from within humanity a perfect offering of obedience and self-sacrifice in face of all adverse circumstances, thereby made 'a full, perfect, and sufficient sacrifice, oblation, and satisfaction' for the

sins of the whole world. This is metaphorical language. It corresponds to a general recognition that in the life of society injury
and debt must be dealt with by an appropriate payment of
recompense however this may be determined. And it corresponds
to the recognition to which Jesus Himself appealed that the greatest
of all offerings was accomplished when He sanctified Himself, i.e.
offered Himself on behalf of others. The measure of the value of the
offering of a perfect obedience cannot be quantitatively determined.
It surpasses all other offerings. By its very perfection it convinces
man that his own massive account of indebtedness has been settled.
By its utter selflessness it assures him that his own entail of damage
has been cancelled. Where damage and debt in relation to the
ultimate constitution of things are empty and meaningless terms,
any reference to the supreme merit of Christ's death, any proclamation of the surpassing value of His obedience, falls on deaf
ears. But where there is any sense of being involved in a universal
failure to deal rightly with God's gifts and to fulfil the duties rightly
laid upon His subjects, the doctrine that through Christ, the surety
and sponsor for all humanity, a perfect offering of the will and of
the body has been consummated, restores hope and confidence and,
cancelling all sense of legal indebtedness, substitutes the deep sense
of indebtedness to the Son of God 'Who loved me and gave himself
for me'.

Turning to the general model of Hebrew Law we find a constant
emphasis upon the authority of the leader (whether he be patriarch
or prophet or chieftain or 'captain of the Lord's host'), on the
delegation of authority to leaders of smaller units within the one
all-inclusive brotherhood, on the absolute necessity for all to remain
faithful to their mutual obligations and commitments (normally
expressed through covenants), on the gravity of any form of disloyalty to the covenant, on the need for judgment to be inflicted upon
anyone who deliberately shatters the social structure by betraying
his trust. There is little regard for hierarchy or for organic structures
related to the life of the land. In theory all men are on the same
level though there are in fact variations through physical strength
and prowess, through wisdom and skill, through the accumulation
of goods and possessions. Laws are concerned with allegiance to
and respect for the leader and the other members of the community:
every man and his family has a share in the common life of the tribe
but at the same time his own identity and well-being must be
preserved by simple laws which forbid any man to trespass on
another's rights.

The archetypal model in this tradition is simply that of two individuals, each respecting the other's identity yet desiring some closer association with him. The essential pattern of action in such circumstances is that of give and take. Each commits himself to give: each, it follows, expresses his readiness to receive. Each deprives himself of some portion of his own strength or skill or possessions: each receives some valued addition to his own limited resources. While the process of interchange continues all is well. But what happens if one party clings tenaciously to that which he has promised to give? Or snatches more than he is entitled to receive? By such acts he becomes guilty of falsehood, treachery, disloyalty to the whole brotherhood. That which he has withheld or snatched he must restore in full measure—an eye for an eye, a tooth for a tooth, a life for a life. And if he has exercised violence towards another— robbery, rape, murder—violence it would seem must be exercised towards him—stoning, burning, hanging. When life is constantly in danger a community's only safety is to be found in complete loyalty between its members. Any breaking of covenant obliga- tions must therefore be summarily dealt with according to the uncomplicated law of direct retaliation.

The basic idea of the *lex talionis* is deeply engraved in the human consciousness. It constitutes the roughest kind of justice when he who causes injury to another has similar injury done to him, when he who steals from his brother has an equivalent taken from himself. By this simple adjustment society appears to restore its own equili- brium. Yet there are obvious complications. Blood spilt cannot in reality be recompensed by the blood of the killer being spilt. A man's loss incurred through the unfaithfulness of his wife is not made good by the woman and her lover being stoned to death. It may, of course, be said that through the extermination of the guilty party a poison or infection is removed from society. It may be urged that the slaying of an offender acts as a powerful deterrent to others. But this is not the same as a full restoration of covenant- mutuality. It cannot be claimed that all obligations have now been met and that due reparation has been made.

The chief survival of the old *lex talionis* has been capital punish- ment for murder but even this has been abandoned except in a severely limited number of cases. Until quite recently beatings were allowed but these, too, have become illegal. The only remaining major *punishment* is the deprivation of freedom through prison sentence. Life in prison is unpleasant enough but it does not normally involve actual bodily suffering. The punishment lies mainly in the negation of free movement and the cessation of free social relationships. It is difficult to ascertain how far the thought of prison acts as a deterrent to crime. It is exceedingly doubtful how far incarceration acts towards reformation. The present situation then is that punishment is regarded as necessary in some form but that grave doubts exist about what is possible or appropriate in particular instances beyond a committal to prison for a limited period of time.

But surely removal to prison alone—without that is any consideration of what can be done for the offender while he is in prison— can hardly be regarded as an enlightened policy. Its only justification would seem to be the protection of society (but if the man does not *change* while he is in prison the situation will be unaltered when he is freed) or the inculcation of fear to prevent others from following his example—an indirect but dubious way of protecting society. The fact seems to be that responsible citizens are increasingly uncertain about the validity of the idea of purely retributive or deterrent punishment. Punishment can only be justified if it is in some way reformatory and if it is to reform offender A it is hard to see how it could be borne in any substitutory fashion by innocent B. It is indeed possible to advance certain psychological considerations and to urge that if A sees B suffering what should have been his own desert he will be moved to change his own attitude and to repent of his past offences. But such considerations are outside the range of judicial processes. At an earlier stage in the evolution of society when the head of a family or the head of a tribe was regarded as gathering up within himself the totality of corporate responsibility it was perhaps conceivable that the one could accept punishment in a strict legal sense on behalf of the many. Even then, however, it was more normal to assume that the whole group must suffer and bear punishment because of the sin of the head rather than the reverse.

My conclusion must then be that no strictly penal theory of atonement can be expected to carry conviction in the world of the twentieth century. The general response of the conscience to the sufferings of one who stands faithful through all external pressures —the conviction that in some mysterious way this heroic sufferer has borne the stripes and the chastisement which should, by strict desert, have fallen upon less worthy members of the community—is spontaneous and psychologically valid. But it does not conform to legal principles which would gain general acceptance and cannot therefore be forced into the service of a penal interpretation of atonement. If the atonement is to be interpreted in terms of given law, the system used for purposes of comparison must be one which will command the full respect of the best-informed juristic minds. To appeal to a system which is either outmoded or seriously open to criticism is to bring the whole doctrine into discredit. At least for the time being it seems wise to leave on one side the traditional association of the death of Christ with ideas of punishment and substitutionary penalties and to concentrate on other modes of comparison which can more readily appeal to the contemporary mind.[29]

29. See H. L. A. Hart: *Punishment and the Elimination of Responsibility.*

CHAPTER VI

THE ALL-EMBRACING COMPASSION

Third Analogue

The fabric of human relationships in God's original plan was designed to reveal an overall pattern of growth through mutual inter-dependence. Within a continuing rhythm of give-and-take, lives would flow together, thereby enriching and fulfilling one another. God and man, man and man, would be linked together within a total organismic structure of developing personal relationships. But self-asserting and self-inturning have disrupted this harmonious rhythm. How can free circulation be restored? How can an un-impeded flow of life be renewed?

In any organismic structure the condition variously described as stale, anaemic, diseased can be changed only by means of some fresh introduction of life-giving energies. But to do this is a supremely diffi-cult operation. Separated elements must come together and be held together; weak elements stimulated and encouraged to reflow together. Moreover this must be done without causing damage to the delicate fabric of inter-connections which constitutes the total life-process.

It is the claim of the New Testament that into the situation where man had withdrawn from free relationship with God, God Himself entered in a new way. This initiative had nothing of the nature of a forced entry. As a child, through lowly doors, in a process of deepening identification, dissolving barriers of suspicion and mistrust, ultimately from within this humanity making the perfect self-offering and reopening the channel through which life could again freely flow. 'God was in Christ reconciling the world to Himself'—drawing it away from its isolation and separation, shaming its proud self-assertiveness and renewing the condition of flowing to-gether in which all can find their true relation to one another by virtue of the enjoyment of an unhindered relationship with God in Christ.

A

We are no longer in the realm of wide-ranging cosmic reconcilia-tion: we have drawn inwards from the customs and laws of clans and tribes: we are now in the more intimate and familiar territory of the human family, an institution as ancient and as universal as any known to man. In this context human relationships can be natural, spontaneous, uninhibited: on the other hand they can be tense, unnatural, hurtful. The structure of the family has passed through many variations in the course of human development and yet no single institution has been more durable. It is probably under a more severe strain today than at any time in human history and yet it retains an extraordinary hold upon the emotional and imaginative life of mankind.

Let us look at some of the basic elements of a family structure. First and foremost there is the relationship of mother and child. The woman conceives a child within her own body but at birth it is separated from its complete physical dependence upon her. Yet almost immediately the new-born babe is reunited with the mother in the process of lactation, sucking in nourishment from the body out of which it was taken. Further there is obviously a flow of blood in the child's body and this blood must be the same as that of the mother. In other words mother and child still in a sense form a single organism. Even though separated insofar as each now occupies a particular position in space, they constitute parts of a single whole which lives and grows within a constant mutual relationship.

But although mother and child together constitute the primal unit there are many other elements in the total family. There is the home and the hearth, the small-holding surrounding the home and the domestic animals—all are included in the family complex. Far more important there are the other children of the mother, and the man who has been bound to her by the marriage-tie. Family structures have varied at different times and places with the mother's sister sometimes occupying a privileged position as her occasional substitute, with the brother sometimes occupying a special role as protector of the children. But whatever structures of this kind may have existed, still the man who has a special marital relation to the woman, whether or not his part in the conception of children is recognized, is regarded as bearing major responsibility for the protection and nurture of wife and children alike. He by reason of his superior strength and his exemption from many of the child-rearing duties easily assumes a position of authority within the household. But it is still authority within *the total living organism*. The primary emotional ties are between the children and the mother. The child grows towards maturity as it maintains its proper place within the total family complex.

Within the intimacy of family life two perversions are abhorred beyond all others. The first is that of incest. It is altogether remarkable that amongst peoples at all stages of development incest seems to have been branded by a universal taboo. To turn inwards, to allow emotion as it were to incurve upon itself, has nowhere been tolerated or approved but rather regarded as a gross offence. The second perversion is that of murder. If one member of a family asserts himself and his own rights to the extent of inflicting bodily harm upon and even slaying one of his own kin, this too is an offence beyond all ordinary imagining. He has, as it were, spilt his own blood: this is unnatural, fearful, sheer madness. There is no obvious way of undoing such a grievous wrong.

The organic character of family life is subjected to strains and even shocks through the crisis of weaning and the still greater stresses of initiation. But the effect has not normally been to disrupt the family pattern entirely but to re-establish it on a more mature basis. The son does not cease to be a son after initiation though he is less dependent emotionally on the mother. The totality of life is maintained and any breaches or misdemeanours are still *within the family*. Where there is disorder or default the combined resources of the total organism flow in, as it were, to restore health and sanity. Every member finds fulfilment as he occupies his assigned place and performs his proper function within the whole.

Nowhere in the literature of the ancient world are family relationships more vividly and more attractively described than in the Scriptures of the Old Testament. The stories of the patriarchs, the judges and the kings all in their own way reveal the conception of the family as it was held in Israel. This conception, Pedersen affirms, is of 'an organism which grows and spreads in the shoots which it is constantly sending forth. The symbol of the plant or the tree naturally suggests itself and the ancients themselves already made use of it. When we speak of genealogical trees, the symbol, properly speaking, can only be applied with certain limitations. We are thinking of the individual as owing his existence to the preceding generation; but he emancipates himself more and more, until as a grown-up man he has his point of gravity entirely in himself. In the eyes of the Israelites, however, the symbol is fully applicable; indeed it is rather more than a symbol, for tree and human species are two entirely analogous forms of life. Just as the branch not only owes its existence to the trunk and the root, but constantly sucks its nourishment from it, in the same manner the individual holds his life only in connection with his family. It is that which is expressed by the sons bearing the name of the father.

'That the son places himself outside the family and raises the standard of revolt against his father, is so utterly unnatural that no law can take account of it. It is more absurd than a kingdom divided against itself; it is a unity, a soul that is at war against itself. If the son sets himself against the father, then he is as a diseased member of a body, and the father who, by the acts of the son, is forced to remove him, is as a man who cuts his own flesh'.[1]

That Pedersen is broadly right may be seen by noting the place that Abraham, the forefather of Israel, occupies not only in Genesis but in the prophets and the New Testament writings: the dramatic relationships between Abraham, Sarah and Isaac and later between Isaac, Rebekah and their two sons: the significance of the stories of Joseph and his brothers: the tensions and struggles within the family of David. In the total picture the mother remains in the background but is never merely a cipher: her influence upon her sons and especially upon a favourite son is obviously great. But the major interest in the stories concerns the relationship between the father and the son. Ideally the blessing of the father is transmitted to the son, the achievements of the son redound to the glory of the father. The father sees the continuity of his own life in the son: the son rejoices if he is able to enhance the dignity and fame of his father's house. The father is the centre of authority but there is little thought of exercising this for his own individual satisfaction. He is the head in whom the whole family coheres and when the time comes his honour descends easily and naturally to the son whom he loves.

This is the ideal. But even in Israel there were defections from this state of harmonious growth. We recall the struggle between Esau and Jacob, the jealousies and intrigues amongst Jacob's sons, the conflicts between Moses and his kinsfolk, above all, perhaps, the cruelties and the treacheries of the sons of David. These aberrations could not be dealt with by external penalties for they were offences *within the family*, breaches within the total life of the organism. They were unnatural and perverse. Moses when he views the defection of his brother Aaron and the apostasy of his people is torn between his sense that righteous judgment must fall and his conviction that being himself part of the total life of God's family he must share the judgment and disgrace. David, when he learns of his son's treachery and above all of Absalom's rebellion, moves hesitantly and uncertainly. The offence cannot be condoned and yet it is an offence *within the family*: all are in a certain sense implicated. How can harmony be restored without doing irreparable harm to the offender? How can he, at one and the same moment, be *against* Absalom and yet also *for* Absalom? Intermediaries try to bring the king and Absalom together but there seems to be no way of overcoming the tension at the very heart of the family's

1. Israel I–II, p. 267.

life. Absalom is determined to usurp the highest place of authority and nothing can save him from his doom.

B

As has often been remarked, the Old Testament uses direct family images to describe the relationship between God and His people only sparingly. Yet the strong assumption is certainly present that it was God Who had called Abraham and his seed, that God's own purpose was bound up with, even incarnated in, this one family, and that its behaviour brought honour or shame, as the case might be, to God's cause in the world. When Israel was unfaithful no third party could intervene. The only hope was that from within Israel itself a man here, a man there, might arise to detach himself temporarily from his nation's perfidy and to reaffirm as it were from God's side the abiding principles of truth and loyalty. In and through the prophets God recalled His people, His family, to the fundamental principles of their own authentic existence. In and through the prophets God expressed His own suffering caused by the faithlessness of His people. At the same time the prophets, by their own identification with the people, experienced in their own lives the suffering and distress which estrangement from God was bound to involve.

The family tension, the prophet's involvement, the suffering of God, the distress of the child, the restoration to organic wholeness all come to dramatic expression in the concluding chapters of the book of the prophet Hosea and illustrate the use of family imagery to describe the relations between God and man.

> When Israel was a child, I loved him and out of Egypt
> I called my son.
> It was I who taught Ephraim to walk,
> I took them up in my arms, but they did not know
> that I healed them.
> How can I give you up, O Ephraim!
> How can I hand you over, O Israel!
> My heart recoils within me, my compassion grows
> warm and tender.
> I will heal their faithlessness;
> I will love them freely.[2]

---

2. The reader of this passage can hardly fail to make the judgment that much of its feeling-tone and imagery belongs more appropriately to motherhood rather than to fatherhood. Occasionally, indeed, in the Old Testament the relation of mother to child is compared to that of Yahweh with Israel. But Hebrew society was so traditionally patriarchal and the role of the father in the family was so dominant that it was natural to attribute to the father attitudes and responsibilities which would normally be associated with the mother today.

All these are the words of the prophet himself. Now he is speaking indignantly, now he is speaking compassionately: now he is speaking in the name of God, now in the name of the people: now in terms of ultimate judgment, now of final reconciliation. He remains always within and a part of the total organic family of God and His people. Through the initiative of God in moving him to speak, the prophet takes his own initiative and opens a way of redemption and restoration. Though the children have forsaken the father's house and turned towards idols, the prophet brings a new revelation of the father's heart of love and invites them to return to their true health and their true home.

But the pattern which appears 'at sundry times and in divers manners' in the Old Testament comes to full expression through the New Testament revelation of Him who is the perfect son within the Divine family. No title of Jesus of Nazareth expresses a greater depth of meaning than the simple name 'Son'. He is 'the beloved Son', the 'only-begotten Son', the Son of His love, the Son of God. No reference to the Divine activity is more significant than that which states with complete simplicity that God sent His Son into the world. This is pre-eminently the imagery used in the Johannine writings though none is more characteristic of the New Testament as a whole. The children of men are seen as unfaithful children: the Son is seen as the bearer of a new initiative who will turn the hearts of the children to their true Father and bring them home to God.

This appeal to family relationships raises one difficult question. It has often been asked whether the New Testament teaches that God is the Father of all men and that all begin, as it were, with the status of children within the divine family: or whether it teaches that all begin as strangers and foreigners in relation to the Divine fatherland and can only gain a new standing through God's creative act and their own willed response. At the risk of seeming illogical I am bound to affirm not only that both conceptions are to be found in the New Testament but that each is valid within its own framework of reference. Even in the Hebrew social structure made familiar to us by the Old Testament the practice of 'adoption' was allowed though in point of fact few instances are to be found. But the very circumstances of the Gentile mission in early Christianity made it necessary to employ this kind of imagery if the already existing body of doctrine and devotion relating to the Divine Fatherhood and Jesus' new revelation of the nature of sonship was to become meaningful. In differing contexts there are differing emphases. But the basic relationship of father to son is common to all.

So far as the New Testament records are concerned the first body of imagery is derived from the unshakable conviction that God had called and chosen Abraham to be the father of God's family on earth, a family through which all the peoples of the earth would receive blessing. With this conviction there existed innumerable questionings about who, at any precise period, constituted the true children of Abraham. All who were circumcised? All who kept the law? All who were of pure physical descent? All who abjured idolatry in any shape or form? All who shared Abraham's faith? The possibilities were almost limitless. Yet in Jewish minds the conviction held fast that the family of God existed in the world. It might only constitute a minority or a remnant but still its marks could be recognized. It was an organism continuous in its life from the past: it was God's flock: it was God's vineyard: it was God's family.

Within such a framework of thought and imagination it was natural to conceive of God's new and climactic initiative in terms of seeking out the lost sheep of the house of Israel, of cleansing and restoring the life of the vineyard, of gathering the children as a hen gathers her chickens under her wings, of bringing back the prodigal to his true inheritance. One writer insists that the Saviour who came into the world had to concern himself with the descendants of Abraham (Hebrews 2: 16). He had to share their flesh and blood, he had to be made like them in every respect so that he might act on their behalf in the things pertaining to their true life and destiny in God. Considerable attention is paid to the genealogy of Jesus of Nazareth in the New Testament writings: he is Son of David, he is Son of Abraham, he is of the tribe of Judah, he is a true Israelite—all of these titles indicating that He could rightly claim to be the brother of those He had come to save, that so far as flesh and blood were concerned He shared the lot of the family of God and was in every way qualified both to be the bearer of the fresh initiative from the Divine side and to act on behalf of the maimed and disordered family on the human side.

This general description of the mission of the Son of God may be developed in greater detail by looking at the several documents from which it is derived. The Gospel of Mark uses the title Son of God sparingly but leaves the reader in no doubt that Jesus was indeed the chosen emissary of God, the unique son, the one who had full authority to declare the words and perform the works of God Himself. Yet his Divine Sonship was not expressed openly, ostentatiously or in such a manner as to enforce an immediate response. Rather He moved as a man (or more characteristically as a

'son of man') amongst men, speaking in homely ways so that the
simplest who had ears to hear could hear, moving in homely circles
so that any who were conscious of need could find in him a ready
help. In these ways He was gathering to Himself a small but highly
significant group of adherents. These were the true family of God—
these who heard the word of God and obeyed it. These were the
true flock who were destined to inherit the Kingdom.

The general pattern of Matthew's redemption-theology is akin
to that of Mark with only slight variations of emphasis. Luke's
range and outreach is, however, wider and his treatment somewhat
different. His concern is for those who had been outcaste from the
regular religious life of Israel, for those who were beyond the pale
so far as the interpretation of the Divine promises and blessings
was concerned. His purpose is to show that Jesus identified himself
with these poor and despised creatures and gathered into the ambit
of his saving ministry all who were prepared in any way to respond
to His words and works of compassion. He does not minimize
the work of Jesus amongst His own people but he misses no opportunity of indicating that it was also designed to bring light to the
Gentiles, to bring salvation to all peoples, to pass beyond the strict
bounds of the children of Abraham and to bestow blessing even
upon a Roman centurion who was ready in faith to receive it.
Luke is not so much oppressed by the mystery of the rejection of
Jesus by His own people as exultant that through their rejection
salvation has come to the Gentiles. There is joy in the presence of
God over one sinner that repents whether he be Jew or Gentile,
Pharisee or publican, respectable or outcaste. Jesus Himself was
cast out and numbered with the transgressors but by that very
identification with them in shame and spitting He was able to include
them in His saving embrace and bring them home to God. There
is less sense of struggle and agonized tension in the Christ of Luke.
He enjoys an unbroken harmony with His Father's will, He delights
to be about His business, He ranges widely as His emissary to call
not the righteous but sinners to repentance. In any mission of this
kind there was bound to be opposition and resistance but God
would vindicate His son and bring Him to His glory. And those
who continued with Him through His tribulations would undoubtedly
share this glory when it came to be revealed.

Of all Luke's pictures which portray the nature of the relationship
between God and man none has exercised so wide an appeal as
that usually called the parable of the Prodigal Son. The danger has
ever been of attempting to make the parallel too exact and to find
correspondences in every detail. The parables and comparisons

recorded from the teaching of Jesus are constantly concerned to lift the imagination of his hearers to the 'How much more'. An earthly father is aware of the needs of his children and provides appropriate gifts to meet them. How much more will your heavenly Father provide gifts from heaven! An earthly father allows each of his sons the freedom to act in the way he desires. If one decides to go far afield and by so doing comes near to complete disaster, he can still be given a royal welcome by an ever-watchful father if he turns his steps homeward. How much more will your Father in heaven be ready to receive the sinner who repents! Not that it would always happen on the earthly level but such a gracious fatherly action *can* be imagined. On the Divine level this is always the attitude and action of the Father whose greatest delight is found in a relation of confidence and trust with His children.[3]

But does this not imply that there is no need to speak of mediation or atonement within a genuine pattern of family relationships? Is not the father *always* ready to welcome back the estranged child? is not the offer of making any kind of reparation swept aside? Such questions tend to overlook the fact that the one who told the parable claimed to speak in the Father's name and that within the parable itself there is the strongest possible resistance to this kind of revelation of the Father's heart of love. Jesus was under no delusion. He came to declare and to represent God's reconciling love for His children who were alienated from Him. But there were vested interests and entrenched attitudes even within the family which were prepared to crucify such an emissary with such a message. The varying alienations within a family situation cannot be *easily* resolved.

The problem of restoring the free flow of family relationships is also underlined in Jesus' references in the Gospels to the constant need for the exercise of forgiveness in family life. 'And when you stand praying, if you have anything against anyone, forgive, that your Father in heaven may forgive you your transgressions' (Mark 11: 25). 'If you forgive men their transgression, your heavenly Father will also forgive you; but if you do not forgive men, neither will your Father forgive your transgressions' (Matthew 6: 14). Above all, in the great prayer addressed to the Father of all, there is the daily reminder that a request for God's forgiveness is only conceivable within the context of a forgiving spirit towards others. Any clinging to a self-love which turns inwards and ignores the claims of others: any manifestation of a self-assertiveness which over-rides the needs of others: both alike are fatal to the free

3. G. Bornkamm: *Jesus of Nazareth*, p. 127 f.

flow of the spirit of forgiveness which brings health to the whole body.[4]

In the Fourth Gospel and the Johannine Epistles the title Son of God is constantly in use. The glory of Jesus Christ in the world was 'as of the only Son from the Father'. The Baptist bears witness that this is the Son of God. Men are condemned because they do not believe in the name of the only Son of God. He who believes in the Son has eternal life. On Him God the Father has set His seal. Of the intimate and continuous and unclouded communion of the Son with the Father we are left in no doubt. But on the other side the matter is not quite so simple. Jesus Christ is the Word Who has become flesh and dwelt among us: He reveals His glory through the signs He performs: He looks with penetrating vision into the hearts of men: He declares the nature of His own being and the character of His mission: He engages in significant dialogues with His own disciples, with individual seekers and with His opponents, the Jews. Yet it is not easy to feel the same identification with His own compatriots as we sense in Mark's Gospel. He comes to His own, it is true, but they do not receive Him. The Jews reject Him. The authorities plot to destroy Him. But through it all the Son knows that the Father has given all things into His hands and that as He came from God so He would go to God. Indications of deep and passionate identification with man in his blindness and perverseness are rare. The Son pursues His predestined path to His final glory irrespective of what man may say or do.

So far as the death of the Son of Man is concerned this is certainly predestined by God. He is to be lifted up on the Cross in order that men may look to Him and be healed, in order that they may come to know who He is, in order that the prince of the world may be defeated and His subjects drawn to the feet of the exalted One: His own travail and death belong to the very constitution of organic life in the universe for except a corn of wheat falls into the ground and dies it abides by itself alone but if it dies it bears much fruit. Jesus will not save His life but will lay it down willingly in order that a more abundant life may be made available for His friends. To be sure the Son brings new life to men, He enables them to be born again as sons of God. He reverses the doom of eternal death to which otherwise they are subject, He releases the Spirit by which men are regenerated and constantly reinvigorated. But all this He does, not so much by standing as man amongst men, by sharing their weaknesses and bearing their sorrows, but rather by fulfilling in complete and utter obedience the task assigned Him by the Father,

4. See T. W. Manson: *The Teaching of Jesus*, p. 311.

by passing even through the dark tunnel of suffering and death on His way to the final light and glory of the Father's house. The Son restores men to a true sonship within the family of God but He does this by submitting Himself to an arduous and costly programme rather than by identifying Himself in depth of feeling with those He came to save. Such seems to be the dominant emphasis of the Johannine writings.

But there is another New Testament document which develops the Markan emphasis in a quite remarkable way. This is the Epistle to the Hebrews, an early Christian exhortation which has been designated by one commentator the Epistle of Sonship. As in those writings already considered, the witness to the eternal divine sonship of Jesus is unmistakable. The first chapter sets him far above all angelic beings and describes Him as reflecting the glory of God and bearing the very stamp of His nature. He was appointed to rule over God's house as a Son and operated as High Priest within the heavenly temple. Yet He so identified Himself with the sons of men that he became like them in every respect save that He in no way fell into that disobedience which is the essence of sin. He was tempted, He experienced every form of suffering; He tasted death. In the most vivid passage of all the author writes:

'In the days of His flesh Jesus offered up prayers and supplications, with loud cries and tears, to him who was able to save him from death, and he was heard for his godly fear. Although He was a Son, He learned obedience through what He suffered; and being made perfect He became the source of eternal salvation to all who obey Him.'

The reference to the Gethsemane scene seems obvious. The Son, who in every respect is in harmony with the will and purpose of the Father, is standing on the side of man, with man, sharing the feeling of dereliction and disarray which is the consequence of faithlessness and 'departure from the living God'. He is wrestling in spirit with man at the same time as in His strong crying He is wrestling in spirit with God. He takes the cold of human meaninglessness and lifts it into a revivifying relationship with the warmth of the Divine passion. Through Him the fresh initiative from the Divine side is expressed in terms of personal energy and through Him the response from the human side begins as it were to take form. He offers Himself once for all and at the same time inaugurates the offering of the ages by which He saves all who draw near to God through Him since He always lives to make intercession for them.

In the striking imagery of the twelfth chapter those who have responded in faith to the pioneer and perfecter of faith are exhorted to rejoice in their new-found sonship even if it does involve a measure of pain and suffering. It is the condition of painless apathy which is so dangerous, even fatal. Those who give up through weariness or because of the roughness of the way are in peril of sinking down into death. To be struggling, to be resisting, to be enduring discipline, to be girding up the loins is to be living. Jesus endured the cross and shame, He wrestled with sweat and tears, He in so doing offered Himself on behalf of His brethren. Those then who follow Him in the way not only grow into life and health and peace themselves, they become intercessors on behalf of their fellow men and open a door for them into health and salvation.

C

Christianity went out from its Palestinian cradle into a world curiously divided in its traditional attitudes to woman and the home. Although at an early stage of Greek civilization represented pre-eminently by the Homeric poems the relations between man and woman are often dignified and moving, by the fifth century B.C. woman has taken an altogether secondary place in the Greek view of life. She is little more than a domestic drudge whose task in life is to bear and nurture children. There is little concern for the life of the home: in fact Plato in the Republic is prepared to jettison the family altogether by the establishment of state nurseries. Lowes Dickinson sums up the general attitude tersely when he says that 'woman in the historic age was conceived to be so inferior to man that he recognized in her no other end than to minister to his pleasure or to become the mother of his children'.[5]

In marked contrast, in the centuries preceding the beginning of the Christian era the home was perhaps the most characteristic and most influential of all the institutions of Roman civilization. The conception of the *familia* had much in common with the British ideal of family life, the only major difference being the wider inclusiveness of the Roman household. Cicero (57 B.C.) might almost have been speaking in nineteenth-century England when he cried on one occasion:

'Is there anything more hallowed, is there anything more closely hedged about with every kind of sanctity than the home of each individual citizen? Therein he has his altars, his hearth, his household gods, his private worships, his rites and ceremonies. For all of us this is a sanctuary so holy that to tear a man away therefrom is an outrage to the law of heaven.'[6] Such an image offered itself to and

5. *The Greek View of Life*, p. 9.
6. Quoted by Hugh Last in *The Legacy of Rome*, p. 213.

was in some measure adopted by early Christians as they viewed the Church as the household of God, the divine family under the protection of the Father of all.

Yet it seems clear that by the time that Christianity reached Rome the whole attitude to woman and the family was changing. Crowds of immigrants from the East had introduced very different ideas which led gradually to the degrading of the status of woman and the growth of moral licence to such an extent that the nobler conceptions of home life were virtually destroyed. Unhappily one result of this was that whereas the Christian attitude as revealed in the New Testament is in general attractive and ennobling, with woman given a place of full dignity within the Christian community and with children regarded as having the right to be brought up in the fear and nurture of the Lord, the time was soon to come when Christian writers would be inveighing against women as being a prime source of temptation and when children would be regarded as having been conceived and born in sin. Tertullian we know was in many ways a fanatic but he was a leader of the Church little more than a century after the Apostolic Age. And he could address the female sex in such terms as these: 'Know that each one of you is an Eve. . . . You it is who so easily destroyed man, the image of God.' A man who could speak in this way was hardly likely to find relationships in the home particularly apt for the purpose of bringing home to his contemporaries the nature of reconciliation through Christ.

Yet while Tertullian was depicting woman as Eve the temptress, destroyer of the image of God, Irenaeus was speaking of her in a more temperate way as guilty indeed of unbelief or faithlessness but as still to be compared with the one who was soon to occupy a pre-eminent place in the theology and devotion of the Church—Mary, the mother of Christ. 'What the virgin Eve bound by means of incredulity', he writes, 'this the Virgin Mary loosed by faith.' And this Mary was 'by her obedience the cause of salvation both for herself and for the whole human race'.[7] What man was failing to experience in his ordinary earthly life—conjugal love and gracious motherhood—he was to find in the world of the imagination through focussing his vision upon the holy family at Nazareth and above all upon the Virgin Mother herself.

Few more remarkable changes took place in the whole ethos of Christianity between the first and, let us say, the seventh century

7. *Adv. Haer* 3:22:4. Christ had from New Testament times been celebrated as the second Adam. Now Mary came to be known as the second Eve, crushing the serpent's head, and soon other identifications were made with Biblical figures —the Woman of the Apocalypse, the Wisdom of the sapiential books and ultimately above all with the Bride of the Song of Songs.

A.D. than the transition from what I might call the model of the father-son relationship to that of the father-mother-son inter-dependence. As we have seen, the New Testament abounds in references to God as Father, to Jesus Christ as Son and to men becoming sons of God through faith in the One Mediator, the only-begotten Son of the Father. The Virgin Mother, except in the stories of the Nativity, is scarcely mentioned. She is seen standing at the Cross, she is with the faithful at Jerusalem in the days before Pentecost but after that the New Testament becomes silent. Of her later life and death nothing is recorded.

But by the end of the second century at the latest apocryphal stories were beginning to appear and soon the details of her whole career from her miraculous birth to her miraculous assumption into heaven were becoming known to the faithful. And with this increasing familiarity with her image went a corresponding increase in the estimate of her significance in the whole economy of redemption. In the second half of the fourth century a Syrian Father of the Church could glorify her by using such a phrase as 'Mediatrix of all the world'. Not that the magnitude of the Son's mediatorial work was doubted. But if He undertook this work by becoming man through Mary then her own role in mediation must have been very great. Mother and son are seen as sharing together in the work of redemption.

In order to show how natural this development was I cannot do better than quote a passage from the first volume of H. O. Taylor's *The Mediaeval Mind*. 'In the third and fourth centuries', he writes, 'the common yearning of the Graeco-Roman world was for an approach to God; it was looking for the anagogic path, the way up from man and multiplicity to unity and God. An absorbing interest was taken in the means. Neo-Platonism, the creature of this time, whatever else it was, was mediatorial, a system of mediation between man and the Absolute First Principle. Passing halfway over from paganism to Christianity, the Celestial Hierarchy of Pseudo-Dionysius is also essentially a system of mediation, which has many affinities with the system of Plotinus. Within Catholic Christianity the great work of Athanasius was to establish Christ's sole and all-sufficient mediation. Catholicism was permanently set upon the mediatorship of Christ, God and man, the one God-man reconciling the nature which He had veritably, and not seemingly, assumed to the divine substance which He had never ceased to be. Athanasius's struggle for this principle was bitter and hard-pressed, because within Christianity as well as without, men were demanding easier and more tangible stages and means of mediation.

'Of such, Catholic Christianity was to recognize a vast multitude, perhaps not dogmatically as a necessary part of itself, but practically and universally. Angels, saints, *the Virgin over all*[8] are mediators between man and God. This began to be true at an early period and was established before the fourth century. Moreover every bit of rite and mystery and miracle, as in paganism, so in Catholicism, was essentially a means of mediation, a way of bringing the divine principle to bear on man and his affairs, and so of bringing man within the sphere of the divine efficiency.'[9]

Man in other words sees himself as set within a divine family in which the figure of the omnipotent Father rules over all but in which there are innumerable members of the household able and ready to assist him as he seeks to be delivered from the wiles of the world, the flesh and the devil and to be made worthy of admission to the glory of the Divine Presence itself. The Son is the great deliverer, the revealer of the Father's nature, the Sacrifice for the sins of the whole world. But behind Him, supporting Him, in all respects sharing with Him, is the Mother of God, 'the Glory of the Universe, Flower of the human race, She who has overthrown the middle-wall of enmity, She who has brought in peace and has thrown open the Kingdom.'[10] He is the champion but she is pre-eminently the compassionate one who takes pity upon those who are harassed by the devil and saves them from the punishment due for their sins. Saints and angels also play their part but it is the Virgin whose assistance is most eagerly sought. She who was deemed worthy to be the mother of God must surely be able to mediate between sinful man and the holy Judge of all.

So it came about that the figure of the Virgin Mother dominated the Middle Ages, its art, its piety, its practical theology, its hymnody. By the thirteenth century she occupied (in sculptured form) the place of honour in the porches of all the great cathedrals of Europe and a noble chapel was normally dedicated to her. Monks and friars made her the subject of innumerable sermons, glorifying her with every conceivable metaphor. And all were gathered up into the title which was most favoured of all: she was Queen of Heaven. As such she could intercede with the Father, she could intercede with her Divine Son. Man's supreme hope of reconciliation lay in constant dependence upon the prayers of the Virgin Mother who was ready to succour all in weakness and distress.

'She was', writes Emile Mâle, 'to the people as grace supreme

8. Author's italics.
9. H. O. Taylor: *The Mediaeval Mind*, p. 54 f.
10. From a hymn of the Eastern Church.

over law. She is seen in the tympanums of the cathedrals kneeling near her Son who is about to judge the world, and she reassures the sinner who on entering dare not so much as look at his Judge. She was the "advocate" who pleaded desperate causes and whose hands held the treasures of God's mercy. And yet the Virgin of the Middle Ages remained very woman. She had regard neither to good nor ill but in love she pardoned all. To be saved it was enough to have daily recited half the Ave Maria. She was present at the weighing of souls and caused the scales to dip on the right side.'[11] What more natural than that in the monasteries seven times a day the cry of the Salve Regina rang out:

'Save, O Queen, thou Mother of mercy, our life, our delight and our hope. To Thee we exiled sons of Eve lift up our cry. To Thee we sigh as we languish in this vale of tears. Be Thou our advocate. Sweet Virgin Mary pray for us, Thou holy Mother of God.' Or that the greatest poet of the Middle Ages, as he approaches the supreme vision of the Divine Majesty, makes St. Bernard supplicate on his behalf to the Virgin Mother in a prayer of surpassing beauty:

> Here thou to us, of charity and love,
> Art, as the noonday torch; and art, beneath
> To mortal men, of hope a living spring.

> Whatsoe'er may be
> Of excellence in creature, pity mild,
> Relenting mercy, large munificence
> Are all combined in thee. Here kneeleth one
> Who of all spirits hath reviewed the state,
> From the world's lowest gap unto this height.
> Suppliant to thee he kneels, imploring grace
> For virtue yet more high, to lift his ken
> To-ward the bliss supreme.

The atonement wrought by the Son of God was not impugned. But in the mediation of its effects to weak and sinful men the Virgin Mother, it was believed, had a sovereign part to play.

One further development in the history of Marian devotion is both interesting and significant. The image of the Queen of Heaven was splendid and inspiring. But it could obviously become a symbol of that which was remote from common humanity. What assurance could a peasant have that a queen would concern herself with his welfare? Doubtless this was only one of the factors promoting the new spirit of humanism which manifested itself in the art and literature of the late thirteenth and early fourteenth centuries. But it was an important one. By the middle of the fourteenth century

11. Emile Mâle: *The Gothic Image*, p. 258.

the Virgin Mother with her child have become, as Male expresses it, both human and intimate. And in the following century an aspect of the Divine motherhood which had already been celebrated in hymnody became dominant in painting and sculpture—the aspect of sympathy and suffering and compassion. The *Mater Dolorosa* was henceforth an object of wonder and devotion.

It was not difficult to find Gospel support for such a conception. Had not her supreme joy at the birth of the Messiah been tempered by the reference in Simeon's blessing to a sword which would pierce her heart? Had she not stood by the Cross and shared in the agony of her Divine Son? (It became a common conceit that the spear which had been thrust into the Saviour's side had reached her own heart also.) Had she not assisted in the deposition of the body from the Cross and mourned over the son of her love? The Gospel foundations could be built upon in such a way as to produce magnificent temples of the spirit suggesting vicarious suffering, sympathetic identification and compassionate support. Into these temples the ordinary worshipper could enter and receive comfort and healing.

In addition to the great works of art in which the theme of the suffering mother is central there were popular hymns, especially associated with the Franciscan movement, which inspired a deep devotion to the woman of sorrows whose tribulation brought blessing to mankind. Of these none became more popular than the Stabat Mater which was current already in the fourteenth century and has retained a firm place in Catholic devotion ever since. Composed in prayer form, it begins with a celebration of the Virgin Mother's compassion, continues with the prayer that the devotee may share her identification with the sufferings of her Divine Son and concludes with an appeal to be brought safely through the Judgment into Paradise. Many translations have been made, some of which reflect the appeals directed to the Mother by the Son Himself. But the central motif of the hymn has remained unchanged—the desire on the part of the devotee to share deeply in the *feelings* of sorrow and compassion which afflicted both Mother and Son in the hour of the world's redemption. A popular translation reads:

> Who on Christ's dear Mother gazing
> In her trouble so amazing,
> Born of woman, would not weep?
> Who on Christ's dear Mother thinking,
> Such a cup of sorrow drinking
> Would not share her sorrow deep?

For his people's sins, in anguish,
There she saw the victim languish
Bleed in torments, bleed and die:
Saw the Lord's anointed taken;
Saw her child in death forsaken;
Heard his last expiring cry.

In the Passion of my Maker,
Be my sinful soul partaker,
May I bear with her my part;
Of his Passion bear the token
In a spirit bowed and broken
Bear his death within my heart.

The significance of such a hymn seems to me twofold. It bears
witness to a growing sense of *family solidarity*. Paul's moving
appeal to the Corinthians to recognize that in the body if one
member suffers, all suffer together, is applied in a specific way to
Mother, Son and the children within the Divine family. It is to a
large extent a turning of the eyes away from the idealized, perfectly
formed, tranquil and joyful Queen of Heaven to the far more
human, sensitive, compassionate Mother on earth—such a mother
as was known in ordinary human life as she toiled, laboured in
travail, cared for and suffered with her children, lamented when
anyone was stricken with disease and death. Whatever dangers and
perversions may have been present in this new attitude it opened the
way to a reinterpretation of atonement in terms of sharing suffering,
and exercising compassion. It suggested Divine inter-relationships
in some measure comparable with those which could be known
within the life of a true family on earth.

In the second place it bears witness to a growing inclination to
celebrate *feeling* rather than intellect. The great intellectual systems
of the eleventh–thirteenth centuries had scarcely touched the common
man. But now the advent of the friars with their popular preaching,
the birth of new forms of poetry and prose in the vernacular and the
changes in the style of religious painting made it possible for the
ordinary human imagination to be touched and indeed deeply
affected by a dramatic presentation of the kind of experience which
was known already to some degree in common daily life. This appeal
to the *feelings* was to grow in intensity both in Catholic and in
Protestant circles. Paul Gerhardt in the seventeenth century translates the *Salve caput cruentatum* ascribed to Bernard of Clairvaux
and thereby makes available in Protestant circles the moving hymn

O sacred head, sore wounded

with its plea:

> In thy most bitter passion
> My heart to share doth cry,
> With thee for my salvation
> Upon the Cross to die.
> Ah keep my heart thus moved
> To stand thy Cross beneath
> To mourn thee, well-beloved
> Yet thank thee for thy death.

Such language is foreign to the academy or the law court or even to the theatre. It finds a place within the intimate family circle or the group of close friends and with all its dangers has provided a vehicle for the soul of man to realize more deeply the meaning of the compassion of God.

Another area in which the appeal to the feelings was to play an increasingly prominent role was that of religious art. The art of Eastern Christendom in the fifth and sixth centuries had depicted the Passion not in terms of humiliation or suffering but rather of heroic endurance and even triumph. Western art showed no appreciable difference until the fourteenth and fifteenth centuries. 'In the thirteenth century', Emile Male writes, 'all the luminous aspects of Christianity are reflected, goodness and gentleness and love. . . . Very rarely does art concern itself with grief and death; and if it does, these are transformed into images of incomparable beauty.' And he continues: 'By the fifteenth century this celestial radiance has long since been extinguished. The majority of works left to us from the epoch are sombre, art offering few images but those of sorrow and death. Jesus is no longer teacher, but sufferer, or rather, He offers His wounds and His blood as the supreme teaching. From now on we find Jesus naked, bleeding, crowned with thorns. . . . It seems that the keyword to Christianity is no longer "to love" but "to suffer". Hence the recurring subject (of the waning Middle Ages) is the Passion. The high Middle Ages rarely chose to depict any but the triumphant Christ; the thirteenth century found in the teaching Christ the subject of its greatest works; the fifteenth century saw in God the Man of Sorrows. The Passion had always been at the centre of the Christian faith but formerly the death of Christ had been a dogma that addressed itself to the intellect. Now it was a moving image that spoke to the heart.'[12]

Yet in the fifteenth century the purely physical agony of Christ Himself has not yet become the centre of emphasis. The suffering is expressed through the sorrow of the mourners, the despair of the women and above all through the passion of Jesus' own mother.

12. *Religious Art*, p. 112 ff.

It is in a real sense the projection on to the eternal plane of that which was being constantly experienced in the circle of the family when a loved one died. At the same time there was the recognition of the responsibility of the human race in general for this rejection of the Son of God. The appeal to the feelings was thus double-edged. The one beholding the picture was encouraged to identify himself in sorrow and suffering with those who had remained faithful to the end: he was also urged to see in imagination the human sins which had crucified the Lord and to recoil from them in horror and repentance.

Probably it was the late fifteenth and early sixteenth centuries which saw the most extreme manifestations of the Saviour's sufferings and dereliction in art. The emphasis on the humanity of the incarnate Son had become more and more pronounced. In addition the plagues and uncertainties of life in Western Europe had become such that men were only too ready to fasten their attention upon a symbol which seemed to gather up their pains and diseases into one dramatic act of Divine sympathy and vicarious absorption. It has been suggested, for example, that when those suffering from the plague and other bodily diseases arrived at the famous hospice of Isenheim and were taken (as was in fact the case) to see the great altarpiece of Grunewald *first* before any kind of physical treatment was administered, it was in the hope that the view of such suffering as was displayed in the terrible picture of Christ in His agony would bring a certain sense of reconciliation to the patient's heart and set him forward on the way to receiving whatever physical relief the hospice could provide. To an alarming extent man was diseased, afraid of the future, forlorn in the midst of what seemed to be an unfeeling universe. To see the Son of God not only sharing his lot but plumbing it to the very depths could bring a ray of hope to his own otherwise despairing condition. This same appeal to the *feelings* was to take many forms in the succeeding centuries but the fundamental motif remained the same: The Son of God was lacerated, wounded, drained of his life-blood on behalf of the sons of men. Is it possible to remain indifferent in face of such suffering? Will not those who behold Him in His sorrows rather seek to be joined in heart and spirit with the faithful few who surrounded Him in time of His agony? To those who allow themselves so to be identified with Him will come a sense of reconciliation with their own lot and of peace with God through His blood. From the fifteenth century onwards the *feelings* take an increasingly large place in the religious life. The intellect is not minimized but illiterate peasants could not respond to rational explanations and logical expositions. By seeing, by feeling, by having the imagination quickened, they could at least enjoy some degree of participation in the fruits of the redeeming work of their Saviour and Lord.

D

It is not easy in the twentieth century to recall imaginatively the long period in European history during which the status of women, the conception of marriage and the ideal of relationships between parents and children were so different from what they are today. In spite of the facts that women play a prominent part in the Gospel records, that in the context of ultimate spiritual relationships the equality of the sexes is upheld, that Jesus Himself loved children and stressed the high importance of childlike trust, and that the father-son relationship constitutes one of the supreme symbols of the New Testament—in spite of the revolutionary implications of all these facts it is still the case that throughout the Middle Ages a very different set of ideas prevailed and largely governed the social life even of the Christian Church. So strong were the traditions derived from Greek, Roman and tribal sources that there was little chance of the radically new principles of the New Testament emerging into social realization, partly indeed because of the existence of ethical directions in other parts of the apostolic writings which seemed to sanction the continuance of attitudes long established in general community life.

In his valuable examination of *The Man-Woman Relation in Christian Thought* Dr. Sherwin Bailey reviews in detail the practices of the patristic age and of the medieval Western Church. The picture, so far as the status of woman and the view of the sexual act are concerned, is almost uniformly sombre. It is true that every effort was made to uphold the sanctity of the marriage relationship and to encourage continency in sexual matters. Moreover in the later medieval period there was a recognition of the ennobling potentialities of romantic love and an artistic idealization of the relationship between man and woman and between mother and child. Yet these factors exercised little effect upon the general patterns of family relations and sexual behaviour which were already firmly established in social life and this meant that little appeal was likely to be made to family relationships by ecclesiastics who were seeking to interpret the Divine act of redemption.

No Christian teachers have had a greater influence upon the developing thought of Western Christendom than Augustine and

Aquinas. Yet Augustine virtually equated original sin, concupiscence and venereal emotion and drew the inference that 'while coitus in theory is good, every concrete act of coitus performed by fallen Man is intrinsically evil—so that every child can be said literally to have been conceived in the "sin" of its parents'.[13] Aquinas, accepting in large measure the Aristotelian view of the man-woman relationship, rejected any idea that woman 'was created to be man's helper in the broad and general sense of partner in all the affairs and enterprises pertaining to human life, for in these he can be aided more effectively by another man; woman is his collaborator simply in that for which she is biologically indispensable—the work of generation'.[14] And their own theoretical teaching both reinforced and gained reinforcement from such factors as the following enumerated by Sherwin Bailey—'the exaltation of virginity as the supreme and truly "religious" state of life; the refusal of marriage to the clergy; the continual insinuation or asseveration that coitus is a defilement and a hindrance to the service of God; the emphasis placed upon the remedial function of matrimony, and the neglect of its relational aspects, and the persistence of a comparatively low view of woman.'[15] In such an atmosphere it is hardly surprising that the atonement was viewed primarily as a means of expiation and purification from sins of the flesh rather than as the means of re-establishing a direct filial relationship between the Father and His erring children or as the initiating action to restore harmony within the family of God.

Although the Reformation seemed at first to promise possibilities of radical change in these attitudes, in point of fact the immediate effect was comparatively small. The most dramatic development was the full acceptance of the ideal of clerical marriage with the consequent depreciation of the state of virginity within the religious life. But this change was to some extent offset by a new concentration on the pattern of family life depicted in the Old Testament, an ideal of domesticity which in the words again of Sherwin Bailey 'intensified the existing androcentricity of society, justified the continued subordination of woman, established the father in a quasi-magisterial role and stringently subjugated children to the wills of their parents'.[16] There is a welcome new emphasis on the 'mutual society, help and comfort' which man and woman ought to enjoy 'both in prosperity and adversity' and upon the right of children to be brought to Christ and then to be nurtured in His faith and

13. Sherwin Bailey: op. cit., p. 55.
14. Ibid., p. 157.
15. Ibid., p. 163.
16. Ibid., p. 181.

fear. But there is still the unremitting stress on the subordination of woman to man, on woman's dominant role as a child-bearer and on the essential taint of the procreative act. Those within the Anglican tradition for instance have never been allowed to forget that 'all men are conceived and born in sin': those within the Reformed tradition that all are 'children of wrath'. The time was not even yet ripe for a new interpretation of atonement in terms of filial and familial imagery.

Yet gradually attitudes began to change. The new possiblities of individual enterprise in travel and trade: of individual learning consequent upon the invention of printing: of individual experimentation by the aid of new scientific instruments—all these led to a growing sense of the place of what might be called the ordinary individual in human affairs. And if the idea of equality began to gain ground what could ultimately prevent the question of the equality of man and woman from being raised at least in matters of status if not in precise function. Further, new discoveries in medical science gradually led to the dissemination of knowledge about the processes of procreation, to safer child birth, and to the relaxation of the strictness of old taboos. And the very fact of the increasing mobility of families through emigration and still more through the beginnings of industrialization meant that the old settled pattern of the patriarchal régime with an unlimited number of descendants held together under the one overlord began to give way to that of smaller family units (often indeed with each possessing a considerable number of children) having to fend for themselves and become integrated into a new social pattern within a new environment. Moreover the gradually increasing power of the mercantile, middle-class section of society over against the traditional, feudal landed gentry meant the establishment of 'comfortable' homes with an almost excessive concern for decorum and domestic propriety. The father was certainly still in control but when adventure or commerce or business took him away from home his wife acted as his surrogate and her status in the family structure advanced accordingly.

An attractive picture of changing attitudes is provided by the book which came to exercise an almost unparalleled religious influence within the English-speaking world—Bunyan's *Pilgrim's Progress*. Here indeed the man is still given absolute priority and falls under no criticism for deserting his family and devoting himself entirely to his heavenly pilgrimage. Yet in the second part of the book Christiana herself, under the guidance of Mr. Great-heart, sets out on the same pilgrimage and the picture of her relations with her children and of their own significance as individual personalities is altogether natural and attractive. We know from Bunyan's own prison writings how deeply he felt the separation from his family and how strong were the ties of affection binding him to each of his children. If, as has been suggested, *Pilgrim's Progress* played a significant part in the growth of the English novel, it is to no small extent by reason of its exploration of those personal and family relationships which have figured so largely in Western literature in the past two hundred years. During this period in spite of reactions and setbacks woman has steadily advanced towards a position of relative equality with man while the rights of children to be loved, nourished and educated have gained an ever-increasing recognition. Child labour would now be unthinkable as also would be child-marriage. The whole concern of our society is to provide for every child the environment and the resources to enable him to fulfil his own gifts and potentialities and to grow in creative relationships with all members of his social group, especially the family.

The changing pattern of the family in society has automatically had its effect upon the use of family models to interpret the relationships between God and man. As I have already indicated the concentration in the Gospels upon the Fatherhood of God and the Sonship of the Christ is quite remarkable. But it still remains to ask how the father-son relationship is to be understood: in terms of generation? of absolute subordination? of unquestioning obedience? And in particular how is the Passion of Christ—His suffering of indignity, His agony in prayer, His faithfulness unto death—to be interpreted in categories which commend themselves to the consciences of those who see little overt evidence of such happenings in ordinary domestic life? There have been some notable attempts to use new psychological insights into the nature of family relationships for the interpretation of Atonement in modern times and it is to these that I shall now turn.

E

Every new interpretation of atonement has been in large measure dependent on earlier formulations. Even when there has been a sharp reaction against accepted doctrine the categories of the past have still been reviewed, criticized and transformed. Yet there have been periods when exceptional changes have taken place, mainly because of the upsurge of revolutionary ideas in the world around. Such a period, so far as Atonement-theology is concerned, was the nineteenth century. As we read the outstanding contributions of this century we are aware of a new atmosphere of thought and of a new view of human relationships. It is true that the traditional and the orthodox remained firmly entrenched and the really original interpretations of atonement gained little honour in their own day. But the future was with them and the dominant doctrine of the early nineteenth century, expressed as it was in terms of unchangeable law and inexorable punishment, made its appeal within ever diminishing circles.

Yet the strength of the existing framework of moral law was formidable. Even where there had been a decline of Christian faith and values there was little diminution—in fact there was often an increase—in respect for the moral law. It seemed that if this was impugned or relaxed in any way, society would be in danger of reverting to anarchy. A vivid example of the general feeling in Church circles may be seen in the outburst of a noted Scottish divine, Dr. Candlish, when confronted by the new teaching of F. D. Maurice. 'I stand', he wrote, 'for the authority of God as Judge, in the plain English meaning of the word, judge. I stand for the authority of his law and its sanctions: apart from which I see no hope for earth, no security against heaven itself becoming as hell. A theology without law—law in the condemnation—law in the atonement—law in the justification—law in the judgment—is to me like the universal return of chaos and old night.'

Such a statement reveals the sense of fear and apprehension which was abroad in the first part of the nineteenth century. Had there not been revolutions in France and America? Had there not been threats of invasion? Were there not the beginnings of vast changes in the social life of Britain as a result of the industrial revolution and of equal changes in the realm of ideas through new explorations of the universe and of man's historic past? Was there not a greater need than ever before to hold fast to the assurance of the absolute Divine government of the world and of the laws of strict retribution by which human pretensions could be held in check? So far as the theology of atonement was concerned it seemed that if any changes were allowed in men's conceptions of law and punishment and remission then the pass would be sold and the whole idea of reconciliation would become meaningless.

In spite of these fears and uncertainties the nineteenth century did in fact produce a remarkable body of creative work on this particular doctrine. It did not in the main attempt to renounce or jettison past thinking but tried to reinterpret it in the light of new knowledge of human associations and relationships. For a variety of reasons the all-important concept was that of *the person* and the all-important questions were those dealing with the nature and qualities of personal relationship. 'Person', of course, allowed a wide frame of reference. It might be the person in the family, it might be the person in some form of wider society. But there was the growing sense that the individual person must be respected, protected, educated. The extension of the popular franchise, the removal of disabilities attaching to particular classes, the growth of educational facilities, the gradual development of a system of rapid inter-communication—all these meant that the individual person became more aware of his own identity and of the nature of his relationships with others. Personal values and personal considerations began to assume a paramount importance.

In the context of the doctrine of atonement this led to new attempts to give traditional concepts a more directly *personal* interpretation and reference. Already in the eighteenth century there had been an application of the penal theory in a more *individual* way through the work of the Pietists in Germany, the Methodists in England and the Revivalists in America. Where social bonds had weakened and individuals found themselves without roots in a new environment: where, moreover, this produced feelings of anxiety and insecurity often deepening to despondency and guilt: the proclamation of God's judgment upon all, but still more of a way of salvation having been made available to every individual who repented and accepted the free pardon procured by Christ, brought new hope and a new sense of self-respect. Now it was the task of theologians in the nineteenth century to question the adequacy of the generally accepted legal model, with its categories of guilt, punishment and penal substitution, to represent the gospel of atonement to those who were becoming increasingly conscious of their selfhood and of their personal relations with their fellow men.

In some ways the adjustment was easier for those who had (e.g. as in England) remained closer to the Catholic tradition and in particular were familiar with the patristic legacy within Christendom. In the East, strictly legal categories had never occupied so prominent a place as in the West. Sacrifice was interpreted as something performed within an existing context of relationships rather than as a means to secure or to radically restore a lost relationship. The kind of succession represented by Cyril and the settled Eastern tradition was taken over in part by Hooker and the seventeenth-century Anglican divines: they conceived the relation between God and men as intimate and sympathetic though as having been perverted and distorted by the negligence and waywardness of sinful man. Humanity they regarded as deprived and lost rather than as altogether rebellious and depraved. Or to put it in another way humanity needed to be healed or mended rather than to be condemned and punished.

But even in circles whose thinking had been moulded almost exclusively by the categories of Anselm and Calvin there began to be a questioning about the nature of sin and punishment, of obedience and sacrifice. Could these any longer be interpreted solely in terms of the law court and legal processes? Or of inexorable, virtually impersonal law and of formalistic, virtually impersonal cultic practices? The significance of the nineteenth century in the history of atonement doctrine is the new prominence given to such relationships as that between father and son or between mother and child, to such concepts as personal sympathy and personal identification with others, to the importance of faith not so much as rational belief but as conscious response to personal gracious activity. This is not to say that none of these had been heard of before. But they begin to occupy a primary rather than a secondary position. And above all they spring out of a new apprehension of the Biblical revelation. The opening up of new avenues of historical investigation was leading men to concern themselves less with dogmatic formulations supported by Biblical texts and more with Biblical accounts of living encounters and personal relationships from which doctrinal deductions could be drawn. In the remainder of this chapter I shall endeavour to draw out some of the new lines of thought appearing in the more 'Catholic' tradition, reserving till the next chapter a consideration of the more 'Reformed' emphasis.

F

In the more Catholic atonement-thinking of the nineteenth century two leading conceptions seem to me to gain a quite new prominence:

1. There is a reconsideration of the idea of *the impassibility of God*. In conditions of life where rhythm and regularity reign supreme it may be possible to retain the thought of God as the source and sustainer of this unceasing motion, Himself relatively untouched by the minor changes and chances of mortal life. But when the universe and man's historical existence are seen to be infinitely complex, with rhythms of orderliness being as it were constantly threatened by disruptive forces, it becomes more realistic to conceive of God as Himself in some way involved in the struggle, as

the One Who is continually bringing order out of disorder, as the One Who is personally concerned to perfect His creation and to fashion His complete image in humanity. To see the Atonement as the process by which the personal travail of God is finding fulfilment in nature and in humanity—this is one of the new visions of the nineteenth century.

2. There is a reconsideration of the idea of *the sacrifice of Christ*. In the tradition of the West sacrifice had been viewed almost exclusively as an offering made by man to God to express gratitude or to win favour. God is assumed to be the One responsible for the proper ordering of all life. Where man has failed to fulfil his obligations, some reparation must be made. Even in order to guarantee the sustained Divine favour some gift is required. Hence sacrifice came to be associated almost exclusively with propitiation and quasi-mechanical operations and the offering of Christ was interpreted accordingly. But with the application of historical methods to the Bible and to the Fathers it became possible to view sacrifice as part of the continuing work of God. God is involved with man in the process of sustaining and renewing life. It is not man who takes the initiative in offering. It is God Who, in and through humanity, makes a continuous sacrifice and thereby carries forward a process of universal reconciliation.

Let us look at each of these conceptions in more detail. As an example of the first I begin with the writings of Horace Bushnell. It may seem surprising to include a New England minister within what I have called the more 'Catholic' tradition but the general pattern of Bushnell's thinking conforms in a remarkable way to the organic conceptions of Eastern Christendom. He was altogether opposed to the bare individualism which was gaining acceptance in his time, the type of religion which regarded the soul of the individual as isolated in its evil fallenness, without life and hope, unless it should be grasped by the extraordinary and apparently arbitrary action of God Himself. Instead he developed an imaginative system of theology in which the all-important categories were the family and the church, nurture and growth, vicarious suffering and organic unity. The goal of the whole process of human life he conceived to be 'that Christ be formed in you': and the agent working continuously within the universal organism to bring about this end was none other than the Holy Spirit Himself.

In opposition also to the Unitarianism of his day Bushnell was deeply committed to a Trinitarian theology, though his concern was for a trinity of revelation rather than for speculation about the relationship between the persons within the eternal Godhead. He readily spoke of the *dramatis personae* of revelation and of the uniqueness of each *persona* as consisting in the aspect of the infinite and eternal God which He conveyed to man. He referred again and again to the unfathomable mystery of the interior nature of God. Yet God has so revealed Himself that the symbols Father, Son and Spirit can alone do justice to what has been made known to us in Christ. In Him the eternal God acts in a glory of manifest radiance and thereby draws us into a response of love and worship, in which activities we know Him ever more deeply as He is.

Such a conception of the Divine Being made it utterly impossible for Bushnell to think in terms of any kind of transaction within the Godhead. To speak as if the Son, in His sacrifice, appeased or propitiated God, even on behalf of others, is blasphemy. 'It is not that the suffering appeases God but that it expresses God—displays in open history the unconquerable love of God's heart.'[17] Or again to speak as if the Son, in His sacrifice, had performed an act of superlative or optional goodness is to misunderstand the Christian Gospel completely. The suffering is not an extra, it belongs to the very essence of God's nature. 'Whatever we may say or hold or believe concerning the vicarious sacrifice of Christ we are to affirm in the same manner of God. The whole Deity is in it, in it from eternity, and will to eternity be . . . there is a cross in God before the wood is seen upon Calvary. . . . It is as if there were a cross unseen, standing on its undiscovered hill, far back in the ages, out of which were sounding always, just the same deep voice of suffering love and patience, that was heard by mortal ears from the sacred hill of Calvary.'[18]

In the opening chapter of his definitive book *Vicarious Sacrifice*, Bushnell sought first to define the phrase itself. He dismissed all views which either underestimate its significance—as, for example, the view that Christ assumed our common liabilities simply in the way that every citizen suffers in some degree for the wrongs of the community to which he belongs—or distorts its meaning—as, for example, the view that Christ Himself became guilty and punishable in our place: instead he affirmed as the true conception that Christ, in his vicarious sacrifice 'engages at the expense of great suffering and even of death itself, to bring us out of our sins themselves and so out of their penalties; being Himself profoundly identified with us in our fallen state and burdened in feeling with our evils'. (He has quoted Matthew 8:7—'That it might be fulfilled which was spoken by Esaias the prophet, saying, "Himself took our infirmities

17. *God in Christ*, p. 216.
18. *Vicarious Sacrifice*, p. 64.

and bare our sicknesses" ' as a key text.) The two most significant
words in this definition are 'identified' and 'feeling'. These were the
notes which Bushnell was to strike again and again. They came out
of the vocabulary of personal relationships as he daily experienced
them. Real identification with suffering humanity, real fellow-
feeling with the sinner in his sinfulness—this is vicarious sacrifice
and this is the highest and deepest revelation of God Himself.
'What then was Christ in His vicarious feeling and sacrifice, what in
His Gethsemane, but a revelation in time of just that love that has
been struggling always in God's bosom, watching wearily for the
world and with inward groanings unheard by mortal ears? . . .
There is a Gethsemane hid in all love, and when the fit occasion
comes, no matter how great and high the subject may be, its heavy
groaning will be heard—even as it was in Christ. He was in an
agony, exceeding sorrowful even unto death. By that sign it was
that God's love broke into the world and Christianity was born.'[19]

In such passages Bushnell writes movingly and eloquently about
the vicarious principle in human experience. But how does he
relate this to sacrifice? Part IV of his book is entitled 'Sacrificial
Symbols and Their Uses' and is in many ways astonishingly modern,
especially in its treatment of language. His exposition runs as
follows. God made man for himself and consequently there is
in a man a constant yearning after God. The fact of sin and the
sense of separation which it entails makes this longing even more
intense though it must never be forgotten that this yearning is
in no sense man's own creation but is rather the result of the
Spirit striving within him. What more natural than that this inward
longing should express itself outwardly in and through the
pattern of sacrifice—a ritual-form which combines movements of
'penitence, self-mortification, homage and the tender invocation of
mercy'. 'Sacrifices then', Bushnell writes, 'are not the mere spontaneous contrivances of men, but the contrivances of men whose
contrivings are impelled and guided and fashioned by God—just
as truly appointed by God as if they were ordered by some vocal
utterance from heaven.'[20] What then is their function in the Divine
economy? Not simply to be types of a mysterious unknown future,
not to be the vehicle of the process of legal substitution, but above
all to be what Bushnell calls a *transactional liturgy*, meaning by this
a pattern of outward action signifying penitence, purification and
finally acceptance with God. To attract men towards Himself God
graciously gives them 'a drill of action' expecting 'by that means

19. *Vicarious Sacrifice*, p. 47.
20. Op. cit., pp. 387–8.

to generate in them an implicit faith, sentiment, piety, which they do not know themselves by definition and could not state in words that suppose a reflective discovery'.[21]

In some respects Bushnell's handling of the idea of sacrifice is idealistic, in some respects it is untrue to the historical evidence which we now possess. He emphasized what he called the altar-form and altar-symbolism in preaching but made virtually no reference to the place of sacrifice in the liturgical and sacramental tradition of the Church. At the same time he showed remarkable originality of thought in emphasizing the necessity of taking the total pattern of the sacrificial act into consideration instead of concentrating attention upon the slaying of the victim alone. Furthermore by perceiving the importance of corporate cultic activity as a means of education and by penetrating to the heart of sacrifice as a divine activity rather than a human perversion he was breaking new ground. He was already wrestling with the question of the significance of symbolic words and deeds and saw the importance of the person as agent in the process of revelation.

The sum of Bushnell's doctrine is that the eternal God—Father, Son and Holy Spirit—is engaged in the activity of love; and love, wherever it is revealed in the universe, involves some form of travail and suffering. Love issues in identification with the other in true sympathy. And the end of love is to transform into the image of the ultimately real which is itself the image of love. Atonement then is the travail of the ages, focussed once and for all in the vivid scenes of Gethsemane and Calvary, but for ever operating in the passion of the Holy Spirit to transform the world into the image of the Son of God. 'To re-engage the world's love and to re-unite the world, as free, to the Eternal Life'—this is the end of all Divine activity. 'It lies in the very scheme and economy of the Gospel to regenerate a Christly virtue in man, a character that bears the type of Gethsemane and the Cross.' These were the twin foci around which all Bushnell's thinking and preaching revolved and although his approach to the interpretation of atonement may be only one among many it is one which impresses the reader deeply as being an expression of personal experience and a key to fuller understanding of ultimate mystery.

So far as I know there was no direct communication between Bushnell in New England and Frederick Denison Maurice in London. Yet it was within the decade 1849–59 that Bushnell's thought was maturing, leading ultimately to the publication of *Vicarious Sacrifice*. It was in the years 1849–54 that Maurice was

21. Ibid., pp. 396–7.

busy lecturing and writing, producing in the later year *The Doctrine of Sacrifice*. Both had been influenced by the thought of Coleridge but each was wrestling with the particular religious and intellectual problems of his own immediate age. It is remarkable that each focussed his attention on the notion of sacrifice and sought to interpret it in an altogether new way within the context of atonement theology.

Throughout his writings Maurice holds fast to two fundamental axioms. One is that Christ, the Son of God, is at all times and in all places, in heaven and in earth, in eternity and in historic manifestation, completely united with the Father in will, purpose and substance. The other is that Christ, in his historic manifestation on earth, became united in all respects with our essential humanity. He did not stand apart from men as their substitute. Rather He was identified with them as their representative, entering with sympathy into a total human experience, revealing Himself as 'the root of righteousness in each man'. Whatever He does He does as the *Son* of God. Therefore whatever else atonement may be it is first and foremost the reconciliation of *sons* to God in and through the Divine Son. This is the principle which Maurice keeps ever in the forefront of his exposition. Every category of atonement thinking—satisfaction, sin, sacrifice—must be interpreted in terms of the relationship existing between the holy Father and the perfect Son.

But one consequence of these initial axioms which is of great importance in his whole theology is that it would be unthinkable to include the perfect Son in any direct rebellion against the Father, any antagonism of the will to the Father's loving purpose for His universe. I shall be looking in my next chapter at the way in which certain modern thinkers have sought to grapple with this difficulty. But in the case of Maurice *sin* was imagined almost exclusively in terms of corporate *evil*. Sin was to him a vast satanic influence permeating human life, a loathsome universal plague infecting every department of human existence. Man is the victim of the ravages of an all-embracing scourge which inevitably leads to his death. In his famous sermon dealing with our Lord's encounter with the man possessed by an unclean spirit, Maurice used such phrases as 'filthy and loathsome', 'impurity and injustice and falsehood and baseness', 'the likeness of a brute', 'the image of a devil'. No words were too strong to describe the dereliction of the human condition brought about through the entrance of sin into the world. And into this situation of horror and darkness the 'pure and holy Jesus' willingly entered. Yet the vocabulary which Maurice does *not* employ is that of rebellion, revolt, contradiction, defiance, even disobedience.

Within his terms of reference, Maurice could speak movingly of the complete sympathy of the Son of Man with fallen mankind and of His complete identification with their lot. He takes up the verse which was so influential in Bushnell's thinking 'Himself took our infirmities and bare our sicknesses'. He speaks of actual participation in man's calamity, of a consciousness of the wickedness of man in His inmost being. He stresses the fact that 'the sense, the taste, the anguish of sin' are infinitely more terrible within the consciousness of one who knows no sin in himself than they could ever be in the mind of the sinner. 'The agony of the spirit which is gathered in the words, "If it be possible, let this cup pass from me", with the submission of the words "Not as I will but as Thou wilt"; above all, the crushing for a moment even of that one infinite comfort, "Yet I am not alone, because the Father is with me" when the cry was heard "My God, my God, why has Thou forsaken me"—these revelations tell us a little of what it was to be made Sin.'[22] Within this complete identification with man's evil condition, the Son of God yet preserves what Maurice calls 'the true sinless root of Humanity'. It is through the perfect response to the Father's holiness and love (which the term 'sinless root' seems to imply) from the very midst of the unholiness and baseness which characterizes the corporate life of humanity that atonement is made.

In a summary statement gathering up his own understanding of the Cross Maurice describes it as the meeting-point between man and man, between man and God. Men at all times have been seeking such a meeting-point but it is God Who has provided it. And the essential nature of that which happened at this meeting-point is 'that in it man is presented as a holy and acceptable sacrifice to the Creator'. In other words Christ, as representative Man, presents in and through the Cross a perfect sacrifice to God the Creator of all. How does Maurice expand this statement in his exposition of the meaning of sacrifice?

Before answering this question it is useful to pause and consider briefly the background of thought against which he (and other pioneer spirits of the nineteenth century) was writing. In Western Christendom the understanding of sacrifice stemmed from two main sources. On the one hand there was the tradition derived from ancient Rome in which sacrifice was essentially a rite to be performed in order to avert the displeasure of the deity and to maintain the well-being of the community. On the other hand there was the tradition derived from ancient Israel in which sacrifice was pre-eminently a rite ordained by God Himself by which the results of

22. *The Doctrine of Sacrifice*, p. 189.

trespasses and transgressions of the law could be minimized and even annulled.[23] In the former tradition the stress was laid upon the godward direction of the act: it was man's chief duty to offer the appropriate gift in order that the natural and social system in which he lived and on which he depended might continue to function harmoniously. In the latter the stress was upon the manward direction of the act: it was God's provision to meet the deleterious effects of human transgression and man, in making the offering, was simply taking advantage of the way of escape which had been provided for him. But whether it were the Roman or the Jewish pattern which governed men's thinking, the whole purpose of sacrifice tended to be expressed in terms of propitiation or satisfaction or expiation. Sacrifice was the traditional or the appointed way for removing the effects and consequences of open offences.

The great change which began to appear in the nineteenth century was the rediscovery of an interpretation of sacrifice having its antecedents in the Bible and in the Greek fathers but coming into new prominence as a result of increasing knowledge of the natural order on the one hand and the course of human history on the other. From each source it became increasingly clear that the surrender of a life to death could in fact lead to an enhancement of life. So, for example, we find the noted preacher of the mid-nineteenth century, F. W. Robertson of Brighton, exclaiming 'The grand law of the universe, Sacrifice, conscious and unconscious, for the life of others'. And a little later Bishop Westcott can appeal to examples in the lives of nations of 'the fruitfulness of sacrifice', of the death of their heroes enabling them to rise to higher levels of being. This was the theme which Maurice made his own and developed with immense power and versatility in *The Doctrine of Sacrifice*.

In this striking collection of sermons the preacher is concerned all the time to turn men's imaginative vision away from the remote Judge, who waits for men to offer the appropriate propitiatory sacrifice, to the compassionate Father who initiates and fulfils the whole sacrifical movement Himself. God, he declares, is the author of life through sacrifice: Christ is the demonstration of life through sacrifice: the Spirit is the inner witness and inspiration of life through sacrifice. This sacrifice is no after-thought invented to meet an unfortunate situation. Rather it belongs to the very constitution of the universe, to the very life of God Himself. It was

23. This is the leading assumption of the Book of Leviticus. I do not attempt here to deal with other views of the intention of sacrifice current at earlier periods.

through sacrifice that the created world came into existence: it is through sacrifice that its evils are thwarted and overcome. And it is only as man identifies himself with the Christ Whose career is the archetype of true sacrifice, and receives the Holy Spirit Who is the inspirer of every act of sacrifice, that he can reach his own true destiny and fulfilment.

How then is sacrifice related to human sinfulness? Not only does Maurice stress the character of sin as an all-embracing loathsome infection. He also exposes it in terms of self-seeking, self-pleasing, self-glorifying. And the most terrible extreme of sin so regarded is the attempt to make God the minister of man's own designs, even his own self-indulgence. He will then go to the length of offering gifts (which are the parody of true sacrifice) to get God on his side. He will seek deliverance from the punishment of evil while the evil itself still persists. But all this is the complete perversion of a humanity created in the image of God. The pattern of this humanity is self-sacrifice, self-outpouring, self-emptying. Sacrifice proceeds from God and is the expression of the very being of God. In his exposition of Romans 3: 25 Maurice insists that it is God who makes the sacrifice, God who justifies, God who makes peace through the blood of the Cross, God who is the beginning and the end of Sacrifice. Moreover it is God Who sends forth the Spirit of His Son and this is the Spirit of Sacrifice. The Son offers Himself to God in the energy of the eternal Spirit and gathers up into His offering those who have received the same Spirit. Thus the Atonement is a process once for all demonstrated but continually enacted. In a fine exhortation Maurice challenges his hearers to identify themselves with Him Who identified Himself with them:

'The might of His own sacrifice is with thee. He Who gave up Himself without spot to God will enable thee to offer thyself an acceptable and reasonable sacrifice, to do His will, to glorify His name.'[24]

Maurice had certainly not said the last word on the doctrine of sacrifice but he had made a most impressive re-statement whose influence was to be felt particularly in the life and practice of the Church of England. I have already touched upon the most obvious defect of his theology. What was to be made of man's deliberate rebellion, the setting of his own will in opposition to that of God? No one could suggest that the perfect Son could be identified with such an attitude. But even man's self-seeking and self-indulgence to which Maurice refers openly—could the Son of God, we still ask, be identified with anything directed self-wards rather than

24. *The Doctrine of Sacrifice*, p. 313.

Godwards? Could His sympathy extend to such a perversion of humanity? These, it seems to me, are the great unanswered questions in what is otherwise a most convincing system of thought. It will be necessary to view atonement from another angle in order to gain light on what is, within Maurice's terms of reference, a baffling mystery.

G

There were to be further attempts later in the nineteenth century to explore the meaning of atonement through an appeal to the nature of the relationship existing ideally between a father and a son and through further examinations of the significance of suffering and sacrifice. Moreover by a new focussing of interest on the Epistle to the Hebrews and the Johannine writings the attempt was made to gain a fuller picture of New Testament teaching than could be obtained from the Pauline Epistles in relative isolation. In 1888 a short series of addresses by Bishop B. F. Westcott entitled *The Victory of the Cross* dealt suggestively with the solidarity of human society, the universality of the law of sacrifice and the place of suffering within the Divine economy. 'Suffering which is welcomed with the response of love, when it is brought to us by the will of God, love for the Creator to whose purpose it answers, love for the creature to whose purifying it serves, illuminates the whole course of this world. In this sense sufferings are a revelation of the Fatherhood of God Who brings back His children to Himself in righteousness and love.'[25] Strong emphasis is laid upon the disciplinary character of sufferings and upon the virtue displayed in bearing suffering trustingly and even joyfully. Christ not only provides the perfect example of such virtue but also 'gives the virtue of His own life to quicken the soul which rests on Him'. By dying to sin in the power of Christ's sacrifice the believer is quickened to righteousness and becomes a true son within the family of God, a son who is now ready and willing to share in the discipline of Christ's sufferings for the sake of others.

Nine years later *The Spiritual Principle of Atonement* by J. Scott Lidgett was published, a book which probably more than any other sought to interpret atonement strictly in terms of the relationship between father and son. What, Lidgett asks, does *fatherhood* mean? It means that God, *out of His own life* called into existence beings at once kindred with Himself and possessing a distinct individuality of their own. In this way they were introduced into a world, a home

25. Op. cit., p. 82.

of love, which environs their whole life and has as its goal the fellowship of mutual giving and receiving which can only exist between those who are spiritually akin, a fellowship which it is the object of fatherly education to perfect.[26]

It is this process of *fatherly education* which Lidgett proceeds to expound. He assumes that a father has the knowledge of the ideal of what the child should become and the power to guide him on the way to its realization. But if the child is disobedient and rebellious the father 'has to assert the sanctity of the law which has been broken and to secure its recognition. He has to bring home to the child the consciousness of wrong doing. All this is the work of punishment and most truly in the interests of the child himself. And satisfaction is made by an act which, in its various aspects, is at once a submission to the father's authority, an offering of homage and reparation to the law, an expression of agreement with the father's mind and a surrender to his love.'[27]

Lidgett seems to have no doubt about the capacity of an earthly father not only to exercise a natural relationship of authority towards the son but also to represent that supernatural authority Who is the source of the ideals and laws of human behaviour. 'By virtue of his fatherhood, the father is the guardian of the law of righteousness which protects the family bond of love and fellowship.' If this law is broken a proper satisfaction as defined in my earlier quotation must be rendered. This is the perfect filial response. But seeing that no son is capable of making such a response out of his own resources it is the father's nature and good pleasure to identify himself as far as possible with the son and direct his mind and will towards the ideal which constitutes his true goal.

But if reparation is to be made for *all* the children of the family there must be a Son universally related to all sons. 'Only such', Lidgett writes, 'could *give complete expression* under our penal conditions to the submission of mankind to God, to make reparation to His law and to put away sin from man.'[28] And it is his conviction that the message of the Incarnation does in fact give the revelation of such a Son, perfectly related to God the Father, universally related to the sons of men. All this is explored with reverent care and devotion and the Father-Son relationship, which is obviously of outstanding importance in the early Christian interpretations of incarnation and atonement, is made central and definitive. Yet it is abundantly clear that Lidgett is still living and

26. See p. 227.
27. J. Scott Lidgett: *The Principle of Atonement*, p. 268.
28. Op. cit., p. 378.

writing within a context of law: the authority of a father to represent a transcendent law, to determine when and how it has been infringed, to judge what constitutes an appropriate reparation or punishment. A son's primary virtue is obedience, even submission. These principles are taken for granted and in consequence we really have a modification or humanization of legal and penal concepts, not an altogether new exploration of the father-son relationship in the light of changing attitudes in the world of the late nineteenth and early twentieth centuries. But ideas which Lidgett was still able to assume as axiomatic were soon to be challenged and exposed to criticism from all sides.

Before this happened however another remarkable attempt was made to reinterpret the Atonement in terms of personal relationships such as could be experienced within the context of a closely integrated human family. Notably amongst the middle classes in England the nineteenth century had witnessed an increasing emphasis upon the ideals of family life. The growing concern for education was making the place of the child in the family more significant and more secure. The status of the mother in the home grew in importance. The intricacies of relationships between man and woman were being explored through drama and novel. The very fact of the greater separation of the father from his home through his engagement in the work of the office, the factory, the business house meant a decrease in his patriarchal status and allowed opportunity for the personalities of other members of the family to develop in their own right. The absence too of boys at boarding school, the development of facilities of correspondence by letter, the increase of opportunities for individual reading—all this led to a growth of awareness on the one hand of the personality of the individual as child, as youth, as reaching maturity and on the other hand of the inter-relationship of individual personalities within the family, the school, the wider community. At their best Victorian homes were nurseries for the development of human personality in relationship with other members of the family and it was from one of these homes that a profound, original and persuasive book appeared, seeking to interpret the Christian doctrine of atonement in terms of the new understanding of the personal which men in so many other ways were coming to apprehend.

Robert Campbell Moberly lived within a family tradition which had distinguished forebears in the earlier part of the nineteenth century. He was doubtless conscious of both the unity and the continuity of the family to which he belonged as well as of the inter-relationship of distinctive individuals within the family complex.

These characteristics made the family an apt analogous symbol for the Catholic Church whose continuity, unity and organic inter-relationships of members have been amongst its most important notes. The Church on earth, especially when viewed as the household of God and the home of the faithful, is a true model of the Church in heaven and the exploration of the nature of personal relations in the human situation can provide valuable analogies for the under-standing of the relationships existing between the three Persons of the eternal Trinity.

These assumptions which could have sprung naturally out of the experience of a strong family tradition and of a satisfying domestic happiness were reinforced in the minds of Moberly and his friends by the idealistic philosophy which was the most influential intellectual movement of their own time. In this school of thought the all-important idea was that within the best gifts of civilization—art, morality, religion—the eternal world was already partially embodied. Reality was to be found neither in the sheer material structures of the physical universe nor in the remote other-worldly structures of a transcendent order. Rather it was to be found incarnated in the structures of truth, goodness and beauty discernible here and now in the life of mankind. This philosophy 'claimed to be in a position to affirm that the great doctrines of Christianity, of manhood taken into God, of life won by the losing of it in death, and the like, were true, not indeed as the record or the anticipation of events miraculous and supernatural in a far distant past or in a remote future quite unlike the present, but rather as statements of the inner significance of the spiritual life of man in every age, of the whole history of civilization itself'.[29]

Moberly's task then was to examine the doctrine of atonement afresh (without questioning for a moment the historic basis of the doctrine or the value of previous explanatory theories) and to show how reconciliation is manifested again and again in human life even if in an imperfect form: above all to show that when the concept of human personality is rightly understood and the delicate nature of inter-personal relationships adequately described the way is open towards a truer and deeper apprehension of what atonement means within the Divine economy. I think that Moberly would have agreed that, to put it quite simply, if there is one key available to us to unlock the door leading to an ever-expanding knowledge of what atonement through Christ can mean to man, it is the key of family experiences, family relations, family ideals.

As is well known the book begins (and the value of its whole

29. C. C. J. Webb: *Religious Thought in England from 1850*, p. 102.

contribution depends upon the validity of the method employed in the opening chapters) with a careful analysis of four leading conceptions—Punishment, Penitence, Forgiveness, Mediation. That these words represent real experiences within the spiritual life of man there can be no reasonable doubt. But, says Moberly, all our experience is imperfect. We can, for example, only experience forgiveness in an inchoate or imperfect form. Yet, he claims, the imperfect can point us towards the perfection of the experience: 'we may, on the basis of imperfect experience, approximately attain a true conception of what perfect realization would mean'. And it follows that it is within the area of the life which we generally recognize as the highest and most ennobling within our experience that we can expect to gain the truest indication of what these conceptions imply in their perfect realization. In other words Moberly's most persuasive analogies are derived from the life of the home and the personal relationships of the members of the family with one another, relationships which involve distinguishable selves within an almost mystical unity of spiritual togetherness.

Within such a context punishment cannot be satisfactorily regarded as a quantitative infliction of pain as retribution. It can only be justified if it is received as 'right' by the punished and thereby transmuted into penitence. Such penitence is the beginning of the expression of atonement. But penitence must develop and grow. All experienced penitence is imperfect for sin holds man back and restricts his capacity for a full penitence. Yet we realize that if only there could be a complete personal self-identification with holiness, penitence would have reached its fulfilment. And the sequence continues with forgiveness. We know forgiveness in many forms— remission of penalty, readiness to forget, treating as innocent. But such manifestations do not take personality and personal relations seriously. Forgiveness only comes to full expression as it relates itself sensitively to every manifestation of penitence. Forgiveness promotes penitence: penitence calls forth forgiveness. Forgiveness in Moberly's phrase, is exactly correlative with 'forgivableness', i.e. with the personal identification with righteousness in which penitence consists. In short punishment, penitence and forgiveness can only be rightly understood as inter-related aspects of the one process by which the sinner is being drawn away from his identification with wrong, with passion, with self-pleasing, to an identification with right, with holiness, with love.

In all this careful examination of terms Moberly keeps personal experience and personal considerations in the forefront and in one notable passage brings his analysis to a climax by describing in detail 'the attitude of a parent, patient, loving, and wise in dealing with the naughtiness of a little child'.[30] Here is the nearest approach that we can conceive to divine forgiveness, the nearest analogy on earth by which we can express the working of Divine love. It is interesting that Moberly does not produce arguments to support this judgment. He assumes it to be self-evident. By appealing to the kind of situation which he had doubtless observed in the life of his own family, he could, he believed, establish principles which though always imperfectly realized on earth belonged to the very structure of Divine atonement. It is worth quoting a few sentences from the description of the process of forgiveness in an earthly family inspired by a spirit of love.

Everything is governed by 'the wise diplomacy of love', a love which always thinks of the child apart from his evil-doing, 'yet cannot wear the aspect of forgiveness while the child is wholly self-identified with its passion'. But 'with the first dim touch or gleam of child-like regret and sorrow, the love which was waiting opens its arms as love. . . . Love dare not, cannot—being love— forgive in the height of the passion. Love dare not, cannot—being love—fail to forgive, from the moment when forgiveness is possible. . . . A child sent away for disobedience offers shyly to come back. Is that shyness the wistful shyness of desire? In that wistfulness, dim, childlike, half-conscious as it is, may be the true germ of what, in its perfected blossom, would be the outpouring of the confession of the penitent. It may be that mere wistfulness, if met with the open-armed embrace of forgiving love, will produce forthwith the faltering word of regret, or the tears without words, which are, so far, the little self's true effort of repudiation of sin, and of personal allegiance to righteousness.'[31] On this kind of basis forgiveness is defined as 'a loving recognition and embrace, on the part of authoritative righteousness, of the first beginning or desire, within the child, towards that condemnation of sin in the self, which is the form through which a personality in which sin is inherent, can become at all again identified with righteousness'.[32]

Clearly the all-important process in Moberly's view of the human situation is *the awakening of a spirit of penitence.* Punishment has no meaning or justification unless it issues in penitence. Forgiveness has no meaning or justification unless it is a response to awakening penitence. Love rejoices when the spirit of penitence begins to appear. Whether in relations between man and man or between

30. *Atonement and Personality*, p. 64.
31. Op. cit., pp. 64–5.
32. Ibid, p. 66.

man and God penitence which moves towards a self-identification with righteousness is the infinitely desirable element. Consequently the all-important question for Moberly is bound to be: How can such a spirit of penitence be awakened in man? How can man so develop in penitence that he can enjoy ever more deeply the forgiveness of God? This is to him the real problem of atonement and it is this problem which leads him forward to the principle of *mediation*.

At first sight, he argues, the very idea of a mediator seems out of the question. If it is the springs of a man's inner character which are to be touched, if it is the very direction of his inner life which is to be changed, how can anyone *from outside* act effectively upon him? No exhortation or example will succeed in penetrating to the inner citadel of the personality. Yet a not uncommon experience makes us pause in our logic. Have we not all heard of a friend who comes into a situation not lecturing, not parading rightness, but *bearing* and *carrying*? 'What heaviness of heart there must be, what anxious thought and care, what hoping against hope, what sense of effort disappointed, and love (as it seems) thrown away, what unwearying prayer to God, what patient bearing with folly, perverseness and sin!' And again to provide his supreme illustration and analogy Moberly turns to the experience of relationships in the home, this time bringing in the mother as the one who constantly exercises the mediatorial role. Assuming that the major problem is the transfiguration of the character of the child Moberly asks: 'Do we not recognize at once that the profoundest hope for the child's real change lies in the reality with which the parents enter into his grief and shame; so enter into it, on his behalf, as to win it to be in him where in fact it was not, until it was first in them, and in him only from them? Do we not recognize in particular, the place, in his discipline and his purifying, which may belong to the voluntary distress and endurance of the mother? This is no question, it is to be observed, of a penalty which the father insists on inflicting upon somebody, and which the mother intervenes to bear. Nothing whatever is inflicted by the father on the mother. Indeed, nothing is, strictly speaking, inflicted on any one by any one. The penalty which the mother bears is the penalty of contrition: it is rather an effort of discipline than a price of satisfaction: it corresponds in idea not to punishment so much, regarded externally as a squaring of accounts, as to the moral discipline which, through self-abasement, self-condemnation and self-surrender to penalty, wins its painful way to victorious goodness and peace. And she bears it, not as an inflicted sentence, but as the spontaneous instinct and outflow of her own intensity of love. And finally, so far is it from being imposed by the relentlessness of an unforgiving father, that whatever she bears in this way, he too bears in her and with her; for in mind, in this matter, and in will, they are one. Whatever he may seem to exact, she exacts as completely as he. Whatever she is willing to endure, his sympathy too, and his will, and his yearning desire, are with her to the full in the enduring.'[33]

This analogy obviously springs out of living experience. It is moving, suggestive, symbolically apt. But Moberly can still regard it as utterly inadequate to represent the ultimate reality of atonement just because the persons of father, mother and child are still distinct. No man can be another. No woman can be her child however closely identified she may be with him in desire and feeling. In human life there may come remarkable changes in human character through the sympathetic influence and concern of a true friend and mediator. But all this falls short of what is required if a sinner is to be turned away from his identification with wrong to an identification with goodness. Only if there be One Who is in a far closer way identified both with God and with man than can be represented in any illustration drawn from the relations of separate human personalities, can a true atonement be made.

This absolute necessity, as he conceives it, leads Moberly to a reconsideration of the basic Christian confession that Christ was perfect God and perfect man. As regards the first part of the confession, Moberly is content to emphasize the unity of the Godhead as Personal and therefore as consisting of a real reciprocity of mutual relation. In regard to the manhood he has more to say. His chief point is that Christ was not simply a man amongst men, another specimen as it were of manhood. 'His relation to the race was not a differentiating but a consummating relation. He was not generically but inclusively man.' Even our own human experience is such that we know that our own selfhood is dependent on our relationships with others. To a minimal degree I am related to the whole human race. But Christ was able to indwell as Spirit the whole of humanity. His was the humanity of Deity. The Spirit of God became through Incarnation the Spirit of Man. What is inconceivable in the relation of man to man, because every man is distinct from his neighbour, becomes real in the relation of Christ to man because He, as personal God, gathers up, consummates and includes within His personal Being humanity as a whole. And because of this fact He is able to effect within humanity that which it would be impossible for any man, however holy and selfless, to do.

However difficult this conception may be it is the vital link in

33. Ibid., pp. 80-1.

the chain which leads forward to Moberly's interpretation of atonement. By an analysis of human experience he has established to his own satisfaction the absolute centrality of penitence in any process of atonement. But a perfect penitence is quite unattainable by man. How then can atonement be effected? Only by the entrance into humanity of the One Who, by embracing this humanity in an all-inclusive way, can make it His own and express within it that perfect penitence which no member of the human race could express either on his own behalf or on the behalf of others. 'He, then, on the Cross, offered as man to God, not only the sacrifice of utter obedience, under conditions (themselves the consequence of human transgression) which made the effort of such perfect will-obedience more tremendous that we can conceive, but also the sacrifice of supreme penitence, that is, of perfect will-identity with God in condemnation of sin, Himself being so self-identified with sinners, that this could take the form of the offering of Himself for sin. He voluntarily stood in the place of the utterly contrite—accepting insult, shame, anguish, death—death possible only by His own assent, yet outwardly inflicted as penal; nay, more, in His own inner consciousness, accepting the ideal consciousness of the contrite—which is the one form of the penitent's righteousness: desolate, yet still, in whatever He was, voluntary; and in that very voluntariness of desolation, sovereign. He did, in fact and in full, that which would in the sinner constitute perfect atonement, but which has for ever become impossible to the sinner, just in proportion as it is true that he has sinned.'[34]

Here is Moberly's central definition of atonement. But such a definition draws the attention away from a transaction in the past and a fulfilment in the future such as had been characteristic of so much of Western thought. Instead it recaptures the emphasis of Eastern thought by concentrating on the present which is in a certain sense the eternal present and on the operation in time of the eternal Holy Spirit. This Spirit is the Spirit of the Crucified, the Spirit of perfect penitence, the Spirit of Human Holiness victorious over sin. It is as we receive the Spirit and live in the Spirit that we become participators in the atoning work of Christ, that we in fact appropriate the perfect penitence of the Redeemer. This, in Moberly's further exposition, is not a purely mystical and unworldly operation. It is carried forward in the world within the Church in the actual experience of its sacramental life. The whole life of the individual Christian within the Body of Christ becomes a perfecting of penitence within the continuous offering of His Sacrifice. 'It is

34. Op. cit., pp. 129–30.

Christ, then, who in the fullest sense, *is* our atonement and our atonement is real in proportion to the reality of Christ in us. Our atonement is no merely past transaction: it is a perpetual presence: a present possibility, of the life and of the self, the consummation of which transcends thought and desire.'[35]

Since Moberly's time vast changes have taken place in the social life of the West. Generally speaking the role of the father in the family has declined, the mother has become involved in far wider interests and responsibilities outside the home and children have matured at an earlier age and sought their codes of conduct outside the family context. Traditional moral standards have been questioned and criticized. Increasing attention has been given to the place of sexual attraction in human feelings and relationships. The novel has explored endless permutations and combinations in family and small social groupings, diagnosing where possible the sources of alienation and occasionally suggesting ways of reconciliation. The drama has focussed attention first upon the drawing room, then upon the kitchen-sink, all with the object of disclosing human situations of tension, personal attraction and repulsion, strong emotion and dynamic action, comedy and tragedy, individual aspiration and social conformity. It has been a time of experimentation and search for new stabilities in a world whose fundamental characteristics seem to be relativism and rapid change.

In such a period the use of family analogies and comparisons becomes highly problematical. Man's interest in the family—its establishment, its sustenance, the right ordering of its relationships —shows no sign of diminishing, certainly in the world of the West. But where is guidance to be found? Not in the philosophies of the past. Not in the authority of religious systems. Can it be found by means of employing the same methods as are in vogue in man's general attitude to the world—observing, experimenting, making statistical analyses, allowing for environmental conditions, using modern means of communication? That these methods cannot be by-passed or ignored seems clear enough. That whatever can be regarded as firmly validated by pragmatic experience must somehow be incorporated into acceptable patterns of behaviour seems only sensible. Yet does this imply that the great tradition of the family—the protective responsibility of the father, the sacrificial sympathy of the mother, the child's growth into maturity through learning, watching, imitating, questioning, all within a context of mutual trust and affection—must be discarded?

I do not think that it need be. But much that was at one time

35. Op. cit., p. 286.

taken for granted is no longer acceptable. In matters of punishment, for example, the assumption that a parent has the right to determine the form that punishment in any particular instance shall take and to proceed then to inflict it has been radically questioned. Unless it is reasonably certain that the child has grasped the nature of a rule of behaviour and has recognized that an infringement of the rule will necessarily bring about a certain consequence, it is meaningless to cause a particular consequence to follow upon the child's infringement of a particular pattern. On the other hand few would deny that a society, however small and intimate, must have *some* rules and conventions of behaviour. And for the sake of the rest of the society contraventions of the rules by any individual cannot pass unnoticed.

So in family, in school, in business-concern the struggle continues to devise reasonable rules and disciplines which combine the maximum of freedom for the individual with the minimum of hurt or inconvenience for the rest of the social group. And in theory at least it is widely agreed that this can only be done if the framers of the rules are willing to make every conceivable effort to see the total situation from the point of view of the child, the pupil, the worker, as the case may be. What is intolerable is that an arbitrary command or set of commands shall be simply *handed down from above*, *dictated*, *enforced*, and that any failure to obey the commands should then be punished by an arbitrary and rigidly imposed sanction. That in the Judaeo-Christian tradition there are evidences of God being conceived as behaving in this way it would be hard to deny. But at least it may be claimed that the heart of the doctrine of reconciliation is that God did not remain aloof as a despotic parent, giving commands and inflicting punishments, but that He did in fact enter into the child's view of his world, saw from within the problems of the child's relationship with his environment, revealed in human terms principles of behaviour which can make life not only tolerable but expansive and fruitful and accepted the pain and suffering which follow from a general social neglect of or contravention of those principles in a spirit of resolute hope and willing endurance.

That there is much still to learn about the nature of true relationships between parents and children at different stages of family development and in varying environmental conditions seems abundantly clear. We cannot take traditional patterns of family interchange and use them uncritically as comparisons to assist in the interpretation of atonement. Any new light which comes from the insight of the artist or from the researches of the sociologist deserves to be welcomed without reserve. Yet the family is a living institution and no artist or social scientist will speak the last word concerning its nature and structure. And it is still possible for the Christian to use family imagery as he confesses that God has spoken by a Son, that this Son partook of the children's nature, that He was made like His brethren in every respect and that by bearing their weaknesses and temptations and above all the results of their shortcomings and misdeeds, He was able to save to the uttermost all those who draw near to God through Him. Unworthy and outworn conceptions of parenthood and the family must be allowed to go. But the result can be the disclosure of a fuller vision of the Father 'from whom every family in heaven and earth derives its name' and of the Son whose earliest recorded saying was 'Did you not know that I must be in my Father's house?'

CHAPTER VII

THE ALL-INCLUSIVE FORGIVENESS

Third Parable

One of the most mysterious and yet one of the most familiar patterns of human relationship is that in which a member of one family or distinctive social group encounters and is powerfully drawn towards a member of a quite different group. They find interests in common, they engage in common enterprises and bind themselves to one another by a formal agreement. In broadest terms there is a free commitment of man to man in friendship and trust. But one of the saddest things of life is that even an intimate relationship of this kind can be shattered by misunderstanding, disloyalty, excessive demands, insufficient self-giving. A slight breach soon becomes magnified until a gulf divides those who have hitherto been bosom friends.

What hope is there of change in this condition of personal alienation? Only it appears if there can be some altogether new initiative by one of the parties concerned. This involves gathering into his own being the contempt and the antagonism of the other and transforming it by a creative act of forgiveness. It involves further the communication of this forgiveness in such a way that it can be accepted and enjoyed without damage to the personal character of the structure which holds the two parties together.

It is the triumphant claim of the New Testament that God was reconciling the world (of persons) to Himself in Christ. In Christ man's attitude of suspicion and active antagonism is accepted into the Divine being. In Christ an outgoing forgiveness and a welcoming acceptance are fully expressed. The word of reconciliation can now be proclaimed by those who have themselves been 'accepted in the Beloved' and in the light of this ultimate disclosure the word of constraint immediately follows: 'Be ye kind one to another, forgiving one another, even as God in Christ has forgiven you.'

A

In Chapter VI, I used as framework of comparison the life of the family. No institution has held a more central or more enduring place in the life of humanity. Within the family, unity and continuity, find unique expression. The relation of children and adolescents and even those of mature age to the parents who begat them and in particular to the father who protects them and orders their way of life, provides a strikingly fruitful comparison to express the nature of the relationship which exists ideally between God and the children of men.

But there is another form of relationship which is characteristic of human life at all times and in all places. It is that which is deliberately willed between individuals who have come to maturity and possess at least some measure of ability to choose and to act. The binding power of customs, of family loyalties and duties, of religious sanctions, of ingrained habits and practices is immensely strong. In early stages of human development the area of freedom is severely limited and this applies to the choice either of a partner in marriage or of a companion when embarking on some new enterprise. Yet the time comes, mysteriously, when a man breaks through custom and ventures forth on his own, even within the sphere of human relationships. He attaches himself in a determined way to a particular woman or he chooses a man to go with him as he follows a particular course. These developments are strikingly new but while they take place within the closed circle of existing family and tribal relationships there is nothing about them that could be called revolutionary. The really radical change occurs when there is a meeting with a *stranger*. Hitherto any special attachment has been within the ordered and the known. With the advent of the stranger wholly new patterns of relationship are created for the *willed* and the *self-determined* now takes precedence over the *natural* and the *socially-determined*. The possibility of a larger freedom begins to emerge.

This larger freedom, however, is a complex condition. It involves not only excitement but also fear. It can produce a strong attachment but it can also create a venomous hatred. The new stirs ambivalent feelings. The very strangeness seems to be a threat, for the regular and familiar routine of life is disturbed and there is no knowing what the outcome will be. At the same time the strangeness holds possibilities of an extended and expanding world with ever new prizes to be won. Wherever there is a real encounter with the extraordinary, there is the inauguration of a dialectic which may indeed quickly subside but which may also lead to new and creative advances in individual and corporate life.

Obviously it is the nomad or the hunter or the refugee or the wanderer who is most likely to encounter the strange and the hitherto unknown. A closed tribal existence or a settled city existence offers little opportunity for meeting the unusual circumstance or the unexpected quality of life. But wherever there is movement, sooner or later a crisis is bound to arise. Some adjustment must be made. Either there is a panic-stricken retreat to the familiar and the long established or there is a coming to terms with the new experience. It is the fascination of the Old Testament that so much of its story is concerned with the relation of the chosen people or the elect individual to new conditions of life and to new social milieux. Only rarely did prosperous and settled conditions prevail. For a brief period under Solomon it seemed that the kingdom was firmly established, though even then there were active contacts with the peoples of the surrounding world. But in the main the narrative is concerned with the way in which a succession of men of faith became aware of new possibilities of existence and sought to deal creatively with them, however costly the process might be.

The forefather of the Jewish people who has always been accorded a place of primacy and honour in their recollection was the patriarch Abraham. In the Genesis narrative and in later references in the New Testament his claim to fame was that he went out from the settled and the familiar, 'not knowing whither he went'. The result was that he encountered strangers, in Canaan, in Egypt and back again in Canaan. He made covenants of friendship: he attacked hostile tribes. He did not ignore the claims of family and kin. At the same time he launched out into a wider world and grew himself in stature by reason of his encounters with others. And it seems altogether natural—though in fact it marks one of the high peaks in the progress of humanity—that he should have made an alliance with the God of the great open spaces by the same general pattern of procedure as would have been used in a covenant with another tribe. In the Biblical perspective it was God Who called Abraham and made a covenant with him and this is indeed the interpretation of events which men of faith descry. Yet the *form* of the covenant or alliance or pact of friendship was that of the covenant made with a stranger of any kind. There was mutual commitment: there was mutual sharing. I promise my loyalty: I receive of your bounty. This is the simplest form of covenant pattern and it is the essential pattern of mature, personal, relationship between consenting adults at all times and in all places. The Bible dares to call Abraham 'the friend of God'. Again and again the meetings between God and Abraham are, in the form of their recording, as between friend and friend.

The most vivid description which the Old Testament contains of personal friendship between men belonging to different tribes and families is to be found in the story of David and Jonathan. Jonathan belonged to the royal household and was heir to the chieftainship. David, a member of a comparatively obscure family but distinguished by reason of his own courage and physical exploits, was brought into the royal entourage. They meet, they feel mutual attraction, they commit themselves to one another in a solemn covenant. They give personal assurances of loyalty: they accept from each other some valued item of personal property. Henceforward they are bound together by ties stronger even than those of family. This is not to say that family duties are neglected but in any conflict of loyalty, personal friendship has the prior claim. And this principle holds even though it led in their case to tragedy and loss. In judgment of many of their contemporaries the claim of family should undoubtedly have prevailed. Yet in the judgment of the narrator the relation of friendship between these two men was a noble and a creative thing. Jonathan rallied to his father's cause and gave his life fighting in his battles. Yet he remained true to his covenant with David and within the interchange of the covenant that which should have been Jonathan's by nature became David's by grace.

In a very real sense Yahweh, the god who reveals himself to the chosen men of the Old Testament, is a *stranger* God. He is not primarily the god of the natural order or even the god of mankind in general. Potentially and in ultimate purpose He is such. But just as Abraham separated himself from a natural environment and a domestic security and went out into the unknown to seek his destiny, so, it is not irreverent to say, Yahweh went forth from the familiar circle of divine existence seeking the man, the succession of men, to whom He could relate Himself as friend to friend. No longer would religion be viewed simply in terms of a family of gods in natural and harmonious relationship with a family of humans. No longer even would it be viewed in terms of a high god or an all-powerful god or a father of the gods holding all mankind within his embrace. Rather the all-important manifestation of religion would be found in the god who comes forth and enters into the human situation, who meets with men, speaks to men, lays his demands upon them and at the same time grants them his favour. This god is in the beginning the Stranger. He encounters Moses in the backside of the desert and speaks to him as man to man yet with words of transcendent power and grace. Moses, already in a profound sense a religious man, finds himself under the constraint of One whose demand is overwhelming yet whose promised grace is boundless. And Moses responds in faith. Moses too becomes the friend of Yahweh.

In such a conception of covenant-friendship the relationship is never an end in itself. The demands and the assurances are always related to some wider context or purpose. Abraham was called to friendship in order that he might become a blessing to the families of the whole earth. Moses was called in order that he might bring a people out of wretchedness to share the covenant blessing bestowed upon him. The Divine Stranger stands, as it were, on the other side of a divide, not having previously been known in his true nature: yet through the new alliance he makes himself known within an intimacy even closer than that of family kinship. He becomes known as the god of the fathers, Abraham, Isaac and Jacob. Yet he is only such because of the revelation of himself in demand and grace to each of these patriarchs of the people. Obviously natural and organic and kin images remain apt and popular. But the images of friendship and fellowship within a common purpose are even more significant within the development of the religion of the Old Testament. Yahweh is the God of the Covenant, the God Who speaks, the God who calls an elect people to a destiny, the God who gives Himself to this people in abounding grace. The Stranger has become the Friend.

But the potential splendour of this pattern of imagery is marred and spoiled by the persistent failure both of individual and of people to remain steadfast within the covenant. No problem so perplexes the prophets and story-tellers of the Old Testament as that of the perfidy and treachery and open rebellion of those who had been granted the inestimable privilege of being called 'friends of God'. How could they turn back to weak and beggarly idols? How could they lose interest in His majestic purpose? How could they seek help from earthly 'saviours' by making alliances with Syria and Egypt and Babylon? Just as 'faith' was the means of entrance into life within the covenant, unfaithfulness was the unforgivable sin, for it was the renunciation of all the grace and favour which God in His mercy had purposed for mankind. No question in the Old Testament becomes more urgent than this: Can the Covenant once broken ever be renewed? Slipping and stumbling, doubt and misgiving—these could be overlooked. But what could be said of treachery to a friend, of the betrayal of one with whom a common table had been shared, of the breach of promises solemnly given? No more agonizing cries break forth from the Old Testament men of God than those which are concerned with the abandonment of true loyalty and personal friendship in favour of some will o' the wisp on an altogether lower level of religious apprehension.

Are there then any pointers in the Old Testament to the way in which a broken covenant can be restored and the sin of the unfaithful forgiven? There are certainly references to occasions when the original covenant was *renewed*. This was not difficult to envisage. The children of Israel were from the time of the Egyptian bondage a people on the move. Though there was always the hope of a firm settlement in the promised land only rarely did the goal seem to come into view. Whenever then a new stage was reached or when a new generation arose, it was altogether natural to enact a sacrificial ceremony by which the covenant could again be made vivid and the Israelites' resolution upheld. Yet to those who saw more deeply into the evils of national life, such outward renewals of an original pattern were not enough. Under the shock of the Exile, which seemed to be a direct judgment on the sin of the nation, the great prophets Jeremiah and Ezekiel began to speak of a *new covenant*. This was in no wise to be simply a re-enactment of that which had been consistently betrayed. Rather it would be a new coming-near by God in judgment and in grace to those who were ready to receive Him. He would draw near to convict, to speak inwardly to the conscience, to forgive, to inspire with His own Spirit. It matters little whether the prophets envisaged this as a possiblity for the whole nation or for an elect remnant. The hope to which they bore witness was that of a new covenant, a more personal covenant, a covenant more searching by virtue of the penetrating power of its words of command, a covenant more enheartening by virtue of the free bestowal of the Spirit of its Creator. When, and exactly how, this new Covenant would be inaugurated are never defined. But the prospect is one of the noblest that the Old Testament contains.

B

Half a century ago it was natural to speak of Jesus' *self-consciousness* and of His claims to fulfil the implications of this or that category or title—Messiah, Son of Man, the Servant of the Lord. Today such language is regarded as highly suspect. Does a particular passage represent Jesus' own self-consciousness or does it simply mirror the confession of faith of the early Church? Did Jesus indeed claim to be the Messiah or is this a reading back of the conviction awakened in the hearts of those who had been witnesses of the Resurrection? These questions raise large difficulties but at least there are some answers which command a reasonable measure of agreement. One is that Jesus regarded Himself as and was regarded by others as standing in the authentic tradition of the Hebrew *prophets*. Whether or not He claimed to be Son of

Man or Messiah there is strong probability that He accepted the role of *prophet* with the inevitable consequences that such a role implied. Professor John Knox, who has grave reservations about all attempts to define the self-consciousness of Jesus, yet commits himself to the statement that 'if a category must be found to which Jesus thought of himself as belonging, that of the prophet is the most likely' and goes on to say: 'Perhaps the real question is not whether he claimed to be a prophet, or indeed consciously thought of himself as being one, but rather whether his consciousness of God, of God's will and of God's relations with men and more particularly with himself, was of the kind characteristic of the prophet. It seems to me highly probable that it was.'[1]

It is unnecessary to marshal the evidence for these assertions. Scattered throughout the Synoptic Gospels are references by Jesus, by the disciples and by the crowd to His words and His works as being those of a prophet. Sometimes the prophet is named. Is he Elijah or Jeremiah redevivus? Is he in the succession of Isaiah? Has the long age of waiting at last been terminated and has God visited His people through a new and mighty prophet? Yet the most striking aspect of the Gospel evidence is not the nature of the prophetic activity there described but rather the nature of the opposition which it aroused. If Jesus was to be regarded as representing the authentic prophetic vocation then it would be as true of Him as of others that 'a prophet is not without honour, except in his own country', and that 'a prophet cannot perish away from Jerusalem'. 'O Jerusalem, Jerusalem, killing the prophets and stoning those who are sent to you.' He like Moses and Elijah had been sent by God. He like them, would experience rejection at the hands of those whom He had come to save.

This, then, was the first aspect of Jesus' *personal* ministry about which we can feel reasonably certain. He came as a prophet, proclaiming the Kingdom of God and promising redemption to all who would turn and believe the Good News. Yet because He called to repentance and gave no assurance of easy salvation His own village, His own countrymen refused to accept Him. Because He preached judgment to the 'insider' and grace to the 'outsider' the 'insiders' rose against Him and thrust Him out and ultimately killed Him. His utter faithfulness to the *personal* character of the demand and the forgiveness of God led to His rejection and death. In humanity He witnessed to God: in humanity He bore the weight of the opposition of all who clung to their own independence and refused to acknowledge their true Lord.

1. *The Death of Christ*, p. 115 f.

Amidst all else that is uncertain in any effort to reconstruct a picture of the historical Jesus, one other characteristic of His earthly career has gained wide recognition as being genuine and authentic. He ate and drank with tax-collectors and sinners. Again references to this aspect of His ministry occur in diverse contexts in the Synoptic Gospels and the analysis of 'forms' in the Gospel tradition has revealed the fact that these references are to be found in many patterns and are recorded, it would appear, with varying motivations. In other words the criticism of the narratives reveals no single conscious purpose for drawing attention in these various passages to this particular aspect of Jesus' ministry. If there is one pattern of His earthly activity which can be regarded as supported by a remarkable cluster of converging evidences it is his going forth to seek and to save that which was lost.[2]

But how in fact did He do this? The converging evidence to which I have referred gives us a picture of Jesus deliberately seeking the company of social outcastes and religious excommunicates and sharing table-fellowship with them in their houses. The whole implication is that the joys of the final Messianic banquet were already being experienced as men and women responded to Jesus' outstretched hand of friendship. He did not wait for them to come to Him, expressing their need or their sorrow. Rather He went out to them and assured them that they were welcome to enter God's house of healing and friendship. He did not hesitate to affirm in His controversy with the Pharisees that 'the tax collectors and the harlots go into the kingdom of God'.

As I have indicated, recent historical criticism, while questioning the authenticity of many details recorded in the Gospels, is prepared to regard this aspect of Jesus' activity as carrying the strongest kind of historical support. This only adds to the significance of the point made many years ago by James Denney in his book *The Christian Doctrine of Reconciliation* that whereas 'there might be a question as to whether Jesus spoke any given word assigned to Him, or as to the circumstances in which it was spoken, or as to its proper application; . . . it is quite inconceivable that the evangelists should misrepresent so new and wonderful a thing as the attitude of Jesus to the sinful, or the reconciling power which accompanied it. . . . The words of his enemies "This man receiveth sinners and eateth with them"—though spoken malignantly, enshrine the ultimate truth of His life and work, and it is through this truth that

2. Amongst the few activities of Jesus which Bultmann regards as well-substantiated is his 'association with the declassé such as tax collectors and prostitutes'. See R. H. Fuller: *The New Testament in Current Study*, p. 63.

His reconciling power is felt.' Such incidents in fact as His gracious reception of the woman who was a sinner (Luke 7: 36–50), His uninhibited acceptance of the hospitality of Zacchaeus the tax-collector (Luke 19: 1–10), His ready sharing of the meal in Levi's house with his former associates and friends (Mark 2: 13–17), all indicate that Jesus' ministry was essentially one of *reconciliation*. He came forth in the name of God to proclaim peace to those who had been enemies, reconciliation to those who were alienated and estranged.

If this quality of Jesus' ministry can be regarded as central— and there seems no good reason to doubt it—it means that we have an important clue to the significance of His death. It has often been the case in the course of Christian history that Jesus' death has been interpreted almost in isolation from His life. Sometimes this has been because categories of interpretation were being used which were indeed related to death in general but had little reference to living activities: more recently it has been on account of un-certainty about the historicity of the Gospel records and the consequent necessity to focus attention upon the death itself about which there could be no reasonable doubt. But whatever the cause the result has not been satisfactory. The death of a man of unknown qualities and character can have little relation to the general human situation. Even if it be claimed that his death was the death of a divine emissary or a divine figure, the force of the claim is minimal unless something be known about the type of divine life which he represents. It becomes far more possible to interpret the death on the Cross as an act of reconciliation if it can reasonably be assumed that the life of Jesus was devoted to forms of *reconciling* activity, if, that is, the Cross can be regarded as the climax and consummation of His own central and deliberate purpose. In other words it leads to coherence if St. Paul's definitive word that God was engaged in Christ in reconciling the world to Himself applies both to the incarnate life and to the atoning death.

No man laid greater emphasis on the significance of the *death* of Jesus than did James Denney. Yet he was at pains to show that the death could not become meaningful in isolation—it was all of a piece with the life. In a later chapter of the book to which I have already referred Denney returns to the subject of what he calls 'the general character of the work of Jesus'. 'In the widest sense', he writes, 'it will not be questioned that it was a work of reconciliation. He received sinners. He declared, bestowed and embodied forgive-ness. He came to seek and to save that which was lost. Whatever else He did, He came to men who were alienated from God by their sins . . . and He brought them back to God and to the assurance of His fatherly love. This was the general character and result of His life work in relation to individuals. . . . We may say that the reconciling virtue of His being was concentrated in His death, or that the reconciling virtue of His death pervaded His being; in any case, that the whole influence exerted upon sinners by Jesus is an influence by which, through penitence and faith, they are won from sin to God—in other words is a reconciling influence— cannot be denied. How He exercised such an influence and what it cost Him to do so are ulterior questions.'[3]

That this reconciling activity was, in fact, a costly enterprise seems clear from the Gospel narratives. It was the identification with sinners in intimate table-fellowship which aroused criticism and active opposition. To express God's love for the sinner in word and in deed brought bitter resistance from those who believed that because of their own devotion to the will of God they were assured of His continuing favour. They could neither bring themselves to accept His prophetic challenge to reform nor allow themselves to be associated with His declaration of God's grace to sinners. So at length they seized the prophet in Jerusalem and put an end it seemed to His reconciling activities. Yet even on the Cross His concern for those who were enemies and outcastes did not cease. 'Father forgive them: they know not what they do.' 'To-day shalt thou be with me in Paradise.' In words such as these Jesus gathers up the attitude of His whole life. Through His death God's full forgiveness and acceptance of the sinner are conveyed. Whatever may be the cosmic or the forensic implications of Calvary, the *personal* are amply demonstrated in these words. God was engaged in reconciling the world to Himself in and through Jesus the Christ.

One other important point arises in this context. Jesus did not attempt to engage in this reconciling activity *alone*. It had been a common practice amongst the prophets of the Old Testament to enlist the co-operation of one or more attendants or assistants in their particular tasks, often with a view to future developments. These companions always ran the risk of being so identified with the master and his work in the popular view that any opposition which He might arouse would recoil on themselves. They might indeed gain the sense of having been chosen to participate in a mission which was God-inspired and God-directed. But it was rare for such a mission to be exempt from the antagonism of the upholders of the *status quo*.

That Jesus·chose a group of men to be with him as learners and

3. *The Christian Doctrine of Reconciliation*, pp. 131–2.

associates in His mission is strongly attested by the Gospel narratives. They were not to be just assistants. Their initial call held out a notable promise—that they would themselves become 'fishers of men', that they would, in other words, serve as God's agents in bringing men into His Kingdom. By Jesus' own words and deeds they were instructed in the nature of the Kingdom and in due time they were sent out on healing and reconciling missions (Matthew 10). Their essential task was to bring salvation to the villages and households which were prepared to receive them. The supreme blessing which they were to offer was that of Peace (Matthew 10: 12). In and through their new activities the Kingdom of God would be brought near to men.

But they are left in no illusions about the opposition which a prophet must encounter or about the privations and hardships which will be the lot of his faithful followers. Their vocation is summed up in the word 'follow'. They can look for no settled charge (the Son of man has nowhere to lay his head). They can expect to travel no smooth and easy road. They must be prepared to abandon any earthly tie which stands in the way of a full commitment to the Kingdom. In fact they must envisage a ministry in which it will seem as if the great weight of a cross has been laid on the shoulder and each disciple is bearing it after Jesus Himself. This is a most intimate covenant into which they have been admitted by their Lord and Master. It contains a magnificent promise—a share in the glory of the Kingdom of God. It also contains an almost overwhelming demand—a resolute 'No' to all self-regarding interests and a willing 'Yes' to the mission of witness to the Kingdom in which Jesus is leading the way.

The nature of this intimate fellowship is made unmistakably clear in the records of the Passion Story. In the Johannine account Jesus uses the terminology of 'friendship'. As I have already indicated, the title 'Friend' was one of great dignity in the Jewish tradition. Abraham and Moses had been accorded the title 'Friend of God' because they were utterly obedient to His commands and unswerving in their trust in His promises. In a late Jewish writing the title is given a wider application when it is said that wisdom, in all ages, entering into holy souls makes them friends of God (Wisdom 7: 27). Here Jesus gathers His disciples within a signal band of friendship by reminding them that He chose them, that He has shared with them all that He has heard from the Father and that He expects them to continue gladly in His obedience. They are His friends— and He will show His love for them even to the extent of laying down His life for them. Yet one is missing from the circle of those designated as friends. He has already gone out into the darkness of the night. He has cut himself off from the loyal trust which friendship involves and he will therefore know nothing of the benefits which Jesus will bestow through the laying down of His own life in sacrifice.

In the Synoptic account the same image is presented through the use of the terminology of the Covenant. It was a familiar practice in Judaism for groups of companions to share common meals together in a solemn fashion, especially on the evening preceding the Sabbath. Whether or not the Last Supper comes within the latter category it seems certainly to have partaken of the character of a ḥabûrah meal. In it and through it Jesus pledged Himself to His followers and they, by sharing in the bread and wine, pledged themselves afresh to Him.

> 'You are those who have continued with me in my trials; as my Father appointed (or covenanted) a kingdom for me so do I appoint for you, that you may eat and drink at my table in my kingdom.' (Luke 22: 28 f.)

For Jesus the immediate sequel was death. But His followers were held together within the covenant-bond, sealed by His blood. They came to the conviction that His living presence was still with them and that the covenant could be continually renewed when they came together for the breaking of the bread.

From first to last Jesus was engaged in an activity of reconciliation and those who became His followers, His friends, His covenant-companions, pledged themselves to the same mission. There were of course defections and failures. The most grievous of all was that of Judas Iscariot, branded for all time as the traitor. Whereas Peter and the other disciples were guilty, as the Gospel story shows, of cowardice, prejudice, self-seeking and worldly ambition; although when the hour of crisis came they all forsook Him and fled; yet they were never guilty of betraying Him or of deliberately apostasizing from the household of God. Minor acts of disobedience and disloyalty were reversed as the perpetrators turned in repentance to their Leader and Lord. But for the man who had broken faith with the fellowship, spurned the covenant and betrayed the Leader for thirty pieces of silver, there was no place for repentance. In the whole tradition of the desert-nomads the betrayal of a friend was the most heinous crime: in the Old Testament it stands out as the most inexplicable, the most blame-worthy of all sins: and in the person of Judas Iscariot it reaches its most terrifying form of expression. It is the final 'No' to the gracious self-giving of a covenant-making God. And the New Testament gives no indication that the work of Christ has forcibly changed such a 'No' into an unwilling 'Yes'. Yet to His friends, however weak and liable to fail in face of testings and trials, Jesus speaks the word of assurance:

> I have chosen you:
> i have prayed for you.
> In the world ye shall have tribulation
> I have overcome the world.

C

The witness of Paul to the meaning of the death and resurrection of Jesus can never be isolated from the record of his own career, first in the religion of Judaism and then within the fellowship of the Christian Church. As he reflected on his own experience he was intensely conscious of the fact that before his conversion he had actually persecuted the followers of the truth. He had sought almost fanatically to establish his own righteousness by fulfilling all the outward commandments of the Law. There was little of personal feeling in all this. The Law and the traditions were clear and objective and encoded: man's duty was to reflect in his own pattern of life the exact regulations prescribed therein. By so doing God's order could be increasingly established and the way prepared for His final Kingdom.

Into this situation came the adherents of a strikingly different kind of faith. Their conception of religion was intensely personal rather than legal. They had companied with a personal leader. They had received his personal instruction, they had pinned their faith upon his personal vindication. After His resurrection they invited others to become related to the Lord Christ, as they themselves had become related, in personal faith and commitment. Individuals who responded to the invitation were baptized and thereby given formal admission into the Christian fellowship. There could not help being certain rudimentary elements of organization but the whole emphasis was upon direct personal encounter and decision.

The activities of these sectaries seemed to Paul to be anti-law, anti-tradition and in the end anti-God. His duty as he conceived it was to resist and if possible destroy the Lord's enemies. So he set himself to search out and to apprehend the followers of Jesus. He persecuted them even unto strange cities. Then came the shattering reversal. His zeal against the enemies of the Lord had, he saw, been directed against the Lord's Messiah. By attacking them he had constituted himself an enemy of God and of His saving purpose. His very zeal for law was the death of personal religion. But as later on Paul spoke and wrote about this reversal he did not doubt for a moment that it had come about through God's gracious approach to him in reconciling love. 'It pleased God to reveal His Son in me.' There had been a direct revelation of Jesus Christ as Reconciler and this revelation had been so overhelming in its implications that henceforward what things had been gain were regarded as loss. There was a complete revolution of religious values. Instead of a righteousness of his own based on obedience to the requirements of the law, he was now concerned only for the righteousness of God made available through faith in Christ. Instead of striving for blamelessness under the law, he was concerned only to grow in the personal knowledge of Christ Jesus the Lord.

Few events of New Testament history are so well attested as this revolutionary change by which the fanatical persecutor of the Church of God became the devoted servant of Jesus Christ. It was a shocking revelation—that he who had boasted of his relationship to God and was sure that he knew His will had in fact been an enemy of God and a persecutor of His chosen people. How could God ever forgive one who had so violently opposed His saving purpose? Perhaps nowhere does Paul more clearly express his own understanding of what had happened than in these words:

'If while we were enemies we were reconciled to God by the death of His Son, much more, now that we are reconciled, we shall be saved by His life' (Romans 5: 10). Here Paul identifies himself with all who must be classed as enemies of God, hostile to His purposes, opposed to His truth. Yet God had come forth to reconcile such to Himself through Christ. He had done this in particular through His death. In some wonderful and mysterious way the death of Christ had reversed the enmity and made it possible for men to be fully reconciled to God.

The vocabulary of reconciliation is employed afresh in a notable passage in 2 Corinthians (5: 14 ff). Here Paul is again speaking in terms of the revolutionary changes which have come about through the work of the Christ. Nothing could be more far reaching than the statement, 'The old has passed away, the new has come'. But this is applied not in any merely general way but in the context of the life of a particular individual. 'If anyone is in Christ he is a new creature.' A man, living on the purely human level, seeking to commend himself as best he can to God, regarding Jesus Christ simply as a man of unusual qualities, is apprehended by God and brought to see that the death of Christ is the death of all human aspirations and judgments. It is, moreover, the death of all that is opposed to God. He so identified Himself with men that in His death they died, thereby severing themselves from all that was effete and hostile to God. This Paul had known in his own individual experience. In Christ's death what had formerly been his highest ambition had proved to be worthless. By accepting identification with Christ in His death (and Christ had made this possible by being identified with him in all the weakness of his human life) he had broken away from old values and old attitudes: he had rejected the whole view of God which the system of the law implied: he had renounced the sin which actuated his former manner of life: he had in short died to all that could be construed as anti-God, and was henceforth committed to the new life in Christ, the life of faith in the Son of God who had loved him and given himself for him.

In this passage Paul's chief object is to magnify the initiative of God Himself. 'All this is from God.' When there was no possibility of change on man's side, seeing that he was content to be living for himself and to be viewing all things from his human standpoint, God through Christ entered into the situation and reconciled us to Himself. The Greek word here translated 'reconciled' seems normally to have been used in connection with the healing of breaches between those who had previously been on terms of close intimacy and friendship.[4] It is a term of a directly personal kind. Its use in this context emphasizes the fact that God's approach in Christ was comparable to a personal intervention in a human situation where two parties have become entirely estranged from one another. God does not hold the past enmity against the offender nor does He allow present hostility to repel His advances. He makes His gracious offer of reconciliation even to the point of accepting death at the hands of those who will not heed His advances. His wounds, His sacrifical death, now speak the word of reconciliation more eloquently even than His life of love. And those in turn who have heard and responded to this word proclaim the message to others: As God appealed to His enemies through Christ, His appointed ambassador, so now, through us who are also ambassadors, He continues to appeal, Be reconciled to God.

The passages Romans 5: 8–10 and 2 Corinthians 5: 14 ff are charged with personal feeling. There is the poignant recognition that it was the hostility of those who had rejected God's friendship which caused the death of the Christ. He died for all. Yet there is no precise account of the connection between the hostility and the death. The all important thing is that the whole situation has been

4. See *The Significance of the Cross*, p. 112 f. It is suggestive that the root-force of the Greek verb is '*to down the otherness*'.

changed. The old with its barrier of trespasses has passed away. The new with its freedom of personal trust has come. And now the reconciling work continues for those who having themselves received it are ready to take the initiative in appealing to others. He had made peace through the blood of His cross: He has reconciled us in his body of flesh by his death: let us then no longer live for ourselves in defiance of God: let us live for Him Who for our sakes died and rose again.

D

Apart from all questions of special revelation and special content the New Testament has a character all its own amidst the other writings of the ancient world. Its form is determined by *personal* problems and *personal* encounters to an extent to which there is no obvious parallel elsewhere. The centre of its interest from beginning to end is a living Person in relationship with others. The utterly new phenomenon to which it bears witness is that a Divine Being came into the world in human form, grew up as a member of a human family and of a human community, engaged in a mission whose essential characteristic was that of direct personal approach in speech and action, met opposition and ultimately rejection at the hands of most of his contemporaries yet passed through suffering and death to a continuing personal existence in Divine power. Even though the writer of the earliest New Testament records— the apostle Paul—had not, it would appear, encountered Jesus in the days of His flesh, he had become vividly aware of Him as a living Person who reveals Himself to those who respond to the Gospel message in faith. In his own efforts to make this Gospel known he had come into intimate personal relationship with men and women in numerous cities of the Mediterranean world and it is largely their personal problems and uncertainties which lead him to send out the letters which came to be preserved for future generations. It would not be too much to say that these letters provide a unique example of a man relating himself to human problems of a personal kind in the light of the new revelation which has come to mankind through the personal career and activity of Jesus the Messiah.

But besides the direct personal correspondence of Paul there are other documents which owe their existence to the challenge of situations of a dominantly personal character. It is now generally agreed that the Gospel-form is in no way to be regarded as biography or history in the modern sense of those terms. Rather it was a form designed to convey the Gospel of salvation and apply it to the conditions in which men found themselves at particular places and times. Originally the Gospel had been revealed through Jesus, the Son of God, entering into human situations, making direct encounters with those in need, speaking words of judgment and grace, acting to banish disease and to promote healing, in short, coming as the personal representative of God to mediate His salvation to all who would respond in personal faith. So in the written Gospel the evangelist was concerned to gather together stories and dialogues of an oral kind which told of Jesus' acts and words and to present them as a total drama obviously related to the immediacy of the situation in which his readers were involved. In a sense every story and every dialogue, having originally sprung out of a living personal situation, had its direct relevance to a similar personal situation at any time and in any place. Yet it was also the case that the total collection constituting the full Gospel story had its application to the whole life and destiny of the members of any particular Christian community. Every part had its significance as a kind of miniature gospel while the whole made its larger impact as embracing the total personal existence of the individual within the community.

I have emphasized the *form* of the New Testament writings because we are largely dependent on literature for the knowledge of any particular period and it is important to recognize what is the character of the sources we possess. In general we may say that the maximum of emphasis upon direct personal relations is to be found in the earliest writings of the New Testament—the unquestioned Pauline Epistles and the Gospel of Mark. Fuller attention is given to community principles and structures in the Gospel of Matthew and the Lukan writings, in Ephesians and Colossians and in the First Epistle of St. Peter. Finally in the other writings the Gospel is applied to general ethical, metaphysical and eschatological questions though the personal reference is not excluded. This does not mean that personal encounters and personal tensions were no longer part of the experience of Church members towards the end of the first century A.D. It does mean that writers were assessing the implications of the Christian faith in more general and less personal areas of existence and that we shall turn to them in vain for interpretations of atonement drawn from the dialectic of person-to-person relationships in daily life.

Further, if this is true of the New Testament, it is still more true of the second and succeeding centuries of the Christian era. That men and women were still meeting, talking, disputing, quarrelling, renewing friendship, offering mutual help in directly personal ways there can be no reasonable doubt. But these were not the events which gained much attention in the literature which has survived and it was not through these patterns of relationship that doctrinal truths were presented. The Gospel and the Epistle (letter), the two eminent forms of the New Testament, eminent in expressing the relations between God and men in *personal* terms, belonged to the past. We move forward into the age of the myth, the creed, the oracle: the apology, the polemic, the treatise: the Church-order, the liturgy, the catechetical sermon. All these had their place to play in the life of the expanding Church but they obviously did not attempt to express Christian truth in terms of dialogue, parable or short story (the supreme forms used in personal engagement). Moreover the forms of Christian literature surviving from the patristic and medieval period had a natural affinity with the general attitude to life and destiny which characterized the age. The over-mastering concern was for permanence in the midst of change, for order in the midst of social confusion, for security in face of threats of dissolution. These were the themes which increasingly determined both the form and the content of Christian writings.

In previous chapters I have appealed to these writings for evidence of the way in which patristic and medieval writers interpreted the doctrine of atonement—cosmically, dramatically, forensically. But it is not easy to find evidence between the second century and the Reformation period for the existence of directly personal images of reconciliation. The whole conception of life was framed hierarchically. Relations between man and man were likely to be viewed as between a superior and an inferior on a social scale. Relations between God and man were certainly viewed as between the exalted, transcendent and impassible One, and the weak, inferior, mortal sons of men. The old Hebrew conception of God covenanting with man and making him His friend or the New Testament conception of God in Christ directly addressing man in a personal appeal to accept reconciliation, these are alike foreign to the imagination of the Middle Ages. Forgiveness is from above mediated through the necessary hierarchical channels. When a personal offence is committed the remedy is largely of an impersonal kind. Through penance and satisfaction, in which direct personal considerations may play little part, adequate reparation can be made. Forgiveness can hardly be called the re-establishment of conditions of peace. Rather it is the process by which offences are continuously remitted and the offender progressively purified. Atonement is the ceaseless application to the Church and to the individual of the fruits of Christ's atoning sacrifice.

But some time in the eleventh century of the Christian era—it is obviously impossible to give a precise date—a change of attitude began to appear in Western Christendom which was destined to affect every aspect of man's relations with his God, his world and his neighbour. It is the attitude usually described as the emergence of a new humanism. Instead of seeing himself as a weak and dependent creature, wholly at the mercy of his natural and social environment except in so far as he had links with the supernatural order and lived within the embrace of the divine protection, man began to realize, however slowly, that he himself possessed certain dignities, certain capacities, certain potentialities which he was permitted to explore and under proper conditions to use. This change may be seen most dramatically in the realm of pictorial art. But it also comes to light in the theological and devotional writings of the eleventh and succeeding centuries. There ideas and attitudes, which at first seemed little more than a trickle, gradually gained in volume until the great stream of humanism was in full spate. It was to be a long process of gradual acceleration but it is not fanciful to locate the springs of the great expansion of the nineteenth century far back in the uplands of the eleventh.

In a fascinating description of the beginnings of this humanistic movement Professor Richard Southern[5] puts first the turning of the attention to the invisible things of the inner self as shown in such writers as Anselm, Bernard and Richard of St. Victor. But this leads on to the recognition of another aspect of human experience— the experience of friendship. 'Without the cultivation of friendship', he writes, 'there can be no true humanism. If self-knowledge is the first step in the rehabilitation of man, friendship—which is the sharing of this knowledge—is an important auxiliary. This was understood by the humanists of the Renaissance; but it was first discovered in the monasteries of the late eleventh century.' And once the experience of human friendship had been discovered afresh it was natural to apply it within the realm of what was still man's largest concern—his relations with God Himself.

'Of all the forms of friendship rediscovered in the twelfth century', Southern continues, 'there was none more eagerly sought than the friendship between God and Man. This may seem a commonplace theme, and one which has been debased by countless sentimentalities and trivialities. But it was once fresh, and it lifted a great weight from men's lives. The God of the period before about 1100 was not seen as a friend. Just and merciful perhaps, but the justice had an appearance of wrath and the mercy was reserved for the very few.

5. *The Listener*, August 26, 1965.

By great labour and exertion, by incredible penances and crippling gifts to the Church, by turning away from the world and eschewing its charms, men might creep into the precarious favour of God. But of God as a friend men knew little or nothing. It was terribly difficult to approach Him. Then quite suddenly the terror faded and the sun shone.'

Yet as is shown later in the article, the terror and wrath did not by any means vanish completely. In fact I cannot help wondering if the sentence about the fading of the terror and the shining of the sun does not tend to give too rosy an impression of the change. Luther's experience in the early years of the sixteenth century shows that the black cloud of terror was still a sinister reality in many parts of Europe. Nevertheless it is true that in the realm of art few things are more significant than the growing recognition from the twelfth century onwards of the beauty and wonder of *light* in a building or in a painting, and certainly in the realm of ethics and devotion attention became increasingly focussed on the humanity of Jesus, His sympathies, His sufferings, His revelation of true friendship, His readiness to lay down His life for His friends.

All this was in harmony with another aspect of humanism which became especially characteristic of the Middle Ages. This was the idea that no life was more noble than that of the knight who committed himself to a cause, went out to fight for it, endured hardship in absolute loyalty to his comrades, and acted constantly under the inspiration of an ideal form of romantic love. Such a man inevitably still lived in a world saturated with ideas of supernatural powers and influences. But in his natural world the idea which above all others captured his imagination and ordered his life was the idea of chivalry. To keep faith with a friend even to death, to defend a comrade even at the cost of shedding one's own blood, to express one's love and devotion by laying down life itself—these became the levers of the imagination and so of action in the eleventh to the fifteenth centuries.

Let us take, for example, one of the clearest figures of the Middle Ages, St. Louis of France (mid-thirteenth century). A not unworthy king in his own domain, he gained far greater fame by engaging in crusading expeditions of a fanatical and disastrous kind. But to his biographers he was the 'perfect knight'. This is how one describes him:

'This holy man loved God with all his heart, and imitated His works: which was evident in this, that as God died for the love which He bore His people, so he (Louis) put his body in peril several times for the love which he bore his people. The great love which he had for his people appeared in what he said to his eldest son, Louis; when very sick at Fontainebleau: "Fair son," said he, "I beg thee to make theyself loved by the people of they kingdom; for indeed I should prefer that a Scot from Scotland came and ruled the people of the kingdom well and faithfully rather than that thou shouldst rule them ill in the sight of all". [6]

This is the spirit of chivalry which stirred the imagination of those newly awakening to a sense of what a man of devotion and courage could achieve. Is it to be wondered at that the mission of the proper Man, the Son of God, began to be envisaged in these terms? The 'Perfect Knight', Jesus, the Son of God, had laid down His life for His friends. He had humbled himself, accepted poverty, performed menial tasks, been weary and distressed, had suffered pains and torments unimaginable in order to give men release and restore them to the liberty of sonship. The poem which Professor Southern calls the greatest of the Middle Ages describes it all in the well-known words:

> Think, kind Jesus—my salvation
> Caused Thy wondrous Incarnation
> Leave me not to reprobation
> Faint and weary thou hast sought me
> Shall such grace be vainly brought me?

The humanism which first appeared in the eleventh century within an almost exclusively religious context was destined ultimately to express itself in ways which are generally described as secular. But the process was slow and before any kind of secularized humanism had taken shape the energies of man's new confidence were poured into the attempt to reform religion by rediscovering and re-establishing the pattern of Christian faith as it was disclosed once for all through the pages of the New Testament. To translate the Bible into the vernacular and to make it available and comprehensible to the common man became the greatest of all the enterprises of the fifteenth and sixteenth centuries.

To the pioneers of Biblical translation nothing was clearer than that God had seen fit to call a man and a nation into covenant with Himself. He had chosen Abraham the individual, Israel the people, not on account of any merits of their own but out of His sheer grace and mercy. He had called them and made far-reaching promises to them. All that He required in immediate response was faith. By this faith those whom God had called gained a new identity as His covenant people. Moreover, they became bound to one another

6. H. O. Taylor: *The Mediaeval Mind*, I, pp. 559, 567.

within the covenant which required the acceptance of mutual responsiblity but gave the assurance also of mutual support. To be related to God and to one's fellow-man within the covenant gave a sense of confidence which enabled those with scarcely any earthly resources to resist tyrannical powers and to go forth adventurously on the quest for a new order.

The immediate aftermath of the Reformation was bitterly disappointing to those who had expected new personal freedom and new patterns of social life. Powerful reactions led to the hardening of authority in the Roman Communion, to the emergence of a kind of Protestant scholasticism concerned for the niceties and orthodoxies of the Reformed faith and to bitter controversies which engendered open wars. It seemed that the ideal of religious liberty for the individual and for the minority-group had been stillborn. Yet in this very period of disillusionment in the seventeenth century other ideas were beginning to ferment which were ultimately to combine with the creative stirrings of the Reformation to produce altogether new possibilities of understanding the nature of the personal in human relationships. The striking results gained by *experimenting* with natural phenomena, the recognition of the need for the exercise of the human *reason* if religious excesses were to be avoided, and the advocacy of the place of *feeling* in the life of the Spirit to offset the cold rigidity of theological orthodoxy, all led in time to new possibilities of enquiry about the relations between man and man and subsequently the relations between man and God. The nineteenth century was in many ways anxious and unsettled. Revolutions, national and industrial, were gathering strength. The natural tendency in many quarters was to strengthen law and authority at whatever cost. Yet nothing could hold back the probing and investigating of the individual, through his experiments, through his travels, through his reason, through his feelings. Man was constantly learning more of his world. He was constantly learning more of his social relationships and his individual identity.

So it is that the nineteenth century brings the first major attempts to interpret atonement in terms of adult personal relationships. Until the end of the eighteenth century the categories of law and justice and punishment and remission held the field. There had been the radical challenge of Socinus and the suggestive reinterpretation of Grotius. There were the logical denials of the rationalists and the devotional affirmations of the pietists but intellectually the orthodox interpretation in terms of the demands of Divine justice stood firm. A brilliant and original development initiated by Schleiermacher I shall consider in Chapter VIII. For the present my concern is with the attempt, especially represented by certain theologians of the Reformed tradition in Scotland, to interpret atonement in the light of the new knowledge of the nature of personal relationships which was beginning to become available. The pattern to which a special appeal was made in the Anglican tradition was that of the family. As we saw in Chapter VI an analysis of the relations existing between husband and wife, parents and children in the family circle provided suggestive analogies for the breaking and the healing of relationship within the Divine family. In the Scottish tradition the father-son relationship is prominent but the pattern is now conceived primarily in terms of an adult son, honouring his father yet possessing his own power of willed action *vis-à-vis* his father. To the classic example of this form of interpretation I shall now turn.

E

Whereas medieval man looked at some vivid picture of the physical sufferings of the Christ or at the sculptured form of his dead body and thereby gained a not unworthy conception of the cost of his own redemption: whereas reformation man heard the dread words which told of the sufferings and death of Christ being borne meekly and patiently as the judgment upon and punishment for his own sin: nineteenth-century man began to turn his attention more to the mental and spiritual anguish involved in the human experiences of the Christ and to explore reverently the inner struggles and agonies which might hold the essential key to the interpretation of the outward manifestations in the body. Might not the spirit and the passion and the personal attitude in which the work of redemption was carried through be of more importance for true Christian understanding than the sheer physical suffering and death, however terrible in their objective form they might seem to be?

Signs of this new approach to the doctrine of atonement are to be seen in the work of Erskine of Linlathen, admirably summarized in R. S. Franks's fine history.[7] But nowhere in the nineteenth century is it more profoundly revealed than in *The Nature of the Atonement* by J. McLeod Campbell. The title itself is significant. It is not primarily an examination of the 'Why' or 'Wherefore' of atonement but rather of the 'How' of the Atonement which, it is assumed, has certainly been accomplished. If we accept the faith of historic Christianity that Jesus Christ, the man of Galilee, who lived and suffered and died was the unique Son of God Who remained always in perfect relationship with his Father, how within

7. *The Work of Christ*, p. 655 ff.

the exercise of this relationship did His earthly activities effect the actual reconciliation between God and men? How did His work make it possible for men to attain their true destiny as sons of God?

In his introduction Campbell gives us a glimpse of some of the newer forces operating in his own time, one of which was the growing influence of 'Science'. Some men, he saw, were employing the laws of natural processes which Science was unveiling for purely practical ends: others were rising above this realm of scientific techniques to the contemplation of the Divine source and sustainer of these laws but were resting content with a philosophic Theism which fell far short of what Campbell called 'Religion' or the exercise of the wisdom proper to the Kingdom of God. Religion for him involved active relationship and this relationship was most adequately described in terms of father and son. He never doubted that God desired above all that men should walk before Him as 'dear children'. But in and by themselves they were as prodigals in a far country, alienated from their true home, living in contradiction of their own well-being, subject to the righteous condemnation of God. Therefore it was beyond all things necessary that the true Son should be revealed for 'we see the Father when we see the Son, not merely because of identity of will and character in the Father and the Son, but because a father as such is known only in his relation to his son'.[8] Yet perfect sonship did not consist simply in an unbroken delight in the Father's love. The Son could not fail to relate himself to those who had been created as sons but no longer enjoyed that relationship. 'He, the perfect elder brother, unlike the elder brother in the parable, sympathized in all the yearning of the Father's heart over his prodigal brethren; and the love which in the Father desired to be able to say to each of them, My son was dead, and is alive again; he was lost and is found, in him equally desired to be able to say, My brother was dead and is alive again; he was lost and is found.'[9]

In these quotations, the key words are perhaps, 'relation' and 'sympathized'. These are the notes of the Kingdom of God in contrast to the realm of Science where the important matters are laws and calculations. And the area of the life of the Kingdom in which these notes come to fullest expression is that of *Prayer*. It is in Prayer that the relation of free spirits is constantly exercised: it is in Prayer that a true fellowship of suffering is made possible. 'What most fixes our attention, in the practical aspect of the kingdom

8. Introduction, p. 52.
9. P. 125 f.

of God is the place which prayer has in it. God is the hearer and answerer of prayer; our aspect toward Him is in its spirit prayer without ceasing. We see a place of free action occupied by God as the Father of our spirits, and a liberty in relation to Him conceded to us as His offspring, which permit direct personal dealing on His part and on ours. . . . That place which the fixedness of law, as what we may always assume, has in our practical relation to the reign of law, the character of God, as the hearer and answerer of prayer, has in our practical relation to the kingdom of God.'[10]

We feel in this section of Campbell's introduction a growing awareness of the onward march of *Science*. The results of its endeavours are to discover laws which give no place to personal relationships and free actions. And it goes without saying that the past century has revealed more and more of these 'laws', even though they may be conceived and described in different ways today. The altogether important question now as then is whether room is still left in a total view of the universe for personal relation and for action which can in any way be called free. I think that Campbell underestimated the possiblities of using the term atonement in a meaningful way in the area generally covered by the term Science. But his basic insight remains valid that it must be pre-eminently in the *personal* realm, where there is the possibility even of rejecting that which belongs to health and well-being, that atonement can be conceived and interpreted. And his further insight follows that the *personal* comes to fullest realization in the direct give and take and sharing and sympathizing and offering and bearing which in the realm of relationships between God and man we call Prayer.

Speaking in the simplest terms, we may say that Campbell had realized afresh that the most wonderful thing known to us in human life is for one person to take another's burdens on his own heart and carry them into the presence of God. If the burden is a burden of sin, then suffering is bound to be involved for he cannot fail to see the sin in the light of God's standard of holy judgment, while at the same time his whole heart is set toward the establishing of a condition in which his brother can live as a free son in the family of God. Campbell received a flood of light on the general problem as he contemplated the incident recorded in Numbers 25: 10–13. When disaster had come upon the camp of the Children of Israel, one man, Phinehas, stayed the plague by performing an act which seemed at first sight cruel and impetuous. But the important thing Campbell says, was 'the moral element in the transaction—the mind

10. Introduction, p. 39.

of Phinehas, his zeal for God, his sympathy in God's judgment on sin—this was the atonement, this its essence'. In other words to share the mind of God toward sin and at the same time to enter into his yearning toward the sinner, that is the essence of atonement, and it is something that must be experienced in the life of prayer, before it can come to expression in the context of historical event.[11]

To expound this idea of atonement Cambell employs a fourfold framework which can be set before the eyes of the imagination in the form of a cross. The upright may be conceived as the Christ dealing with man on behalf of God and reciprocally as dealing with God on behalf of men: the cross-bar may be conceived retrospectively as Christ dealing with the sin from which man needs to be set free and prospectively as exhibiting the good which is God's intended light of life for men.

(1) *Christ's dealing with men on the part of God in its retrospective aspect.* This was essentially 'to witness for the excellence of that will of God against which we were rebelling, to witness for the trustworthiness of that Father's heart in which we were refusing to put confidence, to witness for the unchanging character of that love in which there was hope for us, though we had destroyed ourselves'. In all this section the contrast is underlined. On the one side there is the personal perfection of Christ, His love for God, His love for His fellow-men, His joy in God, His sorrow for the sins of men: on the other side there is the pressure of our sins upon the Spirit of Christ, the enmity of the carnal mind to God, the hatred and dishonour and reproach which were directed towards the perfect Son, all of which He endured 'in sympathy with God', thereby honouring the Father in the sight of men.

(2) *Christ dealing with God on the part of men in its retrospective aspect.* Here undoubtedly is Campbell's most original contribution to atonement theology. He did not question for a moment the reality of the Divine reaction against sin and sinners nor that *some kind of satisfaction* was due to the Divine justice. But the more urgent question for him was this: Was there any way in which the Divine reaction against sin could be stayed, in which the Divine holiness could be vindicated, without direct *penal* sufferings being inflicted? This problem had tormented many other minds before Campbell's day and, as is well known, the clue to a solution came to him from an altogether unlikely source. The great philosopher-theologian of New England, Jonathan Edwards, had in the eighteenth century arrived at the conclusion that there were only two ways in

11. This paragraph I have taken with slight changes from my book *Jesus Christ and His Cross*, p. 63.

which due reparation to the Divine justice could be made: either an infinite punishment must be borne or 'a repentance, humiliation and sorrow proportionable to the greatness of the majesty despised' must be enacted. But seeing that the second of these alternatives was plainly impossible the first was the only imaginable means of atonement.

Campbell, however, was in no way content to dismiss the second alternative so summarily. Did not the whole experience of prayer reveal the fact that contrition and sorrow could be expressed for offences against God? Was not the testimony of Scripture and conscience clear that such repentance was acceptable to God? If then a mediator should appear who could make a *perfect* confession, could utter 'a perfect Amen in humanity to the judgment of God on the sin of man', surely the requirements of the Divine holiness would be adequately met and the name of the Father vindicated. The crucial sections read as follows:

'He who so responds to the divine wrath against sin, saying "Thou art righteous, O Lord, who judgest so" is necessarily receiving the full apprehension and realization of that wrath, as well as of that sin against which it comes forth into his soul and spirit, into the bosom of the Divine humanity, and, so receiving it, He responds to it with a perfect response—a response from the depths of that divine humanity—and *in that perfect response He absorbs it.* For that response has all the elements of a perfect repentance in humanity for all the sin of man—a perfect sorrow—a perfect contrition—all the elements of such a repentance, and that in absolute perfection, all-excepting the personal consciousness of sin; and by that perfect response in Amen to the mind of God in relation to sin is the wrath of God rightly met, and that is accorded to divine justice which is its due, and could alone satisfy it.'[12]

I suppose that the phrase in this statement which causes the greatest difficulty is 'excepting the personal consciousness of sin'. Campbell's constant appeal is to what God *felt*, to what Christ our true brother in humanity *felt*. But the one thing which the Divine Father and Son could not *feel*, he says, was personal consciousness of sin. Could the Son then express a perfect sorrow and contrition for that which He could not *feel*? Is not the very essence of sin its sheer perversity and contradiction, its strange insensitiveness to all finer feelings? We try to understand the character of a Hitler, a Stalin. We make every possible allowance for background and upbringing, for bitter experiences of frustration and disappointment—and still we find it impossible to enter with

12. Op. cit., pp. 136-7.

any depth of feeling into the sheer callousness and lust for power which possessed them. If we were less dulled in our sensitivities by reason of our own sin, could we feel the depth of their sin more keenly? Even if we could, would that enable us to embrace it and confess it unless we had some consciousness of our own implication in the same kind of guilt? Could we feel deeply and confess the majesty of the Divine antipathy if we were conscious of a relatively complete personal separation from this sin?

This is a profound psychological problem on which opinions may differ widely. Yet it is clear that Campbell, through his penetrating insights that Christ from within his humanity made a perfect response to the Divine judgment upon human sin and that it is possible for the relatively innocent to bear the burden of another's sins on his own heart and spirit, brought original and influential impulses into atonement doctrine and opened the way for the whole subject to be approached from the personal and experiential angle rather than from the impersonal and formal context of law. In effect he was saying to his contemporaries: You will never understand the atoning work of Christ in the depths of its meaning so long as you remain within the strictly defined procedure of a court of law: you must rather go to the inner sanctuary and fall on your knees and seek the vision of the holiness of God revealed in Christ. As you acknowledge the rightness and perfection of His holy judgment, seek to take into your own bosom the sin of a single prodigal son and confess it as that of your brother in the presence of the holy Father—do that and you will begin to have some consciousness of the way in which the perfect Son uttered the full Amen in humanity to the Father's holy judgment and took upon His own heart the sin of the whole world.

(3) *Christ dealing with men on the part of God in its prospective aspect.* From confession Campbell moves on to intercession. Confession in his view is specially related to the past (though it is ever within the context of the abiding judgment of God upon all that is sinful). Intercession is specially related to the future (though it is ever within the context of the abiding will of God that in Christ all shall partake of eternal life). As far as Christ's witness to men is concerned, it consisted essentially in the revelation of the true communion which a son can enjoy with the Father in the experience of the full range of intercessory prayer. 'The light that shines to us in the communion of the Son with the Father . . . is the very light of life to us; for this communion is the gift of the Father to us in the Son. In the experience of this communion in our nature and as our brother did our Lord look forward to our

partaking in it as what would be our salvation. The seventeenth chapter of the Gospel of St. John most fully declares this. Indeed the evidence abounds that it was this which was ever in the contemplation of Christ in glorifying the Father on the earth; while of anything like the consciousness of being working out a righteousness to be imputed to men to give them a legal ground of confidence towards God there is no trace.[13]

But how could the Cross be regarded as part of this intercession? How can it be viewed as the supreme witness to God's prospective purpose for men? Jesus' 'own consciousness in humanity witnessed within Him that humanity was capable of being filled with the life of love. The more perfectly He realized that these were His brethren whose hatred was coming forth against Him, the more did He realize also that hatred was not of the essence of their being, that there was hope in giving Himself for them .to redeem them from iniquity—that there was hope in suffering for them the just for the unjust—hope that He would bring them to God.'[14] This was the light in which He lived and to which He bore witness to the very limit. When the enmity of man had manifested itself to the utmost, He still could pray 'Father, forgive them; for they know not what they do.' The hope in His prayer is derived from the light of His own communion as son with Father which men at present do not see. If this light can be fully revealed, revealed in the midst of final contradiction and shame, then will the way be open for men to receive the light and walk in the light as reconciled sons of God. In His intercession is the ground of our confidence and hope.

(4) *Christ dealing with God on behalf of men in its retrospective aspect.* But if our hope is quickened and sustained by the light of the communion which the Son enjoys with the Father still further is it confirmed by the knowledge that Christ in His humanity offered on our behalf the perfect intercession, asking that His own mind and spirit should be reproduced in us. And His offering, we believe was accepted by the Father. 'In the light of what God accepted when Christ through the eternal Spirit offered Himself without spot to God, we see the ultimate ground—the ultimate foundation in God—for that peace with God which we have in Christ.'[15] As we contemplate Him in His intercession 'uttering all that in love to the Father and to us He feels regarding us—all His divine sorrow—all His desire—all His hope—all that He admits and confesses as against us—all that, notwithstanding, He

13. Ibid., p. 173.
14. Ibid., p. 163.
15. Ibid., p. 177.

asks for us, with that in His own human consciousness, in His following the Father as a dear child walking in love, which justifies His hope in making intercession—enabling Him to intercede in conscious righteousness as well as conscious compassion and love —we have the elements of the atonement before us as presented by the Son and accepted by the Father, and see the grounds of the Divine procedure in granting to us remission of our sins and the gift of eternal life.'[16]

Campbell, as we have seen, was not unaware of man's capacity to explore the life of nature around him and to contemplate it as the handiwork of the living God. But far more important to him was man's existence as *a person*, in relation to God and to his fellow-men. If a man never reached the stage of experiencing a personal communion with God through Christ, he had never really lived at all. He set before his eyes the vision of the perfect Son, who came forth into humanity and was made in all points like as we are. He saw Him delighting to do the will of the Father, he saw Him embracing with infinite sympathy His brother-men. The perfect offering in the eternal Spirit he saw as essentially a *personal* offering, an offering infinitely costly yet infinitely satisfying both to the Son who made it and to the Father who accepted it. All is in the light of *personal* relationships, focussed and interpreted within the experience of prayer, prayer being supremely the meeting-place of heaven and earth. Campbell receives from the recorded experiences of Jesus at prayer the supreme illumination which his own mind craves on the mystery of atonement and it is hard to believe that this illumination was not even intensified within his own personal experience of confession and intercession. He had suffered deeply at the hands of his brethren. He had known the trust and support of an earthly father in days when he was himself suffering reproach. His own recourse was to communion with his Father in heaven in the fellowship of the One who was his brother. In that kind of experience his doctrine was fashioned and whatever criticisms may be levelled against it, it remains as a magnificent testimony to atonement as seen in the New Testament portrait of the Christ and to atonement as experienced in the devoted life of one of His faithful followers.[17]

Campbell's insistence that the oratory rather than the law court was the essential context for the clarification of our thinking on

16. Ibid., p. 176.
17. Perhaps the most obvious criticism is the minimal place that the *death* occupies in Campbell's exposition. It is a theology of Gethsemane rather than of Calvary, a theology which finds its centre in the suffering rather than in the death of the Redeemer.

the nature of atonement has received much support, conscious and unconscious, from preachers and writers since his time. As an example of the preacher one might turn to a remarkable series of sermons by the great Alexander Whyte of Edinburgh, published under the title *Lord, Teach us to Pray*. There is no doubt of the intensely *personal* quality of these sermons, obviously created out of his own personal confessions and intercessions on behalf of others and then communicated to his hearers in the intimacy of personal address. He imagines the Old Testament men of God at prayer—Jacob wrestling, Elijah passionate, Job groping, Habakkuk waiting, each in his own way taking on his heart the sin of the world and confessing the holiness of God. But the heart of the book is reached when we read the sermons on the prayers of Christ. The prayer in St. John 17—'for their sakes I sanctify myself': the prayer in the parable of the man who knocked at midnight: above all the prayer in Gethsemane—'this cup! Thy will!'.

In the Markan account of the agony in the garden there are two words in the English version (Authorized Version) on which Whyte fastens attention. We read that Jesus began to be *sore amazed*. Luther in his day had claimed that the original Greek words at this point were the most astonishing in the whole Bible—a judgment reinforced by a modern commentator who affirms that they 'depict the greatest possible degree of infinite horror and suffering' (Lohmeyer). What caused the evangelist to use such an expression? Whyte freely confesses his own sense of bafflement. Yet he is convinced that the shudder of aversion can only have been brought about by one thing. 'It was *sin* "laid upon Himself" till He was "made sin".' It had been amazement and horror enough to stand and see deceit and envy and pride, and all of that kind, as He describes it in terrible words, 'coming out of the heart' of man. But it was a new thing to our Lord to have all that poured in upon Himself. To be *made sin* 'amazed' our Lord; it absolutely overwhelmed Him—cast Him into 'an agony': it 'loaded Him and sickened Him and slew Him'. And it was Whyte's challenge and offer to his hearers that in such prayer they could enter into the fellowship of Christ's sufferings and share in His work of saving the world from sin.

As an example of theologian and writer one might turn to the books of P. T. Forsyth. No one can even glance at *The Soul of Prayer* without sensing that here was a man who knew what it meant to agonize in prayer and who, in that experience, found a key to a door of illumination regarding the mystery of the Atonement. It is significant that in the book which contains what is probably his most systematic treatment of the doctrine, *The Work of Christ*, the central chapter is entitled 'The Cross, The Great Confessional'. In a pivotal passage he affirms that the essential work of Christ, while in a sense it was to confess human sin, was concerned to do something far greater, namely to confess God's holiness in His judgment *upon* sin. 'He stood in the midst of human sin, full of love to man, such love as enabled Him to identify Himself in the most profound sympathetic way with the evil race: fuller still of love to the God whose name He was hallowing; and as with one mouth, as if the whole race confessed through Him . . . He lifted up His face unto God and said, Thou art holy in all Thy judgments, even in this judgment which turns not aside even from Me but strikes the sinful spot if even I stand on it.'[18] 'This', Forsyth continues, 'is the taking of sin away, the acknowledgement of judgment as holy, wise and good and its conversion into blessing; the absorption and conversion of judgment into *confession and praise*, the *removal* of that guilt which stood between God and man's reconciliation, the robbing sin of its power to prevent communion with God.'

Again and again Forsyth returns to the Cross as the supreme act of confession, confession of the perfect righteousness of God. God Himself was in this confession, initiating it, suffering in it. Yet man was in it for Christ was the new Humanity doing the one thing needful viz. justifying the holiness of God. 'In Christ's atoning work', Forsyth writes in his own theodicy, 'we have the one perfect, silent and practical confession of God's righteousness, which is the one rightness for what we have come to be, the one right attitude of the world's conscience to God's. In Him humanity justifies God and praises Him in its nadir.'[19] But besides the activities of confession and praise, he appeals to the human experience of intercession as a further illumination of the nature of the Atonement. He emphasizes the *personal* character of prayer and the way in which the truest thought of God is generated in prayer. He then goes on to say 'Our atonement with God is the pregnant be-all and end-all of Christian peace and life; and what is that atonement but the head and front of the Saviour's perpetual intercession, of the outpouring of His sin-laden soul unto death? Unto death! That is to say, it is its outpouring utterly. So that His entire self-emptying and His perfect and prevailing prayer are one. In this intercession our best prayer, broken, soiled, and feeble as it is, is caught up and made prayer indeed and power with God. This

18. Op. cit., p. 150.
19. *The Justification of God*, p. 174.

intercession prays for our very prayer, and atones for the sin in it. This is praying in the Holy Ghost. This is praying "for Christ's sake". If it be true that the whole Trinity is in the gospel of our salvation, it is also true that all theology lies hidden in the prayer which is our chief answer to the gospel.'[20]

F

We have looked at some striking examples of writers interpreting atonement within the context of and by the help of the experience of prayer. In the commerce of persons in ordinary life there are constant askings of favour, expressions of gratitude, acknowledgements of value, recognitions of obligation. If relationships of this kind are interrupted a way of restoration has to be found if the personal quality of life is to be maintained. By exploring the human situation in this respect and by focussing attention in particular on Jesus' own prayer experiences in the days of his flesh the attempt has been made to shed new light on the meaning of atonement in terms of inter-personal relationships.

But there is another area of human experience which has been subjected to the closest scrutiny during the past century both for its intrinsic interest on the human level and for the bearing it may have on the nature of ultimate reality. In every personal relationship there are occasions of misunderstanding, offences to sensitivity, clashes of purpose. These issue in quarrels, breaches, even separation. When this happens how can the relation be restored? How can reconciliation be effected? The common answer has been that there must be the attitude and acts of *forgiveness*. William Blake likened *mutual forgiveness* to the gates of paradise. Here, it would appear, human nature reaches one of its highest and noblest forms of expression. Here, it would seem, that which is done within the human context points unmistakably to the activity of the Divine. Again it was William Blake who exclaimed:

> O point of mutual forgiveness between Enemies
> Birthplace of the Love of God incomprehensible.

Is not the full and free forgiveness of sons the highest and deepest characteristic of the Divine nature that we can imagine?

Yet the matter is not quite so simple. The inter-relationship of *persons* is so complex and so delicate that the fabric once torn is not so easily mended. This is the point of H. H. Farmer's remark that 'the problem of the atonement is the problem of setting right

20. *The Soul of Prayer*, p. 63.

in a world of inaccessible, non-manipulatable wills the rejection of claims which is already part of history and at work in history. It is the restoration of the fabric of the I-Thou world when it has been torn.'[21] In his discussion of the marriage-relationship, where personal factors may be presumed to be of the highest significance, V. A. Demant states quite bluntly that whereas forgiveness is needed most in marriage it is there that it is most difficult. And even between friends beyond the marriage relationship he is prepared to say that 'forgiveness is an agony'.[22] And it is this very fact of the almost infinite complexity of the attractions and repulsions, the desire to dominate and the desire to submit, the urge to possess and the urge to give, the magnanimities and the pettinesses of personal relationships, which has enabled novelists and dramatists of the last two centuries to capture and sustain the interest of their readers. Increasingly during this period men and women from different backgrounds and experiences have been brought close to one another. They have been compelled to meet, to adjust to new relationships, to rise or to fall within them. And amidst all the possible acts and attitudes which such encounters engender it is doubtful if any is more involved than the movement of forgiveness. Two random examples from modern literature can at least illustrate the problem.

In the midst of all the ludicrous characters and farcical situations which Mr. P. G. Wodehouse has created in his novels one may find shrewd insights into the problems and perplexities of ordinary human relationships. At one place he sees fit to comment on the ambiguity of human forgiveness. 'It is a good rule in life never to apologize. The right sort of people do not want apologies and the wrong sort take a mean advantage of them. Sellers belonged to the latter class. When Annette, meek, penitent, with all her claws sheathed came to him and grovelled, he forgave her with a repulsive magnanimity which in a less subdued mood would have stung her to renewed pugnacity. As it was, she allowed herself to be forgiven and retired with a dismal conviction that from now on he would be more insufferable than ever.' It would be easy to dismiss this as a caricature. But Wodehouse is right that forgiveness without mutual personal respect is an impertinence which is only resented. The whole situation is made worse rather than better by such an act.

A more serious writer exposes the same ambiguity in a great historical poem designed to show the descent from idealism revealed in certain of the descendants of Jefferson. The poem is

21. H. H. Farmer: *The Servant of the Word*, p. 43.
22. V. A. Demant: *Christian Sex Ethics*, p. 77.

entitled *Brother to Dragons* and at one point a gesture of forgiveness
has been made:

> the magnanimous
> Act of forgiveness . . . that
> Act is an index equal of desire
> Gone craven with placation
> And of the self's final ferocity
> Whetted in sweetness as a blade in oil.
> Yes, forgiveness is the one unforgivable.
> Act and . . .
> And so Lilburn forgave his wife.
> Oh yes
> That he might blame her too, in his act of forgiveness.[23]

Again it would be easy to dismiss this as pure cynicism. Yet no
one who has in any measure experienced the possible perversions of
forgiveness could fail to respond to the truth of this author's insights.
How can forgiveness be given and received and through the whole
process an absolute personal integrity be maintained?

Greatest of all I would suggest in his insight into this aspect of
the human situation is Dostoievsky. In his novels we see as in few
other writings the extraordinary complexity of human nature. In a
Mitya there is a combination of nobility and baseness, in a Grushenka
of sensuality and self-sacrifice. Wherever he looks out upon the
human scene Dostoievsky sees the beauty of the Madonna and the
horror of Sodom in constant interplay. And where there is such
ambiguity and dividedness forgiveness is always open to the most
deadly perversion. There is a spurious type of forgiveness which
is the act of a proud, superior, calculating individual who knows
he is on top and will use an apparent generosity for his own ends.[24]
There is a way of receiving forgiveness which is cringing and
fawning and again only concerned to exploit a changed situation
for personal advantage. There is a despair of the forgiveness of sins
('I can never forgive myself for it', 'God can never forgive me')
which is a kind of defiant-weakness protecting itself to the very limit.

One of the questions which tormented Dostoievsky was that of
man's right to forgive. Obviously a so-called forgiveness which
passes lightly over glaring wrongs is trivial. But are there offences
which ought not to be forgiven? Dostoievsky is haunted by the
sufferings of children, a boy bullied by his mates, an infant thrown
to the dogs. Ivan Karamazor cries out:

'I don't want the mother to embrace the oppressor who threw her

23. R. P. Warren: *Brother to Dragons*, p. 49.
24. Cp. T. S. Eliot: *The Cocktail Party* 1. 1—'She might decide to be forgiving
and gain an advantage'.

son to the dogs! She dare not forgive him! Let her forgive for herself, if she will, let her forgive the torturer for the immeasurable suffering of her mother's heart. But the suffering of her tortured child she has no right to forgive, she dare not forgive the torturer, even if the child were to forgive him! . . . Is there in the whole world a being who would have the right to forgive and could forgive?'[25]

In and through the brilliant portrayal of human relationships Dostoievsky exposes man as desperately in need of forgiveness and yet confronted by the desperate difficulty of imagining or receiving a true forgiveness. Man wants to forgive himself, he wants the forgiveness of the other. Yet he also wants to preserve his pride; he wants to retain his own independence over against the other. It is the tension between his essential being as a person free to give and to receive and his existence as a sinner unable to give and in the last resort unable to receive. 'If I am guilty', Raskolnikov exclaims to his sister, 'forgive me (though I cannot be forgiven if I am guilty).' Stavrogin, though wanting forgiveness, clings to the thought that he will forgive himself. He will suffer anything for the chance of forgiving himself rather than receive forgiveness from the hands of another.

Such are the complexities of the human situation. That the human experience of forgiving and being forgiven points to a transcendent way of forgiveness is clear enough. But how can the subtle perversions and deceptions inherent even in the best of human patterns be avoided as we seek to present a picture of the *forgiveness of God*? Only, Christian interpreters have insisted, by a constant contemplation of and rediscovery of the forgiveness expressed in all His personal relationships by the Christ. Through Him we enjoy the forgiveness of sins. We can forgive one another only because God through Christ has forgiven us.

Dostoievsky accepts this fundamental principle but expresses it in his own distinctive and (to Western minds) unusual way. In the first place he affirms, through the encounter between Stavrogin and Father Tihon, that even the first movements of desire to forgive oneself, the first glimmerings of belief that it is possible to forgive oneself, are in fact the promptings of God Himself leading man to faith in *His* forgiveness. 'I will give you joyous tidings', said Tihon with emotion; 'Christ too will forgive you if you reach the point where you forgive yourself. . . . Oh no, no, do not believe that I am uttering blasphemy; even if you do not achieve reconciliation with yourself and self-forgiveness, even then He will forgive you for your intention and your great suffering. . . . Everything will be taken

25. Dostoievsky: *The Brothers Karamazov*.

into account; not a word, not a movement of the spirit, not a half-thought will be lost.' In the second place, through the encounter between Alyosha and Ivan Karamazov, he grapples with the question of the right to forgive sins and affirms that only one who has borne in himself the suffering and torture which wicked acts entail can rightfully speak a word of forgiveness to the sinner. 'Only if it be true that Christ really suffers in all suffering, and if upon him all sin has actually fallen, can He have the right to forgive sin in the stead of those other sufferers who may not forgive us.'[26] 'Brother', said Alyosha suddenly with flashing eyes, 'you said just now, is there a being in the whole world who would have the right to forgive and could forgive? But there is a Being and He can forgive everything, all for all, because He gave His innocent blood for all and everything. You have forgotten Him and on Him is built the edifice and it is to Him they cry aloud: Thou art just O Lord for Thy ways are revealed.'

In William Golding's novel *Free Fall* the verger seeks awkwardly to ask forgiveness of the child he has injured. But, Golding comments, 'an injury to the innocent cannot be forgiven because the innocent cannot forgive what they do not understand as an injury'. This may be true. Yet it is the Christian claim that the innocent Christ did not suffer simply as an individual. He gathered into His embrace all who are the victims of injury and wrong. And because of that, His act of forgiveness (to use Golding's description of what such an act can ideally be) is 'a positive act of healing, a burst of light'.

G

The most extensive attempt in modern times to interpret the Atonement in terms of the central category of forgiveness is Professor H. R. Mackintosh's volume in this series *The Christian Experience of Forgiveness*. This book has won wide recognition both on account of its deep insight into the nature of personal relationships and because of its profoundly religious quality. Mackintosh moved between the poles of a life hid with Christ in God and a life open to the testimony of that which men experience in their relationships with one another. He knew what it was to be forgiven by God in Christ: he knew the cost of forgiving a fellow-man for Christ's sake. Two moving passages in his book illustrate this double frame of reference. Speaking in one place of the different stages of the

---

26. This quotation is taken from an (so far as I know) unpublished paper by Paul Ramsey entitled *Sin, Guilt and Atonement* to which I am much indebted in my references to Dostoievsky.

Christian's union with God in Christ he arrives at the deepest experience of all. 'He (the Christian) may well be obliged to face the shattering discovery that all his moral efforts are vain and that, in the light cast by God, he now appears even to himself as one who, guiltily and unconditionally, has failed. In Christ's presence he learns, gradually or suddenly, the final truth about himself; and the revelation breaks him. It is in such hours of inexorable conscience, when in his lonely responsibility and acknowledged impotence a man has bowed his head and fallen on his knees, that "the word of the cross" can find its most effectual entrance. Nor will any message of reconciliation suffice which does not contain a relief for this, our profoundest and sorest need.'[27]

This is one side. But there is another side. 'We are constantly under a temptation to suppose that the reason why we fail to understand completely the atonement made by God in Christ is that our minds are not sufficiently profound. And doubtless there is truth in the reflection that for final insight into the meaning of the cross we are not able or perspicacious enough. But there is a deeper reason still. It is that we are not good enough; we have never forgiven a deadly injury at a price like this, at such cost to ourselves as came upon God in Jesus' death. . . . Let the man be found who has undergone the shattering experience of pardoning, nobly and tenderly, some awful wrong to himself, still more to one beloved by him, and he will understand the meaning of Calvary better than all the theologians of the world.'[28] The 'shattering' discovery of personal failure: the 'shattering' experience of pardoning personal wrong. It is noteworthy that Mackintosh uses the same word in each case. Each experience he regards as a precondition for a deep understanding of the meaning of atonement. The one springs out of a deepening personal relationship with God in Christ, the other out of an expanding relationship with the world of men for whom Christ died.

The book is concerned with four main themes. First the author invites attention to the place of forgiveness in human life as we know it. The best things in human intercourse are in very truth 'windows into the life of God'. Forgiveness of any kind he declares is 'an active process in the mind and temper of a wronged person, by means of which he abolishes a moral hindrance to fellowship with the wrong-doer, and re-establishes the freedom and happiness of friendship'.[29] Forgiveness at its highest and deepest occurs

27. Op. cit., p. 228.
28. Ibid., p. 190 f.
29. p. 28.

'when by self-conquest which even bystanders can see to be noble the injured man (or, as it may be, woman) refusing to ignore moral realities, yet reaching over and beyond the wrong to knit up the old ties of communion, attains to the act of deep pure pardon'.[30]

Yet he never forgets that forgiveness as it is exercised in human affairs moves within this framework of *moral realities*. It seeks to overcome *moral* hindrances to fellowship. In other words forgiveness is only conceivable where there is the full recognition that something needs to be forgiven and this not merely something which I personally may dislike or resent or find tiresome but something which contravenes moral standards, which, in fact, cuts across the moral principles by which sound human relationships must be governed. Forgiveness only takes on meaning and relevance within a moral universe where sin of every sort, at all times and in all places, is followed by evil consequences.[31] Sin and suffering are inexorably linked together. This may not by any means always be obvious and the consequences may not fall heavily upon the offender. But unless no such thing as a moral order exists and everything in human life is arbitrary it must be possible to assume that somehow evil-doing will work itself out into pain and suffering and that this is more likely to impinge upon the righteous and the innocent than upon those who have no qualms about being identified with evil.

Thirdly, the most wonderful thing of all is the revelation of the Divine forgiveness. It is impossible not to feel the exaltation of spirit with which Mackintosh celebrates this Divine activity. It is the key to the ministry of Jesus in the days of His flesh: it is the central meaning of His cross and passion. One of the striking things about the book as a whole is its constant return to the picture of Jesus deliberately extending the hand of friendship to publicans and sinners, dealing with men and women in *personal* terms as erring and needing to be forgiven, identifying himself with the sinful and conveying to them the assurance of the forgiveness of God. In one particular section[32] Mackintosh paints a vivid picture of Jesus on the one hand reflecting 'God's own mind', on the other hand vicariously participating in human shame. In the days of His ministry 'He sought the company of the sinful habitually and with open eyes, and did so not for subtle reasons, or as an example to anyone, but because by nature He could do no otherwise,

30. Ibid., p. 188.
31. p. 202.
32. Ibid., pp. 97–100.

because it was the only possible outcome of His intimacy with the Father'. Yet 'it is an agony to see vileness eating into the life of those we love' and the supreme revelation of the agony was the Cross itself. 'Of this willingness to suffer in prolonged and faithful proximity to sinners the Cross is the last and highest manifestation. Calvary is the pain, felt in unison with God's mind, whereby the Divine readiness to forgive is sealed.'

Looked at from the other side the Cross is the climax of 'fraternal sympathetic agony'. 'Jesus . . . could not convey the Father's pardon to the guilty in absolute fulness except by carrying His identification with them to the uttermost point; at that point He gave Himself in death. The Bearer of forgiveness perishes in giving complete expression to the mercy and judgment which in their unity constitute the pardon of God. It is tragedy, it is that inscrutable and catastrophic collision of good and evil of which in its measure human life is full. But, if the phrase be permissible, it is not pessimistic but optimistic tragedy; Jesus does not fall along with His cause, He falls that in Him the cause may live.'

This is the twofold affirmation to which Mackintosh constantly returns. God has spoken the Word of complete forgiveness through the personalty of Christ expressed in life-situations and in the final death-agony. Jesus mediates this Word of forgiveness by identifying Himself completely with His brothers in their fallenness, in their shame, in the supreme symbol of that shame, the Cross. In other words Jesus not only *reveals* the forgiving love of God, He *conveys* it. 'It was not that God stretched His hand from the sky, seized the mass of human iniquity, transferred it to Jesus by capricious fiat, then chastised Him for it. God does nothing in that way. But when Jesus entered into our life, took the responsibility of our evil upon Himself, identifying His life with ours to the uttermost and placing Himself where the sinful are by strong sympathy in a fashion so real that the pain and affliction due to us became unspeakable suffering within His soul—*that* was the act of God, that (if we take seriously Jesus' oneness of mind and will with the Father) was indeed the experience of God. In no way other than by letting sinful wills do their worst to Jesus could it be openly demonstrated, and for ever, what sin involves in God's righteous judgment.'[33]

Mackintosh's fourth theme is the fulfilment of the Atonement made by Christ in our own union with Him. The crucifixion regarded purely externally as an event of bygone history has no power to reconcile. It must be manifested and reproduced within us. Its

33. Ibid., p. 205 f.

virtue must mould our attitudes and our actions. The reality of
the whole pardoning activity of God in Christ can only be communicated today through our sharing His spirit and being united
with Him in His constant concern for those who are cutting themselves off and excluding themselves from the love of God. The book
is a deeply religious book, one that breathes the spirit of a humble
love of God and a sympathetic love for the fellow-man. No one
can doubt that this interpretation of God's forgiveness is the fruit
of a long experience of having been forgiven and of seeking to
express that forgiveness to others. There are difficulties, particularly,
I think, in his assumptions about the self-consciousness of Jesus
and in his psychological analysis of human sinfulness. But in
company with McLeod Campbell, Mackintosh will take his place
in Christian history as one who entered deeply into the mind and
spirit of the Christ of the Gospels and who saw the light of the
glory of God in the face of the Crucified. His book might almost
be regarded as an extended meditation and commentary on William
Blake's aphorism: 'The Spirit of Jesus is continual forgiveness of
sins'.

H

One of the most powerful streams of thought flowing through the
theological life of the past half century has been that which has made
the *personal* its fundamental category of interpretation. It has sought
to analyse the relations between man and man and has gone on to
apply the results to a deepening of our understanding of the relations
between God and man. Or alternatively it has begun from certain
aspects of God's relations to man as witnessed by the Biblical
revelation, has accepted these as the norm of the 'personal' and has
gone on to use them as the criterion of health in the relations
between man and man. Already in the nineteenth and early twentieth
century the importance of the concept of the personal and of its
derivative 'personality' was coming to be recognized but Martin
Buber's small book, *Ich and Du*, written during the First World
War, exercised an extraordinary influence by its emphasis upon the
distinction between man's experience of the personal which he
symbolizes as 'Thou' and his more general relationship with the
non-personal which he symbolizes as 'It'. It was a period when
'things' manufactured by man were proliferating and when his life
was being increasingly spent in the midst of a mechanical and
abstract environment. Buber, with profound insight and imagination

sought to recall his contemporaries to the primacy of the 'Thou' world, the personal encounter, the glories and the tragedies of man-in-relationship-with-the-other.

Of theologians who have written since Buber's book appeared I can think of none who has employed the language of the 'personal' more consistently than has H. H. Farmer, especially in his book *The World and God*. Brunner can perhaps be regarded as the outstanding example of a theologian beginning from the Divine side of the relationship. The title of his book *The Divine-Human Encounter* indicates the direction in which his theological construction constantly moves—from God to man, from the Word of God to man's obedient response. On the basis of the Biblical revelation he defines this address as double-sided, making on the one hand an unconditional demand, offering on the other hand an unconditional grace. God in Christ is Lord and Saviour and the nature of the personal is revealed in this double form of the communication. But the Bible itself does not use the category 'the personal' and one is bound to infer that Brunner has taken a convenient term out of the vocabulary of our time and applied it to describe what is undoubtedly the central characteristic of the Biblical testimony. Farmer is more logical in taking the word out of current speech, asking how we employ it in human situations and then enquiring how far it corresponds to realities in the relationships between God and man.

The simplest experience of friendship in human life is enough to convince us that two essential factors are involved. There must be give and take, a willing commitment to the other with at the same time a preservation of one's own identity. Farmer analyses the basic elements of personal relationship as (a) the awareness of a self-activity coming forth from the other man and meeting ours in a certain tension or resistance and (b) the awareness of a certain community of interests which leads to value co-operation, the coming forth from the other man to support me in my own inadequacy. 'The awareness of the other as potentially co-operative in his resistance or as potentially resistant in his co-operation, lies at the heart of our awareness of personality in one another.'[34] From this analysis he passes on to his definition of the personal in the relations between God and man. Believing that God has created an essentially personal order in which it is His will that all should live in personal relationship with Himself and with one another, Farmer argues that what is known partially or imperfectly in human experience is true completely in God's dealings with men. He ever acts towards them

34. *The World and God*, p. 22 f.

in a *personal* way and this implies an unconditional demand upon them (though respecting their autonomy and their ability to resist) together with an unconditional offer of succour (again respecting their right to refuse His gifts).

The very structure of personal relationships, however, their duality and ambivalence, render them peculiarly open to distortion and perversion. By excess in any one direction the essentially *personal* quality is corrupted. Failure on either side in giving or receiving leads to resentment which can grow into hatred. In an illuminating discussion of 'motivation' within personal relationships, John Macmurray employs the terms 'love' and 'fear' to describe what he calls the positive and negative poles of this motivation. Fear is always present because the self desires to preserve its own identity: love is always present because the self desires to be fulfilled in the other. But the very interplay of these two desires inevitably produces frustration, resentment and even hatred—inevitably 'because it is impossible that you should always be able to respond to me in the way that my action expects.'[35] 'The rejection of personal relationship itself is a negative aspect of personal relationship, and itself enforces a reciprocity of negation. In so far as I threaten your personal fulfilment you can only reciprocate by threatening mine. Hatred, therefore, is the emotion by which we can identify the motive of mutual negation in the personal relation. If it completely escapes from intentional control it issues in murder'[36] (of the other or of myself).

So inevitable is the emergence of hatred in the very structure of any relationship that can be called 'personal' that Macmurray is prepared to identify it with what theology has called 'original sin'. If it is once assumed that true mutuality between persons is conceivable then it must also be assumed that its negative is possible. *Corruptio optimi pessima.* Nothing is so fundamental in man's whole distinction between good and evil as the positive and the negative in the bipolar relationship between persons. And because offences are inevitable, human existence will become increasingly at cross-purposes unless there be some way of healing, of forbearance, of forgiveness. That such forgiveness has been manifested in the ordinary relationships of life few would deny. Whence has this come? Can it be claimed that every movement towards forgiveness, every act of forgiveness is directly motivated by God Himself, that His nature and property is always to forgive? Can it further be claimed that because of man's dullness and

35. *Persons in Relation*, p. 74.
36. Ibid.

blindness a superlative, unique expression of this forgiveness was once-for-all given within the very conditions and structure of human personal relationships? This in fact is the Christian claim and it is this which Farmer seeks to substantiate in his chapter entitled 'Sin and Reconciliation'.[37]

He begins by rejecting certain commonly held views of the nature of sin as inadequate in that they do not do full justice to the essentially *personal* quality of the relations between God and man. Sin therefore he defines as 'something through which a man is set against *God*, the word God standing not for an impersonal Moral Order or Creative Life Force, nor for a man's own Better Self, nor for the totality of Social Ideals, but for the Eternal as personal will which enters into relation with the will of man in a polarity or tension of personal relationship'. But this refusal to respond, this rejection of God's demand and succour, arises out of the bipolar relation to which I have already referred. There is always, Farmer says, propulsion of the soul towards the personal advance of God because it is seen to be 'reasonable and right and relevant' so far as the soul's own welfare is concerned. On the other hand there is also a propulsion of the soul away from such an advance because it seems to imperil its own values and preferences and ambitions. Here is the conflict which in an extraordinarily complex way characterizes the total realm of personal relationships.

Farmer lays great emphasis on one other aspect of the situation. In his view the crucial factor determining the movements of the person in his relations with others is the *attention*. What holds the attention, directs the will. The mental image always tends to act itself out. The heart of the conflict then is the human imagination. And the heart and centre of sin 'is going against the light, such light as one has, not in the sense of snuffing it out as a man might a candle-flame between his fingers, for that no one can do, but in the sense of screening it under a veil of excuse and subterfuge. It is "holding down the truth in unrighteousness".'[38] Moreover the darkness is not to be regarded as the sole creation of the individual soul. Every individual is born into an already existent order of personal relationships which has become alienated from the true light. From the beginning he is unable to see clearly because of the encircling gloom; he himself, by his false choices of attention, increases the gloom for others. Like the author of the Fourth Gospel Farmer finds the imagery of light and darkness the most adequate of all to describe the human condition. The preliminary

37. Op. cit., p. 183 ff.
38. Ibid., p. 193.

to speaking of the coming of the light is the awareness of darkness covering the face of the earth.

Such a diagnosis of the human situation leads naturally to the description of the way of salvation. 'Somehow the darkness of his (man's) mind must be broken through so that he can at least begin to see things as they really are—God as He really is, himself as he really is, his neighbours as they really are, within that whole personal order which underlies all the circumstances of his life and in which it is the divine will that he should find his right place.'[39] Further 'the saving revelation must be such that at one and the same time it shows man the truth and makes it possible for him to be sincere with it. It must make him vividly aware again of the searching holy will of the Eternal dealing with him, challenging him, condemning him not to run away from it, but sincerely and humbly to accept it. In short, it must bring a new manifestation of God as both consuming fire and final refuge and strength, only now in such wise that the inner darkness caused by sin and insincerity is broken through and the deepest springs of the soul's life reached. The Christian affirmation is that God has made such a saving revelation of Himself in the personality of Jesus Christ.'

In the remainder of his book Farmer is concerned to draw out the consequences of this saving revelation, particularly in the realms of providence and prayer. He makes the personal dealing of God with man through Christ his touchstone at every stage. And it is when he comes to deal with the most perplexing and frustrating of all human experiences—the suffering and the evil— that he turns to the Cross as the focus of the light of the saving revelation. The power of the Cross to bring light into human darkness springs from two of its aspects. In the first place it stands in the midst of human history and is thereby related to all the historical conditions of human life. Secondly it plumbs the depths of evil. It includes in itself 'something of almost every darkness to which human life is liable—sin, hatred, physical agony, premature death, the innocent suffering for the guilty, the bitter disappointment of high ideals. Yet because the uniquely pure and revealing personality of Jesus is at the centre of it all, the darkness suddenly becomes full of light. The discernment is given that as the holy love of Jesus is in the midst of all this evil, so also is that on which it rests and by which it is sustained, namely the holy love of God. The one is apprehended through the other and both through human history in its most tragic form. . . . The light which man needs is seen shining

39. Ibid., p. 196.

out of the midst of those very events which otherwise overwhelm and defeat his soul.'[40]

To illustrate the way in which the light shines out of the darkness of the Cross Farmer draws attention to three things. In the Cross we see perfect love surrendered to the personal order, for righteousness enters into the same condemnation with malefactors: we see perfect love manifested in the innocent bearing the burdens of the guilty: we see a complete self-commitment to an ultimate purpose of love through the midst of the profoundest darkness and suffering. Such a vision suffices to bring men out of darkness and to lead them to follow the Christ in the way of His Cross, thus bringing light into all their relationships with others. Nowhere is it claimed that the above is a full interpretation of the meaning of the Cross. But throughout the book the testimony is repeated again and again that a revelation sufficient to break through all the darkness which beclouds human relationships has been given in and through the personal life and character of Jesus the Christ and supremely in the culmination of His earthly career in the surrender to the Cross.

The outstanding contribution of this book seems to me to lie in its analysis of the nature of personal relations and in its exposure of that which is needed to effect a reconciliation of a truly personal kind. Today many would find difficulties in the concept of 'the personality' of Jesus and in the adequacy of the psychology of the 'attention' to carry the weight of the argument that rests upon it. By concentrating in each case on a single concept, the author tends to break away from the polarity and the paradox which appear so clearly in his preliminary analysis. Yet whatever difficulties of this kind there may be it remains evident that one who seeks to interpret atonement in terms of *personal* relationships between mature and adult characters comes to the place inevitably where the main emphasis lies on the Cross as

(a) The perfect revelation of suffering love where the Son of God takes upon Himself the burdens—sins, sufferings, infirmities—of His brethren within the personal order and thereby expresses to the limit the unconditional grace of God;

(b) The perfect act of response to holy demand in which the Son of God, standing with His brothers in their condemnation, acknowledges the righteousness of the Eternal Will and thereby lays upon them the unconditional demand to make the same acknowledgement themselves.

Holy demand and gracious succour are revealed both through His response to the Eternal Personal and through His relation to

40. Ibid., p. 243 f.

those who are His fellows within the personal order. And it would not be untrue to say that these are the keynotes of all the attempts we have considered to interpret the act of atonement in terms of personal relationships: The act both constrains and upholds, condemns and saves, judges and forgives, always within the personal order. Jesus in His Cross is the pioneer and perfecter of reconciliation between God and man, between man and man. To respond personally to His Cross is to set out on the pathway of reconciliation in which increasing demands and increasing grace company together and in which the person is both preserved and fulfilled within the perfect personal order which is the Divine purpose for mankind.

CHAPTER VIII

THE IMAGE OF PERFECT INTEGRATION

Fourth Analogue

The pattern of the individual human personality in God's original design was intended to reveal at every stage coherence, integration, depth. In the process of growth towards maturity the spirit, in relationship with the body, would discover its true fulfilment. But man has shown himself prone either to dissipate his energies wastefully or to narrow his attention obsessively into some trivial concern. Playing light-heartedly with the many he fails to discover the one: limiting himself to the pursuit of the particular he fails to grow towards the universal. So the personality remains either dwarfed and stunted or at the mercy of competing objects of desire. How can a true integration be achieved?

The all-important instrument of integration is *the image*. Man's diffused interests begin to find a focus of integration in a constraining image of wholeness. His tendency to devote himself to the trivial can be overcome by the disclosure of an image of greatness. The image transcends his conflicting interests. At the same time it takes form within his own essential frame of reference. Such an image—the only fully adequate and finally compelling image—is that of the Man for others, the Man of transcendent origin who yet descended to the depths of the human situation in order that he might raise humanity to the heights. He laid aside His garments and girded Himself with a towel and began to wash the disciples' feet. Taking His garments again He said: 'Ye call me master and lord and so I am. If I then your lord and master have washed your feet ye also ought to wash one another's feet. For I have given you *an image*.' In the gift of the image lies the hope of reintegration. 'I, if I be lifted up, will draw all men unto Me.'

A

A convenient starting-point as we begin to consider the individual personality is the phenomenon of *initiation*. Wherever social anthropologists have investigated the practices of tribal peoples they have discovered elaborate ceremonies of initiation all of which are related to man or woman *as an individual*. There are innumerable ceremonies with a corporate reference—dancing together, singing together, eating and drinking together—but in every initiation ceremony there is at least a momentary focus of intense concentration upon the individual. It is true that the corporate reference is never absent. The initiand is being brought into an experience of some treasured aspect of tribal life and this very fact serves to remind the community of the nature of its own heritage. Yet the actions are directed towards the individual and in the turning point of the ritual the individual exists for the moment *alone*. In and through a *rite de passage* he experiences a transfiguration from one form of existence to another.

As Mircea Eliade points out in his book *Birth and Rebirth*, initiations can in general be viewed under three categories. First there is the ordinary initiation which every child born into the world is expected sooner or later to undergo: secondly there is the initiation by means of which a more limited number are admitted to the membership of particular groups or societies: thirdly there is a still more limited form by which a highly select category of individual is introduced into the sacred realm of religious mysteries—he becomes a shaman or medicine-man or ecstatic. But although these three types can be distinguished there is a remarkable uniformity in the general motivation and pattern of the ceremonies themselves. These may be described as involving a symbolic death to whatever the present form of existence may be, a death involving a return to the beginnings when life sprang out of inertia, order began to form out of chaos, light began to triumph over darkness. It is by an actual participation in the origins that the initiand can be assured of progress towards his own fulfilment. As Eliade expresses it a 'symbolic return to chaos is indispensable to any new Creation'[1] within every culture and upon every plane of manifestation. Through a mystical death and resurrection a new personality or at the very least a personality of fuller potential is born.

The importance of the ceremony of initiation for the development of the individual can scarcely be exaggerated. As we have had occasion to see in the earlier part of this study the greater part of human life is a shared life—with nature, with other humans, with divine beings. It would easily be possible for the life of the individual to be swallowed up in the totality of natural and social existence, to be a continuous automatic reflection of his immediate environment. Yet the whole object of initiations is to effect a momentary withdrawal—of the individual from his society, of the self from its

1. *Myths, Dreams and Mysteries*, p. 80.

natural surroundings. Such a withdrawal may be painful and terrifying, and may involve a severe strain upon the initiate. Yet if he endures he becomes a new man and becomes capable of playing an active rather than a purely passive part in the community to which he belongs.

In the first place the withdrawal is from the mother and her associates (this is of course specially the case with a boy). No longer must there be the dependence on woman and the soothing elements of life. By a dramatic representation the initiate is transferred to the world of hard reality in which each must struggle for his own existence and that of the society to which he is now responsible. In the second place the withdrawal is from the ordinary and the familiar: this may be symbolized by a forced entry into an artificially induced darkness or by a descent into a cave or by a passage through water or by a period spent in silence and fasting. Customs have varied in detail but the underlying motif has always been the same: to initiate the individual into a world of sacred mystery and to do this through a re-enactment of the tribal myth of origins. By certain initial actions chaos and darkness were originally overcome and the ordered life of the tribe came into being. Now in the life-span of every member of the tribe these actions must be symbolically repeated in order that he may truly participate in the creative life which is his own true destiny. Silence, fasting, immersion in water, entrance into darkness, sexual abstinence—each in its own way is a symbol of death, and no conviction seems to be more deeply ingrained in the consciousness of archaic and traditional cultures than that the way to fuller life is through a symbolic death.

So far I have spoken of initiations largely in terms of their negative aspects. The withdrawal into silence or darkness, the affliction of the body and the emotions are normal aspects of the dramatic ceremonial. But through the recital or re-enactment of a primal myth the initiate is brought into contact with more positive elements of the situation. A divine being is revealed as having passed through a similar experience of suffering or passion or deprivation and by a natural sympathetic response the initiate comes to share this at least in some degree. When other stimuli have been withdrawn the imagination becomes open to receive vivid impressions and these impressions can mould the personality unless other more powerful factors conspire to erase what has been received in the period of emotional intensity.

There can be little doubt that the oldest form of the primal myth is derived from an agricultural and matriarchal culture in which the over-riding concern was the continuing fertility of the fields. The drama of the death of vegetation, so easily taken for granted today, was in earlier times terrifying in its possibilities. Man needed reassurance and hope and this he found in the myth of the dying and rising vegetation-god and in the ritual-forms through which devotees could be identified with their deity in the same process. Through many centuries this essential pattern of the adventures, death and resurrection of a Divinity were represented through myth and drama, and the initiand, who had already been brought into a highly emotional and expectant state, normally submitted without resistance to the impress of the pattern and entered himself into an experience of death to his former, 'profane' existence and of rebirth into a richer, 'sacred' manner of life.

In the general history of mysticism similar motifs are to be found though there is a tendency to lay increasing stress upon the need for a more rigorous purification of the body and the senses to prepare the way for the supreme moment of identification. All forms of mysticism require their would-be followers to begin their quest by setting out on the way of Purgation. This, it has been said, has two main objectives: 'first of all complete detachment from and renunciation of the things of sense, and the death of the egocentric life, so that the divine life may be born in the soul and union with the Godhead attained; and secondly, a continuous cleansing of the perceptions and a scouring of the windows of the soul, so that the light of a new reality may stream in and completely illuminate and transform it.'[2] Sometimes as in earliest Buddhism, the way of purgation involves a complete withdrawal from the body, from every form of involvement with matter: only through the destruction of every kind of carnal attachment can there be release into unconditioned bliss. Sometimes, as in the Hinduism of the Bhagavad-Gita, purgation involves renunciation of world-directed activities, release from all attachment to results which bring earthly advantage: and this is to be progressively achieved by contemplating the example of Lord Krishna and becoming increasingly devoted to him. But whether or not purgation is followed by or combined with a stage of concentration and illumination the ultimate goal is the same: in the final issue the soul reaches the stage of identification with or union with absolute reality, with God Himself.

Before the advent of Christianity, then, a remarkable pattern of human experience already existed. In its most general terms it was the pattern of renunciation or withdrawal, followed by concentration and contemplation, followed in turn by identification and union. The particular manifestations of this pattern had very wide variations

2. F. C. Happold: *Mysticism*, p. 58.

though, as Eliade has shown in his examination of these variations, the underlying motif remained constant, namely, the quest for new or renewed life through some form of symbolic death. The symbolism of death might be realistic, horrifying, cruel: it might be refined, pictorial, escapist: the aim was always the same, to renew life on a higher level of existence. The individual is driven to pursue such a path either through a sense of incompleteness or through a sense of failure. Not all, of course, were prepared to embrace the rigours of the way. But few, until comparatively recent times, doubted that another world, another manner of life, an extrasensory realm did in fact exist. To gain access to that realm and to share in the transcendent life of that realm constituted the highest ambition of all who failed to find a complete satisfaction in the world of the here and now.

<h1 style="text-align:center">B</h1>

How far is the kind of experience which I have been attempting to sketch reflected in the writings of the Old Testament? To such a question one's immediate response is inclined to be: Very little. The Old Testament is first and foremost a record of the acts of God and of the history of a particular people. Surrounded by enemies and threatened by their superior power throughout the greater part of its historical existence Israel was hardly likely to cradle visionaries and mystics. It needed men of action, leaders who would hazard their lives on behalf of the true God and His purpose of blessing for His people. This God was to be seen pre-eminently in those mighty acts which brought deliverance to the oppressed and protected them as they journeyed towards some promised land.

If we examine the Hebrew rite of initiation we find that although it may at a very early stage have had links with the practices of other peoples its reference at the time when the Old Testament records were being committed to writing was dominantly to the covenant which Yahweh had made with Israel. Circumcision was then regarded as necessary for all who were to be admitted to the privileges of the Covenant: children were to be circumcised on the eighth day after birth, servants or resident aliens at any age if they were to share in the Passover. There are indeed indications that at a more primitive stage circumcision was an initiation-rite before marriage; 'purification' and 'withdrawal' motifs would then have been prominent. But the peculiar historical experiences of the Hebrew tribes seem to have led to the transference of the significance of the rite to the context of the Covenant and consequently to its administration at a much earlier stage of life—immediately after birth rather than at puberty or when approaching the age of marriage. Ultimately circumcision became the distinctive mark of Israel's separation from the surrounding world. He who had been circumcised belonged to God and His covenant-people. Proselytes were obliged to accept it though at some stage they were required to add to it the more potentially meaningful ceremony of baptism. But all in all the Jewish rites of initiation can hardly be said to have conformed to the general death-and-rebirth symbolism which characterized the ceremonies of other peoples.

What then are we to say of the New Testament? So far as Jesus Himself is concerned we read of His withdrawal to the wilderness or to the mountain side to grapple with forces opposed to His mission and to strengthen Himself by renewed communion with His Father. The narratives never suggest that self or sin or the flesh needed to be renounced. He may have shrunk from the prospect before Him: He may have been tempted to take an easier way to the fulfilment of His task: He did on occasion exult in ecstasy as He saw the Kingdom being manifested in power. But none of these could be called mystical experiences. It would have been contrary to the whole testimony of the apostles to suggest that there was anything in Jesus which needed to be purged away through stripping or through dying in order that He might enter into a fuller communion with the divine.

Yet few events in the Gospel records are better attested than Jesus' willing submission to John's baptism. And two striking sayings associate the imagery of baptism with His own impending suffering and death.

'I have a baptism to be baptized with; and how I am constrained until it is accomplished' (Luke 12: 50).

'Are you able to drink the cup that I drink or to be baptized with the baptism with which I am baptized' (Mark 10: 38).

Mysterious as these sayings and indeed the acceptance of John's Baptism are, at least they indicate that Jesus was under constraint to go down into the darkness of the waters, to pass through the river of affliction, to follow the pathway of self-humbling and self-identification with the poor in spirit, in the fulfilment of His vocation. Through an initiation, both symbolic and actual, of unparalleled severity He attained the fullness of His glory and revealed the pattern of true manhood according to the will and purpose of God.

But He also presses upon the imagination of His hearers and

disciples the same pattern of renunciation, self-humbling and suffering. At a critical point in the Gospel of Mark, after the first recognition of His Messiahship and His open reference to His destiny of suffering and rejection, He speaks solemnly and emphatically to 'the multitude with his disciples':

'If any man would come after me, let him deny himself and take up his cross and follow me. For whosoever would save his life will lose it; and whoever loses his life for my sake and the gospel's will save it' (Mark 8: 34 f). The great principle here enunciated of leaving self behind, of saying 'No' to the promptings of self-interest, is applied to particular cases in the incident of the rich young ruler and in the response to the request of the two sons of Zebedee (Mark 10). In the first case the postulant to discipleship is bidden to abandon his attachment to worldly possessions. In the second the seekers for positions of prominence in the Kingdom are bidden to take the pathway of humble service and to be ready to accept the darkness and bitterness of the world's rejection in order that others may be saved. The pattern of individual growth to fulfilment which Jesus displays is not exactly that of the mystic or even of the religious initiate. But it is parallel to these in its emphasis on renunciation and self-denial: on the death (take up the cross) to all worldly advantage: on the journey through the darkness to the full light of· glory. It gave no place to any final withdrawal from society or to any self-inflicted bodily pain. But in a new context and through a new orientation the ancient principle of 'death and rebirth', of 'through sacrifice to fulfilment' was accepted and reinforced. Jesus walked ahead on the road going up to Jerusalem (Mark 10: 32). And although those who followed were afraid they continued to follow the 'light by day and the pillar of fire by night' which alone could lead them to their true destiny.

As we go forward to the Pauline and Johannine writings we discover structures of experience and forms of language which have a closer affinity with the general tradition of mysticism. It is true that Paul was primarily a man of action, constantly travelling, constantly in danger, always eager to proclaim the Gospel with which he had been entrusted. But he was also a man of intense self-awareness who recognized his own earth-boundedness, his own evil desires, his own bondage to the flesh. Passages in Galatians 2 and Romans 7 and 2 Corinthians 4 are amongst the greatest autobiographical records in the Bible and they bring us a vision of what has often been called Christ-mysticism, to distinguish it from the types of mysticism which characterize natural religion wherever found.

In these records the recurring words are sin and death. Paul is deeply conscious of a struggle in his own inner nature between the spirit and the flesh. These are contrary the one to the other. His own self, as responsible agent, seeks to suppress the evil propensities of the flesh, but the result is an ever tightening bondage to the law of sin dwelling in his members. Yearning on the one hand to identify his whole being with the will of God, he finds on the other hand that he is unable to resist the forces which drag him in precisely the opposite direction. So there comes the poignant outcry: 'Wretched man that I am! Who will deliver me from the body of death?'

Nothing is clearer from his writings than that deliverance came, not only once for all but progressively, as the vision of the death of Jesus took hold of his imagination and as the assurance of the resurrection of Jesus inspired his hope. He points out that in the very rite of baptism which all Christian initiates had experienced there had been a participation in the death and renewed life of Jesus.

> 'How can we who died to sin still live in it? We were buried with him by baptism into death so that as Christ was raised from the dead by the glory of the Father we too might walk in newness of life' (Romans 6: 3-4).

Here the essential pattern of initiation which we have noted in other contexts is brought to dramatic fulfilment by being related to the actual death and resurrection of the incarnate Son of God. In the Christian ceremony of initiation believers die with Christ to their former manner of life and rise with Him to manifest the new ethic whose integrating characteristic is love.

In another striking passage Paul links together the imagery of water-baptism and flesh-circumcision as he seeks to show how what he calls 'fullness of life' has been made possible in Christ and through Christ. Christ Himself, Paul writes, actually divested Himself of His body of flesh when He submitted to His baptism of death. So believers in their baptism, which can be regarded as the circumcision belonging to the *new* covenant, have put off the flesh with its evil desires and allowed it to be buried in the waters through which they passed. But for Christ death and burial were only the prelude to resurrection and exaltation. So too those who have been united with Him in death have been also raised with Him into glory. Even the prospect of physical death they can now face with confidence. Their gaze is set upon the Christ Who loosed all the bonds which prevent the sons of men from enjoying fullness of life. In union with the Head every member of the Body can grow 'with a growth that is from God' (Colossians 2: 19).

That which Paul conceives as being dramatically shown forth in baptism is continued and confirmed in the liturgical and ethical life of the Christian community. Everyone who receives and eats the bread at the Eucharist participates in the broken body of the Christ: everyone who receives the cup of blessing shares in the blood of Christ. Everyone who suffers on account of his faith enters into the experience of Christ's own suffering. Everyone who pours himself out on behalf of others is thereby conformed to the pattern of Christ's own sacrifice. In all circumstances the pattern established by Jesus' death and resurrection constituted for Paul the controlling image of faith and conduct. Nowhere is this pattern more beautifully and more movingly set forth than in the second chapter of the Epistle to the Philippians. Paul knows that those to whom he is writing have allowed themselves to focus their attention and their energy upon the pursuance of their own selfish interests, regardless of the needs of others. The result is dissension and disintegration in the community rather than harmony and integration. The only way of renewal is to look afresh at the One who emptied Himself, taking the form (or image) of a servant and becoming obedient to death even death on a cross. By allowing the imagination to be transformed into this pattern revealed in Christ Jesus real growth into newness of life will become possible in the experience both of the individual and of the community. And the peace of God which passes all understanding will keep hearts and minds in Christ Jesus.

Just as Paul was passionately concerned to see the principle embodied in the Cross and Resurrection being worked out in every department of human experience so the author of the Fourth Gospel was intent upon so 'lifting up' the Son of Man before men's eyes that they would be drawn to Him and thereby enter into the enjoyment of abundant life.

The unveiling of ultimate reality is a recurring theme in the Gospel but nowhere does it come to more dramatic expression than in the symbolic story of the washing of the disciples' feet. Jesus rises from supper and lays aside His garments and girding Himself with a towel, proceeds to perform the task of outward purification. But quite obviously a deeper cleansing of motive and intention is implied. Jesus' act is so unusual that it shocks and startles the disciples. A servant stooping down and touching the depths, taking away the uncleanness, resisted and misunderstood yet persisting in his task: 'Ye call me Teacher and Lord; and you are right, for so I am. If I then, your Lord and Teacher, have washed your feet you also ought to wash one another's feet. For I have given you an example (an image) that you should also do as I have done to you.' To be united with Jesus in the process of self-emptying and humble service, even to the limit of suffering and death, is to share His glory already and to be assured of entering at length into the glory which Jesus Himself shared with the Father from the foundation of the world.

This is the central dramatic parable of the Gospel. But throughout the Johannine writings the author's purpose remains constant. It is to unveil Jesus as the Lamb of God removing the sin of the world: as the One uplifted on a Cross (as the serpent was lifted on a pole) in order that all might look to Him and be saved: as the shepherd laying down his life for the sheep: as the bread given for the life of the world: as the rock smitten in order that life-giving waters might gush out: as the corn of wheat falling into the ground and dying and thereby bearing fruit: as the vine from whose passion life-giving energies could be derived: as the King through whose sacrifice the whole world is renewed. If only men can truly *see* Him they will be drawn to Him. If they can be drawn to Him they will be purified by His words, illuminated by His example and made one with Him in His death and resurrection. The inner life of the believer is transformed as he abides in Christ and Christ in him. 'As thou, Father, art in me and I in Thee, that they also may be one in us' represents the same experience as Paul's 'I live yet not I but Christ liveth in me'. Through the contemplation of the death and resurrection of Christ the self is transformed into the image of the perfect Son and shares in the glory of God.

In the New Testament, then, we find evidence of what can justly be called a form of Christ-mysticism in which the crucifixion and burial and resurrection and ascension of the Divine Son is held steadily before the imagination in order that this sequence may become the pattern of the whole life of the individual believer. It is true that the records of this intimate religious experience occupy a relatively small space in the writings. In the main these are concerned with the needs of the community—the preaching and teaching, the worship and discipline, apologetics and encouragement. Yet when Paul finds himself confronted by community situations in which the health of the whole depends upon some change in the attitude or dedication of individuals within the whole, he does not hesitate to open his own heart and tell of the way in which he himself has been delivered from slavish obedience to the Law or from bondage to a sinful habit or from fear of outward circumstances. In every case deliverance has come as he has identified himself again and again with the crucified and risen Christ. The vision has gripped him. The image has impressed itself upon the receptive organs of his inner imagination and in this way he has begun to be conformed to the same pattern in his outward behaviour.

The author of the Fourth Gospel gives his witness in a quite different way but it is impossible not to feel that behind his record there lies a similar experience of personal identification with the incarnate serving, suffering, dying and rising Son of God. For this author as for Paul the experience is not simply subjective, a general progress along the mystic way as it had been already defined in certain oriental religions. Rather it is firmly related to the pattern which had been exhibited in the career of God's Messiah, a pattern which indeed had definite correspondences with the threefold purgation, illumination and union of other traditions but which had been once for all engraved upon the consciousness of humanity by the faithfulness unto death of the representative Man, Jesus the Christ. 'Your life is hid in God'—the goal of the mystic quest—has become possible because 'ye died with Christ' and 'have been raised with Christ' and have now 'set your minds on things that are above where Christ is, seated at the right hand of God' (Colossians 3: 1 ff).

C

'In the work of Plotinus is found the fine flowering of Neoplatonism which, in fertile association with the Christo-mysticism of St. John and St. Paul, was the foundation of speculative Christian mysticism. His canvas was indeed an immense and magnificent one, a picture of an "intelligible" world, the real world, timeless, spaceless and containing in itself the archetypes of the sensible world and having its existence in the mind of God; of the sensible world as an image of the Divine Mind, which is itself a reflection of the One; of the whole universe as a vast organism, an immense living being, held together by the power and Logos of God, so that all existence, men and things is drawn by a sort of centripetal attraction towards God.'[3]

This quotation draws together the themes of the two preceding sections and leads us to the consideration of the significance of Christian mysticism in the history of the interpretation of atonement. It is not easy to isolate the stream of mystical writings in Christian history for references to intense inner spiritual experience are often included in the records of more general Christian teaching. For example within the vast range of the writings of St. Thomas Aquinas

3. F. C. Happold: Op. cit., p. 184.

which deal mainly with intellectual problems we encounter periodic upsurgings of deep mystical piety. I shall therefore interpret mystical in a reasonably broad sense and shall look particularly at the ways of release defined by Christian writers, enabling the individual soul to free itself from the ties and inhibitions of its bodily existence and to ascend to the real world which is its true home.

As Happold indicates, a great deal of the inspiration for the long tradition of what can in broadest terms be called Christian mysticism is derived from Plato. Much else was to be brought into Christian thinking from his writings but the particular form of Platonism which came to expression in the third century A.D. in the writings of Plotinus was spiritual rather than intellectual, mystical rather than rational in its emphasis and it was this which exercised an immense influence upon the Christianity of the early Middle Ages. St. Augustine was deeply indebted to Plotinus as also was the Pseudo-Dionysius and it is doubtful if any Christian writers did more to mould the general religious outlook of the millennium between A.D. 500 and 1500 than did these two.

The particular genius of Plotinus has been admirably defined by Dom David Knowles in an important chapter of his book *The Evolution of Mediaeval Thought*. Commenting on his teaching concerning the appropriate end for human endeavour and activity he says this:

'Plato had been concerned to prepare and purify the soul and mind, by moral and intellectual discipline, for a knowledge of the Forms, that is, of essential reality, dimly in this life and more fully in another. With Aristotle, beatitude consisted in the contemplation of metaphysical and physical reality, perhaps in this life only, though later followers of his school made this contemplation in some sense the employment of immortal intelligences. Plotinus, on the other hand, sees the final activity of the soul in a union of knowledge and love with the One beyond being, which can be attained partially and fleetingly even in this life. There is therefore a religious, a mystical character in the thought of Plotinus. Traces or adumbrations of this are certainly present in Plato. . . . Nevertheless Plato in his magisterial passages speaks only of an intellectual employment for the philosopher and of a plurality of Forms for him to contemplate; Plotinus finds employment for what we should call the whole personality in a union of knowledge and love with One ineffably present to the soul. The universe of Plotinus is wholly spiritual.'[4]

Plotinus was not himself a Christian. Yet it is easy to see how his

4. *The Evolution of Mediaeval Thought*, p. 22.

religious philosophy proved congenial to those who, like St. Augustine, wanted on the one hand to do justice to the intellectual framework contained in the books of the Platonists and on the other hand to give honour to the revelation of the living God contained in the Holy Scriptures. As Knowles makes clear, Plotinus did not reject Plato but rather sought to go beyond Plato, to extend the thought of his master into the realm of ultimate spiritual unity, beyond all intellectual forms, beyond all conceivable images. Thus man's constant striving is to be towards the union of the whole personality with the One rather than towards the apprehension of the eternal forms by the mind alone. The ascent of the soul is the very heart of his interest. To quote Knowles once again:

'Just as there is a radiation, a procession, from higher to lower, so there is a yearning and a striving and an invitation to the lower to mount upwards. Life is a discipline and a purification, and we owe to Plotinus and his followers, as an addition to the cardinal virtues and the physical, moral and intellectual discipline of Plato, the three classical stages of incipient, proficient and perfect— purgative, illuminative and unitive—with the various virtues practised in three moods of increasing perfection.'[5]

Here then is a religious philosophy and psychology, immensely subtle in its detailed outworking but capable of providing the Christian thinker with an interpretation of reality not inconsistent with the Christian revelation. He is not content, indeed, to conceive the One in any impersonal way for to him the One is the living God, the I am, the Father of all. He is not content to conceive the Logos as pure mind, as the abstract form of the sensible universe, for to him the Logos has been revealed as the living Word, the agent of creation, the Son of God. But the overall hierarchical framework he gladly accepts and knows that the *summum bonum* of life is to attain union with the God Who transcends all conceivable orders of being. He is aware, in exalted moments, of a centripetal attraction drawing him up towards God. He responds to St. Augustine's great word that God has made us for Himself and that our hearts are restless until they rest in Him. He commits himself to the way whose general characteristics are a withdrawal from satisfactions derived from things of sense and an increasing aspiration towards the delights of spiritual reality.

Yet although through such writers as St. Augustine and the Pseudo-Dionysius the mystic quest was accorded a place of high honour in the Christian way of life, it has to be admitted that there is little direct reference to the Cross and Resurrection or to the

5. Op. cit., p. 27.

sufferings of the Christ in the expositions of the way by which the soul may enter into ultimate union with God. In the scheme of the Pseudo-Dionysius, for example, attention is first given to the knowledge of the Divine Names to be gained through the mediation of the Scriptures and to special revelations granted through the activity of members of the celestial hierarchy. Then comes a closer definition of the normal threefold sequence by which the soul can move towards its ultimate goal. This sequence is, in effect, the realization of purification, illumination and union through participation in the sacraments. Baptism corresponds to purification, the Eucharist to illumination, Chrism to union. For the ordinary or average church member this is as far as he may hope to reach. But for the true mystic who perseveres to the end, another possibility is still open. He may pursue the *via negativa*, abandoning sense-perception and mental activity, 'and as far as is possible mount up without knowledge into union with the One who is above all being and knowledge; for by freeing thyself completely and unconditionally from thyself and from all things, thou shalt come to the superessential brightness of the divine darkness.'[6] This is the true goal. Insofar as baptism and the eucharist inevitably carry a reference to the death of Christ it could not be said that the Cross has no place in the Dionysian scheme. At the same time it is a relatively minor place. There is no reference to the Cross in the final stage. Nor is the image of the suffering Christ held before the soul's attention. The aim of the mystic is to rise above ugliness and conflict and suffering and to be united with the One 'in a supermental way'.

In the mystical writings of St. Augustine also the way of the Cross figures but little. It is true that when he speaks of union in terms of the soul's *love* of God, he fully recognizes that this love has been inspired and drawn out by prevenient Divine Love and that this Love was supremely manifested when, as St. Paul records in Romans 5: 8, Christ died for us, when we were still His enemies. 'This therefore took place, as the end of the precept and the fulfilment of the law is charity, that we should love Him in return, and just as He laid down His life for us, so we also should lay down our lives for the brethren, and if it were difficult for us to love God Himself, at least it should not be difficult for us to love Him in return, when He first loved us and spared not His Only Son but gave Him up for us all. For there is no greater invitation to love, than to be first in loving.'[7] There are other evidences that St. Augustine recognized an essential link between the love

6. *Mystical Theology*, I, pp. 1–2.
7. *De cat rudibus*, 4: 7. Quoted Franks: op. cit., p. 102.

of the One, which is the goal of the soul's quest, and the love of God for man manifested in all its wonder when He sent His Son not only to live with man but to be slain by him. Yet he does not greatly expand the thought nor does he make it central in his doctrine in the way which in certain later writers came to be the case. In fact we may risk the generalization and say that in the first millennium of Christian history, whereas the basic pattern of the mystic way— purification, illumination, union—found a place in literature and in practice, this pattern was not linked in any intimate and inevitable way with the passion and death and resurrection of the Divine Son. The mystic—pagan and Christian—was finally concerned to proceed beyond outward images and mental constructs to the ineffable and the inexpressible. The soul would find its integration in union with the superessential One rather than in contemplation of the Cross as the ultimate manifestation of the Divine Love.

As we move on to the twelfth and following centuries, however, we find ourselves in a very different atmosphere. Mysticism of what might be called the classic type still exists and comes to definitive expression in the works of the Dominican friar, Meister Eckhart. In these we see the basic mystic pattern of the life of God being poured out continuously into the world of space and time and drawing it back purified into His eternal being. But there is a wider and more popular form of Christian mysticism whose goal is the conformity of the soul to the pattern of the career of the Logos in self-humbling and loving self-sacrifice. Here the great names are Bernard of Clairvaux and Peter Abelard and Francis of Assisi though so far as influential writings are concerned none have surpassed those of Thomas à Kempis. Bernard held fast to the mystic pattern of the outflowing Divine life being poured into humanity and thereby redeeming it from its subjection to death and the devil. Such an outpouring involved travail and sacrifice and revealed the extent of the Divine Love. Yielding to the attraction of this Love men are themselves redeemed from the limitations and defects of their humanity and raised to the full enjoyment of Love in union with God Himself. The whole process is viewed in terms of self-humbling, self-outpouring, self-sacrifice. Divine Love is revealed as the Son of God Himself submits to this pattern. Men are moved to become identified with the same pattern and in so doing to become united with God in love and obedience.

Abelard's chief difference from Bernard lies in his stress upon the individual's personal response to the exhibition of Divine Love. In a certain sense God, in Bernard's scheme, takes hold of human nature and thereby brings all individuals, whether they are conscious of it or not, within the scope of the Divine redemption. It is for the individual to humble himself and accept what has been made possible for him through the grace and generosity of the Divine. In other words it is a dominantly passive role that the individual plays: his call is to become identified with the pattern of the Divine outpouring and thereby to enter into a deepening union with God Himself. In Abelard's writing, however, we become aware of something more active and more passionate. Man's eyes are opened to see the greatness of a love which came near to him even when he was its enemy. He responds in devotion to the love of the Cross and seeks to make it the pattern of his whole life.

The place of Abelard in atonement theology has been repeatedly discussed and he is normally distinguished as the arch-exponent of what is called the subjective theory. But such a categorization tends to be confusing and unhelpful. In reality Abelard marks the transition from an outlook which saw God dealing with humanity *as a whole*, either through a legal transaction or through a mystical transfusion, to one in which the ethical and psychological qualities of *the individual within the community* began to receive fuller recognition. With profound psychological insight Abelard saw that nothing is more powerful to move the will from its apathetic acquiescence in some sinful habit than the sight of the One Who actually suffered on account of our sins and bore their penalty in His death. Love begets love and if only the Cross can be seen as the supreme manifestation of vicarious Divine love then man will be moved in his inmost being and will respond in love to his Redeemer. And his response will not simply be an affair of the emotions. It will issue in a new form of ethical living of the same basic pattern as that of the Redeemer Himself.

The stages of the spiritual life set forth in Abelard's writings are not exactly those of the mystic quest but there are significant correspondences. The three stages for Abelard might be defined as: Illumination, Excitation and Unification. In one of his most important statements Abelard affirms: 'I think . . . that the purpose and cause of the incarnation was that He might illuminate the world by His wisdom and excite it to love of Himself'. And in another passage of his exposition of the Epistle to the Romans we find him saying: 'His Son took our nature, and in it took upon Himself to instruct us alike by word and example even unto death (and so) bound us to Himself by love; so that kindled by so great a benefit of divine grace, charity should not be afraid to endure anything for his sake'. The inference throughout is that the love for God enkindled in the soul of man will lead to the transformation of his character into the pattern of love towards all men such as was exhibited supremely in the words and example and passion of the Divine Son.

All is summed up in the oft-quoted passage which occurs in the same context of the commentary on Romans.

'Every man is made more just, that is more loving towards God, after the Passion of Christ than he had been before, because men are incited to love by a benefit actually received more than by one hoped for. And so our redemption is that great love for us shown in the Passion of Christ which not only frees us from the bondage of sin, but acquires for us the true liberty of the sons of God, so that we should fulfil all things not so much through fear as through our love for him who showed towards us a favour than which, as he himself says, none greater can be found: "Greater love hath no man than this, that a man lay down his life for his friends".'[8]

As Sikes points out Abelard's overmastering concern was the clarification of the motivation of the good life. If love was the highest good, if the redemption of the world would consist essentially in bringing men to love their fellows without reserve, then how could such a desirable end be achieved? The Law of the Old Testament had indeed commanded men to love God and their neighbours but this love had lacked warmth and breadth of outreach. It was the coming of Jesus which had revealed the true nature of love and therefore the *summum bonum* of human existence. Previously men had been motivated by fear. Now in the light of Christ's Passion, love could be the motive, love could be the goal. There was no suggestion in Abelard's exposition that the sight of Christ's obedience even unto death would simply evoke sympathy and pity and a general sentiment of gratitude. Rather in his view the exhibition of such a concern for man's welfare as is evinced in the incarnate life and willing sacrifice of the Son of God must surely awaken gratitude and kindle a response in life comparable to that which has been so incomparably shown forth. As Moberly aptly and I think rightly comments: 'The emphasis of his thought is not really so much upon Calvary as a picture exhibited before our eyes, as it is upon Calvary as a constraining and transforming influence upon our characters. It is not so much really upon the love of God manifested to us as upon the love of God generated within us.'[9] At the same time a spirit of love to God and our fellow-men could not have been generated in us except by the demonstration of a love so great that no greater could be conceived by man. Thus the illumination which

8. Translation in J. G. Sikes: *Peter Abelard*, p. 208.
9. R. C. Moberly: *Atonement and Personalty*, p. 381.

is given by the revelation of Christ loving, suffering and dying excites a response which is deeper and stronger than all ordinary movements of the human psyche and leads to a union with Christ Himself in His charity and passion; a charity and passion which are truly Divine.

The obvious criticism which has been constantly levelled against Abelard's doctrine is that he gives no clear indication of why the incarnate life and the heroic suffering of the Christ were such overwhelming demonstrations of love. Unless man was involved in some terrible predicament and unless the whole activity of the Christ was related to that predicament, to help and to save, there could hardly be the hope of man's interest being stirred or his gratitude evoked. Yet any reference to the wider corpus of Abelard's writings shows that he maintained as strongly as any of his contempories that man was burdened and beset by sin, bound under judgment and unable to walk in the freedom of sonship. Similarly he was convinced that Christ had borne the burden and paid the penalty of human sinfulness.[10] But although he gives a kind of general consent to these traditional doctrines he cannot rest content with any view which does not lead to the transformation of the sinner's character into the pattern of faith and love which was revealed by the Saviour of mankind. The establishment of justice for which he looks is not the exacting of a *quid pro quo* nor the restoring of a tarnished honour. Rather is it the willing service of love by man to his neighbour, the reflection in humanity of the very nature of God Himself. This he believes was actually achieved in the ministry and passion of Christ and what He did so marvellously in the very midst of the human situation can be reproduced in the lives of all who are kindled by 'so great a benefit of divine grace'.

The ideal which took shape in Abelard's theology exercised little influence upon his contemporaries or even upon the immediately succeeding centuries. The individuals who attracted attention and gained significance in social life were either the knights of heroic crusading activity or the exponents of extravagant ascetical self-humiliation. On the one side were the men of fiery speech and missionary adventure such as Ignatius de Loyola and Francis Xavier: on the other side were men of dramatic renunciation and

10. Cp. his comment on Romans 4: 25. 'In two ways He is said to have died for our faults: (1) because the faults for which He died were ours and we committed the sins of which He bore the penalty and (2) that by dying He might remove our sins, i.e. might take away the penalty of our sins introducing us into paradise at the price of His own death and might by the display of such grace draw our minds away from the will to sin and incline them to the fullest love of Himself.'

humility of spirit such as Francis of Assisi and Blessed Peter of Luxembourg. All found their inspiration in Christ and his Cross. But whereas for the one group the Cross represented the hardness of the struggle against the forces of infidelity and malignity, for the other it represented the suffering which followed upon the acceptance of the evils of the material world. It may be dangerous to characterize any era as a whole but those who lived in the Middle Ages seem to have been peculiarly aware of the transience of things temporal and of the suffering which belongs to the ordinary human lot. The exceptional individuals therefore were those who mastered the conditions of earthly existence by showing a certain contempt for the worst that these conditions might impose upon them. And no way of achieving this end was surer than to be identified with Christ in His self-humbling, His obedience, His passion and His death.

The book which expresses this attitude more clearly and more influentially than any other is *The Imitation of Christ*. Its author, Thomas à Kempis, was a relatively obscure monk who lived in Holland from 1380–1471. He set forth as the ideal of the spiritual life not so much the ascent into the heights of absolute union with the One in a moment of ecstasy but rather the pursuit of ultimate bliss by being united with the Christ in His progress along the 'Royal Road of the Holy Cross'. For those who found themselves unable to dwell for long in the contemplation of high and heavenly things, Thomas commended the way of the Cross as equally efficacious to bring man to the joys which surpass all human understanding.

The way of salvation which Thomas expounds movingly and imaginatively is essentially that of acceptance. No one can escape ills and griefs and tribulations and trials in the course of ordinary earthly experience. The great question is how they are to be borne. Complainingly? Resentfully? Rebelliously? Always with a hankering after pleasures and comforts? If this is the general attitude, then it is clear that the guiding principle is the love of self rather than the love of Christ, the affection for things on earth rather than the things of heaven. And the end will be condemnation by the Lord when He comes in judgment. But all those who 'in their lives conformed themselves to the Crucified' not only gained strength of mind and joy of spirit during their earthly pilgrimage: they will stand with confidence in the day of judgment. Again and again Thomas returns to the same theme. The way of the Cross, the way of daily self-denial, the way of humiliation, the way of willing acceptance is the way of salvation. 'When you have arrived at that state when trouble seems sweet and acceptable to you for Christ's sake, then all is well with you for you have found paradise upon earth.' 'There is no salvation of soul, no hope of eternal life, save in the Cross. Take up the Cross, therefore, and follow Jesus and go forward into eternal life.'

Such glorification of suffering is obviously dangerous. It can become an end in itself and lead to a kind of masochistic self-immolation. It can breed an excessive passivity which makes no attempt to cure the ills of earthly existence or to improve social conditions. It can lead to an inordinate concentration upon the individual's duty to save his soul by enduring hardship and tribulation. It can view the Cross as the supreme example of human renunciation rather than as the unique act of Divine redemption. Sin can be identified with the seeking of creature comforts and holiness with the passive endurance of every kind of earthly ill. Yet the vision and the words of Thomas à Kempis brought new courage and inspiration to countless men and women. For most life was hard and there was little release from tribulation. To realize afresh that Christ Himself endured contradiction and bodily deprivation and anguish of heart brought the confidence that God was in the midst of those trials and that Christ Himself had revealed the method by which they could be mastered and made the instruments of the individual's salvation. This was not justification by faith but neither was it justification by works. It was an acceptance of life in the light of the perfect example of the Christ. It was an acceptance of the way of the Cross as the only true avenue of salvation into friendship with Christ and union with God Himself.

The period between the twelfth and fifteenth centuries was, it seems, a time of widespread religious subjectivism. The objective elements remained—the great church building, the constantly repeated action of the Mass, the recognized hierarchy of sacred ministers—but the more important and more widely diffused elements were the subjective—the imaginative identification with Christ in His Passion and the sympathetic response in sensibility and action to His sacrifice. Wherever men went abroad they saw direct representations of the Passion in picture, in sculpture, sometimes in drama, sometimes in mime. But they also saw indirect representations either through some scene suggesting an analogy or through some symbol which had come to be associated with redemption. In many cases, perhaps in most, the impression was relatively shallow and it could be claimed that an easy familiarity with holy things bred indifference and even contempt. What is certainly true is that these subjective impressions were far more powerful than any apprehensions of necessity and meaning derived from the disputations of the theologians. By being exposed to the example of the Christ the common people gained at least some vision of God's redeeming grace and reconciled themselves to the hardness of their own lot in conformity with the spirit which had been revealed on the road to Calvary. There was ever the danger of shallow sentiment, of supine acceptance of ill, of unworthy notions of the Divine judgment and salvation. At least the sign of the Cross was engraved upon the imagination and some sense of God's compassion supported men in the struggle of life.[11]

D

The Reformation and the Renaissance, each in its own way, brought about a marked swing away from subjectivism and passive sensibility to a new objectivism and a new concern for the life of action. The great new objectivities were God's word written, the glories of art and literature inherited from the past, the constitutive elements of the natural order of which men were becoming increasingly aware. The challenge to action was heard alike in God's call to obey His word and in the lure of the possibilities of new discovery in the world around. At least in northern Europe it was a time to struggle, to resist, to explore, to reform. And throughout the history of Protestantism the tendency has been to stress the saving activity of God declared through His Word and the responsive activity of man shown forth in faith and obedience. Feelings have been suspect. Meditation and contemplation and the discipline of the inner life of the soul have taken second place to outward witness and active service. The Cross is supremely the means by which God acts towards man and summons man to act in response rather than the revelation of God's inner being to the pattern of which man's own being is to be conformed. The contrast is not absolute but the fact remains that in large areas of Christendom since the time of the Reformation the elements of mystery and inner passion, of purgation and illumination, of contemplation and mystic union which played so prominent a part in earlier ages have been discounted and even at times rejected.

Yet in the writings of the Spanish Catholic St. John of the Cross or of the Anglican mystic, Thomas Traherne, the Cross still occupies the central place and it is through conformity to its pattern that union with ultimate reality is sought. The devotee in his meditation returns constantly to the Christ of Calvary—His humility in accept-

11. Cp. J. Huizinga: *The Waning of the Middle Ages*, p. 192.

ing the way of the Cross, His patience in the presence of His persecutors, His actual bodily sufferings, His steadfast endurance of pain. He does not attempt to construct a theory of atonement or to give any kind of rational explanation of the work of Christ. Rather by a kind of instinct he recognizes his own sinfulness as shown in his self-seeking and self-protecting. The life of God can only be realized in him insofar as this sinfulness is renounced and purged away. But this can only be effected through discipline and suffering which, though far beyond the capacity of any man if left to himself, become possible because God of His infinite grace entered the human situation and revealed the true pattern of humiliation and renunciation. Through conformity to this pattern, apart from any questions about the why and the wherefore, man shares increasingly in the true life of God and is restored to union with his Creator.

In the Catholic tradition the contemplation of Christ's example as He steadfastly pursued the way of the Cross and endured the utmost of human mockery and shame was often intensified by the use of pictures and images bringing some aspect of the Passion before the very eyes of the worshippers. For varying reasons such a use of visual forms was generally rejected by the Reformers but this did not prevent the emergence of another medium by which a profound impression could be made upon the individual's imagination, namely, the hymn. The Pietists, especially the Moravians, in Continental circles, the Evangelicals, especially the Methodists, in England found the Passion-hymn or the hymn celebrating the restoration of a lost humanity through the blood of Christ (a favourite mental image) to be a powerful means of directing their devotion towards the God Who had accepted suffering and shame in the person of His Son and Who had thereby revealed to men the only pathway towards the sanctification of their own lives.

Innumerable examples of such hymns could be quoted. Sometimes they become sentimental and appeal directly to unhealthy emotions. Sometimes they are crude in their language and banal in their form of expression. But at their best they succeeded in capturing the attention and directing it towards the Christ Who had loved men and given Himself for them. And as the attention came to be fastened upon Him in His suffering love, the emotions were stirred, the mind was illuminated and the will was fortified to turn from the service of self and the world to the service of God through Christ.

No hymn in the English language has expressed this Protestant form of mysticism more powerfully and more continuously than Isaac Watts's 'When I survey the wondrous Cross'. With an economy of words and images this Protestant Dissenter, who represented the growing concern for the individual and the minority-group within the life of the nation, gave to his own and succeeding generations a simple yet memorable compendium of the theology of the Cross. The stark bringing together of 'The young Prince of Glory' and 'Died', of 'Wondrous' and 'Cross', of 'Boasting' and 'Death of God', of 'Sorrow' and 'Love', of 'Thorns' and 'Rich a Crown' rivets the attention by the sheer succession of paradoxes. The Divine Sorrow is for man's sin—his pride, his love of vanity and empty delights, his pleasure in the things of this world. The Divine Love reveals itself in a complete outpouring of life (the shedding of blood) the self-humbling to a felon's death, than which no fuller exhibition of love could be imagined. Within the hymn no questions are asked about punishment or cosmic redemption. It is enough to raise the individual's eyes to the unique revelation of the attitude and action of God in the Cross. If this does not capture the heart and move the will to renounce pride and self-seeking, nothing will. This does not mean that in the mind of Isaac Watts and his fellow Protestants the Atonement was unrelated to wider aspects of life. But nothing was more important now than the appeal to the individual with a view to his salvation. Within Protestantism he was not being asked to withdraw from the world in order to pursue a lonely mystic quest for the Alone. Rather he was being summoned to surrender his whole self to God's service in ordinary daily life and to bear witness to the love and sorrow of the Cross in his relations with his fellow-men.

E

Yet ultimately some attempt would have to be made to integrate this intensely personal and individual experience into a body of doctrine which, while faithful to the general tradition of Christian thought, was also related to the contemporary world. The pioneering genius in this respect was undoubtedly Schleiermacher. His achievement was immense. In the midst of a remarkable flowering of culture in Germany he succeeded in giving a reinterpretation of the Christian faith which was vitally related to the interests and vocabulary of that culture. By so doing he ran the risk, it is true, of cutting himself off from all earlier interpretations of the faith and of formulating a system in which the Christ appeared more as a persuasive influence than as a historic Saviour. But whatever may have been his defects, to him more than to anyone else is due the fact that Christian theology at the beginning of the nineteenth century did not simply remain embedded in traditionalism or isolated from the new movements of thought and feeling which were stirring so powerfully in Western culture. He liked to think of his interpretation as essentially mystical but it was a form of mysticism which in no way withdrew itself from the market place of contemporary ideas.

When Schleiermacher uses the term 'mystical' we could without falsifying his meaning employ the word 'psychological'. He was a theologian whose focus of interest was man's inner consciousness rather than the splendours of the starry heavens or the majesty of the revealed Word. He was a man of the finest sensitivity whose initial experiences of the Other came through contemplating and feeling rather than through thinking and acting. He believed that the true spirit of religion was lost in words. The immediate vision, the uninhibited response in feeling—these were the supreme experiences through which the Divine and the human came to be joined together in an undifferentiated unity.[12]

In his actual verbal analysis Schleiermacher spoke of three stages of human consciousness. The lowest he described as animal consciousness though he admitted that we have no exact knowledge of the animal state. But he assumed that in this state there is some form of consciousness without any kind of stable integration—'a consciousness of such a sort that in it the objective and the introversive, or feeling and perception, are not really distinct from each other but remain in a state of unresolved confusion'. This confusion he suggested was characteristic of animals but also existed in children and primitive peoples. The next higher stage, which he sometimes called the middle state, is characteristic of developed adult life. It can truly be called self-consciousness for it includes the awareness of self-identity but its basic structure is best described as a dialectic between two constant factors. On the one hand there is an awareness of free and spontaneous activity directed towards an Other—Other being interpreted in the widest possible sense of personal or impersonal entities. On the other hand there is an awareness of constraint or dependence—a receptivity affected from some outside quarter. Thus normal human self-consciousness may be described as oscillating between feelings of dependence and feelings of freedom, between receptivity and activity. No human being exists except along with an Other and consciousness may be said to consist in the vast web of relationships with this Other in its infinitely varied manifestations.

But now, in Schleiermacher's view, there is a third or highest stage. He is not content to extend the dialectic to the area of life in which

12. See K. Barth: *Theology and Church*, p. 172 f.

relationships with the highest or ultimate Other is conceivable. Rather he assumes that in man's highest stage of consciousness the element of movement towards or action upon the other is excluded. The highest consciousness within the range of human experience is that of *absolute dependence*. In other words to assume the possibility of absolute freedom is to infer that man has the capacity to take an absolute initiative. But such a possibility Schleiermacher finds unthinkable. There is a *given-ness* in human affairs, a priority from the 'outside' or the 'beyond'. All temporal existence is characterized by absolute dependence in the last resort. Insofar as any man becomes immediately self-conscious of his absolute dependence in his own journey through time, in that measure he may be said to be religious, to be in relation with *God*. In Schleiermacher's own words 'the *Whence* of our receptive and active existence, as implied in this self-consciousness, is to be designated by the word "God".' In the more modern interpretation of H. R. Mackintosh: 'By "God" cannot be meant any special reality within the cosmos, or even the cosmos as a whole; God is the dominant Power behind all phenomena, imparting to them reality, unity and meaning.'[13]

As can readily be seen this analysis of human self-consciousness leads Schleiermacher to conclusions very similar to those of earlier mystics who had spoken of God as the Ground of Being or the Divine Abyss. But in his case he does not simply bear witness, by straining language to its limits, that there is a region of human experience in which we have some awareness of ultimate Being. Rather he engages in a process of lengthy and acute analysis of the experiences of dependence and freedom in order to lead his readers ultimately to the recognition of not only the possibility but also the logical necessity of the concept of absolute dependence. We are all, in fact, he declares, aware of the reciprocity of freedom and dependence. But such an awareness could not exist unless it were rooted in a feeling of absolute dependence and that feeling is that which we describe as religious, the feeling of being in relation with 'God' who undergirds and sustains and re-creates the totality of existence.

It has been necessary to refer in some detail to Schleiermacher's initial analysis for out of it the whole of his system develops and grows. If the analysis is in any way correct then it follows naturally and inexorably that the *summum bonum* of human existence is to be found in an increasing awareness of absolute dependence or, as it can be alternatively described, in an ever-expanding consciousness of God. But how is this possible? How can the evil condition be

13. *Types of Modern Theology*, p. 63.

overcome which consists in 'an obstruction or arrest of the vitality of the higher self-consciousness, so that there comes to be little or no union of it with the various determinations of the sensible self-consciousness, and thus little or no religious life'.[14] This condition can best be described as *God-forgetfulness*. It is not the case that God-consciousness or the feeling of absolute dependence is at zero. Rather it is under severe constraint, imprisoned, relegated to the background. The utterly distinctive marks of the Christian faith are first unique concentration upon the removal of all hindrances to the feeling of absolute dependence and secondly its insistence that this removal has been universally and completely accomplished by Jesus of Nazareth. To bring these two into focus Schleiermacher adopts the vocabulary of *Redemption*. The Redeemer has appeared in history, He has set free in human nature the feeling of absolute dependence, He has communicated this God-consciousness to the community which He founded, 'The Redeemer is like all men in virtue of the identity of human nature, but distinguished from them all by the constant potency of His God-consciousness which was a veritable existence of God in Him'. 'The Redeemer assumes believers into the power of His God-consciousness and this is His redemptive activity.' (Titles to 94 and 100 in *The Christian Faith*.)

This concept of redemption Schleiermacher proceeds to work out with astonishing ingenuity and comprehensiveness. The whole system of Christian doctrine is reinterpreted in terms of this governing principle. No longer is the primary focus of attention right belief or right action but rather the perfect God-consciousness of Jesus which was transmitted into His community as a mighty pervasive influence. The negativity, the forgetfulness, the lack of consciousness had to be reversed and this was done in and through the earthly work of Christ. In addition the positive conscious relation to God had to be sustained and extended and this is being done in and through the continuing work of Christ in His community. To describe the latter, the terminology of reconciliation is employed but there can be no doubt that redemption and reconciliation are almost correlative terms. The initial act is followed by a process but both act and process are all of one piece within the eternal providence of God.

What function then can be attributed to the Cross in the redeeming and reconciling activity of Christ? Perhaps the most important thing

14. *The Christian Faith*, 11: 2. It is interesting to note how Schleiermacher swings to and fro between the symbolism of height and of depth. In a paradoxical fashion it is the highest self-consciousness which is aware of ultimate depth.

to note is that Schleiermacher is utterly opposed to all attempts to *isolate* the Cross from the rest of the incarnate life and ministry of Christ or to isolate Him from the humanity of which He became a part and into which He injected so powerful an influence. In regard to the first he refers to the common supposition that Christ's passive obedience began only with His arrest while the active had expressed itself from the beginning of His public life up to that point (and in the common view it was the passive obedience that was specially associated with suffering). In point of fact, Schleiermacher declares, 'every instance of opposition which He experienced during His active life, every snare of His adversaries, and equally the indifference with which many passed Him by, became for Him suffering, because in it He had a sympathetic feeling of the world's sin and thus carried that sin; so that this suffering accompanied Him throughout His whole life' (104: 2). He was at all times and in all places receptive towards everything which came to Him from the corporate life of the sin of mankind: equally He was always ready to bear the suffering involved in His active task of bringing into being a new corporate life in which His own powerful God-consciousness would gain unhindered sway. Thus His life, His passion, His death were all of a piece. In all, intense suffering was involved but it was only through such suffering that God's purpose could be fulfilled.

In regard to the second, Schleiermacher reacts strongly against such traditional terms as Christ honouring the divine *law* or Christ fulfilling the Divine *will* by standing in our place. That Christ in any of His actions or experiences was separate from mankind cannot be allowed. In humanity He bore the painful effects of evil in every shape and form: at the same time He created a new humanity so animated by His influence that it led to an ever more perfect fulfilment of the divine will. 'In order to assume us into the fellowship of His life, it was necessary that Christ should first have entered into our fellowship. He without sin, so that no evil could arise from the presence of sin in Him, must enter into the fellowship of the sinful life where, along with and as a fruit of sin, evil is constantly arising. Hence it must be said of Him, that His suffering in this fellowship, if occasioned by sin—and from merely natural evils He never suffered—was suffered for those with whom He stood in fellowship, that is for the whole human race, to which He belongs, not only because no particular fellowship within the human race can be completely isolated, but also by His own deliberate choice' (104: 4). There is in other words no law separating Christ from God: there is no sin separating Christ from humanity. His perfect God-consciousness undergirds His fulfilment of the divine will: His perfect sympathy with men enables Him to bear their evil.

In his comprehensive interpretation of the work of Christ Schleiermacher offers a brilliant and original reinterpretation of the threefold offices of prophet, priest and king. It is in the second of these official capacities that Christ most obviously deals with human sin though again His work must be regarded as a whole and no one office is separate from the others. Having considered various phrases which might be employed to sum up Christ's priestly work he expresses a preference for *satisfying representation*: 'In the sense, first, that in virtue of His ideal dignity He so represents, in His redemptive activity, the perfecting of human nature, that in virtue of our having become one with Him God sees and regards the totality of believers only in Him; and second, that His sympathy with sin, which was strong enough to stimulate a redemptive activity sufficient for the assumption of all men into His vital fellowship, and the absolute power of which is most perfectly exhibited in His free surrender of Himself to death, perpetually serves to make complete and perfect our imperfect consciousness of sin' (104: 4).[15]

It is exceedingly difficult to summarize Schleiermacher's exposition for it is subtly argued and is concerned all the time to reinterpret traditonal conceptions—satisfaction, punishment, guilt, vicariousness —in the light of his own controlling principle. This principle, which he himself allows could be called 'mystical', implies that the all-important factor in human life is 'consciousness', that the individual shares this 'consciousness' with the rest of humanity and that the supreme blessing both for the individual and the community is to be redeemed from all forms of sensuous self-consciousness into an uninterrupted God-consciousness. The consciousness is primary and determines both thought and action. But man of himself is unable to enjoy the experience of perfect God-consciousness. His situation can only be remedied by the entrance into human life of a 'pervasive influence' which will not force the situation and yet will by its very potency and attractiveness set man free to participate in a new and

15. The phrase 'sympathy with sin' appears strange. It must be interpreted in the light of the previous discussion which focusses attention upon the way in which Christ entered into 'the fellowship of the sinful life' even to the point of confronting and being involved with Judaism and heathendom in the last days of His life, an alliance of sinners sufficient to represent the sin of the whole world. He did not isolate Himself from any section of the human race. He stood in fellowship with the chiefest of sinners and by so doing absorbed their guilt and liability to punishment into His own sinless consciousness. By this means they could become aware of their own misery as sinners and begin to share in the fellowship of His sufferings by which sin is removed.

creative fellowship. Such an entrance was effected by Jesus of
Nazareth who in spite of all opposition and suffering maintained
His unbroken God-consciousness from beginning to end. His
triumphant influence is now at work in humanity, calling out a new
community of blessedness. The way is open for individuals to be
incorporated into this new community and to share in the God-
consciousness of the Redeemer Himself. As Barth vividly remarks,
'A man is touched, seized and carried along by this corporate
life (I would prefer "drawn inwards" to "seized") which flows like
a river through continents and centuries or which circulates like
blood through the veins of humanity. It is this which makes him a
Christian, which puts him in relation to the redemption consummated by Jesus of Nazareth.'[16]

Schleiermacher's reinterpretation of the Christian Faith may seem
over subtle and ingenious. It is certainly one sided in its stress on
the more passive side of the human psyche—its receptivity, its
subjective feeling, its dependence. Yet it constituted the first major
attempt to expound Christian doctrine psychologically rather than
philosophically or dogmatically. It showed itself intensely aware of
the relation between the individual and the corporate, between
active freedom and passive dependence, between the higher and
lower consciousness in mankind, between suffering and evil. That
Jesus the Redeemer and Reconciler had brought completely new
potencies into the human situation Schleiermacher had no doubt.
That He had done this at the cost of constant resistance, physical
suffering and an overwhelming sense of the awfulness of sin,
Schleiermacher also did not question. That He had acted throughout
in complete harmony with the will of God and not in any way
over against or in contradistinction to the Divine requirements
Schleiermacher constantly insisted. Where he laid himself open to
criticism was in his under-emphasis upon commitment-in-faith,
upon freedom-in-action and consequently upon that which bears
witness to decisions and actions, viz. the record of history. The
century which followed the work of Schleiermacher was to bring
an outstanding redress of the first of these defects through the
contribution of Kierkegaard, a more than adequate redress of the
second through the emergence of a host of writers and investigators
concerned to give an orderly account of the history of Jesus and
His Church. But his acute analysis of psychological factors was of
the utmost value and still has much to contribute to our own
thinking in spite of the great advances in psychological theory
which have taken place in the past fifty years.

16. *Theology and Church*, p. 184.

F

Since the time of Schleiermacher, successive efforts have been made to define more clearly the nature of the human consciousness. Not that before his time there had been any lack of attempts to penetrate to the inmost nature of the 'I' or 'self' or 'soul'. Descartes with his famous *Cogito, ergo sum*; Locke with his doctrine of separate individuals each possessing a conscious, mental substance; Hume with his definition of the soul of man as 'a composition of various faculties, passions, sentiments, ideas, united, indeed, into one self or person, but still distinct from each other'—each was seeking to direct attention to man as he is in himself, apart from God, apart from his fellows. A totally new kind of individualism was emerging in which it was believed possible to isolate man as an object of observation and study, simply as he exists in himself. Just as man was seized with the excitement of exploring the starry heavens and the physical world external to himself, so he began to investigate the workings of the inner consciousness and to establish new categories by which behaviour could be explained and in a measure determined.

In the middle of the nineteenth century two philosophers, Sir William Hamilton and John Stuart Mill, engaged in a long dispute concerning the existence and nature of *unconscious* mental processes and it was this distinction between conscious and unconscious (or subconscious) which was now destined to play an increasingly important part in psychological investigations. Gradually men became familiar with the idea of unconscious processes and the genius of Freud established it as a hypothesis open to testing by empirical observations. Since his notable pioneering work became generally known there has been no end to the extensions, modifications and even radical revisions of psychological theories. But all are concerned with the human consciousness, how it is to be represented, how analysed, how diagnosed for possible abnormalities, how integrated. There has been an intense interest in the question of the relation of the consciousness to the body, of the individual consciousness to that of the collective, of the different levels of the consciousness (if such there be) to one another. Theories abound and there is no such thing as psychological orthodoxy. We can therefore only appeal to certain broad areas of agreement as we seek to relate the Christian doctrine of atonement to the psychological needs of the individual soul.

Let us first consider the general question of conflicts and disorders in the human consciousness. A conflict may be in the immediate present and may virtually fill the consciousness of the one who experiences it. He is summoned to act in a particular way: he is threatened by sudden danger: he is thwarted in the carrying out of some design: he is rebuked for some delinquency. In a host of ways an individual may at any time be thrown into a state of turmoil by the very pressure of his environment, personal or impersonal, and for the time being the conflict fills his consciousness. He must find some form of reconciliation if his mind is to retain any measure of stability and health. I shall be more concerned with this kind of conflict in Chapter IX.

But the tension in the mind may be less dramatic and less easy to account for. There may be a feeling of malaise, a sense that something is not right and yet there may be nothing in the immediate situation to cause obvious anxiety. In such a case the normal procedure is for the individual to search backwards into his memory to see if he can remember any event or encounter or chain of circumstances which may have caused him conflict or distress. If something has called for action but has been neglected in the pressure of other concerns: if there has been some slip from the accustomed path of rectitude which has been passed by in the bustle of immediate activity; if, in short, there has been anything to cause unease which has not been resolved at the time of its occurrence, a man, having searched in his memory and become aware of it again, will seek to take what steps he can not only to deal with the precise source of the trouble but also with the consequences which may have followed from it. All these possibilities are included within the traditional concepts of self-examination, penitence and repentance, penance and reparation, punishment and restitution. It is assumed that the individual is capable of looking backwards in memory and of thereby discovering a possible source of his present unease. An apology, a delayed action now performed, an outward acknowledgement of failure, may be sufficient to resolve the conflict.

On the other hand some more extensive procedure may be necessary. If the neglect or the fault seems to have resulted in consequences far greater than can be mollified or undone by ordinary human means, then appeal must be made to some transcendent agent who can absorb the evil which has been engendered. In earlier chapters I have examined some of the ways in which such an appeal to transcendent reconciling activity has been made. Traditional concepts such as forgiveness, absolution, restoration, salvation enable the sinner who has become newly aware of past faults and neglects, to gain the sense of cleansing and confidence through the assurance that these sins have been borne, within the mysterious inter-dependence of humanity, by One who both transcends and is involved in the corporate life of mankind.

The major contribution of modern psychological thought has been in connection with that aspect of the personality sometimes referred to as the unconscious, sometimes as the subconscious, sometimes as the hidden conscious. In a sense these descriptions are paradoxical for strictly speaking the conscious mind can have no contact with the unconscious. What the terminology, however, is seeking to express is the assumption, ever more strongly confirmed by the evidence of dreams, hypnosis, behaviour symptoms and amnesia, that there is in every individual an area of the psyche impenetrable by ordinary conscious processes such as recalling, remembering or re-enacting. A conflict in the unconscious can have grave effects upon the health of the individual concerned. Yet he is utterly unable to locate the source of the trouble himself or to deal with it if simply told of its location by another.

In this context one of the most famous terms of modern psychological theory is the word 'repression'. This has been well defined by David Stafford-Clark when he writes: 'Repression means a particular, compulsive kind of forgetting, which results in forgotten material being neither available to direct recall nor even represented in consciousness or preconsciousness by the vaguest awareness that it ever existed.'[17] We are all aware of the ordinary limitations of memory. Often considerable effort or ingenuity is required to recall information from the past. But in speaking of repression we are referring to something quite different. We are concerned with memories which are not open to recall by any ordinary methods. They are related to experiences of life which were charged with intense emotion and which the conscious self was unable and unwilling to deal with constructively. They were therefore banished into the depths and thereby became sources of potential disturbance. On the one hand they had been simply 'bottled-up', without the emotion attached to them having had any chance to be released: on the other hand they themselves had a constricting influence, preventing the 'drives' which belong to any normal human psyche from coming to expression.

There have been many variations in the theory of repressed complexes but that some process of repression is of universal occurrence has been widely accepted. The originating cause is some kind of conflict. There is the conflict in the mind of the child between satisfying its own pleasure and pleasing the parent by

17. *Psychiatry Today*, p. 144.

conduct which seems to run contrary to its own pleasure. There is the conflict between admiration for the strong and dynamic 'other' —often the father—and jealousy or even hatred towards him because of the threat to self-expression which he embodies. There is the conflict between conformity to the existing pattern of the social unit on which the individual depends and the desire for independence in at least some directions. Certain drives seem to be universal in the individual—hunger, sex, struggle for power, desire to gain approval—but again and again some contrary force operates to thwart the full realization of the 'drive'. According to the strength of the drive so is likely to be the intensity of the feeling engendered by the resistance encountered and consequently the latent explosive potential of the complex buried beneath the consciousness by the act of repression.

How far the insurgent elements in the unconscious are derived from the past experience of the *society* to which the individual belongs is still matter for debate. The existence of similar mythologies in different parts of the world, the emergence of the same symbols in the dreams of different individuals and indeed the whole phenomenon of inherited characteristics seem to necessitate the formulation of a theory of some common patterns within the unconscious being capable of influencing the behaviour of the individual. Here may well be the source of other conflicts within the personal unconscious though it has also been held that through dreams in particular a certain relief or release from the pressure of warring elements can be obtained. Whatever theories of a collective kind may be put forward, the main conclusion, accepted by all investigators of man's psychic life, is that within its hidden depths a struggle is always in progress, a struggle between drives which complement one another and yet exclude one another, a struggle between a self seeking to dominate and possess the other for its own fulfilment and a self seeking to serve and win the approval of the other also for its own fulfilment. If there is one assured result of the modern analysis of the human psyche it is that it seethes with ambivalences and opposing forces and that although from one point of view these are the dynamic source of health and progress, from another point of view they can produce excesses of 'guilt' and disharmony which may issue in some final disruption.

If now it be agreed that sufficient evidence has been forthcoming in modern psychological analysis to support the hypothesis that beneath and beyond the conscious activities of the mind there are hidden forces at work which constitute a threat to its free and full development, what may be said of the means proposed for the relief of the situation? At the source of most therapeutic methods lies the conviction that at all costs the insurgent elements need to be exposed to the full light of consciousness and thereby brought under control. Presumably the grounds for this conviction are that repressed material appears to be striving in this direction during sleep or during day-dreaming or during the process of some forms of artistic expression: that in the parallel case of the human body relief comes when a hidden source of infection is brought out into the open: and that patients who have been helped to gain a conscious apprehension of formerly unconscious tensions have often been set on the way to an apparently healthy and harmonious life. Such reasons are not conclusive and it could be argued that in some cases at least a better policy would be to 'let sleeping dogs lie'. But insofar as our culture is committed to the conviction that the rational is to be preferred to the irrational, the conscious to the unconscious, the controlled to the chaotic, to this extent we must assume that a release from at least the more violent of unconscious conflicts is much to be desired.

How then is such a release to be achieved? Various techniques have been employed by analysts—free association of concepts, interpretation of dreams, encouragement to project feelings on to another—but common to all is that which is ultimately most important, viz. the relationship with the analyst himself. It is assumed from start to finish that the self can only find healing and integration by means of relationship with another and at least in the more complicated cases that other will be the analyst.[18] He on his part must be ready to enter into the life-situation of the one who seeks healing as deeply as is possible without losing control of his own feelings and actions. Such a process is obviously most delicately balanced. As Jung has pointed out, the doctor cannot possibly escape being influenced by the patient if there is to be a real meeting of personalities. 'For two personalities to meet is like mixing two chemical substances; if there is any combination at all, both are transformed. In any effective psychological treatment the doctor is bound to influence the patient; but this influence can only take place if the patient has a reciprocal influence on the doctor. You can exert no influence if you are not susceptible to influence.'

18. There is strong evidence that in ordinary daily life we all tend to identify ourselves in some measure with other figures whom we encounter either in person or in imagination. It is therefore always possible that some unconscious source of feeling will be touched in such an encounter and that by the process of identification the feeling will be released as the self becomes involved in an imaginary situation comparable to that in which the feeling was originally engendered.

Yet it is only through such a meeting, sustained in all likelihood over a considerable period, that the therapeutic process can go forward.

The character of this process has been described in another way within the context of Freudian theory by J. S. Bruner in the composite volume *Freud and the Twentieth Century*. 'The sense of the human tragedy', he writes, 'the inevitable working out of the human plight—these are the hallmarks of Freud's case histories. When Freud, the tragic dramatist, becomes a therapist it is not to intervene as a directive authority. The therapist enters the drama of the patient's life, makes possible a play within a play, the transference, and when the patient has "worked through" and understood the drama, he has achieved the wisdom necessary for freedom.'[19]

The mixing of two chemical substances, the enactment of a play within a play—these are two analogies designed to help as to picture more easily the process technically described as the *transference*, a process which almost all modern psycho-analysts would regard as crucial if successful treatment is to take place. As we have seen the therapist seeks to bring out into the open certain material which has been suppressed and in so doing is bound to stir up feelings of an intense and even violent kind. There will be resistance and resentment and the search for an object upon which the emotions can be projected. What more appropriate object could there be than the analyst? He is seeking to get to the root of the trouble and offering himself as a mediator in the situation. So it naturally happens that 'during the course of treatment the patient comes to feel the love and hatred, the dependence and the rebellion, rivalry or rejection towards the analyst, that he has felt but never fully acknowledged for other people in his life; people whose impact has been earlier and inescapably close, people such as his parents, his first love, or the friends and enemies, heroes and villians, of his childhood. This uncritical and barely understood investment of emotion in the person conducting the treatment is called the transference. Normally it begins by being positive, in the sense that the natural gratitude and respect which the patient feels for someone who is prepared to take a considerable amount of trouble in helping him, is uppermost. No transference ever remains wholly positive throughout the course of treatment, and if it did, nothing of fundamental importance could be achieved, for no unbearably hostile emotions would be uncovered.

'Sometimes a transference may become almost entirely negative, and then the course of treatment, perhaps the patient, and some-

19. p. 277.

times the analyst, will be in danger; but the control of the transference, the regulation of its depth and intensity, are to a great
extent in the hands of the analyst, since he has the underlying
interpretation for use as the occasion demands. To interpret or
interfere with the transference too early is to deprive it of the
strength necessary to enable the patient to carry on with his already
difficult contribution to the treatment. . . . The handling of the
transference situation is thus of vital importance in the course of
psycho-analysis as indeed in the course of all forms of psycho-
therapy. It is the existence of the transference which both enables
the patient to discover the nature of the underlying feelings and then
to acknowledge them. Once this has been done he often finds
himself able to regard them in a far more tolerant and dispassionate
light, and so be liberated not simply from their effect upon his past
but from their influence upon his future.'[20]

The process of transference then is central in modern psycho-
analytical practice even though there may be variations of emphasis
on detailed techniques. Moreover there is now general agreement
that the therapist cannot occupy the position of a detached observer
offering authoritarian advice. He must be involved and yet not
completely involved: he must listen and yet not remain completely
silent: he must accept the exposures of the patient and yet not in
such a way as to leave his own inner being completely untouched:
he must help a man to be himself and yet in a certain sense to be
other than himself: he must be utterly patient and yet ever alert
to take the intiative as occasion arises: he must preserve his own
identity and yet be willing to receive into his own psyche that which
is utterly foreign to his own pattern of life. Such a process is not
hard to describe. To work it out in practice is as demanding as
any task that can be imagined. And to anyone familiar with the
Christian tradition, can any pattern drawn from human experience
seem to approximate more closely to the Divine way of salvation
through Christ? Indeed on the human level one is bound to ask
'Who is sufficient for these things?' It is at least possible for the
Christian to affirm that whereas the human therapist, however
skilful, is inevitably limited—by his own temporality, his own
fallibility, his own physical resources—there is One Who transcends
human limitations and Who in His God-manhood has effected and
does still effect the transference through which the individual can
gain liberation and health.

The suggestive analogies provided by modern psycho-therapeutic
methods have been used by various writers to give a vivid range

20. Stafford-Clark: op. cit., p. 175 f.

of comparison by which the Divine work of reconciliation can be more readily apprehended. For example Dr. R. S. Lee, in his book *Freud and Christianity*, accepts the general Freudian theory of the formation of the Super-Ego through identification with the father and the consequent predicament which arises when the father is defied within the complex of sexual relationships. The threat of death hangs over the ego within the deepest recesses of the human consciousness and liberation from this fear can only be gained through the assurance that in some way the original sin against the father has been expiated. The key to a meaningful doctrine of atonement is to be found, Dr. Lee suggests, in the psychological process (or mechanism) of identification. Jesus, the ideal son, identified himself with his brethren: it is now possible for all who suffer from the sense of being involved in guilt to identify themselves with the ideal man.

'Identification with Him (i.e. Christ) is encouraged first by the way He identified Himself with man and secondly by the fact that He suffered the very penalties that we, in our unconscious, fear as the just punishment of our unconscious crimes, whose derivatives we openly confess. He is our representative, the perfect man accepting that punishment on our behalf, though as an individual He did not merit it. Through that acceptance He finished His life in unbroken obedience. He is perfectly at one with the Father. By identifying ourselves with Him we first of all reap the benefit of His sinlessness because we inherit from Him the Father's forgiveness of our sins and secondly we put on His character. He lives in us and we in Him and our character becomes modelled on His. We gain the strength we need to cease from sin—that is from disobedience and lust. The vicious circle is broken, the burden of guilt drops away from our shoulders. We escape therefore from the condemnation of the Super-Ego inwardly shown in the sense of guilt and outwardly in the fear of God and we know an unspeakable sense of joy, the joy that always comes when the Ego approximates to the Ego-ideal.'[21] Lee goes on to emphasize the necessity of the process of identification being continued after the initial release. A full at-one-ment calls for the assimilation of the total image of Christ within the ongoing experience of life.

Such an interpretation of atonement retains many traditional concepts though it makes use of the vocabulary of modern psychological theory. In his book *Christianity after Freud*, Mr. B. G. Sanders is more daring and relates the Atonement more closely to Freud's own ideas. He focuses attention on the act of killing

21. R. S. Lee: *Freud and Christianity*, p. 169 f.

(the sacred animal in totemism, the victim in developed sacrificial systems, the Lamb of God on Calvary) and claims that in all such acts man is satisfying two drives which surge up from the unconscious. On the one side there is the drive to kill not only the earthly father but also the Divine father who is the barrier to the satisfaction of every one of his own urgent desires (sexual, aggressive, power-seeking): on the other side there is the drive to kill himself because of the feeling of intense guilt which arises through having, it seems, committed an unpardonable sin against a loved one. Only by his own death can the sin be expiated. In the death of the God-man, Sanders suggests, both of these drives gain a full satisfaction. The love-hate feeling, seemingly an inevitable element of a son's relationship with his father and magnified to a transcendent intensity in relation to the Father of all, only finds release and a measure of resolution through being transferred to the Divine Son Who is both the surrogate of the Father and the representative of all sons of men.

Jung's system is more complex and does not easily provide comparisons for use in Christian formulations.[22] He lays enormous stress upon the unconscious and the part which it plays in the life of all men. To accept the unconscious, to understand it, to come to terms with it, is for Jung the essential first step on the pathway to integration. In certain respects this is parallel to what St. Paul describes as justification by faith. Secondly, Jung may be said to have developed his whole system in terms of contraries or opposites. The condition from which man needs at all costs to be released is that of 'a dull and helpless unconsciousness'. In the clash of contraries real life is to be found. Jung is not anxious to attain a complete resolution or reconciliation of the opposites: in fact such a resolution is, he believes, impossible. Rather he wants man to embrace the heights and depths, the lengths and breadths of contrary experiences and in so doing to advance to the fullness of his own potentiality, to what Jung himself calls 'individuation'.

There is a remarkable passage in *Answer to Job*, a book which in some ways seems quite antagonistic to Christian faith. Yet when Jung considers the ways in which Christianity has engendered 'insoluble conflicts' by its ethical demands he grows warm in its praise and acknowledges its power to bring man near to a true knowledge of God. But in what does this knowledge of God consist?

'All opposites are of God, therefore man must bend to his burden; and in so doing he finds that God in his "oppositeness" has taken possession of him, incarnated himself in him. He becomes a vessel,

22. Yet see the various works of Victor White and David Cox.

filled with divine conflict. We rightly associate the idea of suffering with a state in which the opposites violently collide with one another, and we hesitate to describe such a painful experience as being "redeemed". Yet it cannot be denied that the great symbol of the Christian faith, the Cross, upon which hangs the suffering figure of the Redeemer has been emphatically held up before the eyes of Christians for nearly two thousand years. This picture is completed by the two thieves, one of whom goes to hell while the other enters into paradise. One could hardly imagine a better representation of the "oppositeness" of the central Christian symbol. Why this inevitable result of Christian psychology should signify redemption is difficult to see except that the conscious recognition of the opposites, painful though it may be at the moment, does bring with it a feeling of deliverance. It is on the one hand a deliverance from the distressing state of dull and helpless unconsciousness, and on the other hand a growing awareness of God's oppositeness, in which man can participate if he does not shrink from being wounded by the dividing sword which is Christ. Only in the most extreme and most menacing conflict does the Christian experience deliverance into divinity always provided he does not break but accepts the burden of being marked out by God. In this way alone can the *Imago Dei* realize itself in him and God become human.'[23]

Jung was at all times fascinated by the symbols which seem to arise spontaneously in the unconscious and whose distinctive quality is the bringing together of opposites. This 'coniunctio' he regarded as pre-eminently the mark of the Divine. So wherever man in his conscious experience accepts the witness of the unconscious and embraces opposites creatively, there he is identifying himself with the Divine life, is being 'delivered into divinity'. In Jesus and His Cross we see a supreme example of such identification and it is by contemplating and being conformed to the pattern of Calvary that the individual gains release from helpless torpitude and advances towards his true identity. Jung was certainly not a traditionally orthodox Christian but his efforts throughout his life to uncover the nature and structures of the human unconscious led him to the conviction that 'the opposites' constitute its most distinctive feature and that the symbolic representation of 'the opposites' which is best able to bring before the consciousness the *coincidentia oppositorum* is the supreme instrument by which the human may be delivered into the life of the divine. And it seems that he had little doubt that the Cross is in fact the supremely efficient symbol in this context.

23. C. Jung: *Answer to Job*, p. 89 f.

G

It has been the supreme task of modern depth-psychology and psycho-analysis to discover new ways and means of observing, describing and testing experimentally the structures and operations of the human psyche. The results should not be regarded as a body of knowledge utterly unrelated to earlier insights. Much that has emerged as the result of painstaking analysis was expressed in other forms in earlier ages by mystics, poets and preachers. But in a dominantly scientific age it is necessary to re-express and reinterpret truth through images and symbols which convey meaning and carry conviction because of their association with scientific methods of enquiry.

Possibly no modern theologian has given such serious attention to the writings of depth-psychologists as has Paul Tillich. Yet he insists that many of their findings about the constitution of the human psyche were known already to the Biblical authors and the Fathers of the Church. Referring in particular to St. Augustine's doctrine of man he says:

'Monastic and mystical self-scrutiny brought to light an immense amount of the material of depth psychology, which entered theology in its chapters on man's creativeness, sin and sanctification. It also appeared in the mediaeval understanding of the demonic, and it was used by the confessors, especially in the monasteries. Much of the material which is discussed today by depth psychology and contemporary existentialism was not unknown to the religious "analyst" of the Middle Ages. It was still known to the Reformers, notably to Luther, whose dialectical descriptions of the ambiguities of goodness, of demonic despair and of the necessity for Divine forgiveness have deep roots in the mediaeval search for the human soul in its relation to God.'[24] Dante among the poets, Breughel among the painters, penetrated intuitively to the depths of the human situation. It has been the achievement of the greatest amongst modern psychologists to express their insights in terms of complexes and repressions and neuroses and drives within the context of a certain orderliness of description and openness to experimentation such as the scientific method demands. It has been pointed out by Bakan that psycho-analysis drew many of its key traditions from Jewish mystical religion. For a long time the leading psycho-analysts both in Europe and the United States were nearly all Jews and their aims, in and through their methods of scientific therapy, were similar to those which their forefathers had sought

24. *The Courage to Be*, p. 129.

through mystical as distinct from strictly legalistic techniques.[25] Similarly Jung was deeply indebted to the insights and methods of mystical religion wherever found as well as to the alchemistic and cabbalistic circles of the Middle Ages. The fact is that the analysis of the human predicament in modern psychology in terms of anxiety and alienation differs little from the earlier conclusions of religious seers: the fundamental contrast is to be found in the *scientific* character of the theories presented and of the therapeutic techniques advocated.

Tillich, in an eloquent passage, claims that there is one common denominator in all modern psycho-therapeutic theories. I think it is arguable that the same factor is to be found in all great and deep analyses of the human personality contained in biography or fiction. What is this common denominator? It is *anxiety*.

'Anxiety is the awareness of unresolved conflicts between structural elements of the personality, as for instance conflicts between unconscious drives and repressive norms, between different drives trying to dominate the centre of the personality, between imaginary worlds and the experience of the real world, between trends towards greatness and perfection and the experience of one's smallness and imperfection, between the desire to be accepted by other people or society or the universe and the experience of being rejected, between the will to be and the seemingly intolerable burden of being which evokes the open or hidden desire not to be. All these conflicts, whether unconscious or subconscious or conscious, whether unadmitted or admitted, make themselves felt in sudden or lasting stages of anxiety.'[26]

From St. Paul writing 'The good that I would, I do not: but the evil which I would not, that I do. . . . O wretched man that I am! Who shall deliver me?' to Stephen Spender writing 'I could not reconcile my ideals either with myself or with the world. I was tormented by the feeling that nothing was as it should be, single and clear and pure' the story is the same. Man is estranged within himself, divided, in conflict, and therefore anxious, even in despair. Who shall deliver? What process can deliver? What symbolic form can deliver? These are the great questions of modern literature, of modern plays, of modern medicine, of modern psycho-therapy. It is the claim of the Christian that the ultimate reconciliation effected by Christ through His Cross can be related through analogies, models and parables to these ways of reintegration which are advocated in every genuine healing technique. Jesus constantly drew his own images and language concerning the soul's healing

25. See a remarkable article in the Princeton Seminary Bulletin, January 1959, entitled *Religious Overtones in Psychoanalysis*, by D. C. McClelland.
26. Op. cit., p. 60 f.

from the vocabulary of bodily processes. No poetic image more adequately represents the character of Jesus' life and ministry than that embodied in the words 'He took our infirmities and bore our diseases'. No phrase more beautifully and comprehensively describes the reconciliation finally wrought by Jesus' death and resurrection, than 'By His stripes we are healed'.

Not that this reconciliation can ever be fully *explained*. It is characteristic of Jung with his deep sense of the mysteries of life to say that no matter how much he and his patients contribute to an analysis, they can at best only prepare the way, remove the obstacles to healing. Healing itself, he says, always comes in some wholly unexpected way from the unknown, *wie ein Wunder*—like a miracle.[27] Freud never claimed that technique alone would achieve success. The mystery of the 'transference' remains. And it has been the genius of novelists and dramatists to show how some identification in agony and hell can mysteriously lead to a miraculous togetherness in healing and heaven.

W. R. Matthews has suggested that the mysterious experience of telepathy offers a suggestive pointer to the nature of the redeeming work of Christ. The religious value of such phrases as 'He bore the sin of many', 'The Lord hath laid on him the iniquity of us all' is undoubted. But how can these phrases take on real depth of meaning in our own situation? 'Does not some faint gleam of light dawn upon us', he writes, 'when we reflect upon the hidden rapport between selves of which telepathy is one evidence? We could imagine a case where all the barriers of the self are down and all the thought, emotions and desires of all the world flow in—the muddy stream of all human mental life. It does not overwhelm the conscious self, which remains aloof and master of the inconceivable mass of presented material, but all the thoughts are present and are part of the total experience. The conscious self knows them all, not from the outside but from within, yet insofar as they are evil and foolish repudiates them and overcomes them. Would not such an experience be bearing the sins of many and the victory over them?'[28]

Whatever we may think of such a suggestion, there can be no doubt that modern investigations of mental processes have undermined all theories of the individual as isolated or of the self beginning life with a kind of *tabula rasa* mentality. The evidence accumulated from experiments in E.S.P., in telepathy, in psychical research, together with the vast amount of material now available through psychological investigations of projection, identification, empathy,

27. Victor White: *God and the Unconscious*, p. 253.
28. *The Problem of Christ in the Twentieth Century*, p. 54 f.

and the transference, enforces the conclusion that even in the depths of consciousness we are members one of another and that any injection of new impulses into the consciousness of the individual can produce untold effects upon a whole society. As more observations and experiments are made, the range of comparison by which the self-identification of the Christ with humanity can be apprehended will expand still further. The dimensions of the meaning of the supreme act of love will continue to exceed our grasp. For try as we will we cannot fully comprehend the wealth of meaning condensed within that act of love which is, in the Christian view, the final reality of the universe.

James Denney wrote before the impact of modern psychological theories had been felt. He had not studied the human psyche in the light of the vast store of information amassed by recent physiological research. Yet he had a profound understanding of human nature, built up doubtless by a life-long study of the Scriptures, of history and of imaginative literature, together with a wide experience of pastoral relationships. He knew how hard it is to describe an action or movement of one personal consciousness towards another which becomes fully involved yet maintains its own integrity, which proceeds to the limit in sympathy yet retains its own standard of values, which feels the utter shame of another's failure yet never rejects the one who is guilty. In the end the vocabulary of love was alone satisfactory.

'In the last resort', he writes, 'nothing reconciles but love and what the soul needs, which has been alienated from God by sin and is suffering under the divine reaction against it, is the manifestation of a love which can assure it that neither the sin itself nor the soul's condemnation of it, nor even the divine reaction against it, culminating in death, is the last reality in the universe; the last reality is rather love itself, making our sin its own in all its reality, submitting as one with us to all the divine reactions against it, and loving us to the end through it and in spite of it. Reconciliation is achieved when such a love is manifested and when in spite of guilt, distrust and fear, it wins the confidence of the sinful.'[29] Whatever else it was, the Cross was, for Denney, the ultimate assurance that not sin, manifested in the consciousness of guilt, shame, fear, anxiety, alienation, estrangement but sin-bearing love bringing the consciousness of forgiveness, acceptance, integration, reconciliation is the ultimate and the all-victorious reality in the universe.[30]

29. *The Christian Doctrine of Reconciliation*, p. 218. Cp. p. 20.
30. An exceedingly valuable re-interpretation of the Atonement in the light of modern psychology is *The Hope of Glory* by Martin Jarrett-Kerr.
D. S. Browning's *Atonement and Psychotherapy* appeared after the above chapter was written.

CHAPTER IX

THE WORD OF FINAL RECONCILIATION

Fourth Parable

Any study of history or of contemporary life provides examples of individuals who stand out as in certain significant respects different from their fellows. The dominant characteristic in all these manifestations of difference is a certain form of courage— courage to confront the unique challenges which life brings, courage to launch out into the unknown as occasion offers. Through struggle character is strengthened. Through adventure the dimensions of experience are enlarged.

In the course of this struggle and adventure, however, a crisis may arise in which the total existence of the individual may seem to be in jeopardy. Every way of advance may appear to be blocked: every possible retreat may seem to be cut off. No memories derived from the past can give an ultimate assurance for nothing comparable has ever happened before. No anticipations of future fulfilment can give hope for there is no future in view. What then can the individual do? He may simply collapse and allow himself to be finally crushed. He may leap out in a gesture of despair into sheer emptiness. Or, just possibly, he may grapple with that which threatens his existence in the faith that this very concentration of danger embodies the secret of the renewal of life. He may elect to fall into the hands of the fearsome Other rather than into the darkness of a meaningless Void.

It is the Christian claim that the representative Man found himself facing the most terrifying crisis that it is possible to imagine. Symbolically it took form as a Cup—a cup of deadly poison, a cup of bitter judgment. Shall he refuse it? Shall he seek to avoid it? Instead he grasps it, drinks it, absorbs it. Even in the ultimate crisis he maintains his integrity: he takes the total threat into his own bosom: he passes through the jaws of death into the radiance of the fulfilment of life. Existence is transfigured in and through the crisis of faith.

A

Until comparatively recently, tribes in many parts of the world lived under conditions virtually identical with those in which Palaeolithic man eked out his existence. His life, as we know, was surrounded by dangers and uncertainties. His food and water supply was only in the rarest instances assured. He was engaged in a ceaseless quest for roots and plants and meat and was never safe from the attacks of marauding beasts. At any moment a crisis might arise in which his own life and that of his dependants could be threatened with extinction. In such moments he was thrown back upon two resources—his own physical strength, extended through at first crude and later skilfully fashioned *tools*: and his own emissions of sound, extended gradually into skilfully fashioned *forms of communication*. The former of these resources was the more obvious and it can be argued that if man had not become a tool-making animal he could scarcely have survived. At the same time it can also be urged that if man had not developed powers of speech and thereby of intercommunication he could not possibly have advanced to the building up of the social and cultural life which is his chief glory.

I shall not dwell upon man's activities as a tool-maker though I am fully aware of their importance in his development. I am concerned rather to discover the significance of his self-expression in words or at least in sounds in moments of crisis and danger. In what can only be a brief summary of the evidence I am largely indebted to Sir Maurice Bowra's book *Primitive Song* in which extracts of poetry and song from many primitive cultures are recorded and certain general characteristics established.

In simplest terms it may be said that when man is at the end of his tether so far as ordinary resources are concerned: when he can no longer flee away from a danger that threatens: when his own arms and hands are not strong enough to resist the adversary: when not even weapons or tools at his disposal have any chance of providing an adequate defence: then he may *cry out*, either to invoke the aid of some mighty unseen power or to hurl defiance in sound at the apparently all-powerful foe. Even the common experience of a nightmare shows how the sleeping self, hemmed in by hostile forces which gradually draw near to effect its destruction, breaks out into inchoate noise, half crying for help, half shouting resistance to that which would swallow it up. To call in, to ward off, these are the twin compulsions it seems, motivating man's reliance in times of emergency upon sound and (later) speech.

What probably began as the sheer outburst of an immediate reaction came in time to take shape in more orderly forms. Words, phrases, even rhythms could be used to hold fast a particular reaction and communicate it to others. Further, individuals appeared who either through having experienced a crisis of special poignancy

or through possessing a gift of special rhythmical utterance
succeeded in communicating their emotions to other members of
the community and in providing patterns of speech which could
be used to promote confidence in similar circumstances. No exact
account of a process involving innumerable variations can be given
but its general character is revealed through the many song-forms,
often remarkably appealing, which have been translated out of the
language of modern primitives. The 'intense vision of a brief
moment', the 'concentration on a single theme', the 'tendency to
stress it by isolating it', the 'recalling of it in passion and excitement',
the presentation of it as pertinently and as vividly as the singer is
able—all these elements are stressed by Bowra[1] and reveal how
closely the songs or poems correspond to the quality of life which
inevitably was the lot of the Palaeolithic hunter. Into his songs he
projected his whole being and, seeing that life for him was constantly
threatened by death, the songs provide unlimited variations on the
theme: Man's behaviour when facing his final enemy.

In his chapter on 'The Human Cycle', Bowra gives a striking
example of this reaction in a dialogue-song derived from the Gabon
Pygmies. In this the eldest son of a dead man begins and the
maternal uncle replies:

> A. The animal runs, it passes, it dies.
>   And it is the great cold.
> B. It is the great cold of the night,
>   it is the dark.
> A. The bird flies, it passes, it dies.
>   And it is the great cold.
> B. It is the great cold of the night,
>   it is the dark.
> A. The fish flees, it passes, it dies.
>   And it is the great cold.
> B. It is the great cold of the night,
>   it is the dark.
> A. Man eats and sleeps. He dies.
>   And it is the great cold.
> B. It is the great cold of the night,
>   it is the dark.
> A. There is light in the sky, the eyes
>   are extinguished, the star shines.
> B. The cold is below, the light is on high.
> A. The man has passed, the shade has vanished,
>   the prisoner is free![2]

Here is a remarkable example of men facing the stark realities
of death, the dark, the cold,—and yet in their song daring to leap

1. *Primitive Song*, pp. 102 f.
2. Op. cit., p. 202 f.

upwards in hope and confidence that the light will break and the prisoner be freed. Admittedly ancient history and contemporary records contain innumerable examples of despair in face of sickness and death. Yet there are also evidences, especially among tribes compelled to live nomadic and dangerous lives, of a readiness to confront death with words of defiant hope and of faith in some ultimate victory.

As he draws to the conclusion of his survey of primitive song Bowra quotes a further example in which the poet allows his imagination to dwell upon the dark, the night, hunger and nakedness, homelessness and death:

> the Maker is no more there,
> Is no more the host seated at the hearth.

'Such is the dark background', he writes, 'against which primitive life is passed. Yet even in their menaced and divided existence they still find redeeming compensations when they can be themselves as they would wish to be, and then too they turn to song, which reflects and increases their desire to live and to maintain their own place in the world.

'Primitive song is indispensable to those who practise it. Because it is so urgently needed, because it gives order and harmony to their sudden, overmastering emotions and their tumbling, jostling thought, because it is so inextricably part of their lives, it gives to them a solid centre in what otherwise would be almost chaos, and a continuity in their being which would too easily dissolve before the calls of the implacable present. Through it they rise to face the struggle for life and keep their minds and their energies awake at full stretch. Above all it is an art and does what art always does for those who practise it with passion and devotion. It enables them to absorb experience with their whole natures and thereby to fulfil a want which is fully satisfied neither by action nor by thought. In the end, like all true art it enhances the desire and strengthens the capacity to live.'[3]

I have quoted this passage at length because it seems to me to provide a striking summary of one aspect of human experience which finds expression both in the earliest patterns of primitive existence and in the most sophisticated forms of modern life. Man confronted by a crisis whether of minor or of ultimate dimensions gains hope, confidence, the will to overcome through a form of words which somehow represents reconciliation and

3. Op. cit., p. 285 f.

integration in the face of threatening disintegration and chaos. The danger is immediate and overwhelming. There is no time for sustained thought and contrived planning. There is no opportunity of drawing upon the resources of the community or the environment. The only possibilities are the action and the word. Yet even the way to meaningful action may be blocked. The word becomes the final and yet the altogether powerful instrument of reconciliation. Man embraces death within a word of life, gathers threatening chaos into a word of controlled order, overcomes the worst through a word which bears witness to the best. Such is the stuff of great poetry, of enduring song.

B

Whereas there is little to suggest that mystical aspirations or practices flourished in ancient Israel, the case is altogether different in regard to the records of individuals confronted by situations threatening danger, disintegration and even death. Probably in no body of literature known to us are there so many examples of individuals, hemmed in by circumstances, finding a way of hope and confidence through the utterance of the reconciling word. From Abraham the great forefather, on through Moses the great deliverer, continuing with Elijah and Jeremiah and the succession of the prophets, concluding with Job and the Psalmists and the heroes of the Maccabean period—here is an unparalleled succession of men who through faith, expressed in noble words accompanying courageous deeds, gained a place in human history which is never likely to be forgotten. The title once given to a composite work dealing with the legacies of three of these men of faith was: *The Cross in the Old Testament*. Perhaps a still more apt title would have been 'The Word of the Cross in the Old Testament'. It is through the words of poetry and song in which they expressed their hope of triumphing over all adverse circumstances that their names live. In the furnace of affliction their words of life-in-death were fashioned and through these words they both experienced an ultimate reconciliation themselves and set up a guide-post by which those who came after might also direct their steps towards a place of peace.

Take for example the records of Moses. The narrator is concerned to present a picture of a man constantly threatened by adverse forces, by the overwhelming might of a great empire, by the treachery of his own people, by the weakness of his own nature: yet a man who, upheld by the Word, re-created through the

Word, echoing the Word in his relations with stubborn and com-
placent followers, became the central agent in the creation of a
symbol which has nerved and encouraged and upheld a multitude
of others to trust and not be afraid. The story of Moses' encounter
in the remote loneliness of the desert is a superb word-picture. The
man disillusioned and disheartened with no hope for the future:
the bush burning with fire yet not consumed: the voice inspiring
terror and self-despair: the beginnings of new life through integration
into the consuming passion of the Other. Here is a word wrung
from man's confrontation with ultimate reality and it is a word
of salvation-through-passion, reconciliation-through-suffering, life-
through-death. There were to be further experiences of crisis in
Moses' career when death—the death of his hopes, the death of his
strivings—again stared him in the face. But out of each crisis the
Word was reborn. He was renewed in his own identity and integrity
through the Word of God and the word born out of his own travail
became a word of reconciliation to others set in the crisis of their
own particular time.

Or again the three individuals whose experiences Wheeler
Robinson examined in the monographs linked together in *The
Cross in the Old Testament*. The dramatic poem which bears the
name of Job tells of a man who was in every way prosperous and
faithful in his cycle of religious observances. Yet suddenly and unexpectedly death visited him. Death removed his cattle, his servants,
his children: the plague, symbol of decay and death, afflicted his own
body. Brought face to face with the ruin of all his hopes and the
shattering of all his peace what would be his reaction? To curse God
and go out into nothingness? To take refuge in a facile theory of the
operation of moral laws? Neither of these will Job entertain. Instead
he struggles with his friends, with his fate, with his universe, with his
god. He struggles but does not prevail—at least not outwardly.
Through the experience of terror, pain, stripping, bewilderment,
man discovers his own identity in relation to the mystery and
majesty of the living God. He refuses to settle for half, for anything
less than the ultimate. He allows himself to be fully tested and fully
known. And when all the props of tradition and convention and
pious theorizing have been removed he is really known by God
and made an instrument of reconciliation for the rest of mankind.

The message of the anonymous poet contained in the Servant
Songs of the Second Isaiah is not dissimilar. Yet of all Old Testament
figures, with the possible exception of Moses, none is more clearly
revealed in the depths of his personal struggles and anguish than
is Jeremiah. Through the devotion of his companion and disciple,

Baruch, oracles spoken by the prophet were committed to writing and to these were added accounts of events in his life-history. Though it is impossible to construct a biography in the modern sense of the term, events and utterances can be linked together to form a relatively connected whole. At the very least the poetic cries and ejaculations can be set within a context which makes them vivid and meaningful.

The dominant impression conveyed by the book is of a man of deeply sensitive nature who shrank from public life yet felt compelled to challenge the policies of rulers and the inclinations of his people in the name of God. In his own inner consciousness there was the intense struggle between the desire for withdrawal into obscurity and the compelling sense of responsibility to become engaged in political life: in his outer experience there was the agonizing tension between his ceaseless concern for his people and their welfare on the one side and his recognition of his duty to proclaim judgment and woe upon them on the other. At times the tension becomes almost unendurable and words break out from his despair which by a strange paradox are transfigured through the very act of speaking into an instrument of life and hope.

> Without healing is my sorrow
>   My heart upon me is faint
> For the breaking of my people am I broken
>   Seized by horror, I mourn.
> O that my head were waters
>   And my eyes a fountain of tears
> That day and night I might weep
>   Over the slain of my people.   (8: 18, 21. 9: 1).

> Broken is my heart within me
>   All my bones are strengthless
> I am like a drunken man,
>   Like one overcome by wine
> Before Yahweh and His holy words.   (23: 9).

Again and again this extraordinary tension is revealed. Jeremiah's senses are strained to the limit on one side as he hears Yahweh's words of judgment, sees the earth made desolate, hears the sounds of battle, looks at the result of the invader's destructiveness: on the other side he makes the people's cry of distress his own, feels their misery, pleads for their deliverance, and so identifies himself with them that in a real sense he takes the judgment into his own inner being and absorbs it. He is *for* Yahweh and yet he is also *for* the objects of the divine judgment. His heart reaches breaking point and he cries a bitter cry of anguish. Yet even in this cry which holds together as it were the opposing poles of holiness and dereliction a promise of reconciliation can be discerned.

And this tension which is so characteristic of Jeremiah's experience is directly paralleled in many of the Psalms. Often indeed it is the Psalmist's own distress of body or mind which causes him to cry out in anguish.

> I cry with my voice to the Lord, with my
>   voice I make supplication to the Lord,
> I pour out my complaint before him,
> I tell my trouble before him.
> In the path where I walk they have hidden
>   a trap for me
> I look to the right and watch but there is
>   none who takes notice of me; no refuge
>   remains to me, no man cares for me.   (Psalm 142).

At other times, however, he becomes the mouthpiece for his people's anguish

> 'Sorely have they afflicted me from my youth'
>   let Israel now say—
> 'Sorely have they afflicted me from my youth
>   yet they have not prevailed against me.
> The ploughers ploughed upon my back; they made
>   long their furrows'.   (Psalm 129).

As we read the Psalms we enter into the distresses of the total society as well as of the individual: persecution and oppression from envious outsiders, betrayal and treachery from trusted insiders. Here are human spirits deeply sensitive to the struggles and the tensions of life in the world and as they react to the extremes of physical suffering and mental despair they become vicarious representatives of a universal humanity. They do not cloke their cries in sentimentality or unreality. They confront life at its most threatening and most intractable. But by a daring and seemingly impossible leap of faith they affirm and reaffirm the rule of Yahweh, His constant loving-kindness to His children and the final triumph of His Kingdom. He will save the soul of His servant, He will redeem Israel, He will turn the night of weeping into a morning bright with joy.

Probably no psalm approaches more nearly to the limits of human anguish and distress than does the 22nd. It matters little whether the poet is referring primarily to his own or to his people's suffering. He describes the scorn and derision of the bystanders, a company of evil-doers who pierce his hands and his feet and divide his garments amongst themselves. He exposes his own sense of utter weakness:

> I am poured out like water and all my bones
>> are out of joint;
> My heart is like wax, it is melted within
>> my breast;
> My strength is dried up like a potsherd
> And my tongue cleaves to my jaws.

Worst of all he tells of the bitterness of the feeling of having been forsaken by God:

> I cry by day but thou dost not answer and by night
>> but find no rest.
> 'He committed his cause to the Lord; let him deliver
>> him
> let him rescue him, for he delights in him!'

Yet it is in the very expression of his despair and dereliction that he finds his salvation. He does not sink down in silence, he does not wrap himself round with his own hopelessness, he does not content himself with shouting defiance at his enemies. Rather he cries out and continues to cry out to the God Who delivered his fathers, the God Who preserved him from his mother's womb. In face of all that would deny faith, he refuses to abandon his hope that God will yet come to his aid

> But thou, O Lord, be not far off!
> O thou my help hasten to my aid!

And in the cry is the resolution. When all human props have been removed, when the heart and the flesh have failed, God makes Himself known as man's strength and portion for ever (Psalm 73). In man's end is his beginning. In entering vicariously into the experience of total blackness the poet becomes the medium through whom the light of glory can be revealed.

C

In the Gospel-records, no sections are more significant for our enquiry about the interpretation of atonement than those which bear witness to sayings of Jesus in which the notes of tension and conflict become acute. Early Christians were constantly confronted by situations of stress and danger: any word which showed how Jesus reacted to such situations was utterly relevant to their own struggle. From the beginning they had confessed Jesus as Messiah and Lord. It is unlikely therefore that words suggestive of inner conflict would have been attributed to him unless there had been unusually strong evidence to support them.

Few sayings are more striking than those recorded in the account of the Temptations. Here we are presented with three vivid word-pictures of the struggle between traditional conceptions of Divine Sonship and the particular vocation which Jesus dedicated himself to fulfil. It was a struggle of peculiar intensity. Could not miracle, mystery and authority (in Dostoievsky's words) be used to save and heal mankind? And Jesus refused all three because the end-result would not have been a real salvation into a developing and expanding communion with God but rather the establishment of a perpetual childhood. Yet each time the conflict was resolved only in and through an agonized cry. 'Man doth not live by bread alone.' 'Thou shalt not put the Lord thy God to the test.' In such cries the conflict is transcended and the contraries momentarily reconciled.

From the initial conflict so graphically portrayed in the Temptation story the narratives move forward with constant references to Jesus' struggles—with his family, with his fellow-citizens in Nazareth, with scribes and Pharisees, with demonic powers; with unbelief, with misrepresentation, with envy, with impatience: and supremely the conflict between his deep concern and desire for the well being of His own people and His recognition that their accepted way of life was bound to lead to disaster. Perhaps the key-passage revealing Jesus' own innermost tension is Luke 12: 49–50.

> I came to cast fire on the earth;
>   would that it were already kindled.
> I have a baptism to be baptized with;
> How I am constrained until it is accomplished.

Such cries and ejaculations give us a glimpse of the tension under which Jesus continually laboured. They are wrung from his lips at moments when the conflict approaches the limits of endurance. Earth's contradictions are resolved in a cry which pierces heaven. The sinful resistance of the world is overcome in and through a perfect confidence in and obedience to the Divine Will. In His cry is our hope and peace.

The Gospel-records reveal a steadily intensifying conflict as Jesus moves forward to Jerusalem. He was convinced that it was God's Will for Him to bear witness in the Holy City: He was equally convinced that no prophet perished outside Jerusalem. So within the Passion-stories we encounter words of peculiar significance, throwing as they do light on the nature of Jesus' final wrestling with treachery, failure and death. There are three groups which I shall examine in succession.

(a) *The Words at the Last Supper:* Few sayings in the world's literature have been subjected to such intense scrutiny as have these words attributed to Jesus. They appear in four New Testament narratives and in no two of these are they in exactly the same form. Yet there is enough material common to each to enable us to point with great confidence to an original core which may indeed have gathered to itself interpretative phrases in the course of its transmission. And this original core is of the utmost significance. It consists of two definitive phrases:

(a) This is my Body.

(b) This is my Blood of the Covenant.

Jesus has seen the growth of opposition without, the likelihood of defections within the ranks of his own closest followers, the virtual certainty that events would move to a crisis during the festival season in Jerusalem. The whole atmosphere is full of memories of another great crisis, the crisis in Egypt when after long struggles and many uncertainties the hour of reckoning drew near. On that occasion every family took a lamb, killed it, and roasted it for eating: and at the same time took the blood, which had been separated from the body, and smeared it on the framework of the door to preserve the household from the destruction and death which were to be abroad in the land that night. The atmosphere in Egypt and at every successive passover was redolent with death—the oppressor's cruelty, the succession of natural disasters which had befallen the land, the brooding sense of something still worse about to happen. Yet for the Hebrews there was also the promise of life through death, of the long-delayed deliverance becoming actual, of a new era about to begin in their national destiny. It was on such a night that Jesus, instead of taking the flesh of a lamb, took a loaf, broke it and said 'This is my Body': instead of taking a bowl of blood, took a cup of wine and said 'This is my Blood of the Covenant'. In face of the accepted certainty of his own death and what appeared to be the end of his own mission, He affirmed through act and word the triumph of God's purpose and the consequent salvation of the new Israel. Not through the flesh of a lamb but through sharing in His own broken body His followers would gain sustenance for their journey into freedom: not through the blood of a lamb but through sharing in His own outpoured blood His followers would be sealed within a new covenant under the assured protection of the God Whose mercies would never fail them.

No words could have been more daring, more expressive of a final trust in God and an ultimate concern for His own friends. Faced with death he leapt over death, out into the new era of the Spirit. The keynote of the Supper is the *new*. The old is at an end. The *new* has come. The new bread to sustain the new life: the new wine to establish the new covenant. In face of the crisis which outwardly spelt disaster and the end of all his hopes, Jesus dared cry out triumphantly: This broken bread is bringing life to all men: This cup is the assurance of the new order in which the prophecy will be completely fulfilled, 'I will be their God and they shall be my people'. In and through this acted parable Jesus becomes the cause of eternal salvation to all who follow in the steps of His faith and obedience.

(*b*) *The Words of Gethsemane:* The narrative describing the intense struggles in the Garden of Gethsemane has an extraordinarily dramatic quality. The triple sequence from the challenge to three to stay awake to the second discovery of their stupefaction through sleep to the final acceptance of their complete insensitivity: the reiteration of the phrase 'the Hour'—the Hour of doom, the Hour of destiny: the Greek words translated into English as 'deep amazement and anxiety', suggestive of horror and shuddering and profound agitation: all these provide a setting for Jesus' words which serves to intensify the sense of inner conflict which they portray.

As far as the authenticity of the reported words is concerned there are slight differences in the three Synoptic accounts and there are verbal echoes of the Lord's Prayer which may have influenced the precise formulation. Yet the general character of the scene and of the words spoken is such that it is exceedingly difficult to imagine any motive for pure fabrication. A romancer would surely have depicted Jesus in an attitude of facing death with confidence and fearlessness and ready acceptance of the will of God. Instead there is the fearful encounter with horror and darkness issuing in the cry: My soul is weighed down with sorrow, even to the point of death. And whatever links there may be with the clauses of the Lord's Prayer, there is one outstanding image which seems to be the key to all, namely 'the cup'. Each evangelist reports the agonized plea that the cup might be removed. Matthew refers to it a second time— 'The cup' represents that from which Jesus shrinks back in horror and amazement. For the significance of this cup-symbol we naturally look to the Old Testament. It is true that in the Old Testament 'the cup' is used in two different senses. On the one hand the cup represents joy, salvation, new life, refreshment.

What shall I render to the Lord
For all his bounty to me?
I will lift up the cup of salvation
    and call on the name of the Lord.   (Psalm 116: 13).

On the other hand, and even more frequently, it represents suffering, punishment, dereliction, woe: it is a 'cup of wrath' and a 'bowl of staggering'.

> 'For not from the east or from the west and not from the wilderness comes lifting up; but it is God who executes judgment, putting down one and lifting up another. For in the hand of the Lord there is a cup, with foaming wine, well mixed, and he will pour a draught from it, and all the wicked of the earth, shall drain it down to the dregs.' (Psalm 75: 6–8)

There has already been a reference to the cup in the incident recorded in Mark 10: 35–45. In that context the cup is certainly the symbol of tribulation and suffering. And now in Gethsemane it is psychologically understandable that an image which had been gathering associations in Jesus' mind should become overwhelmingly real and full of foreboding. The Cup. The Cup to be drained to the dregs. The Cup containing the final judgment upon human sinfulness. Must He drink this Cup? Must He face this Hour? He wrestles and prays, He falls prostrate on the ground, He agonizes in a sweat of blood. Yet the final word that issues as a cry from the depths, as simultaneously the acceptance and the overcoming, is the utter paradox of two wills made one:

Nevertheless not what I will but
    may Thy will be done.

Here again it is in the cry itself that the promise of final reconciliation is contained.

(c) *The central Word from the Cross.* The words spoken by Jesus while hanging on the Cross have brought encouragement and inspiration to His disciples and worshippers at all periods of history. The spirit of forgiveness towards His persecutors, of sympathy towards His fellow-sufferers in body and mind, of child-like trust in God through every kind of adversity—this quality of spirit breathes through the words which the Evangelists report and, whatever criticism may be applied to their exact formulation, that they represent the impression made by Jesus upon His devotees can hardly be doubted. There is, however, one other word, the only word to be reported by more than one evangelist, a word described as a loud cry or a great shout out of the darkness, the word in fact which in the view of Mark the earliest evangelist was the altogether memorable and representative cry of the crucified Messiah. In Mark's version the Aramaic form is given, in Matthew's the Hebraic. Obviously it is taken from Psalm 22 and we find ourselves confronted by this mysterious cry as the concentrated expression of Jesus' ultimate experience of suffering and rejection: My God, my God, why hast Thou forsaken me?

Attempts have been made to deny the authenticity of the saying in its historical context and to regard it as the result of the early Church's meditation upon Psalm 22. The tradition was strong that Jesus had uttered a loud cry. What more likely than that it should have been the opening words of the Psalm which so vividly represents the suffering of a righteous man? Yet such an argument does not carry full conviction for at least it can be said that the loud cry could have been one of triumph, comparable to that which is included in the later part of the Psalm. The very difficulty of imagining that such a cry of desolation should have come from one who was immediately thereafter to be acclaimed by the centurion as son of God (he having been convinced and converted by the manner of Jesus' death) is in itself testimony to the truth of the tradition that Jesus had in fact uttered these words.

But when every effort has been made to examine the background of this cry and its appearance in this particular setting it seems impossible to resolve the mystery which surrounds these words logically or historically. One alternative is to regard them as a substantially correct record of this central moment in the experience of Jesus on the Cross. Darkness has enveloped him. Death is in sight. Spontaneously he cries out, using words which have burned themselves into his inner consciousness. The other alternative is to regard them as the interpretation of the cry of Jesus by the early Church: the Psalm is viewed as the record of a momentary eclipse of the Divine presence and approval being turned into a renewal of trust that God would vindicate His faithful servants.

Strong arguments can be advanced in favour of each of these alternatives. But whichever is adopted, reconciliation is only to be found in the sheer utterance of the word itself. Whether looked at from the point of view of Jesus Himself or from that of the early Church, the climax of death by crucifixion was terrible in the extreme. The darkness, the pain, the sense of desertion by all earthly friends, were symbolic of something deeper—that here the Divine reaction against every form of human sinfulness had come to its ultimate expression. Yet the One Who bears on His own spirit the crushing load of this Divine reaction, Who faces the threat of final annihilation, still cries 'My God, my God'. The question of how much of the rest of the psalm was uttered can never be resolved. But in the words *My God*, cried out in face of all that symbolized the withdrawal of the grace and favour of God, the crucial act of atonement is expressed. God through man reverses all that is contrary to God in man. From the human point of view the loud cry is the last word of dereliction. Within a Divine economy it is the word which opens gates of new life and begets an altogether new hope. In this one word the Atonement of the ages is effected. God has stood with man in the anguish of abandonment and by the utterance of one word has restored the joy of His presence to the afflicted.

D

In Chapter VIII, I drew attention to experiences of St. Paul recorded in his autobiographical writings which could be roughly classified as mystical. I turn now to those which could more properly be described as existential. I recognize that it is impossible to draw any hard and fast distinction of this kind but whereas the evidence indicates that in his life, even after his conversion to the Christian faith, the struggle between the flesh and the Spirit, between the pull of the lower and the attraction of the higher, never ceased and had constantly to be reconciled by a new identification with Christ in His death and resurrection, there were also moments of urgent and unforgettable crisis in which the only way of salvation was to be found through a daring cry of resistance to the forces threatening his very existence and through a concentrated act of faith in the power of the risen Lord.

The records of his conversion which occupy so prominent a place in the Acts of the Apostles do not in fact make any direct reference to the Cross. They portray a man shattered and bewildered by a blinding vision of One whom he acknowledges as Lord: a man turned from the fierce pursuit of those who submitted to the Lordship of Christ to become himself a humble servant of the same master. There is a complete reversal and this reversal was certainly to be later interpreted by Paul in terms of death and resurrection. But the accounts in the Acts are primarily factual, bearing witness to the amazing change and to the way in which it occurred but not relating it directly to that which was its source and its validation.

It is in the Epistle to the Philippians that Paul gives his own passionate interpretation of the revolutionary change which had completely altered the direction of his life. The context is a recurring situation of early Christianity: converts from paganism were being cajoled by Jewish teachers who, though bearing the name Christian, still gave priority to the demands of the Jewish law. Just because this had been so compelling a demand in his own earlier existence, Paul reacts against such an attempted imposition with all the vehemence of which he was capable. No one could have been a stricter devotee of the Law or a more determined practitioner of its stipulations than he. By birth, by upbringing, by conscious commitment, by intensity of zeal he was the Law's man. If ever a man could rest assured of his right standing with God on the basis of his fidelity to the Law it was he.

Yet a man does not act with such an excess of zeal and fanaticism unless he is in fact being threatened by that which he fears may destroy his very existence. For Paul the only bulwark which he could raise against the terrifying possibility that the judgment of God would crush him was his own complete obedience to the way of life formulated in the Jewish legal system. Yet was his obedience complete, impregnable? Suddenly, he tells us, his whole outlook was transformed. 'Whatever gain I had I counted as loss for the sake of Christ. Indeed I count everything as loss because of the surpassing worth of knowing Christ Jesus my Lord. For his sake I have suffered the loss of all things, and count them as refuse, in order that I may gain Christ and be found in Him, not having a righteousness of my own, based on law, but that which is through faith in Christ, the righteousness from God that depends on faith; that I may know him and the power of his resurrection, and may share his sufferings, becoming like him in his death, that if possible I may attain the resurrection from the dead' (Philippians 3: 7–11). Confronted by the terror of being rejected and banished from the presence of God, Paul abandons the way of meticulous conformity to a written code and casts himself upon the Christ of the Cross and Resurrection as the ultimate revelation of the judgment and mercy of God. In place of every kind of dependence upon his own achievements or merits or exact obedience he now cries: 'Far be it from me to glory except in the cross of our Lord Jesus Christ, by which the world has been crucified to me and I to the world' (Galatians 6: 14). Every eventuality of life is referred to the ultimate criterion: Jesus Christ and Him crucified.[4]

4. R. Bultmann gives a striking summary of Paul's doctrine of redemption in his essay on *Jesus and Paul*. 'Paul's basic idea', he writes, 'is that in the cross of Christ God has pronounced judgment on the world and precisely by so doing has also opened up the way of salvation. Because a crucified one is proclaimed as Lord of the world, it is demanded of man that he subject himself to God's judgment, i.e. to the judgment that all of man's desires and strivings and standards of value are nothing before God, that they are all subject to death.

But this principle had to be reaffirmed again and again in face of the many attempts to undermine his mission and to discredit his authority. A notable example is to be found in the Epistle to the Galatians, a letter written in response to an urgent and critical situation. Christians in the newly founded churches of Galatia were under strong pressure to submit themselves to Jewish legal disciplines in order to bring to fulfilment what had begun when they accepted the good news of salvation through Christ. Such a step in Paul's view would have been altogether retrograde. It involved building up again what had once for all been destroyed. And to reinforce his appeal to the Galatians to stand fast in the liberty with which Christ had set them free, Paul recalls his own painful experience when he was compelled to resist Peter to the face on a similar issue.

A pattern of social behaviour had been established in which Jewish and Gentile Christians in Antioch shared freely together in common meals. Suddenly this pattern was torn asunder by the arrival from outside of rigid segregationists who demanded conformity with Jewish dietary regulations. Peter, poised between two loyalties, decided for the old and thereby, in Paul's judgment, jeopardized the very truth of the gospel. Not that Paul himself was unaware of the attraction of the old. Had it not been that the whole ethos in which he had been nurtured and to which he had for so long given his whole-hearted allegiance still exercised an almost irresistible appeal to certain parts of his nature, Paul could hardly have reacted with such vehemence to the complexities of the situation. Peter, Barnabas and other Christians of standing and integrity were committing themselves in one direction. It would have been the easiest thing in the world for Paul to go with them. Instead he saw in a flash that this was a death and life issue. He cries out in words of terror and yet of supreme courage. The crisis of Calvary is re-enacted in these particular and existential circumstances. Whatever may seem to be the pressures of expediency and conformity, however frightening may be the threats of ostracism

---

If God reconciled the world to Himself through the cross, then this means that he has made himself visible in the cross and, as it were, says to man, "Here I am". All of man's accomplishments and boastings are at an end; they are condemned as nothing by the cross.

'But the cross cannot be separated from the *resurrection*; i.e. precisely he who accepts as valid for himself the judgment that is spoken in the cross, who, as Paul puts it, lets himself be crucified with Christ, experiences the cross as liberation and redemption, and is able to believe that, by giving Jesus up to the cross, God thereby led him into life—a life in which all share who let themselves be crucified with him. It is precisely death that frees us for life.' (*Existence and Faith*, p. 234.)

and disunity, I cast myself towards the Christ on His Cross. I am crucified with Christ afresh. I reaffirm my death to the Jewish law. I reclaim my independence of its regulations. I refuse to build up again what in the Cross has been destroyed. Yet I know that in this agonizing moment of reidentification in death with the Christ Who loved me and gave Himself for me I am living again. The life of Christ is being manifested in me afresh. In the eyes of the world, even in the eyes of those who are bringing worldly considerations into the discipline of the Church, I am a traitor and a fanatic. But I believe that death is the gateway to new life and that the Word of the Cross is the only word which effects reconciliation and peace.

E

At first sight it may seem quite extravagant to suggest that no outstanding example of an existential conflict comparable to that of Paul is to be found in Christian literature until the sixteenth century of our era. Yet in point of fact I know of no writer earlier than Martin Luther who left behind him any record of such a life-and-death struggle as is portrayed in Philippians 3 or Galatians 2. The obvious candidate as an exception to this generalization is St. Augustine. Has he not, in his Confessions, given us a classic and in many ways unique account of a divided self which at last found healing and reconciliation through commitment to Christ and His Church? Does he not appeal to the experience of St. Paul, especially as this is recorded in the great autobiographical statement of Romans 7? The answer to both these questions is clearly 'Yes'. Nevertheless I do not find in the Confessions that extreme tension, that sense of crisis in which a man's total existence is at stake, that agonizing recognition that what has formerly been revered and obeyed must now be dethroned and rejected, such as I find in the writings of Paul and, in a new setting, in the earlier writings of Luther. And if this is true of the Confessions it is equally true of any less developed fragments of autobiography to be found in the patristic period or in the Middle Ages.

Although it can, of course, be argued that a lack of explicit references in writing does not mean that no individuals did in fact share this kind of experience, our general knowledge of the cultural history of this period—say from A.D. 100 to A.D. 1500—leads us to infer that social conditions were such as to make such an individual reaction unlikely and unnatural. For the altogether determinative factor in the case of Paul was that he had been living within a *system* which he profoundly believed had been provided by God for man's salvation, that he had striven to the utmost capacity of his being to conform in every respect to that system and that he had come a long way towards what was normally regarded as success in his efforts. It was not that he had been living as a heathen, worshipping idols: nor that he had been following a way of ethical discipline and philosophical illumination which could find its fulfilment in a more comprehensive revelation. Rather he had given his whole hearted allegiance to the true and living God, as he believed, but had done so by submitting himself to rules and prescriptions which he now was being called upon to acknowledge as irrelevant to, if not downright inimical to, salvation, i.e. to being accepted and approved by God. Here was a crisis which involved a complete reversal within the pattern of his own existence. But it meant the renunication of that which carried an immense weight of authority and which included associations of an overwhelmingly attractive kind. And such a process could be spoken of only in terms of death, crucifixion, utter loss. It was the abandonment of so much that seemed good and holy in order that the truly good and truly holy might be received in faith and humility.

Such an individual experience, however, could hardly be conceived in the early Christian world once the break with Judaism had been made and the coming of Jewish converts into the Church had virtually ceased. Now the pattern of conversion was of the two kinds to which I have already briefly referred. On the one hand an individual (though more often a family or a community) might come to recognize the futility and immorality of idol worship (including the cultus of a deified man) and might turn to the living God Who had sent His Son to be the Saviour of mankind. Such a break would not be easy. It might involve persecution and threats from the defenders of the *status quo*: it might require the discarding of practices which had become part of the very fabric of social life. But in a sense the change was simple and clear-cut. It was from the false, constricted and lifeless to the true and expansive and life-giving. The gods left behind were in no way to be compared with the God and Father of our Lord Jesus Christ Who was now to be the object of worship and obedient service. Once the decision to embrace the new faith had been made, suffering might have to be endured in the outer world of social life but there was unlikely to be the deep inner suffering which comes when one honoured and intense loyalty is being challenged by another and when what seems on any count to involve death and loss must be accepted.

The second pattern of conversion tends to be of a more sophisticated kind. It is represented pre-eminently in the first two centuries of the Church's life when those who had been reared in the general milieu of Greek culture found a deeper satisfaction and fulfilment through embracing the Christian faith. They had already become aware of the inadequacy of the older polytheistic cults and were concentrating their attention upon the One—whether in the form of the ideal good or of the ultimate cause or of the innermost meaning. Yet this One tended to be abstract, ideal, eternal in the heavens but with no direct manifestation on earth. The message that the Logos had indeed become flesh, that the eternal Son in the bosom of the Father had indeed been delivered up to the death of the Cross, that the One through Whom the universe was made had indeed come amongst men as a humble servant—this, though at first startling, proved to be the revelation of ultimate truth to countless souls. To accept its full implications was often far from easy. But the transition could not normally be described as radical crisis or as existential encounter.

All this, however, is very different from the situation which arises when a man begins to feel dissatisfaction and disillusionment with the *system* which claims to be the earthly representative of the authority of God and to be the medium through which the activity of the Word of God is continued in history. Paul had grown up to believe that the Jewish system of his day existed to affirm and declare the Law of God and that those who sat in Moses' seat could mediate the Word of God to whatever situation might arise in contemporary life. This was the faith of his fathers. This was the religion to which he had dedicated his own life. Even to question it was painful. To turn against it was unthinkable.

Many centuries were to pass before a *Christian* system could hold such a comprehensive authority in a cultural milieu as the Jewish system held in Palestine and amongst the faithful in the Diaspora. But by the end of the first millennium of the Christian era a roughly parallel situation existed on a much larger scale. The Catholic system, centred in the papacy, represented it was believed the unchanging authority of God on earth. Through its sacramental activities the work of the Christ, God's Eternal Word, was continuously mediated to men. There might be human failures and abuses spoiling the practice of the system, there might be questionings about certain aspects of the theory of the system, but how could any individual dare to challenge the system itself, to defy the authority of its central spokesman through whom the Word of God was mediated? A king might claim for himself a more significant role in the exercise of the divine authority, a reformer might cry out for the removal of practices which seemed to contradict the Gospel entrusted to the Church. But how could any man whose very salvation depended on submission to the Church and receiving grace through the Church rise up in revolt against the system itself? Would this not be to invite death and final damnation? Would this not be the equivalent of murdering the father who had begotten him, the mother who had nurtured him, to whom he was deeply devoted and on whose continuing favour his very existence depended?

Humanly speaking young Martin Luther could never have reached, let alone surmounted, the central crisis of his life had it not been for the parallel experience of Paul about which he read and pondered and read again. Earlier interpreters had focussed their attention upon particular aspects of Paul's writings—his account of his struggle with fleshly desires, his witness to the righteous judgment of God, his exposition of the love of God manifested in the Cross—but there is no record of which I am aware which reveals a man before Luther wrestling for his very identity, his ultimate existence and selfhood, with an all-embracing system bearing the stamp of God's authority in the way that Paul did. To do this he had to follow Paul to the depths, committing himself to that which seemed folly, even blasphemy, in the eyes of men and to that which constituted the maximum of risk in relation to God. If what he was saying and doing should prove ultimately to be mere pride and presumption on the part of a misguided individual, how fearful would be his responsibility and how terrifying his final condemnation!

Both Paul and Luther gained courage to make the final assault by fortifying themselves with the word of the Cross. For Paul the very notion of a Messiah crucified was, by all the standards of his cultural heritage, sheer folly. As the first two chapters of the First Epistle to the Corinthians clearly show, the event of the Cross went clean contrary both to Jewish expectation and to Greek sophistication: 'a stumbling-block to Jews and folly to Gentiles'. Yet the final negation of the two overwhelmingly powerful systems of his day was for Paul the ground of a new personal existence and a new hope for mankind. The defiant cry 'Messiah crucified' was the word which spelled death to all former judgments and ambitions but which opened a gateway into a new life to the man of faith.

The significant thing, as Erik Erikson has so convincingly shown, is that in the critical years 1513-14 Luther was returning again and again to these early chapters of 1 Corinthians.

'Twenty-five times in the Lectures on the Psalms . . . Luther quotes two corresponding passages from Paul's First Epistle to the Corinthians. The first passage:

22. For the Jews require a sign and the Greeks seek after wisdom;
23. But we preach Christ crucified, unto the Jews a stumbling-block, and unto the Greeks foolishness;
25. Because the foolishness of God is wiser than men; and the weakness of God is stronger than men:

'This paradoxical foolishness and weakness of God became a theological absolute for Luther: there is not a word in the Bible, he exclaimed, which is *extra crucem*, which can be understood without reference to the cross; and this is all that shall and can be understood, as Paul had said in the other passage:

1. And I, brethren, when I came to you came not with excellency of speech or of wisdom, declaring unto you the testimony of God.
2. For I determined not to know anything among you, save Jesus Christ and him crucified.
3. And I was with you in weakness, and in fear, and in much trembling.

'Thus Luther abandoned any theological quibbling about the cross. He did not share St. Augustine's opinion that when Christ on the cross exclaimed *Deus meus, quare me derelequisti*, He had not been really abandoned, for as God's son and as God's word, He *was* God. Luther could not help feeling that St. Paul came closer to the truth when he assumed an existential paradox rather than a platonic fusion of essences; he insists on Christ's complete sense of abandonment and on his sincere and active premeditation in visiting hell. Luther spoke here in passionate terms very different from those of mediaeval adoration. He spoke of a man who was unique in all creation, yet lives in each man, and who is dying in everyone even as he died *for* everyone. It is clear that Luther rejected all arrangements by which an assortment of saints made it unnecessary for man to embrace the maximum of his own existential suffering. What he had tried so desperately and for so long to counteract and overcome he now accepted as his divine gift—the sense of utter abandonment, *sicut iam damnatus*, as if already in hell.'[5]

Luther did not only reject the 'arrangements by which an assortment of saints' could deliver him from 'his own existential suffering'. He rejected all the provisions made by the ecclesiastical system of his day—penances, scourgings, indulgences, purgatorial disciplines.

5. E. H. Erikson: *Young Man Luther*, pp. 204–5.

He even rejected the rationalizations made by the imposing Thomistic intellectual system which had been accepted by the Church. Instead he staked his whole existence on the Cross, on the Man Who had Himself been stripped of all outward supports, human and divine, and had gone out into the utter darkness with the cry on His lips: 'My God, my God, why hast thou forsaken me?' This was the verse which gripped Luther's attention in the same lectures on the Psalms in which the repeated references to 1 Corinthians appear. Here I turn to the discerning commentary of Roland Bainton:

'What could be the meaning of this?' he writes. 'Christ evidently felt himself to be forsaken, abandoned by God, deserted. . . . The utter desolation which Luther said he could not endure for more than a tenth of an hour and live had been experienced by Christ Himself as he died. Rejected of men, He was rejected also of God. How much worse this must have been than the scourging, the thorns, the nails! In the garden he sweat blood as he did not upon the cross. Christ's descent into hell was nothing other than this sense of alienation from God. Christ had suffered what Luther suffered, or rather Luther was finding himself in what Christ had suffered, even as Albrecht Durer painted himself as the Man of Sorrows.'[6]

Obviously in such ways of thinking there lurks the possibility of a colossal self-deception. To reject and be rejected by a system, theological, ecclesiastical, intellectual or social—and to be called upon to suffer, in consequence, a sense of complete dereliction and abandonment, *may* be the outcome of *hubris*, pride, self-conceit. To feel aggrieved and misunderstood is a not uncommon experience and *may* be due simply to one's own ineptitude and awkwardness. It is easy enough to adopt a martyr-role and to interpret suffering as the vindictive onslaught of an unjust universe upon an innocent victim. But Luther never claimed to be innocent. Indeed the exact opposite was the case. He was almost frantically concerned to reach the rock bottom of his own sinfulness. He could vie with Paul himself in being the chief of sinners. But instead of accepting any kind of palliatives or therapies or rationalizations from existing systems to ease his situation he cast himself with a kind of despairing cry on the Christ of the Cross, on the God Whom he saw in the Cross, on the utter paradox that 'God hides his power in weakness, his wisdom in folly, his goodness in severity, his justice in sins, his mercy in anger'; this, to use Erikson's phrase, was the existential paradox to which Luther clung or on which he stood. 'Here I stand', he is alleged to have cried in the moment when all the world

6. Roland Bainton: *Here I Stand*, p. 62.

seemed to be on the other side. I stand on the Cross because God has confronted me with the Cross, has spoken to me the word of the Cross, has (incredible though it may seem) identified Himself with my condition in the dereliction of the Cross. In such a moment of existential affirmation Luther not only died to himself and to the whole world and rose again in Christ but also became the representative figure for a new age, a new culture, a new era in the history of mankind. For as Erikson suggests in a later section of his analysis this *single man*, encompassed by heaven, hell and earth and crying 'Here I stand', established a new credo 'for men whose identity was derived from their determination to stand on their own feet, not only spiritually, but politically, economically and intellectually. No matter what happened afterward—and some terrible and most terribly petty things did occur because of it—Luther's emphasis on individual conscience[7] prepared the way for the series of concepts of equality, representation and self-determination which became in successive secular revolutions and wars the foundations not of the dignity of some, but of the liberty of all.'[8]

As in the case of Paul, the word of the cross was not heard and responded to in faith once and for all. It was the word which spoke to his own condition of despairing sinfulness, opening his eyes to the meaning of 'justification by faith'. But it was also the word which spoke to his dark nights of doubt, of weakness, of apprehension, of perplexity. No part of his life henceforward was *extra crucem*. Whatever mistakes he may have made, whatever extravagances he may have committed, Luther brought again before the eyes of the world the picture of a representative man who, through the constantly renewed constraint of a crucified Lord, received strength to defy all human and demonic powers and to reaffirm his own identity within the pattern of the Cross. Again and again he knew what it meant to be delivered to death for Jesus' sake but in that death he rediscovered his life, in the moment of fearsome alienation his foretaste of final reconciliation.

F

From the seventeenth century, out of a very different context, comes an extraordinarily intimate and personal record of a man involved in the same kind of tension as that which almost destroyed Martin Luther. Blaise Pascal was born in 1623, and spent most of his life in Paris. It is probable that in his early years the religion

7. I would prefer to say 'existential commitment'.
8. Op. cit., p. 224 f.

of his family was that of conventional Catholic conformity but it appears that in the year 1646 it assumed a far deeper seriousness through the influence of the works of Saint-Cyran and Jansenius, leaders of a movement of reform in the religious life of France. In these works was to be found both an intense concentration upon the efficacious grace of God and a searching demand for rigorous spiritual exercises in preparation for receiving this divine grace. Pascal became a man dedicated to the pursuit of truth at all costs.

At the same time he was fascinated by the nature and structures of the world around. He published a book on Conic Sections, he performed notable experiments in physics and he engaged in philosophical studies thereby becoming acquainted with Descartes and his work. Thus it would be true to say that Pascal's life and thought were developing within the context of two major *systems*— the total religious system of the Catholic Church, controlled by the authority of the Pope, and the intellectual system of rationalism, brilliantly upheld by the authority of Galileo and Descartes. And these two systems had something in common. In the first God was seen as manifesting himself through the total hierarchical and sacramental system of mediation, a system in which every man could co-operate with the divine in an ordered and regulated way. In the second God was seen as manifesting himself through the rational order and general laws of the world, a system in which any man could by the exercise of his own reason and activity proceed with confidence to construct his patterns of thought and behaviour. The two systems did not necessarily contradict one another. Trouble would only arise if either sought to encroach on the territory which the other regarded as peculiarly its own.

Now it is clear that Pascal was powerfully attracted towards both of these imposing structures. On the one hand he was devoted to the Church and deeply desirous of experiencing the sense of the presence of God through its ministrations. On the other hand he was an enthusiastic mathematician and experimental scientist and was ready to receive divine truth through his involvement in both of these disciplines. Yet it is equally clear that through neither of these systems could he receive that ultimate relationship with the living God which his inmost being craved. So Pascal moves forward to two major crises in which first one and then the other of these apparently divinely given systems is brought to radical questioning and in a certain sense to final rejection.

The first of the crises has become famous through the words used by Pascal to record it. On the night of 23rd November 1654 he opened his Bible at the seventeenth chapter of the Fourth Gospel and found himself confronted by Jesus preparing himself for his sacrifice in Jerusalem. Then he writes:

FIRE
God of Abraham, God of Isaac, God of Jacob,
  Not of philosophers and scientists.
Certainty, joy, certainty, feeling, peace, joy
  God of Jesus Christ.
My God and thy God
Thy God shall be my God.

My God, wilt thou leave me?
That I may not be separated from thee eternally
This is life eternal that they may know thee
The only true God and him whom thou hast sent
  Jesus Christ.

Innumerable commentaries have been written on these words but for our purpose one point is all important. Until this time Pascal had set his mind upon discovering God through His manifestations in the natural world, on learning about the ways of God through the disciplines of the abstract sciences. Now suddenly the presence of God is revealed in a totally new way. Fire, Jesus Christ, joy, peace—there is no systematic coherence but there is the ecstatic cry of recognition, the whole-hearted surrender to the living God Who has come to men in Jesus Christ. At least for the moment Pascal knows peace, joy, reconciliation in God Himself.

Yet although this crucial experience came as a climax to Pascal's growing disillusionment with the results of his enquiry after God in and through the study of the structures of the natural world, it did not in fact lead to his complete abandonment of the world or of his scientific interests. He was still fascinated by the problems which the space-world presented though he was terrified by the silences of infinite space. He still loved the system on to which he had pinned his hopes though he just as decisively rejected the system as able to reveal to him the presence of the living God. He saw that he must stand forever in the tragic situation of knowing God and yet of not knowing Him, of being aware of His presence and yet at the same time of His absence, of being reconciled to Him and yet of being separated from Him. Only in the cry of anguish is the paradox resolved: 'Be comforted. You would not seek me if you had not already found me.'

But there was a second system to be wrestled with. In this struggle something of a crisis seems to have arisen when a Bull of Pope Alexander VII condemning Jansenius arrived in Paris in 1657. The tension which had already existed in Pascal's mind between the sense of God's grace working in the depths and mysteries of human existence and the recognition of the Pope as the supreme authority in matters spiritual and therefore, as it were, the guarantor of the activity of God in human life and experience—this tension was brought near to breaking point as he found himself faced by a conflict between God and God's representative in the world. In the concluding part of the Provinciales published in 1657, he uses a striking phrase: 'The anguish of finding oneself between God and the Pope!' He could not (as Luther did) make a final breach with Rome. Yet he was constantly conscious of the gracious movements and searching demands of the God Who seemed to be independent of the activities of His representative on earth. Again and again Pascal was torn between his allegiance to the Catholic system within which he had grown up and to which in many parts of his being he was devoted *and* his loyalty to Truth as truth was revealed to him. This in fact constituted the second major crisis of his life.

In his brilliant exposition of the *Pensées* of Pascal and the Tragedies of Racine, Lucien Goldmann uses the term 'Tragic Vision' to describe the inner conflict which never, in Pascal's case, gained any final resolution. In the chapter entitled 'The Tragic Vision: Man',[9] he illustrates from various sources the nature of the dialectic in which tragic man finds himself involved. He turns to the world, experiences its delights but finds in it no final satisfaction: he turns to God, glimpses the nature of true value only to realize the width of the gulf which separates him from the object of his desire. Turning back to the world there comes a still deeper realization of its inadequacy in the light of ultimate reality —and so the paradoxes take shape that 'God is permanently absent in his continual presence' and that 'the soul finds its only rest in uncertainty and its only satisfaction in perpetual seeking.'[10] The perpetual dialectical movement attains its final expression in a phrase from Pascal's own *Mystery of Jesus*: 'Jesus is suffering the torment of death until the end of the world. We must not sleep during all that time.' This book is, in fact, a meditation on the passion and death of Jesus but the significant thing is that the intense concentration of interest is upon those precise elements in the story to which I have drawn attention in this chapter—the record of Gethsemane and the portrayal of the utter loneliness and dereliction on the Cross. It is by identifying himself with the Christ in these

9. Lucien Goldmann: *The Hidden God*, p. 62. I am deeply indebted to this book which I have found both illuminating and convincing.
10. Lucien Goldmann: op. cit., p. 75.

experiences, by making Christ's words his own words that Pascal found joy in the midst of suffering, life in the midst of death.

Mystery of Jesus makes much of the tragic nature of the experience in the Garden. 'Christ seeks at least some consolation from his three closest friends, but they are asleep; He begs them to watch a while with him, but they leave Him with complete indifference, having so little compassion that it cannot keep them even a moment from their sleep. And thus was Christ forsaken, left alone before the anger of God.' 'Christ seeks company and consolation among men. This happens only once in His life, I think. But He receives no comfort for His disciples are sleeping.'[11] In this critical situation, unique so far as Christ is concerned, Pascal sees his own anguish crystallized. He cries to God but is aware only of the inexorability of the cup of trembling: he cries to men and is aware only of a complete indifference. He is alone, completely alone. Yet what He endures is not for Himself alone. It is for the whole of mankind. 'He was made sin through me and for my sake: all your stripes have fallen upon Him. . . . He has cured Himself and thus will He certainly cure me.' But although this cure was wrought by Christ in His loneliness while men were asleep it can only become effective in human life as an individual, knowing something of His tragic loneliness, identifies himself with the prayer of the Christ and by taking His words upon his lips enters into the experience of His 'cure'.

Pascal is a figure who towers above his contemporaries by reason not only of his intellectual genius, but also of his total dedication to the search for the true and living God. In a comparatively short but intense period of mental and spiritual activity which is mirrored in his remarkable autobiographical writings, he became an archetypal figure of tragic man whose very existence is at stake in struggles and conflicts. Pascal never attained any final resolution yet no man has left behind a more moving and impressive record of a moment of reconciliation than that which bore witness to the event of the night of 23rd November 1654 and which remained sewn into his doublet until the end of his life. In this account the figure of the God-man, Jesus Christ, is central. In Him and in His words, Pascal found the key to his own existence. This Jesus, in His utter loneliness and dereliction, had acted on behalf of man. Man, in his own loneliness and dereliction, identifies himself with the Christ and thereby in a sense goes to His help in a way which His disciples refused to do. Yet in projecting himself towards the Christ and in the sharing of His experience man gains a momentary foretaste of reconciliation

11. Quoted Goldmann: op. cit., p. 79 f.

even though the 'cure' cannot be fulfilled except in the eternal order of redemption.

The cry of dereliction on the Cross expressed perhaps the deepest and most obvious tension of Pascal's human existence. Yet from the *Mystery of Jesus* there comes a message which I have already quoted and which, as M. Goldmann finely says, 'when the soul doubts, gives it certainty; when it is afraid, gives it hope; when it is wretched brings it greatness and when it is weary, rest. A message which amidst the perpetual anxiety and anguish of the soul, is the only valid and permanent reason for confidence and hope.

'Be comforted. You would not seek me if you had not already found me.'[12]

G

After Pascal, Kierkegaard. Within the period of 250 years between 1660 and 1910 the Western world saw the steady growth of an attitude to life which may be described as rationalistic and humanistic. Man grew in confidence as he became aware of his growing powers to gain knowledge and understanding of his past history, to analyse and systematize his present physical environment and to criticize and change his social forms. It was the age of immense systems of the mind—Goethe, Hegel, Marx—and of a virtually unlimited faith in the capacity of man to investigate, to manipulate and to re-create. Yet, paradoxically enough, almost at its midpoint a man was born whose destiny it was to question, to mock, to reject outright the whole conception of a world-history or of a universal system. Not that he was uninstructed in the history of mankind and in the culture of his time. A man of genius both in thought and imagination, Kierkegaard refused to follow the prevailing fashions of bourgeois humanism and instead concentrated all his energies on affirming afresh the place and significance of the individual and his inwardness in the total structure of reality.

Born in Copenhagen in 1813, Kierkegaard spent almost all of his relatively short life in this small town which nevertheless had the distinction of being the political and religious centre of the state of Denmark and the home of the intellectual leaders of Scandinavia. He was pre-eminently a writer and his output between 1843 and his death in 1855 could not easily be paralleled amongst the world's great authors. He seemed completely at home in the history of philosophy, in the realms of Biblical and confessional theology and in the cultural issues of his own time. He could exercise an

12. Op. cit. p. 86.

extraordinary psychological insight and could use a variety of literary forms—parable, paradox, irony, dialectic—with brilliant resourcefulness. Above all whatever he wrote came freshly minted from his own intense experience or from his sympathetic imaginative outreach. Scarcely anything could be called ordinary or second-hand or the product of book-learning. Kierkegaard lived in and through his written words. They expressed the 'passion' which like an inextinguishable fire raged continuously at the very centre of his being.

The story of his relationship with his father and with Regina, his fiancée, is well known. Through these his mental and emotional life was strained almost to breaking point between the rival demands and attractions of fear and love, of passion and duty, of social conformity and self-discovery. But he was also involved in a struggle with the intellectual and religious systems which held sway in his environment. Up until 1848 the focus of his attack was the Hegelian system of world history which seemed to Kierkegaard to result in the annihilation of 'the individual'; after 1848 his attention turned more directly to the established Church and its utter failure to bear witness to what he regarded as the only form of authentic Christianity. Yet through all that seems at first sight extreme, bitter, denunciatory and uncompromising we can detect a passion which loves that which it condemns and feels compellingly attracted to that which it attacks. He could have occupied a high position in the academic world, he could have been ordained and proceeded to a place of eminence in the State Church. Yet he remained all his life a controversial figure and at the end was virtually cast out by the society whose ultimate welfare was his deepest concern.

The tide of human thought, as I have already suggested, was flowing strongly towards a total world picture, towards a panorama of world history, towards the emergence of a universal society. Kierkegaard took his stand on the here and now, the point and the instant, and cried out in the name of every individual that if inwardness and subjectivity were lost then all was lost. No universal system of the mind, however noble and impressive, could compare with the wrestling of the individual for his authentic existence in the moment of crisis. No theory of reconciliation, however well supported by reason and logic, could compare with the individual's 'leap of faith' by which his existence *may* gain an actual momentary reconciliation or *may* for ever be lost.

Kierkegaard's concentration on the individual, his moment of decision, his leap of faith, comes to most poignant expression in the book *Fear and Trembling*. He calls this a dialectical lyric—it is, in fact, a poetic approach to the deepest crisis of his own experience. It is wrung from him out of the silence (the preface is signed with the pseudonym Johannes de Silentio). It is a dialectical movement between the urge to reveal the innermost secret of the heart and the obligation to remain absolutely silent: between the temptation to shriek aloud, letting all and sundry know the agony of the moment and the constraint to turn inward into 'the abyss of inwardness, where alone fear and trembling are really fearsome'.[13] He describes the experience as 'existential collision' and claims that it would have been impossible to represent it in an existing individuality for 'lyrically it extorts the extreme limits of passion, dialectically it keeps its expression back in absolute silence'. The book is in fact the expression of a repeated collision between the reflective consciousness and the understanding brought to a focus in the story of Abraham's journey to Mount Moriah there to offer up his son Isaac as a sacrifice to God.

Although Kierkegaard was profoundly aware of his own identification with the Christ in the sufferings of Gethsemane and Calvary he did not elect to explore the consciousness of the Son of Man passing through His own fearsome experience. Instead he approached the matter indirectly through Abraham. Abraham's experience was the paradigm through which the nature of faith and passion and inward suffering could be represented. His desire was to follow on the three days' journey 'when Abraham rode with sorrow before him and Isaac by his side. His wish was to have been present at the moment when Abraham lifted up his eyes and saw Mount Moriah afar off, at the moment when he sent the asses away and climbed the mountain, alone with Isaac: for his mind was busy, not with the delicate conceits of the imagination, but with the terrors of thought.' To enter into the experience of faith— this was all that mattered to this man of intensity and passion.

The book begins with four brilliant word-portraits of Abraham in his crisis, each suggesting ways in which he may have thought about the event which confronted him. In such a fearful situation there could be no certainty, no final appeal to universal standards or morality, no comparison with well-established precedents of religious behaviour, no recourse to the highest known human feelings of parental love and compassion. Abraham stood as an individual between the standards and the new command, between the feelings and the Divine imperative. No intellectual intuition could help. No appeal could be made to any method or system. Abraham was shut up to the inexorability of a single decision:

13. *Concluding Unscientific Postscript*, p. 234.

either he must *leap* or he must withdraw. As Kierkegaard was himself to say in his later book *Concluding Unscientific Postscript*: 'According to *Fear and Trembling*, all Christianity is rooted in the paradoxical, whether one accepts it as a believer, or rejects it precisely because it is paradoxical. Aye, it lies in fear and trembling, which are the desperate categories of Christianity, and of the leap. . . . Christianity was a desperate way when it first came into the world and in all ages remains such; because it is a desperate way out for everyone who really accepts it. A once fiery and spirited steed may come to lose its mettle and pride of carriage when it is held for hire and ridden by every bungler. But in the world of the spirit, sluggishness never gains the victory; it always loses and remains outside.'[14] Kierkegaard gives no place to morbidity or sentimentality. His 'individual' is the 'hero', the 'knight of faith'. Inevitably he must suffer. But it is through his readiness to suffer to the uttermost that he bears witness to ultimate reality. 'The hero becomes a hero precisely through the passion with which he apprehends in himself the terrible, and its decisiveness for his life.'[15] 'Faith has in fact two tasks: to take care in every moment to discover the improbable, the paradox; and then to hold it fast with the passion of inwardness.'[16]

Although he fastens upon Abraham and his relationship with Isaac to represent the terror that confronts a man in the crisis of faith, he constantly turns in others of his writings to Christ as the pioneer and finisher of faith and the pattern for every Christian believer. In his meditation on the lilies and the birds, he points out that the bird *is* what it is. For the bird there is no pattern. But for the Christian a pattern is in existence and he is in existence for his Pattern—he can constantly grow to resemble it more and more.[17] The Pattern reveals lowliness, poverty, contingency, obedience, weakness, suffering, misfortune. Yet through these alone can the glory and the triumph of the eternal be realized. In one place he holds before his readers' eyes a picture of two angels holding out to Christ the cup of suffering. You may go on looking at it almost indefinitely, Kierkegaard in effect says, but there will still come a moment when everything becomes infinitely changed, when the realization dawns that Christ did in fact take the cup obediently from the hand of God, drained it, suffered intensely in the instant, but thereby triumphed eternally. Can the artist depict the eternal triumph? Would a

14. p. 96 f.
15. Ibid., p. 237.
16. Ibid., p. 209.
17. *Christian Discourses*, p. 45.

beholder ever tire of seeing it if he could and wish it to come to an end? 'No, God be praised, it never comes to an end! And yet this triumph is only *once*; but the "once" of triumph is eternity, the "once" of suffering was the instant. It may, no doubt, be impatience which cannot endure to look at the picture where the cup is held out to Him; but it may also be faith, which consequently does not turn away impatiently, but believingly substitutes the picture of triumph for that of suffering.'[18]

To make the leap of faith through the experiences of weakness, poverty, suffering, misfortune, may be paradoxical but there is a Hero of Faith Who has triumphed and He is our Pattern. What is to be said, however, of the far more terrible reality of human life— the reality of sin? Sin, says Kierkegaard, is man's ruin. Sin is man's destruction. Sin is not (like suffering) the instant, but 'an eternal fall from the eternal'. It is not 'once'. It is timeless in its corroding and consuming power. In his intensely searching meditation on the text 'Keep thy foot when thou goest to the house of the Lord' he expresses vividly the terror of being infinitely close to the infinitely exalted One, the terror because 'even if thou hast come from the most dreadful experience that ever befell a man, fleeing from the horror without into God's house—·yet thou dost come to a still more dreadful place. Here in the house of God the subject talked about is a danger the world does not know, a danger in comparison with which all that the world calls danger is child's-play: the danger of sin. Oh, here in God's house what essentially is talked about is a horror which never was encountered before nor will be later, in comparison with which the most terrible thing that can befall the most unhappy of all men is an insignificance: the horror that the race crucified God.'[19]

No earthly need can compare in importance, Kierkegaard continues, with the fact that man is a sinner before God. It is not a question of what we may suffer in the world by way of a little bit of injustice. 'No, here in God's house it is first and foremost a question of the horror the like of which was never seen and shall not again be seen in the confusion of the world, about the injustice which cries to heaven, such as never before was committed and never shall be again, more dreadful than the sea at its wildest, an occasion when the human race did not as usual rebel impotently against God, but triumphantly as it were laid hold of Him and crucified Him . . . And Christ's suffering is not to be remembered as a past event—oh, waste not thy sympathy! No, when this horror is

18. Ibid., p. 109.
19. Ibid., p. 180.

represented it is a present fact, and thou art present, and I, with a present One—and as accomplices.'[20]

Man can only come into the house of God then as in the wrong, as guilty, as an accomplice to the suffering and death of the innocent One. He dare not come save in fear and trembling. Yet the ultimate paradox still stands. Man comes to receive the grace of God in Christ Jesus. Even this, however, inspires fear and trembling also for there is everything to gain, everything to lose. Guilty before God: comforted by God, through Christ Jesus. The tension and the paradox are never finally resolved within the dimension of the finite and the temporal. Over against God we are always in the wrong. The discrepancy of the finite and the infinite can only be brought finally to rest 'in an enthusiastic reconciliation in the infinite. It is the last enthusiastic cry in which the finite spirit appeals to God, within the sphere of freedom. "I cannot understand Thee, but still I will love Thee, Thou art always right; even if it seemed to me as if Thou didst not love me, I will nevertheless love Thee".' Only through such a final act of courage can man's fundamental estrangement be annulled.

Kierkegaard would not have called this a *doctrine* of reconciliation but rather an existential communication.[21] The existential contradiction can never be finally overcome in the conditions of finitude and temporality. There are only moments of action, instants of faith, flashes in which the existential contradiction is overcome. The system, the institution, the universal ethic will ever and again make their appearance and within limits they have a part to play in human affairs. But in the last resort it is the individual who matters, the individual before God, the individual guilty and justified, the individual leaping to meet his destiny after the pattern of the One Who for the joy set before Him endured the cross, despising the shame and is now set down at the right hand of the throne of God. In His act and in His word we find our reconciliation and our peace.

H

The twentieth century has witnessed an extraordinary revolt against systems of all kinds and in particular systems of thought and organization which aspire to be universal in their outreach. At the same time it has seen the emergence of one universal system—communism—which has gained the allegiance of a greater number

20. Ibid.
21. *Concluding Unscientific Postscript*, p. 339.

in a shorter time than any other in the history of mankind. With this latter phenomenon I am not immediately concerned. There have been signs of resistance to the totalitarian character of this régime, especially by poets and artists. Yet no single individual has stood forth as a representative figure in opposition to the system and it is not possible therefore, at present, to draw lessons from the words and behaviour of a non-conformist in a well-established communist society.

But in the Western world many warning notes have been sounded and individuals have been prepared to go into the wilderness rather than accept the system proposed for their allegiance. Dramatic examples have been presented in time of war. For the first time in human history whole societies have been placed on a war footing and universal conscription has been enforced. This has posed an agonizing dilemma for those whose consciences cannot allow them in any circumstances to destroy human life. Normally they have been devoted citizens of their own country and supporters of its general pattern of life. Yet in the final crisis they have felt bound to say 'No' and to bear the consequences however painful. Each way open to them has been fraught with danger, misrepresentation and apparent futility. The perils of over-simplification and sheer personal obstinacy surround them all the time. Yet they have felt bound to make their protest in the name of a value more demanding than everything which society has a right to lay upon them.

These are examples from the world of action. But this century has also brought struggles with systems of *thought* which have seemed massively impressive and all-embracing to their devotees and yet which an individual here or there has come to regard either as true only over a limited area or as downright false to reality as he knows it. Such has been the case with the system of philosophic idealism which held so secure a position in the academies of Europe in the early years of this century or with the system of liberal humanitarianism which so governed the intellectual outlook of the American peoples A Barth arises to challenge the intellectual system in which he has grown to maturity and to which he has been deeply attached: a Niebuhr arises to raise radical questions about the validity, in the light both of history and of contemporary experience, of the system in which he has been nurtured. But the way of the pioneer is not easy either in the social milieu to which he belongs or in the inner sanctum of his own heart and conscience. He is suspended between two worlds—the world of apparent security which has failed him, the world of bewildering uncertainty which beckons him. He knows that he must go forward and yet it is at the cost of breaking valued ties, of assuming an attitude which all too easily can be construed as arrogant and perverse, and of living with radical insecurity which ever threatens him with death. To remain true to his calling is to move constantly within the dialectic of death and life.

It would be absurd to suggest that the whole course of the nineteenth century was one of smooth and easy progress in thought and in life. There were disappointments and setbacks, there were gross cruelties and insensitivities, there were struggles between nations and classes and group-interests. There were vast areas of experience still to be tamed or brought under control. Yet it was possible for the theorizer to integrate his world in terms of such concepts as organic synthesis, historical inevitability, survival of the fittest, evolutionary progress or the coming of the kingdom of God. The objects and events which man studied could still be viewed within what seemed to be manageable limits. In most quarters the conviction held firm that what was perceived could be comprehended within a single rational structure and that it was therefore both possible and legitimate to build systems of thought for the habitation of the human imagination.

The most obvious change in twentieth-century thought has been the breaking through of the limits which encircled nineteenth-century observation and experience and the consequent breakdown of the systems which corresponded to them. Destruction has become possible on a scale undreamed of before. All forms of human communication have been speeded up to an almost unimaginable degree. Man cannot penetrate to the limits either of the universe which surrounds him or of the mysterious world which belongs to every minute particle of matter. The range of past history is too vast to enclose within any single system while the workings of the human psyche are too diverse to be reduced to any single rational formula. Idealism, Marxism, Evolutionism, Utopianism, Scientific materialism, Liberal humanitarianism, Democratic Socialism, Christian universalism, all the varying 'isms' which invited men's allegiance in the nineteenth century have been radically questioned, substantially modified or deliberately rejected. And nowhere has the rejection been more dramatic and outspoken than in the writings of the existentialists who, both in secular and Christian contexts, have cried out against all universal and timeless systems and have staked everything upon the significance of action in the here-and-now. Whether it be a leap into nothingness or a heroic step into an unknown future or an act of commitment to a dimly envisaged Christ or a response of faith to a faintly heard word of God—the basic nature of the action is the same. It is existential. It is a 'standing forth'. It is the affirmation of identity, of reality, of meaning, of value in face of all that threatens man's existence. It is a constantly reiterated 'No' to all securities and systems which have been available or which may still be forged in this world. It is a constant reaffirmation of 'Yes' to the unexperienced and the unknown.

I am not here concerned to criticize the writings of those who would generally be regarded as 'existentialists' within the span of the past half-century. I want only to emphasize the point that these men do not constitute a school of thought nor do they stand for a new ideology. They have been most impressive when their words have been directly linked with actions, when their cry of protest has coincided with an act of faith. Yet the existentialist constantly faces a dilemma. He cries out in protest and leaps into the unknown. He renounces all past securities of thought and life and acts in the situation of the moment. But if he survives the moment and finds himself standing on firm ground is he not immediately inclined to magnify the memory of the moment and to cling to his newly established stance, however limited its area may be? How can the existentialist refrain from bearing witness to his experience and so initiating the process by which a new system might come into being? The strain of any break with the past is intense. To be committed to a constantly renewed break with every past is to find one's life broken into tiny fragments with all coherence gone.

The result is that what might be called the consistent existentialist is non-existent. His words may hold out the possibility but his acts deny his words. Yet his moments of crisis, when he declares his 'No' to all enfolding securities and renews his 'Yes' in the action of unsupported (so far as this world is concerned) faith, can be of immense symbolic significance to those who look to him as a representative figure, a man who can interpret the meaning of existence to them and encourage them to 'stand forth' into their own identity by confronting their own crisis in a similar way.

Some of the outstanding contributions to Christian theology in the twentieth century have been made by those who have been called existential or 'dialectical' thinkers. Barth, Brunner, Tillich, Bultmann has each in his own way cried 'No' to the systems of the nineteenth century, systems which had laid their spell upon them and within which they could have lived and worked with distinction but which no longer constituted for them the authentic interpretation of new depths of reality of which they had become aware. Each has said 'Yes' to a new and exceedingly concentrated focus of revelation: in Barth's case the word of God in Jesus Christ, in

Brunner's Divine Truth as encountered in Jesus Christ, in Tillich's the picture of the New Being in Jesus the Christ, in Bultmann's the Kerygma which testifies to Jesus the Christ. Each has stood in danger of building up a new temple of the reason in place of the one which in a decisive moment he has destroyed. Yet each has sought to return again and again to his criterion and to test every word and every action in the light of the revelation in Christ. And in this revelation no event is so crucial, so determinative of all human experience, as is the event of Cross-Resurrection. The reconciliation of any moment in history, any situation in human life is made possible only through the reproduction within it of the death-resurrection conjunction uniquely enacted by the word of God in Jesus the Christ.

Probably of the four it is Bultmann who has tried most consistently to guard himself from erecting any new system of theology or comprehensive interpretation of doctrine on the basis of his understanding of the essential Christian Gospel. Theology he believes always tends to express itself mythologically, that is in the general concepts and language-patterns of a particular age. But it is the task of the Christian interpreter to penetrate beyond all mythological statements to the 'fundamental idea' that lies behind. And, Bultmann claims, this idea must be constantly rediscovered in and through the preaching of the Gospel, the Kerygma of Christ's death and resurrection. 'Faith', he urges, 'does not relate itself to historical or cosmic processes that could be established as free from doubt, but rather to the *preaching* behind which faith cannot go and which says to man that he must understand the cross as God's act of salvation and believe in the resurrection. Only in preaching is the cross God's saving act and therefore the preaching that is based on the cross is itself God's act of salvation and revelation. . . . This preaching of God's saving act, however, is not a communication about events that one can also establish outside of faith; rather in speaking of God's act of salvation, it at the same time addresses the conscience of the hearer and asks him whether he is willing to understand the occurrence that it proclaims as occurring to him himself and thereby to understand his existence in its light. For this reason, preaching has the possiblity of working death as well as life (2 Corinthians 2: 14–16; 4: 1–6). Thus the event of preaching is itself the eschatological event of salvation (2 Corinthians 6: 1 f).'[22]

Through the Cross, Bultmann continues, 'All of man's accomplishment and boasting are at an end; they are condemned as

22. *Existence and Faith*, p. 163 f.

nothing by the cross.' It is not for man to ask for or about resurrection. It is rather that as he accepts for himself the judgment spoken in the cross, the miracle happens and he is brought out into newness of life by the power of God. Faith in the cross and resurrection is not the acceptance of some irrational mythological doctrine but rather is primarily submission to the judgment of God, the renunciation of all boasting.

'Faith is the trust in God that arises precisely where to the eyes of man there is nothing but darkness, but death. But such trust presupposes the obedience that is willing to surrender to death all that is one's own.'[23]

To read Bultmann's lectures, expositions or sermons is to be in touch with a man wholly opposed to any kind of systematization, philosophical or historical. It has often been noted how deeply he has been influenced by the philosophy of Heidegger but this is in fact the negation of philosophy in the nineteenth-century sense of the term. He is, by all normal standards, a great historian but he refuses to relate faith in any way to historical reconstructions. All that matters is the Word of the Cross. In the original event God's Word of reconciliation was spoken. That Word has continually been heard and proclaimed. Wherever it has been heard as the Word speaking to man's *existence*-in-death, there experience has authenticated itself, there the eschatological event of the Cross has been re-enacted. Faith is created in the moment of response to the Word and man's existence is transformed. 'We cannot speak of an act of God', Bultmann has frequently said, 'without speaking simultaneously of our own existence'. Only in existential encounter which is brought about through the coming of the Word to the individual, calling him to decision (which is an inescapable part of his human nature) *for God* as against his own ideas and possessions and ambitions, only in such an encounter does the cross become real event and only in this way is its true meaning revealed.

Who can doubt that Bultmann has himself heard the Word of the Cross and continues to hear it? Clearly he is deeply concerned that this Word shall be proclaimed to our contemporary world, unfettered by past formulations or speculations. No one can read his sermons preached in times of world-crisis and personal-crisis without a sense of being in contact with a man who has himself heard the Word which interprets his own existence and consequently the existence of all men. Yet it is hard to avoid the feeling that the words of Jesus and the kerygma of the apostles are being forced through too narrow a funnel of infiltration into the human situation.

23. Op. cit., p. 236.

Judgment, obedience, surrender to death, renunciation, all in the context of a despairing trust in the God Who raises the dead—these are words and categories too limited, it would seem, to do full justice to the Word of reconciliation. There is one other interpreter of our own time who, while utterly faithful to this Word, succeeded both through his life and his writings in interpreting the meaning of atonement in a more comprehensive and in the judgment of many in a more convincing way. To him I shall finally turn.

I

Dietrich Bonhoeffer grew towards his own maturity within the context of two great systems of thought—that of Ernest Troeltsch and that of Adolf von Harnack. The first may be epitomized in a sentence from Troeltsch's own writing:

> 'Christianity is not the only revelation or redemption, but the culminating point of the revelations and redemptions which are at work in the elevation of humanity to God';

the second in a sentence from an address given by Bonhoeffer in appreciative memory of Harnack's influence:

> 'He thought that in the holy spirit of Christianity the spirit of every age found its destiny and that the message of God the Father and the human child had eternal validity and therefore validity for us also.'

Both were men of astonishing erudition and a passionate concern for Truth. Both believed that by using the method of patient historical investigation the vast panorama of the development of religion in the experience of man could be revealed and that thereby an idealistic philosophy of Spirit could be developed.

Bonhoeffer was enormously attracted by this type of thinking but he was not entirely satisfied, as became evident when, at the age of twenty-one, he produced his first major theological work. In this he sought to construct a sociology of the Church, not within the framework of idealism and immanentism but rather upon the basis of the concrete individual person, responsible to God, called to decision in every moment of time, and therefore responsible to his neighbour in such a way as to make true community possible. Already we see a deep concern for responsible relationship, for ethical action, for existential decision. There was to be no floating with the stream of universal history or of inevitable social evolution. Bonhoeffer was preparing himself to take the place of lonely opposition over against his teachers, his Church, his country—a loneliness which would be often painful, sometimes agonizing, just because his love for each was deep and strong and because the slightest willingness to compromise could have placed him at once in a position of leadership and eminence within the beloved community.

From the first he was gravely suspicious of the National Socialist movement and of the German Christian party in his own Church. His growing influence in ecumenical circles, his many links with Great Britain and the United States, would have made it comparatively easy for him to sever his connections with the church and land of his birth but such a possibility he refused even to consider seriously. He must be with the Confessional Church in opposing the new paganism in ecclesiastical circles: he must be with the resistance movement ultimately in opposing the fanaticism of an apostate political régime. In all his thinking and acting the figure of the Christ assumed an ever more dominating position and formative influence. Almost unconsciously in following Christ he was taking the way which would lead to a cross.

In his earliest written work Bonhoeffer accepts the traditional interpretation of the Cross though he approaches it in a fresh and interesting way. First he relates the death of Jesus to the Law— the Law which was the standard and strength of the old community but which man has universally broken. Jesus dies in loneliness, 'surrendering to the law and taking upon himself the curse of the law for us!' But in His resurrection 'his death is revealed as the death of death, and thereby the limit upon history imposed by death is removed, the human body has become the resurrection-body, the mankind of Adam the church of Christ'. 'In the resurrection the heart of God has pierced through guilt and death and has truly conquered his new mankind, subjected man to his lordship.'[24]

In principle, then, the victory has been won and a new community has been created. But still two things oppose the full establishment of the divine lordship within the community. There is obviously the will for evil still existing in the world. In addition, however, there is what Bonhoeffer calls the burden of *time*, the inexorable law that 'what has happened, has happened'. If man is really to enjoy communion with God then 'what has happened must by God's decree be judged as not having happened. Now man's guilt cannot be regarded by the God of truth "as if" it did not exist; it must truly be made "unhappened", that is eradicated. This cannot come about by a reversal of time, but by divine punishment and the re-creation of the will for good. God does not "overlook" sin; otherwise it would mean that he was not taking man's personal being seriously in its very guilt, in which case there could not be any re-creation of

24. *Sanctorum Communio*, p. 110 f.

the person, or of community. But God takes man's guilt seriously and for that reason only the punishment and the overcoming of the sin can avail. Both must be accomplished at a point in time, and they happen in a way valid for all time in Jesus Christ. He takes the punishment upon himself, obtains forgiveness for our sins and, to use Seeberg's expression, goes surety for man's renewal. Thus Christ's vicarious action can be understood from the situation itself. In him concrete action within time and its being "for all time" really coincide. There is vicarious action for guilt and punishment. Here the one demands the other, for "punishment" does not mean to take the consequences of sin upon oneself, but to judge these consequences to be a "punishment" for sin. The idea that the Passion of Jesus was in the nature of a punishment has frequently been disputed. Luther laid all possible stress upon this. It is conceivable that someone might take the consequences of sin upon himself even in the moral life of society. The unique quality of the Christian idea of acting vicariously is that this action is strictly vicarious with regard to guilt and punishment. Jesus, being himself innocent, takes the others' guilt and punishment upon himself, and as he dies a criminal, he is accursed, for he bears the sins of the world and is punished for them; but on the felon's cross, vicarious love triumphs; obedience to God triumphs over guilt and thereby guilt is in fact punished and overcome. Such, briefly, is our way of seeing Christ's vicarious action.'[25]

I have quoted this passage at length to show how closely Bonhoeffer at this early stage was approximating to the traditional Lutheran theology of atonement. He was indeed stressing the relevance of atonement to the creation of true community and the crucial significance of vicarious action. But his main emphasis was upon the utter uniqueness of Christ's vicarious act as constituting the sheer gift and offer of God's love. It was the one act in time which reversed time. It was the one supreme punishment which eradicated human guilt. It was an act performed in utter loneliness so far as all human fellowship was concerned but it was altogether within the will and gift of God as the means by which the new community, the Church, was to be brought into existence and a real fellowship between man and God was to be restored.

This early and dominantly theoretical formulation Bonhoeffer did not abandon. But whether through the pressures of the time or through his own developing experience his later works tend to place a far greater emphasis on the disciple's participation in the suffering of Christ and upon the necessity for him to be conformed

25. Op. cit., p. 113 f.

in every way to His likeness. Whereas perhaps the earlier emphasis was upon the creation of the new community through the vicarious act of the Son of God, the focus of attention was now the nature of the life and service of the new community in the world and for the world. For at Calvary not only was the *Church* created; the whole *world* was reconciled. In the very midst of history, God and the world become one *in Christ*. It became possible for the individual, the Church, the world to be conformed to the likeness of the Crucified and in its ultimate expression this means to die daily before God for the sake of sin and to bear all suffering with the knowledge that God uses it for a purpose of redemption.

In his book *The Cost of Discipleship* Bonhoeffer applies this in particular to the life of the individual. He quotes the basic word of Jesus: 'If any man would come after me, let him deny himself and take up his cross and follow me.' This must be taken quite concretely to mean a real sharing in the Lord's sufferings and rejection and crucifixion. It is true that Christ's sufferings alone are redemptive and yet in his grace the Lord allows his disciples to share in the fruits of his Passion 'by bearing the burdens of others and by participation in the work of forgiving men their sins. In fact, the only way to bear the burden or sin of another, and thereby fulfil the law of Christ, is by forgiving it in the power of the cross of Christ. By drinking the cup of suffering to the dregs on the cross, Jesus overcame the suffering of mankind in its separation from God and made fellowship with God again possible, and the Church that follows Christ beneath the Cross will find itself suffering before God on behalf of the world.'[26]

In his preaching and his writing Bonhoeffer had set forth his understanding of reconciliation in and through the Cross. It remained for him to seal his testimony in two ways: in poetry and in action. To mention his poetry may seem strange but it is not, I believe, unimportant and it constitutes a link with the earlier material of this chapter. In a striking review of *The Truce*, by Primo Levi, war-time partisan and survivor of the notorious Auschwitz concentration camp, Philip Toynbee points out how difficult it is for anyone to find words to describe what are after all ultimates or extremities of human experience. Even people who lived in the camps and endured to the end found themselves lacking in concepts or verbal terms adequate to express what ney had seen or felt. Levi's book, he goes on to say, is a great book 'because this man was able to match his experiences both with his character and with his words. It was a poetical book: and another reminder that it

26. John D. Godsey: *The Theology of Dietrich Bonhoeffer*, p. 155.

is only by poetical means that the impossible can ever be described. . . . If Signor Levi had not been a man who was capable of finding such words for his experiences, one cannot help doubting whether he could, in any logical sense, have "had" the experiences at all.'[27]

It is from Bonhoeffer's prison cell that his poems came. But even beyond his formal poetry some of his letters and occasional writings are truly poetical, matching as they do images and language with the experiences through which he was passing. They are veritable *cris de coeur*. We follow him in imagination into his Gethsemane, the loneliness of his own rejection by his fellow countrymen, the binding of the vivid spirit which had gloried in God's gift of freedom. Two in particular reveal him being formed in the image of the Christ to Whom he had wholly committed himself—sharing the experience of Gethsemane, sharing the experience of condemnation to death.

The first is entitled 'Christians and Unbelievers':

'Men go to God when they are sore bestead,
Pray to him for succour, for his peace, for bread,
For mercy for them sick, surviving or dead:
All men do so, Christian and unbelieving.

'Men go to God when he is sore bestead,
Find him poor and scorned, without shelter or bread,
Whelmed under the weight of the wicked, the weak, the dead,
Christians stand by God in his hour of grieving.

'God goeth to every man when sore bestead
Feedeth body and spirit with his bread,
For Christians, heathen alike he longeth dead:
And both alike forgiving.'

In his letter of 18th July 1944, Bonhoeffer saw fit to offer a commentary on the poem. He defined as the central idea:

'Christians range themselves with God in his suffering; that is what distinguishes them from the heathen.'

'As Jesus', he continued, 'asked in Gethsemane: "Could ye not watch with me one hour." That is the exact opposite of what the religious man expects from God. Man is challenged to participate in the sufferings of God at the hands of a godless world.

'He must therefore plunge himself into the life of a godless world, without attempting to gloss over its ungodliness with a veneer of religion or trying to transfigure it. He must live a "worldly" life and so participate in the suffering of God. He *may* live a worldly life as one emancipated from all religions and obligations. To be a Christian does not mean to be religious in a particular way, to

27. *The Observer*, 24th January 1965.

cultivate some particular form of asceticism (as a sinner, a penitent or a saint) but to be a man. It is not some religious act which makes a Christian what he is, but participation in the suffering of God in the life of the world.'[28]

In a letter two days earlier he had written more about the suffering of God in the world. 'God allows himself to be edged out of the world and on to the cross.' . . . God is weak and powerless in the world. He 'conquers power and space in the world by his weakness.' Only a suffering God can help the world. The outstanding testimony to this principle can be seen in the weakness and suffering of the Christ Who in His days in the world bare our infirmities and took our diseases (Matthew 8: 17). And this may mean, for the Christian who identifies himself with his Lord, even the extremity of living without God at the very moment when he is most fully living with God and before God. 'The God who is with us is the God who forsakes us.' The Christian must allow himself to be edged out of the world onto a cross if he is to participate in the supreme task of saving the world (Mark 15: 34). Bonhoeffer was never more certain that God was with him than in the moment when he appeared to be forsaken by God and as it were abandoned to an existence wholly in the grip of the world.

The second, written shortly after he had learned of the failure of the plot against Hitler, he called 'Stations on the Way to Freedom' (I quote Dr. Godsey's translation):

Self-Discipline
If you set out to seek freedom, you must learn before all things
Mastery over sense and soul, lest your wayward desirings,
Lest your undisciplined members lead you now this way, now that
    way.
Chaste be your mind and your body, and subject to you and
    obedient,
Serving solely to seek their appointed goal and objective.
None learns the secret of freedom save only by way of control.

Action
Do and dare what is right, not swayed by the whim of the moment.
Bravely take hold of the real, not dallying now with what might be.
Not in the flight of ideas but only in action is freedom.
Make up your mind and come out into the tempest of living.
God's command is enough and your faith in him to sustain you.
Then at last freedom will welcome your spirit amid great rejoicing.

28. *Letters and Papers*, p. 166.

Suffering
See what a transformation! These hands so active and powerful
Now are tied, and alone and fainting, you see where your work ends.
Yet you are confident still, and gladly commit what is rightful
Into a stronger hand, and say that you are contented.
You were free for a moment of bliss, then you yielded your freedom
Into the hand of God, that he might perfect it in glory.

Death
Come now, highest of feasts on the way to freedom eternal,
Death, strike off the fetters, break down the walls that oppress us,
Our bedazzled soul and our ephemeral body,
That we may see at last the sight which here was not vouchsafed us.
Freedom, we sought you long in discipline, action, suffering.
Now as we die we see you and know you at last face to face.

'Only in action is freedom.' On this the apt comment seems to
be the words of his letter of 21st July: 'This is what I mean by
worldliness—taking life in one's stride, with all its duties and
problems, its successes and failures, its experiences and helplessness.
It is in such a life that we throw ourselves utterly in the arms of
God and participate in his sufferings in the world and watch with
Christ in Gethsemane. That is faith, that is *metanoia* and that is
what makes a man and a Christian. How can success make us
arrogant or failure lead us astray, when we participate in the
sufferings of God by living in the world.'[29]

His poems with their accompanying commentary cannot be
pressed into a logical scheme or interpreted by appealing to less
extreme situations. He had chosen to throw himself utterly into the
midst of the world's struggles in the belief that it was there that he
would share in the experience of the true God. His prison cell
became to him a Gethsemane and a Calvary and he cried out in
words comparable to those which still echo and re-echo from these
two foci of the extremity of human experience. Yet who could
dare say that these cries of agony are not also cries of affirmation?
That in the No is the Yes—that in the final separation is the final
reconciliation? Bonhoeffer endured to the end. Few men have
so obviously inherited the Lord's promise that he who endures
to the end will be saved—and, we may add, by so enduring share
in the glory of reconciling the world to God.

29. Ibid., p. 169.

CHAPTER X

THE IDEA AND THE EVENT

On the day before I began to write this chapter in which I am seeking to summarize the results of my long enquiry I picked up a publishers' catalogue and read the title of a forthcoming book: *Is Sacrifice Outmoded?* On the following morning I opened *The Times* newspaper and saw on the court page a picture. It showed a man wielding a chisel and mallet. His attitude was one of intense concentration. He was about to make an incision into a huge block of wood which was already taking shape as a body with the head wreathed in thorns. It was a crucifix, the reader was told, 'above life size and hewn in oak'. On other pages he could learn about wars in Pakistan and Vietnam; threats from China; terrorism in Aden; the prospect of the doubling of the world's population; plans for economic growth and the raising of the standard of living. But here, near the centre, he could see an individual still wrestling with the rough wood of a tree, trying surely to make the work of his imagination speak to the world of his own day: shocking it, shaming it, inviting it, healing it. Traditional and conventional images of sacrifice may have become outmoded. In a mysterious way the Man upon the Cross retains His place in the human imagination as the timeless symbol of reconciliation through sacrifice.

I propose now in this final chapter to look back over the path which I have pursued and to offer some concluding reflections on the task of interpreting atonement within the terms of the Christian revelation today.

A

My starting-point was the theme of alienation. At that time, more than ten years ago, I tried to develop the theme historically by showing how it came to prominence in the nineteenth century and how it has remained a dominant category of social analysis since that time. My impression now is that this category has attained even greater prominence in the last few years and that it is scarcely possible to take up any interpretation of the human situation, scientific or artistic, without soon encountering the concept of alienation and finding it being used as the chief means of bringing some degree of order into a scene of complexity and even confusion.

In the early part of 1964 a useful article appeared in the magazine *New Society* recognizing the widespread use of the concept, pointing out the danger of its becoming a vague and facile catchword but concluding that 'it remains . . . a potent idea, an attempt to come to terms with a deep-rooted condition of man which requires an equally deep-rooted appraisal of man—of the underlying reasons why he cannot realize himself happily and effectively in the kind of society in which most of us now live'.[1] Psychologically the basic condition of the average human being is diagnosed as anxious, lonely, above all as lacking in any sense of self-identity or of personal integration. In other words the most common characteristic of the *individual* is self-alienation: he neither knows who he is nor can he become what in moments of illumination he would like to be. Sociologically the condition of the average society is diagnosed as mechanical, deterministic, above all as lacking in any sense of personal interdependence within a living organic whole. In other words the most common characteristic of the *social group* is mutual alienation: man is alienated from his work, from his surroundings and most obviously of all from his fellow men.

In such an analysis two important points arise. First of all there is clearly an underlying assumption that the individual or the social group possesses, in a generally undefined way, an original wholeness or an original potential wholeness which has somehow been shattered or at least prevented from reaching its true fulfilment. Now this is a large assumption. It has been basic in Christian theology where the concept of the *imago Dei*, however interpreted, has exercised a controlling influence. It has appeared in countless philosophies as they have sought to come to terms with the self and the not-self, the I and the Thou, the individual and the society, the one and the many. Whatever arguments may be advanced in favour of collectivism, behaviourism, automatism, there still remains in most hearts the conviction that originally or ideally or potentially a pattern of integration does exist and that insofar as man is divided or fragmented in his inmost being he is alienated from his 'real self' or his 'instinctual self' or his 'spiritual self'. And what holds for the individual can be extended to the group. It is conceivable that originally or potentially human society possessed a pattern of wholeness, expressed for example in organic terms, and that insofar as there is inner tension and conflict within the group it is alienated from its true 'image' or 'design':

But even for those who have difficulty in imagining any original wholeness or potential wholeness there is evidence in plenty of

1. *New Society*, 27th February 1964, p. 29.

stresses and strains in individual and social life. Why then is man not content to live for ever in a free-for-all, with every man's hand against every other man, with every momentary desire of every individual being allowed to indulge itself to the uttermost? Why have libertinism and anarchy and internecine conflict and pure sensualism not been allowed to run riot in human affairs? Partly, it may be urged, because of man's sheer struggle for survival. He discovers that unless there is *some* control life itself becomes unbearable. But is this all? Is there not in man a built-in sense that integration is better than disintegration, that harmony is better than cacophony, that friendship is better than enmity? Is there not also an instinctive recognition that the self cannot find fulfilment in isolation? That in a strange way the self that seeks its satisfaction solely within its own impulses and activities fails to find it? The concept of alienation has been formulated not simply on the basis of a theory of potential or ideal wholeness but in direct response to the demands of man's day-to-day empirical experience. The fact that philosophers and theologians, social anthropologists and social historians, psychologists and psychiatrists have all found the concept useful for purposes of analysis and reconstruction bears abundant testimony to the existence of some form of alienation in human life, however precisely it may be defined or explained.

The second important question concerns the intensity and universality of the phenomenon as it is manifested in our contemporary world. Is there good reason to think that the sense of alienation has become more poignant and more widespread within the context of the particular conditions of twentieth-century life? It is often said that the coming of industrial society, its organization under a capitalistic régime, its increasing mechanization leading ultimately to automation, its steady dehumanization particularly in the area of inter-communication, has brought about an acute sense of alienation both in the heart of the individual and in the communal experiences of social groups. Has man lost something of surpassing value, viz. his power to organize his own activities, to gain satisfaction in his own work, to possess his own property however small? Has he been transformed into a cog in the machine, his labour into a measurable commodity, his highest role into that of smooth efficiency?

It is easy to romanticize the past. It is easy to exaggerate the significance of tendencies in the present. There were manifold occasions for alienation in the life of the medieval peasant; there are manifold alleviations of alienation in the life of the industrial worker today. Yet it would be pointless to disregard the effect of large-scale planning and of the fuller organization of production and communication techniques. The small society has a greater hope of preserving intimate personal relationships than has a large collective. The automatic mechanical process gives little occasion for personal confrontation and co-operation such as is common in the small business, the corner-store and the factory employing a score of workers. But the pattern of large-scale computerized industry is bound to be adopted more and more as all the nations of the world seek to improve their standards of living. Man will be increasingly separated from his material, his work, his fellow workers, from any conception of the significance of the total operation in which he is involved. It seems, in fact, that expansion in size, numbers, efficiency inevitably leads to contraction in man's living relationships with his world and his fellow creatures. And this means a deepening sense of alienation leading to frustration and even despair. Man feels that he is helpless in the service either of the machine itself or of the machine-like state. His only weapon for self-assertion is political revolution (now an almost impossible enterprise) or the industrial strike. The easier way is to retreat into the isolation of his home or his room in the hope of gaining some satisfaction through watching the panorama of human affairs while engaging in life as little as possible himself.

In the light then of the researches of the psychologist and the sociologist there seems no reason to qualify the central place which I gave at an early stage in this study to the concept of alienation. That man is unable to integrate his world and his inner self, to reconcile his aspirations and the actualities of his existence, is widely recognized by the social scientist. He speaks of man's powerlessness to achieve the role that he believes is rightfully his, of his inability to act meaningfully in particular situations, of his isolation, physical and psychological, of his estrangement from self-identity and authenticity.[2] One of the most vivid of modern psychological descriptions is the 'split personality': one of the most revealing of modern sociological book-titles is the Lonely Crowd. Each bears witness to the fundamental nature of the alienation which characterizes human life today. Each raises the question of whether a way of reconciliation can be found.

But if alienation has become a popular and acceptable term in psychological and sociological analysis, it has I think figured even more prominently in the realm of literary and artistic criticism. For example William Barrett in his book *Irrational Man* can write: 'The themes that obsess both modern art and existential

2. Cp. New Society. loc. cit.

philosophy are the alienation and strangeness of man in his world: the contradictoriness, feebleness and contingency of human existence; the central and overwhelming reality of time for man who has lost his anchorage in the eternal.'[3] And Ernst Fischer, out of his own Marxist background can say: 'Alienation has had a decisive influence on the arts and literature of the twentieth century. It has influenced the great writings of Kafka, the music of Schoenberg, the Surrealists, many abstract artists, the "anti-novelists" and "anti-dramatists", Samuel Beckett's sinister farces; and also the poetry of the American beatniks.'[4] Alienation has become a key-word in literary criticism. Man still has his old longings but the cadence of modern life, the perspective of modern life, the tempo of modern life are all different and a sense of alienation seems inevitable.[5]

Possibly no artist in the twentieth century has felt the sense of alienation more keenly and thereby exercised a greater influence on his successors than Kafka. By means of two vivid images he expresses his own feeling which gains fuller expression, of course, in his novels. 'I am separated from all things by a hollow space,' he wrote in a letter in 1911, 'and I do not even reach to its boundaries.' Again writing about himself he says: 'He is thirsty, and is cut off from a spring by a mere clump of bushes. But he is divided against himself; one part can see the whole, sees that he is standing here and that the spring is just beside him, but another part notices nothing, has at most a divination that the first part sees all. But as he notices nothing, he cannot drink.'[6] If man were only exiled in the desert, away from his fellows, away from a world of interest and fruitfulness, that would be bad enough. But still worse he is divided in his own inner being, seeing and not seeing, moving and getting nowhere. And this is the artist, Auden has said, who comes nearest

3. p. 56.
4. *The Necessity of Art*, p. 86.
5. 'One of the most compelling traditions of sensibility in contemporary literature—one which is perhaps best identified by the terms isolation, estrangement, alienation, and one which has engaged some of the most interesting and sensitive talents in our recent literary history. Even the most cursory catalogue of representative monuments of recent expression—which might include Kafka's *The Castle*, Graham Greene's *Brighton Rock*, Djuna Barnes's *Nightwood*, Sartre's *No Exit* and W. H. Auden's *The Age of Anxiety*—immediately reveals, beyond all differences of style and genre, an underlying unity of temperament and experience which is consistently organized into a description of the contemporary tragedy in terms of dereliction and estrangement and exile, not in terms of an alienation within a stable world, but in a world where "things fall apart", where "the centre does not hold", where man's deepest tension is not social or economic but an *angoisse métaphysique*.' Nathan A. Scott: *Rehearsals of Discomposure, Alienation and Reconciliation in Modern Literature*, p. 1 f.
6. See E. Heller: *The Disinherited Mind*, p. 175 f.

to defining the spirit of our age in the way that Dante, Shakespeare and Goethe defined theirs.

More recently the note of alienation has become altogether dominant in what can lay claim to being the most creative movement in modern drama. Whether it is called the theatre of the absurd as in the title of Martin Esslin's fine book or the theatre of protest and paradox as in George Wellwarth's, the underlying characteristic which each is describing is the alienation which exists between the characters and the audience, between the characters and their environment and worst of all between the characters themselves. Esslin points out that Bertolt Brecht had attempted to produce an effect of alienation by inhibiting, as far as possible, the traditional identification of the audience with the characters on the stage and replacing it by a cool, detached, critical attitude. But paradoxically his own genius as a playwright was so great that willy nilly the audience found itself caught up in the action and the passion and the old identification was resumed. In the *Theatre of the Absurd*, however, 'the audience is confronted with characters whose motives and actions remain largely incomprehensible. With such characters it is almost impossible to identify; the more mysterious their action and their nature, the less human the characters become, the more difficult it is to be carried away into seeing the world from their point of view. . . . What is the audience to make of this bewildering confrontation with a truly alienated world that, having lost its rational principle, has in the true sense of the word gone mad?'[7]

Although motives and actions may appear to be largely incomprehensible it is at least clear that the characters are alienated from their surroundings. A favourite device is to make the setting in which they operate a room or a cellar or a cell. Within this womb-like environment, a relative and momentary feeling of safety may be experienced. But not for long. There are always threats, sinister movements, mysterious messages from outside. We become aware that the individual or the two or three companions are in the midst of an alien world. It is incomprehensible but it is menacing. It is uncontrollable but some action must be taken. It is terrifyingly alien and yet there is no escape from it.

Worst of all, as I have suggested, the characters are alienated from one another because all normal and time-honoured means of communication have broken down. Man can face all kinds of danger in company with his brother if there is a mutual trust engendered by and sustained by meaningful looks, gestures and specially words.

7. *The Theatre of the Absurd*, p. 229 f.

But in the *avant-garde* drama of the mid-twentieth century characters constantly engage in conversation in which there is no meaningful connection between one sentence and another. The grammar, the vocabulary, the sequence of words may at first sight seem familiar and functional. And then we realize that there is no real sequence, no real dialogue, only a series of unconnected phrases which may be witty or banal in themselves but have no coherent connection with one another. And who can deny that the dramatist, even if in an exaggerated way, is in fact reflecting an all too obvious feature of our modern world. It is an age of doublespeak, catch-phrases, resounding words whose effect is no more than a tinkle,[8] gestures towards the other producing not even a glimmer of a response. The artist, the novelist, the dramatist is deeply conscious of the alienation of his time. To make this our starting-point is to be related at once to genuine concerns within both the world of the social sciences and the world of the arts.

B

Beginning with the universal phenomenon of alienation it is natural to pass next to the question of reconciliation. The very word alienation itself suggests either that two parts of an original whole have become separated from one another or that two elements, designed for one another, each lacking fulfilment apart from the other, are at present isolated and unrelated. If man is the subject of alienation on the one side we must view the other side either in terms of an original Paradise, Perfect Harmony, Ideal Relationship, to be restored, or in terms of future Blessedness, Peace and Fellowship to be attained when man's separation from God has been overcome. Reconciliation is concerned either with restoring a lost good or with attaining a potential good. Man needs to be reconciled to the totality of which he was originally or is potentially a part.

In the face of the world's alienation the Christian Gospel has been expressed in memorable and concentrated form: *God was reconciling the world to Himself in Christ*: and in order to make this proclamation meaningful I have tried to expand it through the use of eight concrete ranges of comparison. Actually these have constituted four pairs, the first and second member of each pair having corresponded to the two alternatives in the structure of alienation which I have just described. And by using these eight ranges I have attempted to cover the main aspects of human life as we have come to know

8. Cp. N. F. Simpson's *A Resounding Tinkle*.

them through history and experience: man in relation to his universe, man in relation to his total society (tribe, city, nation, state), man in relation to his kin-group (family, friends), man in relation to himself. I recognize that life cannot be parcelled up as neatly as this may suggest. There are bound to be overlappings and mergings of symbols and images. But in any set of his circumstances and at any stage in his history man is likely to find one or other of these ranges of comparison the most serviceable to interpret the meaning of his existence and his aspirations. By following the development of each through recorded history I have inferred that none is dispensable and that each has its part to play in a full-orbed interpretation of atonement.

One almost paradoxical aspect of our survey, however, is the way in which it appears that the smaller the dimensions of man's world, the more wide ranging is likely to be his systematic account of reconciliation. As his world expands, so his system seems to contract. When the limits of his universe have vanished into far-off distances, his concentration of concern tends to be focused upon the small-scale world of the isolated inner self. Such a sequence can certainly be seen in the history of theories of the Atonement.

In the Graeco-Roman view, the universe was comparable to a sphere of limited dimensions. It was regarded as a closed system. 'Since it is a unity, it must in the last analysis lie within the range of observation. Its unity embraces gods and men. There is no place for any transcendent sphere, no room for miracles, or any other interference with the rational laws of cause and effect. Authentic existence is for the Greek mind limited on every side, a closed system with a well-defined shape of its own. True, the universe, or the series of events which take place in it, is regarded as unlimited in time. But it is definitely limited in space. The unlimited, space and matter—where these are reckoned with—is not really existent. It is the indefinable, unknowable, the 'non-existent', which acquires existence only when it is given definition and form. Since the sphere is regarded as the perfect figure, the universe itself must be spherical in shape.'[9]

For those who conceived the universe in this way it was not difficult to believe that what had been wrought by the Son of God in space and time could affect the whole universe. Was not harmony the very soul of the universe? If then the harmony had been disturbed either, according to one view, by man's lapse into corruption and ignorance or, according to another view, by the malignity of superhuman forces within the universe, it was altogether

9. R. Bultmann: *Primitive Christianity*, p. 152.

imaginable that restoration would and could only take place by the activity of the Divine representative who came to reconcile all things to their true unity in God Himself. From the second to the fifteenth centuries of the Christian era man lived within this general world-view. His universe was limited, observable, unified. This did not mean that it was controllable by man but it did mean that a Divine act could readily be regarded as having universal consequences. Since the fifteenth century this has become more and more difficult for man to envisage.

The expansion of this limited world took place in at least three ways. New methods of observing the heavenly bodies led to the gradual abandonment of the earth-centred spherical model. Next, man's growing ability to explore his own world by sea-travel led him to realize that there were territories and peoples within his own world hitherto undreamed of. Finally the rapid spread of information about the world of the past, above all the Biblical and the Classical world, brought a wholly new perspective on man's existence in time and the possibilities of social change. So far as Western Europe was concerned the closed world had gone for ever. And such a revolution aroused not only excitement but also fear.

If everything around him was now open to further exploration in what direction could man look for stability and security? The chief answer for the time being was in terms of Law. Man's eyes were being opened to unsuspected vistas in space and time but he clung to the conviction that these were not lawless and chaotic. The universe, though extending far beyond what he had formerly imagined, was governed by Divine laws. The inhabiters of the earth, though more numerous and varied than had been generally known, were also subject to rules framed for their welfare in society. Here then was the sheet anchor to which man could cling at a time when his world seemed to be extending indefinitely. There was the Law of Nature: there was the Law of Nations: there was the Law of the particular society—the nation—to which he belonged. The focus of interest became the Law—its nature, its administration, its enforcement, its penalties, its rewards. While man could live within the boundaries of law and especially within the legal system of a particular society, he could gain a sense of security and confidence. His expanding world was not without form. Whenever breaches of the law occurred he possessed at least some knowledge about the way in which things could be put right.

In this changed situation it became far more difficult to envisage any kind of *cosmic* reconciliation. But if there were laws, either already revealed or possible of discovery, and if man's welfare, temporal and eternal, depended upon conformity to these laws, the all-important matter was *juridical* rather than cosmic reconciliation. And here existing systems of law seemed to provide an invaluable court of appeal. They showed the measures that had to be taken to honour and restore a law which had been broken. Hence on a larger scale it was possible to think of the judgment of God, of His attitude and activity in face of disobedience to His law, of the possibility of His personal representative entering into the broken situation to make satisfaction and reparation and finally of the full restoration of harmony and concord. The universe had expanded but in a real sense man's view of reconciliation had contracted. Nevertheless it seemed definite and concrete: it was undergirded by the relevation of God's particular dealing with a representative people in the past: and although the Divine justice had its terrifying aspects it also gave a sense of security and hope.

Yet even more drastic changes in man's world-view were still to come. In the history of science the next step was the advance towards a new conception of laws in the universe. Were these as firm in their given-ness as had been imagined? Could it be that man's formulation of these laws would need to be constantly readjusted to the new knowledge gained through his observations and experiments? Similarly in regard to history—were the codes of Law (including the Biblical codes) inherited from the past valid for all societies for all times? Could it be that man's formulation of social law would also need constant readjustment in the light of his growing knowledge of the factors influencing general social development? The whole concept of Law was being transformed in an almost frightening way.

In such a period of expansion and extension of horizons the tendency, especially in religious circles, was to contract the range of interest still more and to concentrate attention upon *experience* within limits of direct encounter and intercourse. The laws necessary for the ordering of the great society might be open to question. But in the small-scale society, the family, the guild, the cultural group, the association of friends of a common mind and purpose, a pattern of intimate community life could be accepted and actually experienced. The individual could grow in relation with the other. Dissensions and disputes could be resolved by direct confession and apology. Neglect of recognized obligations could be remedied by proper restitution. All could share in a common heritage and a common task. All could share in a common sorrow and a common remorse. Reconciliation, in fact, was conceivable not so much on a cosmic or a juridical scale but rather on a family or brotherhood scale. The locus of intensive and treasured experience was the group of companions bound together in a common pattern of life. Was it not altogether conceivable that the Son of God had taken His place within just such a group, had shared their common life, entered into their joys and sorrows, borne the shadow and disappointment of their dissensions and selfishnesses and ultimately had, by His own vicarious action on behalf of His brethren, brought reconciliation into their common experience? Such a view seemed firmly based upon that which belonged to the very stuff of daily living. It appealed to the imagination and the feeling. But another set of revolutionary changes was still to come.

Rapid advances in the biological and psychological sciences compelled men to ask whether it was possible any longer to assume that patterns of intimate social experience remained unchanged from age to age. If man has developed by a process of evolution from remote animal origins: if moreover his progress has been enormously influenced by his 'work' environment: and if finally he is constantly under pressure from forces operating in what is usually called his unconscious then he would be a bold man who attempted to establish an unchanging pattern of human social experience, even within the most limited and intimate circles, throughout the whole course of history. The past century has witnessed a constant expansion of the framework within which man-in-relation must be viewed. He is related to his animal past, to the structures of his natural environment, to the total society of which he is a member and to the unconscious with its mixture of what appear to be collective and individual features. Is it possible any longer to think in terms of regular and observable patterns of human experience? It may be possible to estimate statistical regularities by mechanical aids but can we appeal any longer to patterns certain to recur within limited areas of personal life?

Within such a situation where the universe at large can ultimately be described only in terms either of probability or of mystery: where the experience of man in society can be described only in terms either of environmental conditioning or of unconscious motivation: the tendency has arisen particularly in religious circles, to concentrate attention upon sheer *existential event*. Patterns or norms of individual experience may be open to question. But finally all that matters for me, for anyone, is what happens in the moment of crisis, how I react when my very existence is at stake, what I do when all the props of life are taken away from under me —laws of nature, patterns of history, regular structures of relational experience—and I am left alone, facing the void.

In such a moment, reconciliation can be conceived only in terms of the self. The estranged and divided self, the fragmented and disintegrated self, may achieve a momentary reconciliation when closed in by the crisis which allows no escape into space or time. And it is also conceivable that the Son of God so identified Himself with the human situation as to become hemmed in by just such a crisis. The event in which every security and tangibility of earth is stripped away from Him becomes decisive for everyman. *From the eternal cosmos to the existential moment* seems an apt title for the story of man's long enquiry about the possibility of reconciliation.

C

I return to the two major possibilities outlined at the beginning of the previous section. It is fundamental to the whole thesis of this book that reconciliation between God and man, man and God, cannot be expressed through any single shape or pattern. It has often been admitted that there cannot be any single *theory* of atonement in the sense that a basic pattern can be represented by many kinds of analogical human situation. But this is not precisely the point I am now anxious to make. Rather it is that there are *two* basic shapes or patterns which we find in the course of history, clothed in many appropriate forms of imagery. My final aim is to bring out the essential features of these two patterns.

The first assumes that there is *a determinative cosmic idea* in the very constitution of ultimate reality. Being itself is a constant pulsation of life and death, a going forth into life counterpoised by a retraction into death. This general conception is one of the oldest and most widely entertained in the history of mankind. The soul of the universe, it is imagined, breathes out and breathes in, gathers itself up into an ecstasy of life, retreats again into the womb of death. In its beginning is its end: in its end is its beginning. In the thesis is the antithesis: in the antithesis the thesis is renewed.

So enduring and so universal does this pattern seem to be, that it becomes altogether natural to imagine that this is in fact the essential pattern of the life of God Himself. This is the eternal idea beyond which no other can be conceived. And if this is the essential pattern of deity, it is unthinkable that man can truly exist unless the pattern of his own essential being conforms to that of ultimate Being. On the phenomenal plane of existence it is painfully obvious that man and the total environment to which he belongs do in fact move forward constantly from birth to death. In the beginning is certainly the end. But is the second part of the aphorism equally assured? Does death lead forward to the renewal of life? There is much to suggest that it does. But is it certain?

And another factor is involved. Sometimes vaguely, sometimes poignantly, sometimes resignedly, sometimes rebelliously, man clings to his life and its extensions, hugs it to himself, strives to preserve it at all costs. Yet in the very clinging there is a sense of being out of harmony with the essential rhythm of life. And once the rhythm is broken, man seems to lurch forward to the point of no return. His existence becomes governed by the principle of death-in-life rather than by that of life-through-death. How can he hope to be reintegrated into the original, the creative, the constitutive pattern of all existence?

The cluster of questions that I have posed in the last two paragraphs have all found their resolution in one essential idea worked out in a multiplicity of forms. It is the idea most conveniently verbalized in the word *Sacrifice*. In all its many forms sacrifice has involved some kind of deliberate offering which appears to deprive the original owner of some valued possession. In this sense it is a deliberate acceptance of a symbolic death. It is a renunciation, a surrender, a conscious recognition through a sacramental action that the ultimate principle of existence, the highest that we can conceive, is *through-death-to-life*. But is it possible to conceive such an activity taking place within the being of God Himself? If the very nature of His being is in fact life-through-death, how could we conceive of something which might be deemed an *extra*, an addition to what is eternal in its expression? And logically no such addition, it must be admitted, can be justified. It is irrational, it is absurd.

Yet if there is one thing clear in the history of human thought and action it is that man will not abandon the idea of sacrifice. When the context has been cosmic, man has offered a victim which within his total world-view has attained a supremacy of significance because his whole life appears to depend upon its continuance *in type* (i.e. not necessarily in individual manifestation): a king, a son, a camel, a horse. When the context has been that of the large-scale society—the tribe, the state, the nation, the empire—man has offered his sacrifice through a victim which within the social organization has gained a place of outstanding honour, the victim designated in the most general sense the *tragic hero*. When the context is that of the small-scale society—the family in its varying forms of manifestation—man has offered his sacrifice through the travail and suffering of one of the members—father, mother or child—acting in a representative capacity in sympathy with all.

Finally when the context is that of the individual psyche, man has offered his sacrifice through the deliberate renunciation of the delights of experience and what appear to be the noblest fulfilments of his personality in the conviction that he is thereby following the path to the renewal of life on a still higher plane.[10]

That the retention of the idea of sacrifice does not necessarily depend upon the acceptance of its *Christian* formulation could be abundantly illustrated by appealing to works of philosophy, of art, above all of living action. However wasteful a deliberate acceptance of death, actual or symbolic, may appear to be, however antithetical to the general trend and direction of our own self-preserving existences, we respond at least in a minimal degree to this revelation of what we dimly recognize to be the truth of our own ultimate existence. What the Christian disciple has been constantly concerned to reaffirm is that the essential idea, partially expressed in all forms of human self-offering, has been fully expressed in human terms by the self-offering of the Son of God: further that the essential sequel, partially expressed through all forms of human response to this outward manifestation of the sacrificial idea, have been gathered up and directed towards its true fulfilment through the continuous self-offering of the Son in the power of the eternal Spirit.

As I have already pointed out such a claim cannot be encompassed within the bounds of a strict logic. But neither, I think, can sacrifice of any kind. We recognize in moments of illumination that there is something *more* than humanity in humanity, however we may try to definite humanity. There is also something less. All this admits of no fully satisfying explanation. But what cannot be finally explained may gain final reconciliation in and through the idea of comprehensive recapitulation, of inclusive guilt-purgation, of representative suffering, of total renunciation being assumed willingly by the Divine in the person of the God-Man and being reintegrated into the Divine Being in the energy of the eternal Spirit.

What more can be said? The temptation is to rest in such a formulation and to acclaim Sacrifice as the unifying principle of all knowledge and all experience. Yet to do so would, I believe be false to the full-orbed testimony of the Christian tradition and to the witness of the widest ranges of human experience. Whenever man has sought his final unification in a Logos, an Idea, an Ideal, A Myth, a System of the intellect, someone has arisen to challenge

10. In this series it is, I think, clear that there is an ascending scale of *conscious* and *willing* acceptance on the part of the victim.

him with dark, violent and inhuman deeds which seem to wreck the unity and to point to an even starker irreconcilability than had been imagined at an earlier stage. It is the kind of situation which leads to the outburst of Ivan Karamazov:

'It's not that I don't accept God—it's the world created by Him I don't and cannot accept. I believe like a child that suffering will be healed and made up for . . . that in the world's finale, at the moment of eternal harmony, something so precious will come to pass that it will suffice for all hearts, for the comforting of all resentments, for the atonement of all the crimes of humanity, of all the blood they've shed . . . but though all that may come to pass, I don't accept it. I won't accept it.'[11]

Dostoievsky was prepared to blow any system to pieces which threatened the freedom of the individual to say 'No' to God. Marx was prepared to stand the superb system of Hegel on its head in order to affirm the reality of the world and the necessity to come to terms with its glaring alienations.

The second pattern, then, reflects a state of affairs which lies at the heart of the world's *historical* development. Life is constantly threatened by death, is engaged in a ceaseless struggle with death. Storm and tempest, fire and flood, frost and famine—the stars in their courses fight against Sisera. The wild beasts of the earth and the monsters of the deep are allied against man. Nature is red in tooth and claw. Must it not be that man's guardian deity is himself forever engaged in a struggle with the forces of evil and subject to their vicious intents?

So prominent and so recurrent does this pattern seem to be that it has become natural for man to conclude that this is in fact the constitutive structure of the world of ultimate reality. This is the actuality from whose iron grip there is no release. If the deity who protects him and to whom he owes allegiance is constantly involved in this dialectical struggle, it is unthinkable that man himself can be exempted from it. Indeed in the arena of history is it not obvious that man is

> on a darkling plain
> Swept with confused alarms of struggle and flight
> Where ignorant armies clash by night?

His life is nasty, brutish and short. Even if he can dare to believe that his deity somehow contrives to gain a succession of victories in the conflict and never yields to final defeat, is there any assurance that he can do the same? Will his death be reversed by a new access

11. Dostoievsky: *The Brothers Karamazov.*

of life? There is a possible hope that it will but the hope is vague and slender.

And there is a second ugly fact which cannot be avoided. Man does not always find himself on the side of the protagonist whose banner is the light. Though summoned to take his part in the struggle for righteousness by the God to Whom he owes all that he is and has, he yet finds himself all too often with no zeal for the conflict, seeking ease and self-indulgence, even betraying the cause that he knows in his inmost heart is concerned for his own highest interests. And the result is resentment and rebellion. Sick with himself for his craven and cowardly retreat, he projects his rancour on to his own true leader and saviour, accusing him of being responsible for his own inner conflict and estrangement. Instead of discovering his true life in a struggle with death, man drifts towards death as he struggles against the only lord and giver of life.

Can his situation in any way be retrieved? Can he be reinvigorated for the struggle and reassured concerning its final outcome? The answer which alone faces the situation realistically is expressed in terms of a critical confrontation between good and evil on the plane of history, when the good having been wounded, seemingly defeated and even killed still emerges victorious and all-powerful. In such an encounter the good so involves himself in the struggle that his virtue goes out first to save those around him from disaster and then to gather them into the fellowship of his own saving action. The critical event is most conveniently described as an act of *Redemption*. In all its many variations, redemption has involved some kind of heroic initiative in which the leading protagonist risks his own life, submitting himself entirely to the perils and dangers of the situation, all in order to liberate that which by right belongs to him but has been brought into bondage by the adversary. It is a willing submission to death in order that the doomed may have life. It is a passion, an agony, a willed acceptance of actual suffering in the faith and conviction that to save others is better than to save oneself.

But is it thinkable that such an adventure is part of the activity of the living God Himself? How is it possible to imagine Him as One Who, in the vivid word of the Epistle to the Hebrews *tastes* death for everyone? I doubt if the paradox has ever been expressed more forcibly than in the words: He partook of their nature, that through death he might destroy him who has the power of death, that is, the devil, and deliver all those who through fear of death were subject to lifelong bondage. It *is* a paradox. On the face of it it is sheer contradiction.

Yet throughout his long struggle with cosmic forces of overwhelming resourcefulness and power, with world-rulers whose systems of law seem to be impregnable, with foes of his own household and with the inner fear which paralyses his own actions, man has never entirely abandoned the hope of redemption. In all parts of the world man has looked for a Messiah. The coming revolution has been one of his key categories. The death struggle has somehow been transfigured into the instrument of freedom and life. His cosmic myths of a Divine combat have pictured the Champion as pierced, wounded, even slain but emerging victorious. His records of kingdoms and empires have told of a heroic substitute who bears the ultimate penalty of the social law in order that the condemned may be set free. His stories, fictional and historical, of romance and adventure, have celebrated the passion of the hero who hazarded his own life for his friends. His autobiographical confessions have revealed the struggles of representative men who, gripped by their own weaknesses and fears until it seemed that they must be crushed, have yet won victory and peace.

Again I readily admit that the persistence of the story of redemption achieved does not necessarily depend upon commitment to its Christian formulation. We are convinced that whenever, in limited and imperfect fashion, man submits himself to the pressure and the onslaught of powers obviously greater than his own, with the object of achieving a fuller freedom, somehow, somewhere, this action is of superlative value, even if on the plane of history it ends in apparent disaster. In our own imperfect and limited fashion we are prepared to commit ourselves to this pattern of action as alone worthy of emulation and ultimate praise. What the Christian evangelist has ever been concerned to proclaim is that such an event in space and time received its altogether definitive and final enactment when the Son of God willingly exposed Himself to the hosts of evil on Golgotha—cosmic and social, personal and psychological: further that the necessary sequel of Golgotha, expressed in the Resurrection event, has opened the gate of everlasting life to those who receive His Spirit and walk in His ways.

Such a claim cannot be made except in language which appears paradoxical to the point of contradiction. But is this not also true of all stories of redemption in some degree? Is not this the secret of their attraction, their underlying excitement, their dynamic of hope? We believe that the assassination of an Abraham Lincoln was not the extinction of the fire which he had kindled: that the crushing of the Hungarian rising was not the last word in human affairs. It is true that the chain reaction initiated by such events can often seem to be irresistible. But what on the grounds of a straightforward interpretation of history can gain no final guarantee, is open to an interpretation of faith in a Divine Redeemer Who, through exposing himself to the full impact of the cosmic conflict, accepting the full penalty of social law, submitting to complete rejection by the community to which he belonged, experiencing a total separation from the object of his inner devotion and love, achieved the final reconciliation for man, overcoming all alienation and establishing full freedom of communion in the Holy Spirit.

D

The Idea and the Event, Being and Action. We cannot, I have urged, rest in one pole *or* the other. We cannot express what we feel bound to say about the Christian Interpretation of Atonement by means of words or categories or images drawn from one pattern *or* the other. Both are essential. By their very juxtaposition in a continuing dialectic these pairs point to that which is *beyond*— beyond expression as myth or as history, beyond dramatization as tragedy or as epic victory, beyond communication as image or as word. To illustrate this duality I turn to two outstanding poets of the twentieth century, T. S. Eliot and Edwin Muir.

Eliot was steeped in the tradition of the mystics. He had suffered deeply in his own inner world. His greatest poem expressing the reconciliation of opposites is the *Four Quartets*. And I suggest that a key phrase for the interpretation of the poem occurs at an early stage: 'But reconciled among the stars'.

> We move above the moving tree
> In light upon the figured leaf
> And hear upon the sodden floor
> Below, the boarhound and the boar
> Pursue their pattern as before
> But reconciled among the stars

These are the concluding lines of a short lyric in which a series of opposites follow one another in rapid succession. Reconciliation is to be found not in the mind, not in the blood, not on the sodden floor but among the stars, in the realm of the Idea and the Ideal and the Image of Perfection.

But this does not mean that Eliot in any way shrinks from a real involvement with the mud and the sodden floor. In fact the constant cry of the poem is that we must go deeper, descend lower, into the world of perpetual solitude, through the dark cold and the empty desolation, down the sea's throat, by the way which is the way of ignorance and dispossession and emptiness. He finds no

place for 'facile solutions'. He clings to no 'cherished illusions'.
He is ready to go to 'the limits of the human condition'.[12] But from
the depths of the human condition man catches sight of the light
of a star and this reconciliation among the stars is celebrated in
what I believe to be one of the most vivid symbolic representations
of *atonement through sacrifice* in modern poetry.

> The wounded surgeon plies the steel
> That questions the distempered part;
> Beneath the bleeding hands we feel
> The sharp compassion of the healer's art
> Resolving the enigma of the fever chart.
>
> Our only health is the disease
> If we obey the dying nurse
> Whose constant care is not to please
> But to remind of our, and Adam's curse,
> And that, to be restored, our sickness
>   must grow worse.
>
> The whole earth is our hospital
> Endowed by the ruined millionaire,
> Wherein, if we do well, we shall
> Die of the absolute paternal care
> That will not leave us, but prevents
>   us everywhere.
>
> The chill ascends from feet to knees,
> The fever sings in mental wires.
> If to be warmed, then I must freeze
> And quake in frigid purgatorial fires
> Of which the flame is roses, and the
>   smoke is briars.
>
> The dripping blood our only drink,
> The bloody flesh our only food:
> In spite of which we like to think
> That we are sound, substantial flesh
>   and blood—
> Again, in spite of that, we call this
>   Friday good.

The general image of the hospital is a sombre one: wounded,
steel, distemper, bleeding, question, enigma, fever: disease, dying,
curse, sickness, worse: ruin, chill, quake, blood—the human condition is probed to its very depths. The knife, the thermometer, the
painful tests, the discipline, the limitations of food—all are vividly
portrayed. There is certainly no easy solution. And yet there *is*

12. I take these phrases from a striking passage in Martin Esslin's *The Theatre
of the Absurd* used in another connection.

resolution, there *is* healing and it is to be found in the *idea* of the *compassion* of the healer. Through the surgeon's sacrifice, through the nurse's travail, through the self-beggaring of the benefactor, through the transmission of heat, through the transfusion of blood, the patient is *restored*. There is no direct reference to the Cross. Friday is more the day of regular fasting than of unique crucifixion. The bloody flesh is the food of the Eucharist rather than the body on the Tree. Yet the whole effect of the poem is to renew and confirm faith in that Divine Passion, expressing itself throughout the ages in the movement which penetrates to the depths in order that it may exalt to the heights, the Passion supremely realized in the One Who bore our sicknesses and carried our diseases. Here is a compelling modern reconciliation of opposites which points us to that *reconciliation among the stars* which is the final truth of the human situation.

Edwin Muir came from a more primitive and rugged background. He had seen terrible suffering in man and beast, he had encountered poverty and anxiety and despair as the dominant characteristics of the social situation in which he lived. He saw the advance of tyranny in society, the eclipse of freedom, the iron grip of terror. Could the succession of historical events which he had watched and in which in no small measure he had participated, find any meaning within the total sweep of human history. Was there any meaningful centre of history to which his own sector of history could be related? I suggest that the key-phrase for the understanding of his poetic testimony is to be found in the words:

Did a God indeed in dying cross my life that day?

There *is* a cross-roads in history and there the paths of men and nations find their meaning and their goal.
The poem is entitled:

THE KILLING

That was the day they killed the Son of God
On a squat hill-top by Jerusalem.
Zion was bare, her children from their maze
Sucked by the demon curiosity
Clean through the gates. The very halt and blind
Had somehow got themselves up to the hill.

After the ceremonial preparation,
The scourging, nailing, nailing against the wood,
Erection of the main-trees with their burden,
While from the hill rose an orchestral wailing,

They were there at last, high up in the soft spring day.
We watched the writhings, heard the moanings, saw
The three heads turning on their separate axles
Like broken wheels left spinning. Round *his* head
Was loosely bound a crown of plaited thorn
That hurt at random, stinging temple and brow
As the pain swung into its envious circle.
In front the wreath was gathered in a knot
That as he gazed looked like the last stump left
Of a death-wounded deer's great antlers. Some
Who came to stare grew silent as they looked,
Indignant or sorry. But the hardened old
And the hard-hearted young, although at odds
From the first morning, cursed him with one curse,
Having prayed for a Rabbi or an armed Messiah
And found the Son of God. What use to them
Was a God or a Son of God? Of what avail
For purposes such as theirs? Beside the cross-foot,
Alone, four women stood and did not move
All day. The sun revolved, the shadow wheeled,
The evening fell. His head lay on his breast,
But in his breast they watched his heart move on
By itself alone, accomplishing its journey.
Their taunts grew louder, sharpened by the knowledge
That he was walking in the park of death
Far from their rage. Yet all grew stale at last,
Spite, curiosity, envy, hate itself.
They waited only for death and death was slow
And came so quietly they scarce could mark it.
They were angry then with death and death's deceit.

I was a stranger, could not read these people
Or this outlandish deity. Did a God
Indeed in dying cross my life that day
By chance, he on his road and I on mine?[13]

The imagery is controlled by the central axis of reference. The killing is 'by Jerusalem', the traditional and in many respects the actual centre of the earth, the place where the world's cross-roads meet. As a vacuum sucks in the elements around it, so this central *event* exercises a universal attraction. The heads revolve around the central axis. The thorns surround the central head. Even the pain swings in an envious circle. The sun revolves, its shadow wheels, still around the central event. Four women stand unmoved, guarding as it were the four directions of the universe. And there at the heart of the world's life, at the centre of the world's history, death-wounded, cursed with one curse, the Son of God died.

Here the opposites of history are brought together at a central meeting-place, at a critical moment of time. The Son of God nailed,

13. Edwin Muir: *Collected Poems*, p. 224 f.

tortured, cursed, killed. What use a God of this kind? What significance in so outlandish a deity? Yet his heart moves on accomplishing its journey. Did a God indeed cross that day the world's journey through time? Did the spite and envy and hatred inspiring the inhumanity of man to man exhaust themselves in the death that day of the Son of God? Muir asks the question. On the face of it a positive answer seems absurd. Yet the poem is such that its very recital of unadorned facts is strangely eloquent. There is certainly reconciliation in the poem. The cross-roads of the world's history becomes the place and time of the ultimate reconciliation of God and man as the Son of God takes upon Himself the full rage of the world's sin. God was in Christ reconciling the world to Himself.

E

The two poems which I have used to illustrate the Idea and the Event were written before the disclosure of two sinister possibilities in the history of the development of man. On the one hand there is the possibility of mass destruction on an unprecedented scale, even the *annihilation* of man through atomic war. On the other hand there is the possibility, more remote it is true, of the ultimate *dehumanization* of man through an accelerating process of automation. Each possibility extends the width of the alienation between God and man almost to breaking point. To find in such a situation a range of comparison for the phenomenon of reconciliation seems almost impossible.

Yet in the first area of possibility words and images born of faith have not been entirely absent. Edith Sitwell was deeply moved by the news of the totem pole of dust which seemed to her to symbolize the murder of mankind. 'All the moulds of generation died beneath that Ray'.

> For the machine that generated warmth
> Beneath your breast is dead . . . You need a fire
> To warm what lies upon your bone—
> Not all the ashes of your brother Men
> Will kindle that again—
> Nor all the world's incendiaries!

There is nothing but famine, darkness and cold. And yet this is not the final word.

> But high upon the wall
> The Rose where the Wounds of Christ are red
> Cries to the light
> See how I rise upon my stem, ineffable bright
> Effluence of bright essence—From my little span

I cry of Christ, Who is the ultimate Fire
Who will burn away the cold in the heart of Man—
Springs come, springs go . . .
'I was reddere on Rode than the Rose in the Rayne'.[14]

Even more impressive, I think, is the response of Robert Lowell
in his poem 'Crucifix'. He faces the inroads of time, the assaults
of demonic elements, the sentence of doom. How can man imagine
that the unleashing of atomic war will generate anything *new*?
There is no salvation that way. And yet, stripped to the naked
essence of sticks and bones, there is a Cross. The Cross is still a
signpost. In a magnificent leap of faith the hazily perceived symbol
on the bare road becomes the pointer to

VIA ET VITA ET VERITAS

How dry time screaks in its fat axle-grease
As spare November strikes us through the ice
And the Leviathan breaks water in the rice
Fields, at the poles, at the hot gates to Greece;
It's time: the old unmastered lion roars
And ramps like a mad dog outside the doors,
Snapping at gobbets in my thumbless hand,
The sea-ways lurch through Sodom's knees of sand
To-morrow. We are sinking. 'Run, rat, run',
The prophets thunder, and I run upon
My father, Adam. Adam, if our land
Become the desolation of a hand
That shakes the Temple back to clay, how can
War ever change my old into new man?

Get out from under my feet, old man.
            Let me pass;
On Ninth Street, through the Hallowe'en's soaped glass,
I picked at an old bone on two crossed sticks
And found, to *Via et Vita et Veritas*
A stray dog's signpost is a crucifix.[15]

Approaching this limit where the earth lies waste and desolate,
it may still be possible to envisage man casting himself upon God
as his final refuge. But if the inner structure of man is desensitized,
if all his actions are governed by automatic controls, if his behaviour
patterns are deliberately built-in by robot laws, what possibility
remains of the highest experience ever known to man—the experience of the reconciliation of opposites? Immensity and insignificance, tears and laughter, friend and foe, light and darkness, sin
and holiness, mortality and immortality, I and Thou—all these
become meaningless. Reconciliation is unthinkable.

14. Edith Sitwell: *Selected Poems*, Penguin Poets, p. 10 f.
15. Robert Lowell: *Poems 1939–47*, 'Crucifix'.

In one of Isaac Asimov's science fiction stories a man who has remained human and fallible tells Daneel Olivaw, the prince of the robots, the story of the woman taken in adultery. He responds

'What is adultery?'
'That doesn't matter, it was a crime for which the accepted punishment was stoning . . .'
'And the woman was guilty?'
'She was.'
'Then why was she not stoned?'
'None of the accusers felt he could after Jesus' statement.
The story is meant to show that there is something even higher than the justice you have been filled with. (Certain laws of 'justice' have been 'built into' Daneel.)
There is a human impulse known as mercy, a human act known as forgiveness.'
'I am not acquainted with these words, partner Elijah.'

A human impulse known as mercy (and yet it droppeth as the gentle rain from heaven). A human act known as forgiveness (and yet to err is human, to forgive divine). These are the final realities, *compassion* and *forgiveness*, which if lost from the vocabulary of humanity will surely mean the end of man.

Over against this gruesome concept of science fiction I set what seem to me some of the most beautiful words ever spoken and written by man.

Through the tender mercy of our God
Whereby the Dayspring from on high hath
                             visited us
To give light to them that sit in darkness
                          and in the shadow of death
And to guide our feet into the way of peace.

Atonement, Reconciliation, Peace. The long journey is ended in which I have tried to look at these great words from many different vantage-points along the way. I conclude with the words of the aged Simeon in Auden's *Christmas Oratorio*:

'Because of His visitation we may no longer desire God as if He were lacking: our redemption is no longer a question of pursuit but of surrender to Him who is always and everywhere present. Therefore at every moment we pray that, following Him, we may depart from our anxiety into His peace.'

MUSICAL EXPRESSIONS OF ATONEMENT

Music expressing the drama of estrangement and reconciliation, of guilt and the removal of guilt, has attained great popularity in Reformed Christianity since the seventeenth century.

The custom of singing in plainsong the four Gospel accounts of the Passion in the liturgy of Holy Week is known to have existed as early as the fifth century of the Christian era. But until the fifteenth century this had normally been the responsibility of one man, the deacon, who by changes of tone and voice distinguished the parts of the various principals in the drama of the Passion. During this century, even in the Roman Church, a dialogue form was introduced and in the sixteenth century many composers of varying nationalities were producing choral versions in which the words were still in Latin but the music was a mixture of plainsong and polyphony, with individuals singing the parts of the Christ, the Evangelist and so on, a chorus singing the words of the crowd.

The altogether new development in the sixteenth century was the introduction in Germany of settings in the vernacular. By this means a fuller congregational understanding and participation were made possible, for the settings included opportunities for the people to join in the singing and in forms of meditation. But the tradition of plainsong and the Latin tongue remained powerful and this tended to play down the dramatic movements and contrasts in the Passion narratives. It was not until the beginning of the seventeenth century that a revolution in musical theory made possible the development of the oratorio type of Passion Music which has played so large a part in Protestant art and worship ever since. This revolution originating from Florence had as its main object to work out a new relationship between words and music, music being given the function of expressing and emphasizing the dramatic qualities of the words. On the secular side this was to result in the creation of *Opera* in which myths of Greece and Rome normally provided the dialogues. On the sacred side Biblical stories provided the words for the creation of *Oratorios* of which the Passion Oratorios constituted a particular genre. Both opera and oratorio turned away from the formal, liturgical, unemotional musical tradition of the Middle Ages and used music instead to give full force to the dramatic qualities of the text—the fear and the pity, the steadfastness of the hero and the fickleness of the crowd—and thereby to stir the emotions of the audience.

It was the Lutheran composers of North Germany who created Passion music of outstanding excellence with the masterpieces of Bach attaining the position of pre-eminence. Through corporate participation in these artistic forms, particularly during the sequence of Holy Week, men and women were able to share in the tragic drama of the Saviour's Passion through the whole range of emotions which are stirred by words and music intimately related to one another. It is true that the visual elements of the Passion drama, which had been prominent in the plays of the late Middle Ages, were reduced almost to vanishing point. The setting of the church retained some importance though ultimately performances came to be given in concert halls. The relation to Holy Week and Good Friday, particularly to the latter, could increase the solemnity of the occasion though ultimately that link was also destined to be broken. But there was no emphasis upon dramatic action, colour, movement, costume. Effects were produced through words and music only and by general consent none has surpassed the achievement of Bach in his St. Matthew Passion where these elements and these alone were to be used.[1] When, as on Good Friday at Leipzig, the gathered congregation took part in a service where hymns and sermon were combined with the full performance of the Passion Music, European Protestantism came to its fullest and most characteristic experience of tragic drama. The repetition of the great Passion hymn 'O Sacred Head sore wounded' brought the worshippers to the heights and depths of tragic experience: the constant emphasis on the direct connection between the grievous sins of mankind and the sufferings of the Son of God, a connection inspiring fear and horror and shame, brought them to a profound experience of reconciliation as they realized afresh that by His stripes they had been healed.

A different development of oratorio which is associated above all with the name of Handel includes tragic elements but can hardly be called tragic in its total conception. Handel began his career as a German Lutheran church musician but soon devoted himself entirely to the study and composition of operas. Largely because he failed to attain success in this particular medium he turned his attention to oratorios and ultimately came to England. Here his works were produced first in genuinely dramatic form but through opposition to the presentation of sacred themes as theatrical pro-

1. In this whole section I have been greatly indebted to the excellent small book by Basil Smallman entitled *The Background of Passion Music: J. S. Bach and his predecessors* (S.C.M., 1957).

ductions the oratorio in England was denuded of costume and
action and made a pure concert piece. This had the effect amongst
other things of rendering it specially acceptable to the non-conform-
ing and evangelical sections of English Christianity. With their
antagonism to the theatre they would have been quite unwilling to
accept a form designed for production on the stage. But when the
oratorio confined itself to a Biblical subject, included a firm acknowledgement of dependence upon God and was performed by soloists
and choir in ordinary dress singing in English no objection was taken.
Instead the singing of *Messiah* in particular came to be the great
dramatic (even if the drama were unacknowledged) event of the year.
Presbyterians and Puritans, Methodists and Anglican Evangelicals
have through most of their history been deeply suspicious of colour
and costume, action and movement, whether in church or in the
place of public entertainment. On the other hand the emotional side
of their natures, individual and corporate, has been satisfied through
rhetoric and singing, music and choral works, and the Passion
in particular has made its impact upon the inner consciousness
through hymn and sermon and to a less extent through oratorio.

The oratorio as developed by Handel was less directly dramatic
than the Passion oratorios of the earlier Lutheran composers. He
did indeed write a Passion of his own but his characteristic medium
was opera and his oratorios were composed on the grand scale.
It was not a question of dwelling upon intimate and moving details
of the Passion narrative and revealing the dramatic tensions and
conflicts between the *dramatis personae* of the story. Rather his
aim was to present notable figures and great events of the Bible
in the grandeur of their theological setting. This might involve
intensely dramatic moments. Yet the total presentation was not
that of a single drama but rather that of a choral epic. The chorus
had an exceedingly important part to play and Handel's brilliance
was shown in his development of nearly every form of choral
technique. Time and again the triumphant declaration of the
chorus brought a work or a section of a work to its appropriate close.

Greatest of all the oratorios in its Christian significance is *Messiah*.
Can this in any way be regarded as a presentation of Christian
tragedy in the manner of the Passion oratorios? Quite clearly its
aim and character are different. Let me quote some valuable comments by Professor Jens Larsen in this connection:

'*Messiah* is not, as is often popularly supposed, a number of
scenes from the Life of Jesus linked together to form a certain
dramatic whole, but a representation of the fulfilment of Redemption
through the Redeemer, Messiah. It is "the first instance in the

history of music of an attempt to view the mighty drama of human redemption from an artistic standpoint" . . . the contents can be summarized as follows:

(i) The prophecy and realization of God's Plan to redeem mankind by the coming of the Messiah.

(ii) The accomplishment of redemption by the sacrifice of Jesus, mankind's rejection of God's offer and mankind's utter defeat when trying to oppose the power of the Almighty.

(iii) A Hymn of Thanksgiving for the final overthrow of Death'.[2] Commenting later on Section II Larsen continues:

'Here is no description of the Passion as in Schutz or Bach, based on the Evangelists' account of Christ's suffering and death, but a reflection on suffering and its meaning, based on the union of Isaiah, Chapter 53, and a few verses from the Psalms. A detailed account of the Passion, depicting the crown of thorns, the walk to Golgotha, the Crucifixion, or the Seven Words on the Cross is outside the scope of the work. This chain of episodes, which gives the account of the suffering its stamp of living reality and has been firmly linked to the traditional interpretation of the Passion for centuries, is repressed here because it is of no direct importance for the representation of the work's central idea; the redemptive power of Christ's suffering.'[3]

This does not mean that the tragic note is absent from Sections I and II. Such an aria as that containing the words 'A Man of Sorrows and acquainted with Grief' draws us into the experience of deep tragedy. Throughout these parts we are aware of constant contrast and conflict, light and darkness, life and death, the defencelessness of the central figure and the power of his enemies. But the total movement, especially when Part III is included, cannot be called Tragic. Many doubtless who have entered deeply into the music of Parts 1 and 2 have come to the realization of reconciliation and peace before ever Part III is presented. As we have already seen, in a paradoxical way reconciliation can be regarded as achieved by His suffering and death as the archetypal tragic figure, apart altogether from the resurrection and exaltation. Yet for Handel Part III was essential for it brought the whole work of man's Redemption to its proper conclusion. As in the Apocalypse of John, we hear the heavenly choruses singing their praises to the

2. Handel's *Messiah*, 96–7. This interpretation of Redemption belongs to the range of comparison considered in Chapter III. The oratorio grew out of the opera which was itself concerned to express the great myths of mankind in musical terms. So the victory of Messiah over Satan and all the powers of evil is the myth which Handel so powerfully presents.

3. Ibid, p. 137.

Lamb who was slain and has redeemed us by His blood from every tribe and tongue and people and nation. We are reconciled in His passion: we are reconciled in His victory. Neither affirmation can by itself express the full Christian faith. The music of Bach and the music of Handel each has its part to play in the task of mediating to men through art the mighty drama of man's redemption.

Developments in the world of music since the death of these two great composers have been less directly related to the theme of redemption through Christ's sufferings and victory. In the nineteenth century great religious music grew out of the Mass and the Requiem rather than out of the Passion and the Redemption drama. In the twentieth also, when the world has twice been overshadowed by the dark cloud of war, the Requiem has formed the groundwork of a composition[4] which has already been recognized as likely to find a place amongst the world's greatest musical treasures. But there have also been attempts—some little known—to express dramatically through the music and songs of the modern world and through dramatic action the Passion Story of the ages. Michael Tippett in *A Child of our Time* related the tragedy of man's inhumanity to man to the Gospel Story, using negro spirituals as chorales. And in a remarkable experiment described by Canon J. V. Taylor in the book *The Passion in Africa*, we see how the Passion Drama was transferred to African soil one Holy Week and how the singing of the spirituals brought a heightening of spiritual awareness scarcely experienced at any other time, revealing as they did a new depth of meaning and mystery when sung in the context of the Passion story.[5]

So the original drama, recited in some form at celebrations of the Lord's Supper, recorded in each of the Gospels, sung in the liturgies of Holy Week, acted in the passion plays of the Middle Ages, sung with increasing choral and instrumental accompaniment in the churches of Germany, adapted in the great oratorio singing of the eighteenth and nineteenth centuries, in process of rediscovery through experiments in the music and drama and even ballet of the twentieth century—this original drama invites not simply to detached observation but to active participation. Those who can share in such participation experience not only the fear and the compassion and the catharsis of which Aristotle wrote: they experience expiation and justification and peace through the blood of the cross, a peace, as St. Paul wrote, which passes all understanding for it is in very truth the peace of God.

4. By Benjamin Britten.
5. *The Passion in Africa*: Introduction by John Taylor (Mowbray, 1957).

BIBLIOGRAPHY

Auden, W. H.: *For the Time Being: Christmas Oratorio*, Faber & Faber, 1945.
Aulén, G.: *Christus Victor*, S.P.C.K., 1931.
Aulén, G.: *The Faith of the Christian Church*, S.C.M. Press, 1961.
Aylen, L.: *Greek Tragedy and the Modern World*, Methuen, 1964.

Bailey, D. S.: *The Man-Woman Relation in Christian Thought*, Longmans, Green, 1959.
Bainton, R.: *Here I Stand*, Hodder & Stoughton, 1951.
Barrett, C. K.: *From First Adam to Last*, A. & C. Black, 1962.
Barrett, W.: *Irrational Man*, Heinemann Educational, 1964.
Barth, K.: *Theology and Church*, S.C.M. Press, 1962.
Berdyaev, N.: *Freedom and the Spirit*, G. Bles, 1935.
Bloch, M.: *The Historian's Craft*, Manchester U.P., 1954.
Bonhoeffer, D.: *Sanctorum Communio*, Collins, 1963.
Bonhoeffer, D.: *Letters and Papers from Prison*, S.C.M. Press, 1956.
Bornkamm, G.: *Jesus of Nazareth*, Hodder & Stoughton, 1960.
Bowra, C. M.: *Primitive Song*, Weidenfeld & Nicolson, 1962.
Bradley, A. C.: *Shakespearian Tragedy*, Macmillan, 1957.
Brandon, S. G. F.: *The Saviour God*, Manchester U.P., 1963.
Brunner, E.: *The Christian Doctrine of Creation and Redemption*, Lutterworth Press, 1952.
Brunner, E.: *God and Man*, S.C.M. Press, 1936.
Buber, M.: *I and Thou*, T. & T. Clark, 1937.
Bultmann, R.: *Existence and Faith*, Hodder & Stoughton, 1961.
Bultmann, R.: *Primitive Christianity*, Thames & Hudson, 1956.
Bultmann, R.: *Theology of the New Testament*, S.C.M. Press, 1952.
Buchan, J.: *Augustus*, Hodder & Stoughton, 1937.
Bushnell, H.: *God in Christ*, London, 1850.
Bushnell, H.: *Vicarious Sacrifice*, Alexander Strahan, London, 1866.

Caird, G. B.: *Saint Luke*, Pelican Gospel Commentaries, 1963.
Campbell, J.: *The Masks of God*, Secker & Warburg, 1960-62.
Campbell, J. McLeod: *Nature of the Atonement*, J. Clarke, 1959.
Chambers, E. K.: *English Literature at the Close of the Middle Ages*, Oxford U.P., 1945.
de Chardin, T.: *Le Milieu Divin*, Collins, 1960.
de Chardin, T.: *Letters from a Traveller*, Collins, 1962.

de Chardin, T.: *The Phenomenon of Man*, Collins, 1961.

Chase, R.: *The American Novel and its Tradition*, G. Bell & Sons, 1957.

Cullmann, O.: *Christ and Time*, S.C.M. Press, 1951.

Daube, D.: *The Exodus Pattern in the Bible*, Faber & Faber, 1963.

Daube, D.: *Studies in Biblical Law*, Cambridge U.P., 1947.

Davidson, R.: *The Old Testament*, Hodder & Stoughton, 1964.

Davies, W. D.: *Paul and Rabbinic Judaism*, S.P.C.K., 1955.

Demant, V. A.: *An Exposition of Christian Sex Ethics*, Hodder & Stoughton, 1963.

Denney, J.: *The Christian Doctrine of Reconciliation*, J. Clarke, 1959.

Dickinson, L.: *The Greek View of Life*, Methuen, 1896.

Dillistone, F. W.: *Jesus Christ and His Cross*, Lutterworth Press, 1953.

Dodd, C. H.: *Historical Tradition in the Fourth Gospel*, Cambridge U.P., 1963.

Dodd, C. H.: *The Interpretation of the Fourth Gospel*, Cambridge U.P., 1953.

Dodds, E. R.: *The Greeks and the Irrational*, University of California Press, 1951.

Drewery, B.: *Origen and the Doctrine of Grace*, Epworth, 1960.

Eliade, M.: *Birth and Rebirth*, Harvill Press, 1958.

Eliade, M.: *The Myth of the Eternal Return*, Routledge & Kegan Paul, 1954.

Eliade, M.: *Myths, Dreams and Mysteries*, Harvill Press, 1960.

Eliot, T. S.: *The Cocktail Party*, Faber & Faber, 1950.

Eliot, T. S.: *Four Quartets*, Faber & Faber, 1944.

Erikson, E. H.: *Young Man Luther*, Faber & Faber, 1959.

Esslin, M.: *The Theatre of the Absurd*, Eyre & Spottiswoode, 1962.

Farmer, H. H.: *The Servant of the Word*, James Nisbet, 1941.

Farmer, H. H.: *The World and God*, James Nisbet, 1955.

Fischer, E.: *A Marxist Approach: The Necessity of Art*, Penguin Books, 1963.

Forsyth, P. T.: *The Justification of God*, Independent Press, 1948.

Forsyth, P. T.: *The Soul of Prayer*, Independent Press, 1949.

Forsyth P. T.: *The Work of Christ*, Independent Press, 1946.

Frankfort, H.: *Kingship and the Gods*, University of Chicago Press, 1948.

Franks, R. S.: *The Work of Christ*, Nelson, 1962.

Fuller, R. H.: *The New Testament in Current Study*, S.C.M. Press, 1963.

Galloway, A. D.: *The Cosmic Christ*, James Nisbet, 1957.

Gelfant, B. H.: *American City Novel*, University of Oklahoma Press, 1954.

Godsey, J. D.: *The Theology of Dietrich Bonhoeffer*, S.C.M. Press, 1960.

Gogol, N.V.: *The Divine Liturgy of the Russian Orthodox Church*, Darton, Longman & Todd, 1960.

Goguel, M.: *The Birth of Christianity*, Allen & Unwin, 1953.

Goldmann, L.: *The Hidden God*, Routledge & Kegan Paul, 1964.

Grensted, L. W.: *A Short History of the Doctrine of Atonement*, Manchester U.P., 1920.

Guthrie, W. K. C.: *The Greeks and their Gods*, Methuen, 1950.

Happold, F. C.: *Mysticism*, Penguin Books, 1963.

Hart, H. L. A.: *Punishment and the Elimination of Responsibility*, L. T. Hobhouse Memorial Lecture, 1962.

Heller, E.: *The Disinherited Mind*, Penguin Books, 1961.

Henn, T. R.: *The Harvest of Tragedy*, Methuen, 1956.

Herbert, A. S.: *Worship in Ancient Israel*, Lutterworth Press, 1959.

Higgins, A. J. B.: *New Testament Essays in Memory of T. W. Manson*, Manchester U.P., 1959.

Hofmann, H.: *The Theology of Reinhold Niebuhr*, Scribners, New York, 1956.

Hooke, S. H.: *The Labyrinth*, S.P.C.K., 1935.

Huizinga, J.: *The Waning of the Middle Ages*, Edward Arnold, 1924.

Jarrett-Kerr, M.: *The Hope of Glory*, S.C.M. Press, 1952.

Jaspers, K. T.: *Tragedy is not Enough*, Beacon Press, Boston, 1952.

Jones, G. V.: *Christology and Myth in the New Testament*, Allen & Unwin, 1956.

Jung, C. G.: *Answer to Job*, Routledge & Kegan Paul, 1954.

Jung, C. G.: *Modern Man in Search of a Soul*, Routledge & Kegan Paul, 1933.

Kelly, J. N. D.: *Early Christian Creeds*, Longmans, Green, 1950.

Kierkegaard, S.: *Concluding Unscientific Postscript*, Oxford U.P., 1941.

Kierkegaard, S.: *Christian Discourses*, Oxford U.P., 1961.

Kierkegaard, S.: *Fear and Trembling*, Oxford U.P., 1939.

Kiddle, M.: *Revelation*, Hodder & Stoughton, 1940.

Knowles, D.: *The Evolution of Mediaeval Thought*, Longmans, Green, 1962.

Knox, W. L.: *St Paul and the Church of the Gentiles*, Cambridge U.P., 1939.

Knox, J.: *The Death of Christ*, Collins, 1963.
Kreiger, M.: *The Tragic Vision*, R. & W. Holt, 1960.

Larsen, J. C.: *Handel's Messiah*, A. & C. Black, 1957.
Last, H.: *The Legacy of Rome*, Oxford U.P., 1923.
Lee, R. S.: *Freud and Christianity*, J. Clarke, 1948.
Lidgett, J. Scott: *The Spiritual Principle of Atonement*, Charles H. Kelly, London, 1898.
Leivestad, R.: *Christ the Conqueror*, S.P.C.K., 1954.
Lowell, R.: *Poems 1938–49*, Faber & Faber, 1950.

Mackintosh, H. R.: *The Christian Experience of Forgiveness*, James Nisbet, 1927.
Mackintosh, H. R.: *Types of Modern Theology*, James Nisbet, 1937.
Macmurray, J.: *Persons in Relation*, Faber & Faber, 1961.
Mâle, E.: *The Gothic Image*, Fontana, 1961.
Manson, T. W.: *The Teaching of Jesus*, Cambridge U.P., 1935.
Marcuse, H.: *Reason and Revolution*, Routledge & Kegan Paul, 1964.
Matthews, W. R.: *The Problem of Christ in the Twentieth Century*, Oxford U.P., 1950.
Maurice, F. D.: *The Doctrine of Sacrifice*, Cambridge U.P., 1854.
McGiffert, A. C.: *A History of Christian Thought*, Scribners, New York, 1932.
McLuhan, M.: *Understanding Media*, Routledge & Kegan Paul, 1964.
Moberly, R. C.: *Atonement and Personality*, John Murray, 1917.
Moule, C. F. D.: *The Epistles to Colossians and to Philemon*, Cambridge U.P., 1957.
Muir, E.: *Collected Poems*, Faber & Faber, 1964.
Murry, J. M.: *Love, Freedom and Society*, Jonathan Cape, 1957.

Nelson, B.: *Freud and the Twentieth Century*, Allen & Unwin, 1958.
Neumann, E.: *The Origins and History of Consciousness*, Routledge & Kegan Paul, 1964.
Nicoll, A.: *The Theatre and Dramatic Theory*, Harrap, 1962.
Niebuhr, Reinhold: *Beyond Tragedy*, James Nisbet, 1938.
Nisbet, R. A.: *Community and Power*, Oxford U.P., 1962.

Pedersen, J.: *Israel I–II*, Oxford U.P., 1926.
Prestige, G. L.: *Fathers and Heretics*, S.P.C.K., 1940.
Pospisil, L.: *Kapauku Papuans and their Law*, Yale U.P., 1963.

Rankin, O.S.: *Israel's Wisdom Literature*, T. & T. Clark, 1936.

Raphael, D.D.: *The Paradox of Tragedy*, Allen & Unwin, 1960.

Raven, C. E.: *Natural Religion and Christian Theology*, *II*, Cambridge U.P., 1953.

Raven, C. E.: *Teilhard de Chardin*, Collins, 1962.

Robinson, H. Wheeler: *The Cross in the Old Testament*, S.C.M. Press, 1960.

Robinson, H. Wheeler: *The Cross of the Servant*, S.C.M. Press, 1926.

Rupp, E. G.: *The Righteousness of God*, Hodder & Stoughton, 1953.

Sanders, B. G. et al.: *Christianity after Freud*, Geoffrey Bles London, and The Macmillan Company, New York, 1949.

Schulz, F.: *Principles of Roman Law*, Oxford U.P., 1936.

Scott, N., Jr.: *The Tragic Vision and the Christian Faith*, Association Press, N.Y., 1957.

Scott, N.: *Rehearsals of Discomposure, Alienation and Reconciliation in Modern Literature*, Columbia U.P., 1952.

Sewall, R. B.: *The Vision of Tragedy*, Yale U.P., 1959.

Shepherd, M. H., Jr.: *Worship in Scripture and Tradition*, Oxford U.P., 1963.

Sikes, J. G.: *Peter Abelard*, Cambridge U.P., 1932.

Simpson, N. F.: *A Resounding Tinkle*, Samuel French.

Sitwell, E.: *Selected Poems*, Penguin Poets.

Smallman, B.: *The Background of Passion Music: J. S. Bach and his Predecessors*, S.C.M. Press, 1957.

Soothill, W. E.: *The Hall of Light*, Lutterworth Press, 1957.

Southern, R.: *St. Anselm and his Biographer*, Cambridge U.P., 1963.

Speaight, R.: *The Christian Theatre*, Burns, Oates, 1960.

Stafford-Clark, D.: *Psychiatry Today*, Penguin Books, 1952.

Stauffer, E.: *New Testament Theology*, S.C.M. Press, 1963.

Steiner, G.: *The Death of Tragedy*, Faber & Faber, 1961.

Sundkler, B.: *The Christian Ministry in Africa*, Swedish Institute of Missionary Research, 1960.

Taylor, H. O.: *The Mediaeval Mind*, Macmillan, 1919.

Tillich, P.: *The Courage to Be*, James Nisbet, 1952.

Tillyard, E. M.: *Some Mythical Elements in English Literature*, Chatto & Windus, 1961.

Tinsley, E. J.: *Christian Theology and Frontiers of Tragedy*, Leeds University Press, 1963.

Thornton, L. S.: *The Common Life and the Body of Christ*, A. & C. Black, 1963.

Thornton, L. S.: *Revelation and the Modern World*, A. & C. Black, 1950.

Thornton, L. S.: *The Incarnate Lord*, Longmans, Green, 1928.
Toynbee, A.: *A Study of History*, Oxford U.P., 1934.

Warren, R. P.: *Brother to Dragons*, Eyre & Spottiswoode, 1954.
Webb, C. C. J.: *A Study of Religious Thought in England from 1850*, Oxford U.P., 1932.
Weiser, A.: *The Psalms*, S.C.M. Press, 1962.
Westcott, B. F.: *Hebrews*, Macmillan, 1920.
Westcott, B. F.: *The Victory of the Cross*, Macmillan, 1888.
White, V.: *God and the Unconscious*, Harvill Press, 1952.

INDEX

435